The Complete BMAT Specification Explained

Copyright © 2022 6med. All rights reserved.

ISBN 978-1-915091-62-8

No part of this publication may be reproduced or transmitted in any form or by any means, electronic or mechanical, including photocopying, recording, or by any information retrieval system without prior written permission of the publisher. This publication may not be used in conjunction with or to support any commercial undertaking without the prior written permission of the publisher of this book, the publisher and author assume no responsibility for errors or omissions of any kind. Neither is any liability assumed for damages resulting from the use of information contained herein. This does not affect your statutory rights.

Published by RAR Medical Services

www.6med.co.uk

The Complete BMAT Specification Explained

**Eleanor Cooley
Charlotte Lee
Samuel Lowe
David Mackney
Alex Thomas
Deekshitha Umasankar**

Contributions from: Ria Bansal, Noah Chandler, Helena Jankowska, and Aaron Johnston

Edited by Dr Toby Bowman

About the authors

Eleanor is a 3rd year medical student currently studying at UCL. She has had previous experience in BMAT tutoring, question writing and editing.

Charlotte is a final year medical student at Green Templeton College University of Oxford. She previously completed an undergraduate degree (Medical Sciences, BA Hons) at Balliol College, University of Oxford.

Sam is in his final year studying medicine at Imperial College London. During his time at university he has tutored students preparing for admissions tests and has led summer schools for students applying for Medicine.

Having initially applied to study Maths with Music at university he made a last-minute decision to reapply for Medicine and take the BMAT. He is thrilled to be contributing to a resource which would have helped him and hopes you find it useful!

David is a 3rd year medical student at Newcastle University. He also enjoys competitive hockey and rugby, and is an experienced BMAT and UCAT tutor.

Alex is a 5th year medic studying at the University of Oxford, with still no real idea of what he wants to specialise in (but something related to surgery or paediatrics would be nice). He is a keen teacher and is just starting to branch out into some research in sports and exercise medicine. A firm believer in a good work-life balance, he plays way too much cricket for the university.

Deekshitha is a 5th year medical student at Kings College London. She scored highly on the BMAT and, in addition to coaching it with 6med, she is passionate about expanding medical education to younger learners.

Contents

Introduction 7
Section 1 – Thinking Skills 22
Section 1: Thinking Skills - Overview 23
Section 2 Part 1: Biology 37
B1 - Cells 37
B2 – Movement Across Membranes 42
B3 – Cell Division and Sex Determination 46
B4 – Inheritance 51
B5 – DNA 56
B6 – Gene Technologies 58
B7 – Variation 61
B8 – Enzymes 63
B9 – Animal Physiology 66
B10 – Ecosystems 78
Section 2 Part 2: Chemistry 81
C1 – Atomic Structure 81
C2 – The Periodic Table 87
C3 – Chemical Reactions, Formulae and Equations 91
C4 – Quantitative Chemistry 97
C5 – Oxidation, Reduction and Redox 103
C6 – Chemical Bonding, Structure and Properties 106
C7 – Group Chemistry 111
C8 – Separation Techniques 114
C9 – Acids, Bases and Salts 119
C10 – Rates of Reaction 122
C11 – Energetics 126
C12 – Electrolysis 129
C13 – Carbon/Organic Chemistry 132

C14- Metals 139
C15- Kinetic/Particle Theory 142
C16 – Chemical Tests 145
C17- Air and Water 149
Section 2 Part 3: Physics. 152
P1 Electricity 152
P2 Magnetism 161
P3 Mechanics 175
P4 Thermal Physics 191
P5 Matter 197
P6 Waves 203
P7 Radioactivity 214
Section 2 Part 4: Mathematics. 221
M1 - Units 221
M2 - Number 224
M3 - Ratio and Proportion 233
M4 - Algebra 239
M5 - Geometry 253
M6 - Statistics 263
M7 - Probability 269
Section 3 – The Writing Task 275
Biology Practice Questions 288
Chemistry Practice Questions 298
Physics Practice Questions 315
Maths Practice Questions 323
Answers 328
Final Words 362

Introduction

Welcome to the Complete BMAT Specification Explained, from 6med! This book is a compendium, teaching you absolutely *everything* that you need to know in order to ace every single question in the BMAT exam, and will give you plenty of information and practice on the different sections of the exam. Before we can get started with the nitty gritty though, we're going to walk through the details of the test itself.

Why do universities use the BMAT?

Students from all over the world will apply to the same university – whilst academic qualifications are a great way of showing a student's ability, different systems are used around the world. Thus, using a standardised test that is done by everyone regardless of country, gives universities a single measure that differentiates each candidate. The BMAT tests a candidate's critical thinking skills, application of knowledge and communication skills. These are all key skills any healthcare professional needs to ensure their patients receive the best care. For example, a doctor will need to be able to look at an X-Ray, interpret it using the knowledge they've gained in medical school, match it to signs and symptoms the patient has come in with and communicate their findings to the relevant teams.

To show universities that you already possess a basic knowledge of skills, you need to be confident with the test. Revising and practising in a good amount of time is key getting those top scores so that you stand out amongst the thousands of applicants. That's why we've created this book.

What is the BMAT?

Section	Skills tested	# of Questions	Time given
1	Critical thinking and problem solving	32 multiple choice questions	1 hour
2	Application of scientific knowledge	27 multiple choice questions	30 minutes
3	Communication, organisation, language	1 essay	30 minutes

BMAT stands for Biomedical Admissions Test. This exam is taken by medical, dental, biomedical and veterinary students, applying to competitive universities. It is two hours long and consists of three sections.

The Complete BMAT Specification Explained
Introduction

The BMAT is used by universities to provide a different measure of ability – students applying for the subjects listed above often have similar grades and thus, using another, standardised component will help them choose the right candidates.

Deep Dive – BMAT Sections

1. Section 1
   - As above, this section tests problem solving (PS) and critical thinking (CT). This is a multiple-choice question (MCQ) section, with 16 of each type. Each question is formatted with a stimulus, followed by the stem and then 5 options. Candidates must choose the right option. In the CT questions the stimulus is text, whilst in PS questions, the stimulus is a data set of some sort (i.e., diagram, table, graph, etc).
2. Section 2
   - Section 2 covers application of knowledge and is an MCQ section. It covers GCSE Biology, Chemistry, Physics and Maths content but rather than recall, you'll need to apply what you've learnt. There is a BMAT specification that can be found on the official website, which will give you the list of topics you'll need to know.
3. Section 3
   - Section 3 is the essay section, in which you'll get one A4 piece of paper (it has strict margins, so it's not entirely A4) to write an essay. This section assesses your communication skills and to ace this section, you'll need to know how to present arguments clearly, concisely, and logically. You'll have three questions to choose from (you only need to choose one) and the format will generally be a statement followed by three questions. Typically, you will be asked to explain your understanding of the statement, argue to the contrary and provide your own opinion on the matter.

When is the BMAT sat?

The BMAT is sat in two sittings. In 2022, they are in February and November. Check which sitting the universities you are applying to accept (some accept both and some accept only one) as you can only sit the BMAT once in an application cycle. This information can be found on the official BMAT website and on the individual university websites.

The Complete BMAT Specification Explained
Introduction

Frequently asked questions

We've included some common questions here that may come up so you have all the information you may need before you sit the exam.

How is the BMAT scored?

Section 1 and 2 are given standardised marks out of 9.0. 2021's average for section 1 was 4.0 to 5.0.

Section 3 is given a number and a letter score. The number corresponds to the content of the essay and the letter corresponds to the quality of English used. 2021's average for section 3 was 3A.

To really stand out, you want to be aiming for **6.0+ in sections 1 and 2 and 4A+ in section 3**.

How do different universities use the BMAT?

University	How they use the BMAT
Cambridge	The BMAT is used to shortlist candidates after the interview process (90% of students will get to the interview stage). Each college is slightly different, however, so do your research!
Oxford	The BMAT is used to shortlist candidates for interview. Their algorithm includes percentage of A*s at GCSE and BMAT scores to produce a ranking.
UCL	The BMAT is used to determine when applicants are interviewed – higher scores = earlier interviews
Imperial	There is a BMAT threshold which changes every year but is usually around 4.0-5.0 for sections 1 and 2 and 2.5B for section 3.
Leeds	Candidates will be allocated marks and the BMAT makes up 15%. The weighting for the sections are 40% each for sections 1 and 2 and 20% for section 3.
Brighton and Sussex	The entire paper is assigned a score out of 28 (9 marks each for sections 1 and 2 and 5 marks each for each component of section 3) and this is then ranked.

How to prepare

Start a good few months in advance. There's a load of content to learn and you'll find it easier to balance alongside schoolwork and other extracurricular commitments. Practice as many questions as you can and time yourself doing the past papers.

Remember the content of the syllabus should be what you've already covered. Think about investing in some textbooks and workbooks, particularly if you don't study any of the subjects covered in the BMAT (for most people, this is physics).

Write essays and have people mark them according to the mark scheme. Ask around at school to see if there are teachers who are willing to have a look at a couple, to give you some honest feedback on your writing style and essay content. Work with your peers too – are there any points they would add? Is there a different way they'd phrase the point you've made?

In the exam, prioritise the questions. Work through the easy questions first so you know you've got some of those marks in the bag and then tackle the harder, more data heavy questions. Spending time trying to answer a difficult question for a couple of marks could lose you easier marks elsewhere. There's no negative marking in the BMAT so really try and capitalise on the marks you know you'll definitely get.

This is a very brief run through of the BMAT, but hopefully it's helpful. Make sure you use this book to its full capacity – it's got a bunch of tips and tricks in it that'll help you ace the exam and leave you well-prepared. Now, onto section 1.

Now... after this you might be thinking, should I bother with the BMAT? Read below on why we think you should.

Introduction – Science and Medicine

Medicine is a scientific subject. The BMAT tests the application of your scientific knowledge. In medicine, even in clinical work, we apply scientific practices. For example, a patient presenting with a cough and fever, will have a working diagnosis of a pneumonia (hypothesis), which is confirmed with blood tests and x-rays (experiment). This is then treated accordingly. Drug trials are a brilliant example of medical science in action. The rigorous testing process ensures that the drugs are safe to use and will do treat what they are meant to treat.

What is the scientific method?

1. The researcher asks a question
2. They do some background research and gather information on the topic to identify what the field already knows
3. They formulate a hypothesis based on what the information gathered
4. The test the hypothesis with an experiment and collect the data
5. They analyse the data
6. They interpret the results and form a conclusion
7. The paper is peer-reviewed to check for reliability and validity
8. They publish their results
9. Other scientists repeat the experiment to see if they can reproduce the data

Steps 7-9 are important as they ensure that the data being published is reliable. There are many historical cases of false data being published and subsequently affecting the general population's health. For example, a study published by Andrew Wakefield in 1998 linked autism to the MMR vaccine. This was widely publicised, and many parents opted out of giving their children the vaccine. Later, the data was reviewed, and many inconsistencies were found. Thus, the conclusion was unfounded, and the paper was recalled. Unfortunately, the damage was already done and there was a rise in MMR cases in the children who hadn't had the vaccine.

In the BMAT, you are expected to apply the principles of the scientific method to your work and identify certain elements of it in the questions presented to you. You may have questions that discuss an experiment conducted by a student so make sure to be familiar with the process. A little further on, we've actually included a full syllabus checklist for Section 2 that you can tick off once you've revised the key topics. It's a general overview, designed to be easy to read – for the official syllabus, visit the official BMAT website

Introduction – Why The BMAT?

First, what is medicine?

Medicine is defined as the "science or practice of the diagnosis, treatment, and prevention of disease". It is a vocational subject i.e., the syllabus is geared towards preparing you for a particular job and in most countries, is studied for a longer number of years at university than most other subjects.

It is a highly competitive field, with many people starting the application process well before they even put in university applications. Those that are successful become medical students, studying anatomy, physiology, pathology and many other subjects, before shadowing experienced clinicians on placement to learn how to do the job.

Once qualified, the students become practicing doctors, moving through different training stages and gaining experience. Here they can choose to branch off into clinical or academic (research) work and eventually they become consultants in their chosen specialist field.

What makes medicine competitive?

Medicine is a highly revered career choice due to the nature of the work. The number of years and the amount of hard work it takes to even secure a place to study it is an admirable feat. After gaining acceptance, the course is a further 6 years of learning before achieving qualification.

Even then, if you get a great grade and get accepted - you are not a fully registered doctor as when entering the foundation programme, each doctor receives a provisional GMC licence (the licence that legally allows you to practice as a doctor). This becomes a full licence after your first year of foundation training provided you meet all the competency requirements. After that, you are free to continue training.

At each stage of entering training, there is an application process. After foundation training, doctors who choose to go into a general training programme which requires passing multiple exams and sitting interviews. After two-three years, they will then apply again to enter specialist training. Some specialties like paediatrics or obstetrics and gynaecology, only require one application process at the beginning – these are known as run-through programmes.

What this means is that, every year, there are many more applicants than there are places at medical schools. The intensity and duration of medical training limits how many people any university can train to be a doctor – and the BMAT is one of the ways that medical schools filter their applicants, and informs their decision on who to make offers to. Your performance in the BMAT will directly influence the decision of the admissions team to make you an offer, because it is indicative of how you will perform *in comparison to all of the other medical students applying*. You're all hard working, clever people – and that makes separating you out with things like A Level or IB grades almost impossible. The BMAT is so important because it lets the people making those calls turn a solid block of high achievers into a new spectrum of academic skill.

What is the salary like?

Another pull of medicine is the stable income. The base salary for foundation year 1 doctors starts at £28,000. This is further supplemented by pay for extra hours such as evening or night shifts. As a doctor progresses, their salary will increase year on year, with consultants earning up to 100,000 depending on where they work and how many responsibilities they take on.

Furthermore, doctors can work locum or bank shifts, which are extra shifts they may take on that are paid at an hourly rate. These are popular and are well paid – some shifts can earn up to £50-60/hour depending on the staffing need. This can really boost the income of doctors, especially those living in areas with a higher cost of living.

So, why should you choose medicine?

Medicine is a varied, interesting subject and there are plenty of options to choose from. There are plenty of career options within medicine that don't involve clinical work. It's highly flexible, with plenty of time to move in and out of training should you wish to do so. You also have the option to practice abroad. Since it's such a universal subject, you'll have a job anywhere in the world – of course you may have to take a few conversion exams, but it's nothing a bit of revision can't cover. If you don't want to make a big move, you can also take time out to go travelling. Many doctors take extra foundation years to locum, save up and then go on long holidays.

Moreover, wherever you are, it's a pretty stable job with a guaranteed income that garners a lot of respect. Many doctors live quite comfortably on their salaries and though it is busy, have time for social events and have a good work-life balance. You'll make plenty of long-lasting friendships throughout your career!

Another reason is that you may like helping people – as cliché as it may be now, this is a valid reason to choose the career and you do make an impact in your patient's lives. I'm going to break the fourth wall here a bit and tell you, as a graduating medical student, there's nothing better than a patient thanking you for your time and effort. Although you may not be able to do much as you're not fully qualified, some patients will simply appreciate the time you've given them to listen to their concerns.

The process is gruelling and trust me, you'll have moments where you want to pull your hair out, but at the end of the day, it is a highly rewarding job, and you'll feel like you've accomplished a lot.

The 6med BMAT Specification Checklist

Topic	Sub-topic	☑
Biology	Cells - Animal and plant cell components - Bacterial cell components - Organisation of cells in a system	
	Movement across a membrane - Diffusion - Osmosis - Active transport	
	Cell division and sex determination - Mitosis - Meiosis - Asexual/sexual reproduction - Sex determination	
	Inheritance - Chromosomes - Genetic terms: gene, allele, dominant, recessive, heterozygous, homozygous, phenotype, genotype, chromosome - Monohybrid crosses	
	DNA - Structure - Protein synthesis - Gene mutations	
	Gene technologies - Genetic engineering - Stem cells - Selective breeding	
	Variation - Natural selection/evolution - Sources of variation	
	Enzymes - Enzyme mechanism: activation and specificity - Factors affecting rate of enzyme action - Role of amylase, lipase and protease in digestion	

	Animal physiology - Respiration - Organ systems: nervous systems, respiratory system, circulatory system, digestive system, excretory system - Homeostasis - Disease and body defence: communicable and non-communicable diseases	
	Ecosystems - Levels of organisation within an ecosystem - Material cycling	
Chemistry	Atomic structure - Structure of an atom - Relative masses - Atomic/mass numbers - Write atomic configurations of the first 20 elements - Isotopes	
	The periodic table - Structure of the table: rows and groups, arranged in order of size of atomic number - Positions of alkaline and non-alkaline metals - Know the characteristic of an element depending on where it is in the table	
	Chemical reactions, formulae, and equations - Chemical formulae - Symbols: solid, liquid, gas and aqueous - Reversible reactions	
	Quantitative chemistry - Molar masses - Avogadro's constant - Percentage compositions - Empirical formulas - Calculate masses of reactants and products from balanced formulae - Concentrations - Percentage yield	

	Oxidation, reduction and redox - Oxidation and reduction - Determine the oxidation states of atoms in simple inorganic compounds - Disproportionation - Oxidising and reducing agents	
	Chemical bonding, structure, and properties - Elements, compounds, and mixtures - Ionic bonding - Covalent bonding - Metallic bonding - Intermolecular forces - Melting point and conductivity	
	Group chemistry - Alkali metals: reactivity and physical properties - Halogens: reactivity and physical properties - Noble gases	
	Separation techniques - Simple/fractional distillation - Chromatography - Centrifugation - Dissolving - Filtration - Evaporation - Crystallisation	
	Acids, bases and salts - Acids: strong, weak, diluted, reactions with metals, carbonates, metal hydroxides and metal oxides - Bases: strong, weak, dilute and concentrated, reaction with water - Salts	
	Rates of reaction - Exothermic/endothermic reactions - Interpret energy level diagrams - Calculate energy changes from specific heat capacities and changes in temperature in calorimetry experiments - Be able to use bond energy data to calculate energy changes	

The Complete BMAT Specification Explained

Complete Syllabus Checklist

	Electrolysis - Cathode, anode, electrode, electrolyte - Direct vs alternating current - Predict products of electrolysis: aqueous solutions and molten binary compounds - Write half equations - Explain electroplating
	Carbon/organic chemistry - Hydrocarbons: crude oil, boiling points, viscosity, flammability - Cracking: balanced equations - Structural isomerism - Molecular formula, full structural formula (displayed structure) and condensed structural formula - Complete and incomplete combustion - IUPAC guidelines for the systematic naming of carbon compounds, and apply the guidelines in order to be able to name all the compounds in this section of the specification - Homologous series and functional groups - Alkanes - Alkenes - Polymers - Alcohols - Carboxylic acids
	Metals - Reactivity of metal - Displacement reactions - Metal ores - Transition metals
	Kinetic/particle theory - Solid, liquid, gas - Freezing, melting, boiling, evaporating
	Chemical tests - Hydrogen, oxygen, carbon dioxide, chlorine - Carbonates, halides, sulphates - Al^{3+}, Ca^{2+}, Mg^{2+}, Cu^{2+}, Fe^{2+}, Fe^{3+} - Flame test: Li, Na, K, Ca, Cu - Test for anhydrous/hydrous copper

The Complete BMAT Specification Explained
Complete Syllabus Checklist

	Air and water - Composition of air - Distillation - Gaseous pollutants - Chlorine and fluoride ions in drinking water	
Maths	Units - Mass, length, time - Speed - Rates of pay, unit pricing - Density and pressure	
	Number - Positive and negative integers, decimals and fractions - addition, subtraction, multiplication and division: integers, decimals, simple fractions (proper and improper) and mixed numbers - prime numbers, factors (divisors), multiples, common factors, common multiples, highest common factor, lowest common multiple, and prime factorisation (including use of product notation and the unique factorisation theorem) - BIDMAS - square, positive and negative square root, cube and cube root - Simplification - Convert between decimals, percentages and fractions - Surds and multiples of π - Simplify surds - Upper and lower bounds - Round numbers - Approximation of calculations	
	Ratio and proportion - Scale factors, diagrams, and maps - Ratios - Proportion - Percentages - Inverse and direct proportion - Lengths, areas, and volume - Growth and decay	

The Complete BMAT Specification Explained
Complete Syllabus Checklist

	Algebra - Algebraic notation - Index laws - Substitution - Expressions, equations, formulae, identities, inequalities, terms, and factors - Quadratic equations - Rearrange equations - Graphs: roots, intercepts, turning points, reciprocal, exponential, distance, speed, acceleration, gradients - Simultaneous equations - Quadratic formula	
	Geometry - Points, lines, polygons, rotational symmetry - Angle properties: parallel lines, intersecting lines, triangles and quadrilaterals - Square, rectangle, parallelogram, trapezium, kite and rhombus - Pythagoras theorem - Circles: centre, radius, chord, diameter, circumference, area, volume, tangent, arc, sector and segment, arc lengths, angles - Area and volume: triangles, parallelograms, trapezia, cuboids, and other right prisms - SOHCAHTOA - Scalar and vector quantities	
	Statistics - Tables, charts, and diagrams - Discrete and continuous data - Mean, median, mode - Scatter graphs	
	Probability - Tables and frequency trees - Mutually exclusive and dependent events - Tables, grids, Venn diagrams, tree diagrams - Conditional probability	
Physics	Electricity - Electrostatics: friction, electron, charge - Electric circuits: current, charge, voltage, power, energy, conductors, insulators - Components of a circuit - V-I graphs	

	- Thermistors, LDRs, diodes - Resistance	
	Magnetism - North pole, south pole, attraction, and repulsion - Magnetic fields - Soft vs hard magnets - Electromagnets - Motor effect - Electromagnetic induction - Transformers	
	Mechanics - Kinematics: scalar vs vector quantities - Distance, displacement, speed, and time - Forces - Extension - Newton's laws - Mass and weight - Momentum - Energy	
	Thermal physics - Conduction - Convection - Radiation - Heat capacity	
	Matter - States - Ideal gases - State changes - Density - Pressure	
	Waves - Properties - Behaviour - Optics: mirror and ray diagrams - Sound waves - Electromagnetic spectrum	
	Radioactivity - Atomic structure - Radioactive decay - Ionising radiation - Half life	

The Complete BMAT Specification – Scientific Knowledge and Applications

Section 1 – Thinking Skills

Problem solving and critical thinking

For section 1, there's less science, but you'll be assessed on two very important skills: problem solving and critical thinking.

Problem solving

For problem solving, common question types include comparison (time, money, recipe, journey, percentage, and quartiles), spatial (seating arrangement, measurements), speed/distance/time (leaving, arriving, bus/train timetables), logic (pins, voting, safe combinations, passwords, pie charts), shape/abstract reasoning (dice, nets, 3D shapes, visual problems), ratios/percentages and finally a combination of all of the above.

To approach a problem-solving question:

1. Read the question
2. Identify the question type
3. Eliminate incorrect answer options
4. Pick the right answer

Critical thinking

This part of section 1 tests your ability to identify reasoning, assumptions, conclusions and flaws. To approach these questions:

1. Skim the passage
2. Identify the question type
3. Look at the options and identify whether they are supported by the passage
4. Eliminate incorrect answers
5. Work out the answer

Hopefully this very brief insight into how to approach section 1 questions was helpful – we go into more detail in the section 1 part of the book.

The Complete BMAT Specification – Thinking Skills

Section 1: Thinking Skills - Overview

In order to succeed in any section of the BMAT, it is essential to know the structure of the exam:
- Section 1: Thinking Skills contains **32 questions**, made up of:
    o **16 problem solving** questions
    o **16 critical thinking** questions
        ▪ These questions are mixed together which requires you to swap mindsets quickly.
        ▪ Practise both styles of question in random orders to get used to the exam format
- Each question will have **5 answer options to choose from**
- There is **60 minutes** to complete this section
    o This works out as 112.5 seconds per question
- Each question is worth 1 mark
    o The raw marks are then converted into a score between 1 and 9.
        ▪ The median score is around 5.0
        ▪ Top candidates generally score around 7
- There is **no negative marking**
    o If you get stuck on a question, choose your best guess and move on

> **6Med Tip:** No negative marking means that even guesses will give you a 1/5 chance of getting the correct answer!

Most students find section 1 the most difficult part of the BMAT as it:

- focusses on skills that are less familiar, unlike the Scientific Knowledge and Applications questions in Section 2.
- Requires application of knowledge and logic rather than just remembering knowledge

However, students can improve their section 1 marks significantly by doing targeted preparation, as outlined in this chapter!

The Complete BMAT Specification Explained
Section 1 – Thinking Skills

Note, BMAT section 1 changed format in 2020. Section 1 now has:

- Fewer questions (there used to be 35 questions)
- Individual questions each have their own question stem
    - Previously, there were several questions based on a single chunk of information or text.
- No official data inference questions
    - Questions can still involve data interpretation or extraction

> **6Med Tip:** Because of the changes to the BMAT in 2020, be careful if you use other resources to revise from

Section 1: Timings

Section 1 of the BMAT is known to be a time pressured section. Consider using a digital watch to accurately keep track of time.

- Equally dividing time per question allows 112.5 seconds per question.
- Use this timing when you first start to practise section 1
    - Change the timings to suit you:
        - If you find a problem-solving question more difficult than critical thinking, take some of the time allotted to critical thinking questions and use it for problem solving questions
        - Many students find giving roughly 90 seconds for their stronger questions and 130 seconds for their weaker question type can be effective
        - Try different timings to find out what works specifically for you
    - Consider if you want to have time to check your answers
        - Some people find that they second guess themselves when checking and do worse!
            - Compare your results when checking your answers or just going with what you put down first
            - You might want to just check one type of question, like the problem-solving questions where students can make mistakes with mental maths and conversions
        - If you want time to check, figure out how much time you want to use.
            - You might want to have 10 minutes to check
            - This means you will have
                - 60 – 10 = 50
                - 50 / 32 = 1.5 minutes per question
                - 1.5 x 60 = 90 seconds per question

The Complete BMAT Specification Explained
Section 1 – Thinking Skills

- Don't be afraid to move on from questions you are struggling with!
    - Select your best guess and make a note of the question number
        - You can always come back to the question if you have time at the end
        - Just by selecting an answer, you have a 1/5 chance of getting the correct one!
- Once you're familiar with Section 1 style questions, practise them in timed conditions to get used to the time pressure
    - Some students practise with 10 – 20 seconds less than what they plan to have in the exam to get used to the feeling of being behind the clock
    - Almost every student finds the BMAT to be a quick test – don't panic if you don't finish. Take a deep breath and move onto the next section.
    - Don't waste time stressing about things you can't solve

> **6Med Tip:** Dedicating time to work out how much time you need per question is a key part of BMAT preparation you shouldn't skip out!

Problem Solving Questions

These questions require you to use basic mathematics to solve logic-based problems:
- Candidates are not allowed calculators for the BMAT, so strong mental arithmetic skills are crucial to finish the section within the allocated time and do well

It can seem like these questions are impossible to prepare for, as they vary hugely each year. However, they are all based on core mathematics and logical reasoning. Knowing how to approach and having a foundation of maths knowledge that you can apply to each question is the best way to prepare for section 1 problem solving questions – as well as doing lots and lots of practise questions!

Useful Maths Skills to Revise

- 12 times tables
    - Knowing these fluently will save you a lot of time when working out questions
- Unit conversions
    - Information may not be given to you in the same units or the answers may be presented in different units to the question information. Confidence with conversions can save you time and enable you to get the right answer!

The Complete BMAT Specification Explained

Section 1 – Thinking Skills

You will not need to convert between metric and imperial measurements, but may be asked questions using both forms

Metric	
1 centimetre	10 millimetres
1 metre	100 centimetres
1 kilometre	1000 metres

Imperial	
1 foot	12 inches
1 yard	3 feet
1 yard	36 inches
1 mile	1760 yards

- Appropriate rounding and estimations
    o Saves time and effort
    o Can be useful when the data and answer options are spread apart
        ▪ Will not be accurate (or useful!) if the data is close together, for example 1.6, 1.7 and 1.9
- Mental maths
    o Make sure you can correctly and quickly carry out calculations including addition, subtraction, multiplication, and division
- Conversions between fractions and percentages
    ▪ For example, 1/3 = 33%, 1/8 = 12.5%

> **6Med Tip:** 112.5 seconds per question isn't a lot – use your time to figure out the question, not maths you could prepare and learn before sitting the BMAT!

Problem solving questions can include:

- Spatial reasoning
- Calculations involving speed, distance, and time
- Logic and deductive reasoning
- Data tables and graphs
- Multi-step calculations

The Complete BMAT Specification Explained
Section 1 – Thinking Skills

- Spatial Reasoning questions
  - Using information within the questions to derive
    - missing pattern pieces
    - missing dimensions of shapes, like table lengths or chair height
    - manipulations of 2D and 3D objects
      - including rotations, translations, and reflections
  - Some students find these questions very difficult
    - Consider leaving these questions to the end
    - If you get stuck, give your best guess as your answer and move on
      - Always remember there is no negative marking for BMAT questions

- Speed, Distance, Time Questions
  - These are similar to questions asked in some A-Level Maths syllabuses
    - They will not be simple one step calculations, but might require several calculations and comparison of answers to find the quickest or longest route.
  - You will need to apply formulas to answer the questions – these formulas are not given to you in the exam!
    - Also practise rearranging them so you can quickly and confidently use them in the exam

> **Key Formula to Know**
> - Distance = Speed x Time
> - Velocity = change in position / time

- Logic and deductive reasoning
  - Translating information given in the question stem into algebra is the key to answering these problems

> *Example:* Amy is three times as old as Jessica but half as old as Kevin can be:
> - A = 3J
> - 2A = K
> - Therefore, 3J = 0.5K

- Data Tables and Graphs
    - There is usually at least one question using visual representations of data
        - Can be linked to speed, distance, and time questions
        - Can ask you to interpret the data presented
            - Just like the logic and deductive reasoning, translate the question into what it may look like in table or graph format. This can be a rough estimate, like a positive trend or a very extreme data point
        - Can require you to quickly read tables to select the right answer
    - Try to understand *how* the data is presented before learning what the data *is*
        - For graphs, determine what the axis, symbols, and general trend it
        - For tables, look at the headings and see how the information is laid-out:
            - Tables can be read like graphs – read both the columns and the rows
    - Take a breath if you get overwhelmed by the data
        - Lots of extra information can be included in tables and graphs to make the question more difficult and time-consuming
        - Remember, you don't need to read all of the data, you just need to extract the relevant pieces!

- Multi-step calculations
    - These questions can be confusing as they require
        - Making the correct calculations, in the correct order, to reach the right answer
        - Correct identification of which numbers to in each step of the calculation
    - It's important to know what you're working out at each step:

For Example: A rectangular chocolate bar weights 100g. Each section in the bar is made up of 3 squares. There are 10 sections in the bar.

- You should try to label your calculations like this
    - 100g / 10 = weight of a section = 10g
    - 10g / 3 = weight of a square = 3.3g

This will save you time when checking over your answers too!

> **6Med Tip:** The best way to do well in the problem-solving questions is to:
> - Practise mental arithmetic skills outlined in this section
> - Know key formulas
> - Practise applying your knowledge and skills with lots and lots of practise questions!

Critical Thinking Questions

These questions are much easier to prepare for than the problem-solving questions, as there are 6 main question types that are generally asked:

1. Identifying the main conclusion
2. Identifying an assumption
3. Identifying flaws in the information or false conclusions
4. Identifying if additional information can strengthen or weaken the conclusion
5. Matching arguments
6. Applying principles

There is also a standard structure each critical thinking question will follow:
- 100 – 150-word paragraph
- 1 question per paragraph
- 5 answer options to choose from in each question

Approach to Critical Thinking Questions

A key step in answering the Critical Thinking questions is to identify which thought pattern to apply to the question (please see below for more information about thought patterns). Each question format uses a slightly different process to analyse and get the right answer, so identifying what process to apply is a key step.
- When you do practise questions, it can be helpful to practise identifying what type of question is being asked
    - This means that you learn to recognise what type of thought pattern to apply to the question

In addition to practising your approach to the Critical Thinking questions, it's important to plan the best way to approach the questions. There isn't a lot of time to read the question stem, work out the answer, and read the answer options.
- Once you're more familiar with the question styles and thought patterns, time yourself doing practise questions and work out:
    o The order to read the question and answers
        ▪ Some students are faster when they read the answer options first and then the question stem
    o Work out if faster = more marks for you
        ▪ Lots of students get more marks by attempting more questions with the same error rate.
        ▪ Other students find they get higher scores by carefully completing each question and guessing any questions they don't' have time to do properly
            • Remember there is no negative marking in the BMAT

- **Reason/Conclusion Thinking Pattern:**

Critical thinking questions are a good place to earn marks because they are based on a single thinking pattern:
1. The questions are only based on what is written in the question stem/paragraph.
    o External knowledge or reasoning has no place in section 1 critical thinking!
        ▪ Only use the information you are provided

2. For every good argument, conclusions are made from reasons
    o Here, if the reasons are valid, then the conclusion is valid
3. For poor arguments, conclusions are not based on reasons
    o Here, if the reasons are not valid, then the conclusion is not valid

6Med Tip: Only use the information provided to you in the stem to answer each question

You should apply this thinking pattern for each paragraph, by first identifying the conclusion and the reasons
- Conclusion:
    o often highlighted by key words
        ▪ Therefore
        ▪ So
        ▪ As such
        ▪ In conclusion

The Complete BMAT Specification Explained

Section 1 – Thinking Skills

- o Can be at the beginning, middle, or end of the stem paragraph
- o There may be no conclusion written in the question stem, instead, you might need to pick the correct conclusion from the answer options
- Reasons:
    - o We are all familiar with 'reasons' but it's important to have a single and solid definition of a 'reason' for the BMAT.
        - Remember, a reason is the explanation of *why* something happened

Example: Gareth said they would bring either cake or brownies to the party. They didn't have any chocolate to make brownies with. So, Gareth will bring cake.	
Reasons	We know that Gareth will bring either cake of brownies Gareth did not have any chocolate to make brownies
Conclusion	Gareth will bring cake

- **Identifying the Conclusion Questions**

Some questions will ask you to identify the conclusion of the question stem. Use the reasons/conclusion thought pattern to help you with these questions.
- Identify the key reasons in the text
- Read through the answers
    - o Which answer is the logical and natural next step using the reasons presented in the stem?
        - Some questions will require you to do a little basic maths. The stem might say "87% of hens have red feathers". The correct conclusion could be "13% of hens do not have red feathers".
            - Look for mirrored statistics in the answer options to help quickly narrow down the correct answer.

- **Identifying Assumptions Questions**

Some questions will present you with a stem and ask what assumption is being made. Section 1 assumptions generally rely on your intelligence and prior knowledge to trick you out!

- An assumption is something taken for granted in order to reach the conclusion
    - Assumptions are not written in the stem
    - Assumptions require you to add in information (usually subconsciously) to make the reasons and/or conclusions more logical
    - One key pattern to remember is that assumptions are not *assertions*
        - Assertions are written within the stem.
        - If a stem states 'All women are clever', this is an assertion and not an assumption

- Only use the information in the question stem to answer the questions
    - Assumptions are not written within the stem
    - As such, assumptions rely on the reader to add in information or extra reasons to allow a good conclusion to be made from the stem

Example: Gareth said they would bring either cake or brownies to the party. They didn't have any chocolate to make brownies with. So, Gareth will bring cake.	
Reasons	We know that Gareth will bring either cake or brownies
	Gareth did not have any chocolate to make brownies
Assumption	Gareth will make brownies using chocolate
	Gareth will not go and get chocolate to make brownies
Conclusion	Gareth will bring cake

- **Weaker/Stronger Questions**

Some Critical Thinking questions can require you to pick what answer would make the argument in the stem stronger or weaker. As such, the first step for these questions is always identifying what argument the stem is trying to make.

Then, applying another thought pattern on top of the reason/conclusion pattern will enable you to answer these questions:

- Good reasons provide:
    - Evidence
    - Logic
    - Balance
        - These three things can be achieved by looking at all the reasons together, rather than individually
- Bad reasons have:
    - No evidence base
    - Little logic
    - Bias

So, to approach the weaker/stronger questions:
- first apply the reasons/conclusion pattern and identify any assumptions made
- Then, identify if the reasons have (or lack)
    o Evidence, logic, and balance
- Look at the answer options and see which one will make it stronger by adding in
    o Evidence, logic, or balance
        ▪ Or which answer takes evidence, logic, or balance away from the question stem

- **Matching Argument Questions**

In these questions, you will be given 5 answer options that are arguments. You will be asked to choose an argument that is similar to the argument made in the stem.
- Usually, these questions are phrased as 'which most closely parallels the reasoning used in the above argument'
- This doesn't mean choosing the argument focussing on a similar concept. You need to choose the argument that follows the same logic or pattern made in the stem

---

For Example:

Josie did not come to my party. She didn't tell me if she was coming. Either she forgot about the party or she didn't want to come. She must have forgotten as she wouldn't have not told me.

Which of the following most closely parallels the above argument?

Here, the question relies on two ideas:

- Josie didn't come to my party
- She must have forgotten about the party
-

Replacing these with a generic symbol or letter can help you see the structure of the argument:

- Josie forgot about the party
    o This can be A
- Josie didn't want to come to the party and didn't tell RSVP
    o This can be B
- Either A or B is true
- B cannot be true
- A must be true

The Complete BMAT Specification Explained

Section 1 – Thinking Skills

	Answer Options	Explanation

1	It is thought that the Ancient Romans ate a variety of food, although we don't know their specific diet. They could have eaten meat or fish. The distance of the main cities from the sea and lack of storage options imply that eating fresh fish was impossible.	Here, the argument does not follow the same structure as the question stem:
		    A: The Romans ate meat
		    B: The Romans ate fish
		In the stem, A or B is true. Here, A can be true when B is true. As such, this isn't the matching argument

2	If you have talent and train hard enough, you can be a professional athlete. There are many sports you can play including hockey, fishing, running, or chess. At high levels, athletes specialise and focus on one sport	Here, the argument structure is
		    A: you can play hockey
		    B: you can fish
		    C: you can run
		    D: you can play chess
		At high levels, A or B or C or D is an option. As such, the stem has a similar argument to this option but is not the same

3	Andi wants to go on holiday. Within their budget, Andi can go on one holiday this year, either to Greece or Italy. Andi wouldn't go to Italy as they are going there with their family next year.	Here, the argument structure is the same as the stem:
		    A: Andi will choose to go to Italy
		    B: Andi will choose to go to Greece
		    A and B cannot both happen
		    Either A or B is correct
		This answer is the best fitting to stem structure and is the correct option

4	Kristen likes fish fingers but has bought chicken for dinner tonight.	This option does not match the stem structure. Often there is at least one answer option that obviously does not fit the stem structure and can be easily ruled out

5	I would not have missed the bus if I skipped brushing my teeth or eating breakfast	This structure is:
		    A: missing the bus
		    B: skipping brushing my teeth
		    C: skipping eating breakfast
		    A would not be true if either B or C happened
		This structure does not match the argument structure in the question stem

The Complete BMAT Specification Explained
Section 1 – Thinking Skills

- **Applying Principles Questions**

1. Applying principles questions are similar to the matching argument questions. Here, you will have to find the answer that is the same as the logic presented in the question stem. As such, these questions have two steps: identifying the underlying logic in the question stem and finding the answer that applies this logic to another argument

Example: **People who are addicted to substances should be allowed free healthcare. This is because addiction is caused by many factors, including genetics and environment.**

Here, the question stem presents an underlying principle that so called 'self-inflicted' diseases are not truly 'self-inflicted' and those patients should receive free healthcare similarly to other health conditions that are not 'self-inflicted'. The answer grid presents the possible answers and a worked through explanation:

	Answer Options	Explanation
1	Smokers should pay for their own healthcare, including for conditions that their smoking status may have contributed to	This presents the opposite principle to the question stem, and therefore, is an incorrect answer
2	Children should receive free healthcare	This answer option does not have the same or similar underlying principles as the question stem
3	People who are injured whilst doing something illegal should receive free healthcare	The underlying principle similar to the question stem: regardless of the cause of injury, the patient should receive free healthcare. This is the correct answer option
4	People who exercise should get priority healthcare access	The principle in this answer is similar to option 1, however rewards those who do health-positive activities, rather than penalises those who have habits that may negatively impact their health
5	Private healthcare should be more affordable	This answer option is unrelated to the underlying principle presented in the question stem.

The Complete BMAT Specification Explained
Section 1 – Thinking Skills

Overall Tips and Tricks for Section 1

- **Timing is everything**
    - Spending some of your preparation time working out your unique strengths and weakness is crucial for section 1 success
    - Allocate the right proportion of time according to which questions you find more difficult
    - Make sure you move onto the next question if you run out of allocated time for a particular problem

- **Guessing is OK**
    - This section is particularly time pressured as you have to read a lot of information and interpret data
    - Remember there is a 1/5 chance of getting the right answer by just selecting one option

- For the Problem-Solving questions, practise your basic arithmetic skills and gain confidence in doing them quickly (and correctly!)

- Do lots of practise questions
    - Make sure you're used to doing a mix of critical thinking and problem-solving questions in a random order, just like in the exam!
    -
- Learn the format of critical thinking questions.
    - In addition to doing lots of the practise questions, make sure you can confidently identify what type of question is being presented
        - This means you can then apply the right thought pattern to the question

- Take a deep breath if you're feeling stressed or out of control
    - This is useful whilst preparing for the exam and actually during it!
    - Remember, the exam is time pressured for everyone
    - You can only do the best you can – don't stress about things you can't control!

The Complete BMAT Specification – Scientific Knowledge and Applications
Section 2 Part 1: Biology.

B1 - Cells

We start the biology section by looking at cells. Cells are the basis for every living organism, however that does not mean all cells are alike. Animals, plants, and bacteria all have different features to their cells, which relate to the different functions each class of organism needs its cells to do.

The first classification divide is between eukaryotic and prokaryotic cells. Eukaryotic cells include plant and animal cells, and the key feature is that they contain membrane-bound organelles, like a nucleus. Prokaryotic cells don't contain a nucleus, which means their DNA is able to float freely in the cytoplasm.

Eukaryotic cells

There are some features found in all eukaryotic cells, and then some features unique to plant cells.

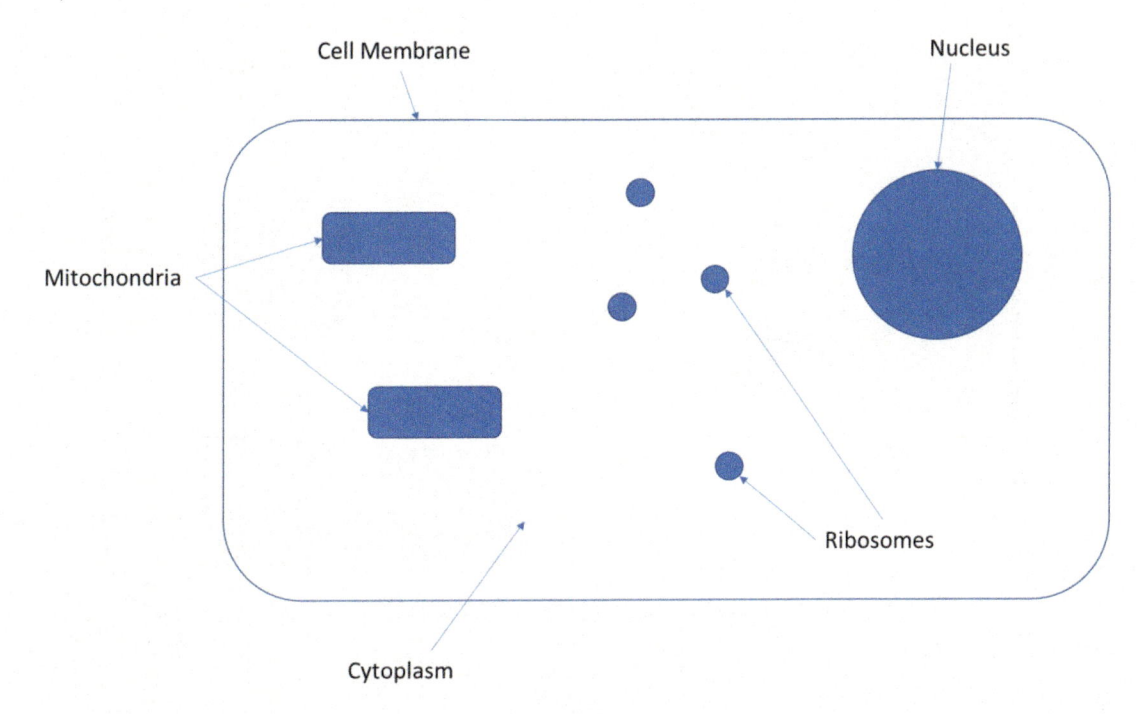

The Complete BMAT Specification Explained

B1 - Cells

Found in all cells are:

- Cell membrane -
    - a semi-permeable boundary around the cell
    - controls the movement of substances into and out of the cell
    - made of a phospholipid bilayer, which prevents charged or large substances from diffusing across
- Cytoplasm -
    - the fluid that fills the cells, which consists of mostly water but also contains organelles, nutrients and other molecules and ions
    - most chemical reactions in the cell take place here
- Nucleus -
    - this is where the genetic information of the cell is stored, in the form of DNA coding for proteins
- Mitochondria -
    - specialised organelles with a double membrane, where aerobic respiration takes place
- Ribosomes -
    - organelles in the cytoplasm that carry out protein synthesis

> **6Med Tip:** Did you know that the *Mitochondria* are the powerhouse of the cell?

Plant cells have several extra features:

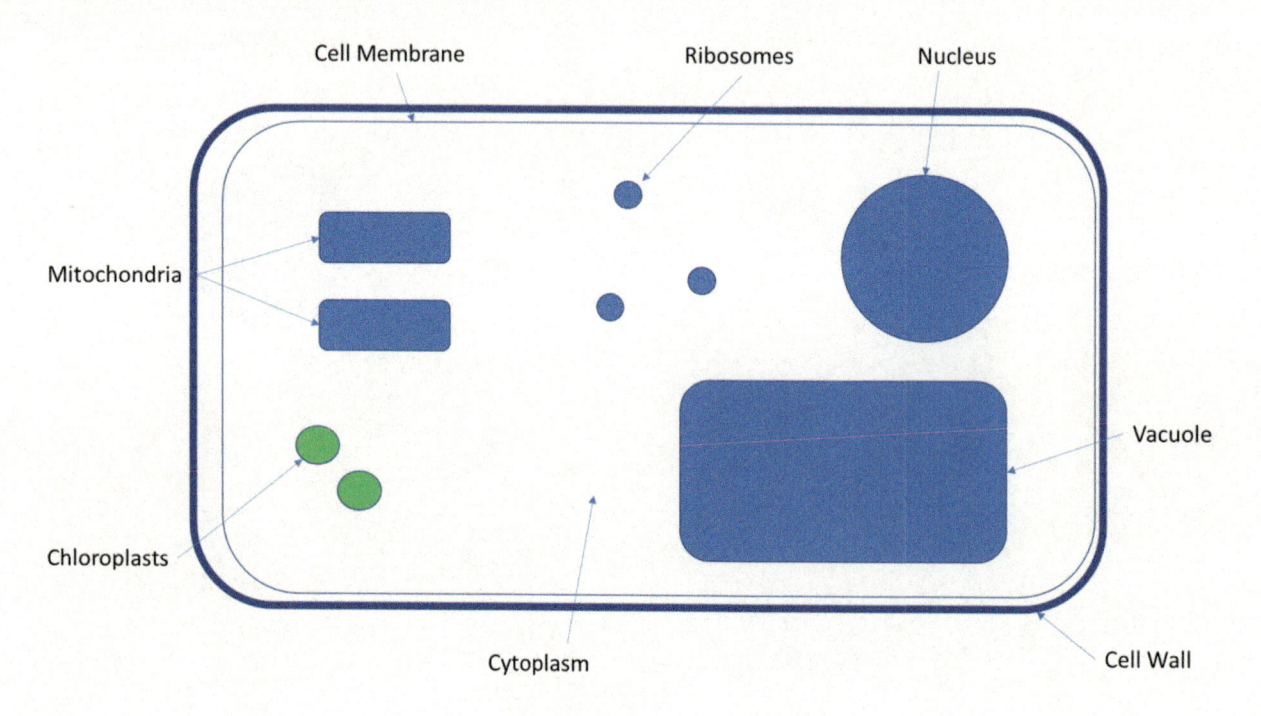

[Diagram of a plant cell with labels: Cell Membrane, Ribosomes, Nucleus, Mitochondria, Chloroplasts, Cytoplasm, Vacuole, Cell Wall]

- Cell wall –
    - made from cellulose, a polymer of beta-glucose
    - provides structural support to the cell, and stops the cell from changing shape due to water movement
- Chloroplast –
    - specialised organelles with a double membrane where photosynthesis takes place
    - contain a green pigment chlorophyll, which absorbs light using photosystems
- Vacuole –
    - contains cell sap, made of sugars, water and nutrients
    - surrounded by a special membrane called the tonoplast
    - keeps the cell turgid to retain its shape

Prokaryotic Cells

Without membrane-bound organelles, prokaryotic cells have had to come up with different ways to meet the same cellular functions as eukaryotic cells.

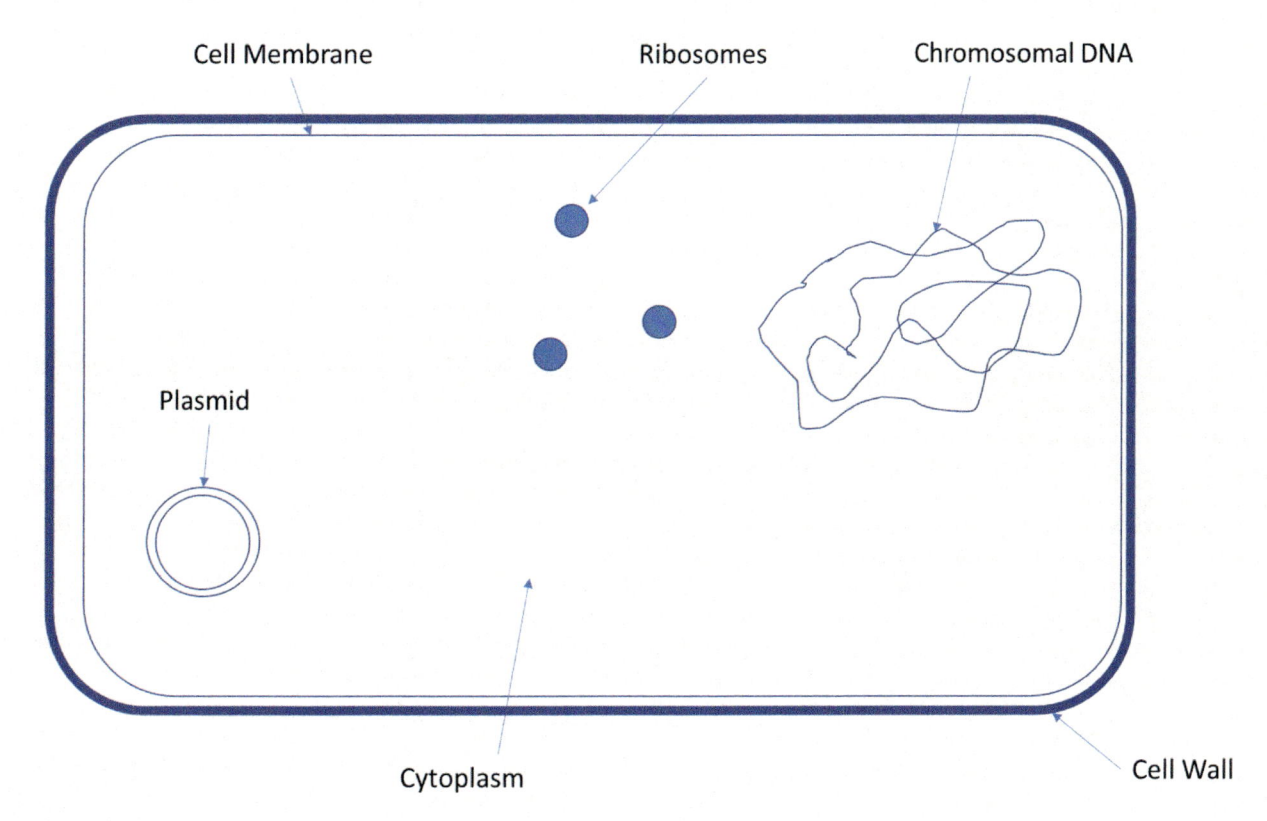

Diagram of a prokaryotic cell with labels: Cell Membrane, Ribosomes, Chromosomal DNA, Plasmid, Cytoplasm, Cell Wall

- Cell membrane –
    - some have a single cell membrane, whilst others have a double cell membrane

- Cell wall –
    - prokaryotic cell walls are made of peptidoglycans, not cellulose
- Chromosomal DNA –
    - prokaryotic cells do not contain a nucleus, so the circular DNA is free to move in the cytoplasm
- Plasmid DNA –
    - a extrachromosomal ring of DNA that is separate from the main chromosomal DNA
    - it is small, circular and double-stranded
    - prokaryotes can exchange plasmids with each other
- Ribosomes –
    - prokaryotic cells have smaller ribosomes than those in eukaryotic cells

A classic BMAT question is to compare the differences between the cell types, so here's a simple summary table:

	Animal	Plant	Prokaryotic
Size	Most 5-100 microns	Most 5-100 microns	Most 0.2-2.0 microns
Cell membrane	✓	✓	✓
Cytoplasm	✓	✓	✓
Cell wall	✗	✓ Cellulose	✓ Peptidoglycan
Mitochondria	✓	✓	✗ Mesosomes
Chloroplasts	✗	✓	✗
Nucleus	✓	✓	✗ Circular DNA and plasmids
Ribosomes	✓ 80S (larger)	✓ 80S (larger)	✓ 70S (smaller)

The Complete BMAT Specification Explained

B1 - Cells

Organisation of cells and tissues

When one looks at a simplified drawing of a cell, it is amazing to think how they come together to form large multi-cellular organisms. There is a hierarchy to how this happens. Groups of cells with a similar structure, working towards the same function, form tissues. Groups of tissues then come together to form organs, and finally several organs come together into organ systems. Here's a couple of examples just to make it clearer:

Cells -> Tissues -> Organs -> Organ Systems

Muscle cells -> muscle tissue -> heart -> circulatory system

Epithelial cell -> epithelial tissue -> stomach -> digestive system

Knowledge Check

Test your knowledge with these questions (if this is your book, don't be afraid to doodle in the margins). Your answers will always be upside down underneath.

1. Which of the following statements about prokaryotic cells are true?
    a. Some contain an extrachromosomal section of DNA called a plasmid
    b. Most of their DNA is stored in the nucleus
    c. Their cell walls are made of peptidoglycans

2. Fill in the gaps in the diagram below:

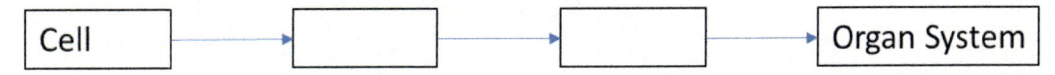

| Cell | → | | → | | → | Organ System |

Answers:
1 = a and c
2 = Cell → tissue → organ → Organ System

B2 – Movement Across Membranes

It's great having cell membranes, but for cells to function properly there needs to be a way for stuff to cross them. For example, the cells lining the digestive system need to be able to absorb nutrients from the food we eat, or nerve cells being able to control the movement of ions to fire off action potentials. Luckily, cells have a few neat tricks to be able to do this.

Diffusion

Hopefully, this one is pretty straightforward, and one I bet you have seen maybe without even realising it. Imagine you drop a bit of dye in a glass of water, or spray a bit of perfume in a room. Over time, the dye spreads to fill the glass, and the smell of the perfume reaches every corner of the room. That's diffusion!

The formal definition is:

<u>The passive movement of particles from an area of high concentration to an area of low concentration</u>

So what does this mean? Exactly what it says! If we take the perfume examples, when you spray perfume, there will be lots of particles in a small area by the bottle – **high concentration**. Over time, the particles will move into the rest of the room, where initially there are very few particles in a large area – **low concentration**. **Passive** means it does not need any energy to make it happen.

This same thing can happen across a membrane in cells. As long as the membrane allows a particle through, and there is a difference in concentration either side of the membrane, then particles will move across the membrane.

Eventually, there will be the same number of particles either side of the membrane. When this happens, we say the system has reached equilibrium. It is important to say here that this does not mean particles are not moving from one side of the membrane to the other, but that the same number of particles are moving over from each side, so the overall number/concentration does not change.

Direction of Diffusion   Dynamic Equilibrium

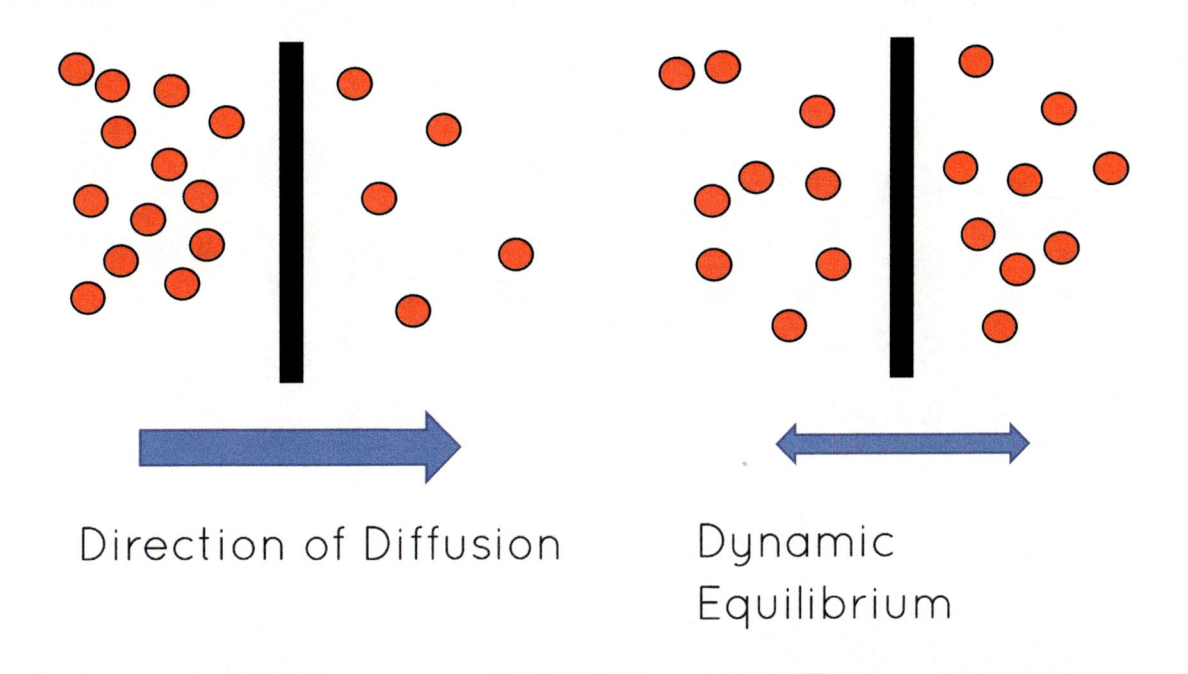

> **6Med Tip:** Remember diffusion is the movement of small particles down a concentration gradient, which means it doesn't require any energy

Osmosis

The next concept we need to cover is osmosis. Simply, this is a special form of diffusion, but often students can get in a right muddle about it. So, let's start with the definition and work through it.

Osmosis is the movement of water particles from an area of high concentration of water (or low concentration of solute) to an area of low concentration of water (or high concentration of solute) across a partially permeable membrane

So just like before, this is diffusion of particles (in this case water) from an area of high to low concentration. However, what makes it special is this **partially permeable membrane**. This is a membrane that allows some things through – water – but not others – solutes.

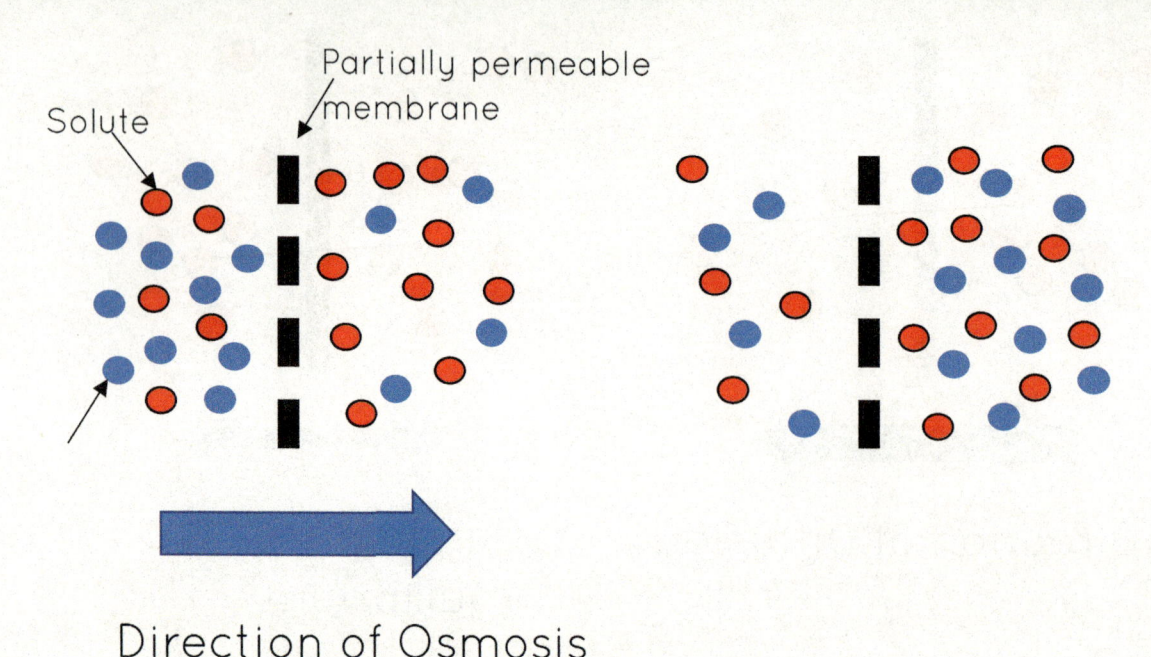

The Complete BMAT Specification Explained
B2 – Movement Across Membranes

Direction of Osmosis

> **6Med Tip:** Osmosis needs a partially permeable membrane that stops the solutes from moving across the membrane

Active Transport

This is the final way of getting stuff across membranes. What happens if there's something you really want, but it goes against the concentration gradient? Well, then you're going to need to expend some energy to get it. As you'll know from the previous chapter, cells have mitochondria that make energy in the form of ATP. This can be used to power pumps or channels, that can move ions and solutes against a concentration gradient.

The Complete BMAT Specification Explained

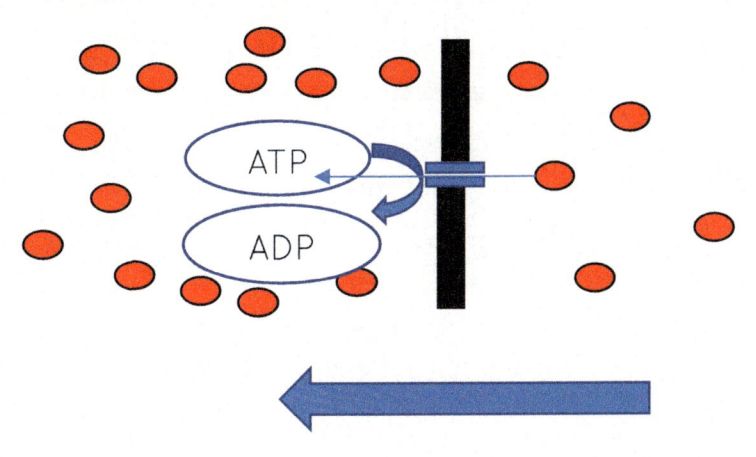

B2 – Movement Across Membranes

Direction of Active Transport

6Med Tip: Because active transport requires energy, cells that use this process a lot will need to have more mitochondria to provide the ATP to power this process

Knowledge Check

1. Match the terms to the correct definition

   Osmosis — The passive movement of particles from an area of high concentration to an area of low concentration

   Active Transport — The movement of water particles from an area of high concentration of water (or low concentration of solute) to an area of low concentration of water (or high concentration of solute) across a partially permeable membrane

   Diffusion — The movement of particles against a concentration gradient, which requires energy to do so

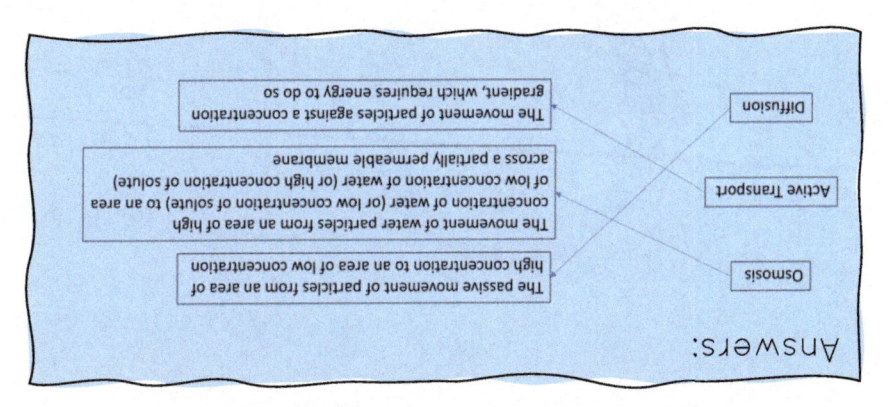

Answers:
- Osmosis → The movement of water particles from an area of high concentration of water (or low concentration of solute) to an area of low concentration of water (or high concentration of solute) across a partially permeable membrane
- Active Transport → The movement of particles against a concentration gradient, which requires energy to do so
- Diffusion → The passive movement of particles from an area of high concentration to an area of low concentration

B3 – Cell Division and Sex Determination

Hopefully the last two sections have been a gentle introduction into Biology for the BMAT. Now that's get into a meatier topic – cell division!

Mitosis

Cells are pretty neat, but they do some tough jobs and not all of them can last forever. Therefore, cells need the ability to replicate for repair. Now think about you, and how much bigger you've got since you were a baby. Cells need to be able to replicate to allow an organism to grow. Finally, some organisms take this further and can reproduce just by cell replication. So how do cells replicate to carry out all these functions? By mitosis.

Cell Cycle

To begin with, let's think about what a cell will need to do to replicate into two. It will need to make more organelles, so each daughter cell will have all the components to function independently. It will need to double the DNA content in the nucleus, so each cell will have right amount of genetic material. But even more so, it needs to make sure each daughter cell ends up with the right bits of DNA – which makes the daughter cells genetically identical to the parent. Finally, the cell membrane needs to be able to split the cell into two. All these processes happen at different points during the cell cycle.

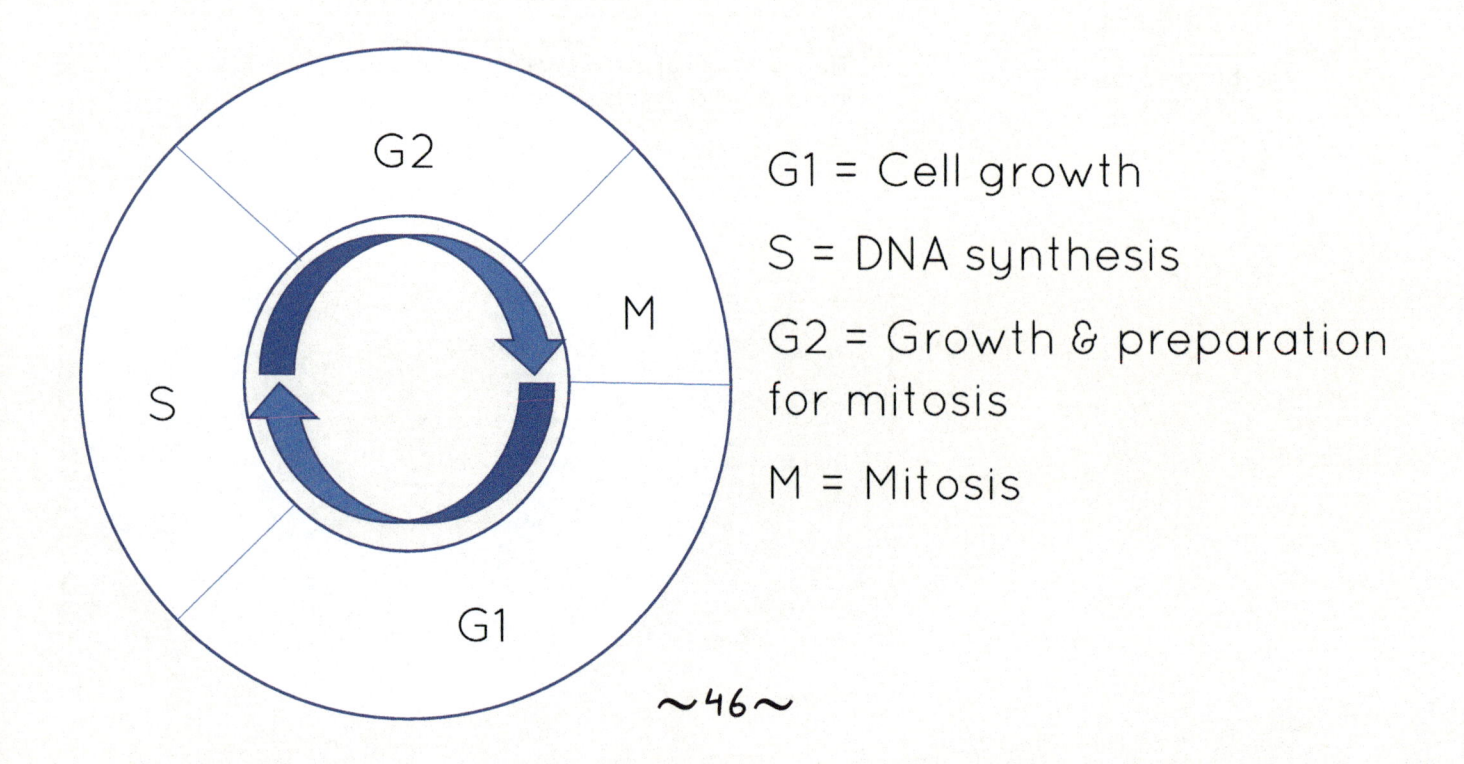

G1 = Cell growth

S = DNA synthesis

G2 = Growth & preparation for mitosis

M = Mitosis

The Complete BMAT Specification Explained
B3 - Cell Division and Sex Determination

G1, S and G2 form the interphase. This is all about preparing the cell for mitosis, so this is where the cell grows and makes more organelles, and DNA is replicated. If we are being really technical, mitosis is the splitting of a nucleus into two genetically identical nuclei, each with the same amount of DNA. Mitosis has its own four stages – prophase, metaphase, anaphase and telophase.

Interphase – DNA content doubles

Prophase – Chromosomes pair up

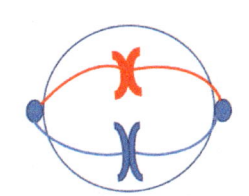

Metaphase – Chromosomes line up along the centre of the nucleus, and spindle fibres branch out from the centrosomes to attach to the centromere of each chromosome

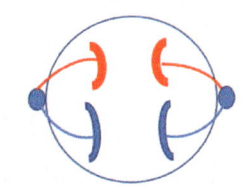

Anaphase – The spindle fibres contract to pull the sister chromatids apart

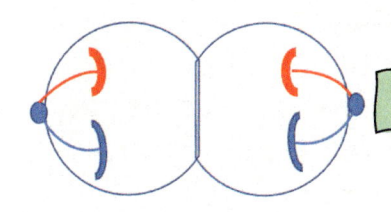

Telophase – The nucleus splits into two

Finally, the cell membrane dividing the two nuclei into their own individual daughter cells is called cytokinesis.

6Med Tip: Mitosis isn't always perfect, and when cell replication goes wrong it can lead to the development of cancers

~47~

The Complete BMAT Specification Explained

B3 – Cell Division and Sex Determination

Meiosis

Some organisms use mitosis for reproduction, but others (like us) do something a little different. We'll talk briefly about the pros and cons of each a bit later on, but for now let's focus on the process of meiosis. This is where a cell splits into not two but four daughter cells. Each daughter cell has half the original amount of DNA, and is called a gamete. But why make a cell with not enough DNA? Because, that means two gametes can come together in a process called fertilisation to form a completely new organism!

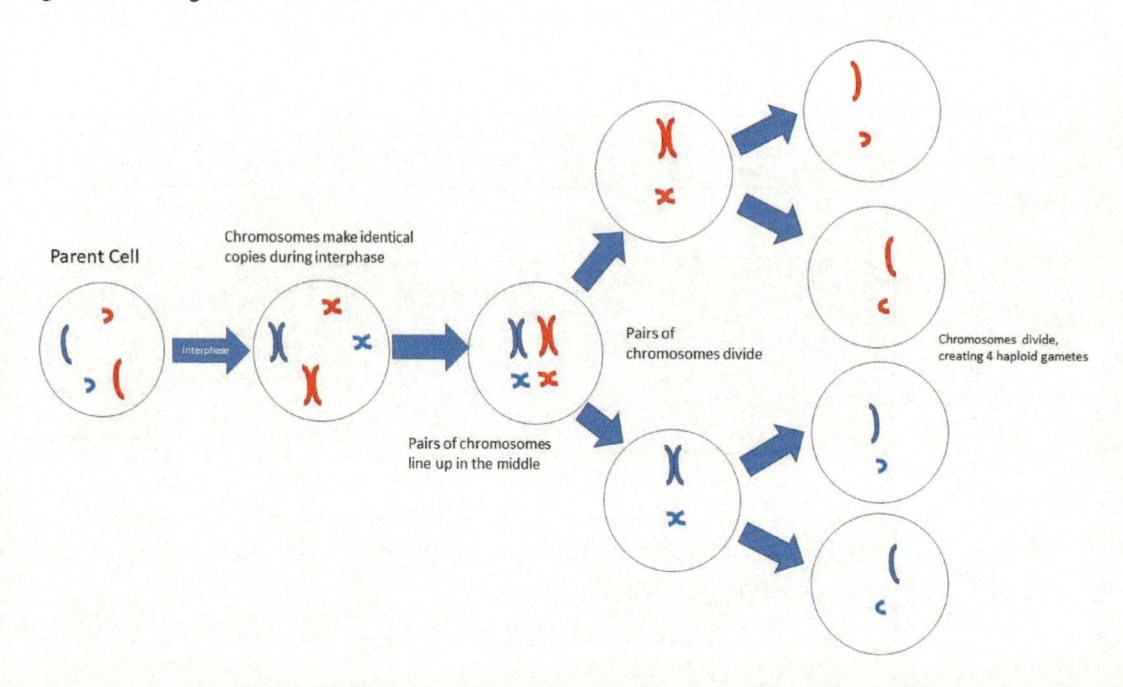

Parent Cell → interphase → Chromosomes make identical copies during interphase → Pairs of chromosomes line up in the middle → Pairs of chromosomes divide → Chromosomes divide, creating 4 haploid gametes

> **6Med Tip:** A really common BMAT question is to ask you how the amount of DNA changes during mitosis and meiosis. Using human cells as an example, each cell has 23 pairs of chromosomes (so 46 chromosomes in total). During interphase, the chromosomes all make identical copies of themselves, so now there will be 46 pairs (92 in total). In mitosis, the cell divides once, so now each daughter cell will have 23 pairs (46 total). In meiosis, the cell divides twice, so now each daughter cell will have 23 individual chromosomes.
>
> We can display this algebraically as well. A parent cell will have $2n$ chromosomes. After interphase, there will be $4n$ chromosomes. Mitosis will produce two daughter cell with $2n$ chromosomes in each, while meiosis will produce four daughter cells with n chromosomes in each.

The Complete BMAT Specification Explained
B3 - Cell Division and Sex Determination

Reproduction

When an organism reproduces just by mitosis, we call this asexual reproduction. If an organism uses meiosis, then this is sexual reproduction.

Asexual Reproduction	Sexual Reproduction
Offspring are genetically identical	Creates genetic variation
Only needs one parent	Requires two parents
Requires less energy	More energy intensive (lots of wasted gametes)

6Med Tip: Sexual reproduction isn't just better than asexual reproduction, each have their own advantages and disadvantages that make them more suited for particular environmental challenges

Sex Determination

One of the particularly cool things about meiosis is the role it plays in sex determination. Organisms that use sexual reproduction have a special set of chromosomes, called the sex chromosomes. Unsurprisingly, these are what determine the sex of the offspring. If an offspring has two X chromosomes, then it's female. If an offspring has an X and a Y chromosome, it's male. You should be able to draw genetic crosses to work out if it's male or female (we'll cover this in more detail in the inheritance section).

6Med Tip: Some diseases can only be passed on through the X or Y chromosome

The Complete BMAT Specification Explained
B3 – Cell Division and Sex Determination

Knowledge Check

One healthy female ovarian cell undergoes meiosis. How many chromosomes, in total, are present after meiosis is complete?

23

44

46

92

184

Match up the stages of mitosis

Anaphase		Chromosomes pair up
Prophase		Chromosomes line up
Telophase		Chromosomes are pulled apart
Metaphase		Nucleus splits

Answers:

1: d (at the end of meiosis, there are four gametes each with 2e chromosomes);

2:
- Metaphase — Nucleus splits
- Telophase — Chromosomes are pulled apart
- Prophase — Chromosomes line up
- Anaphase — Chromosomes pair up

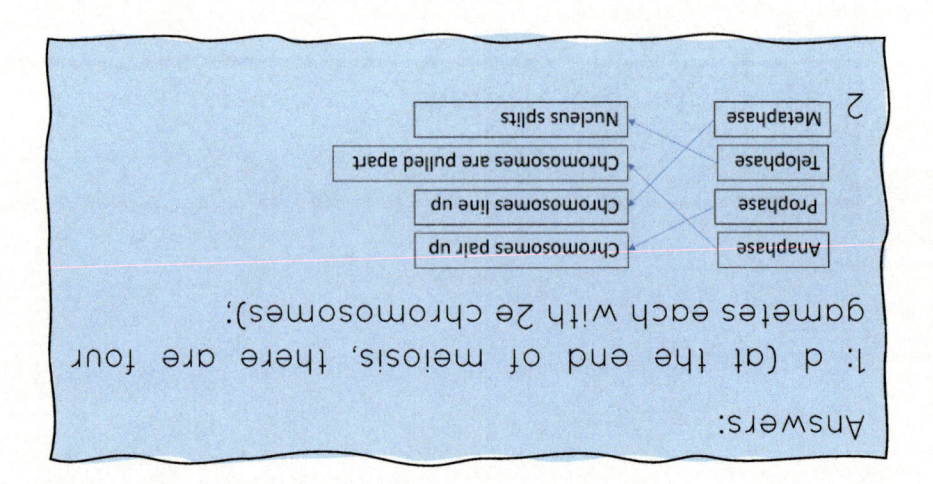

B4 – Inheritance

Long before we knew about mitosis and meiosis, about DNA and genetic engineering, a monk called Gregor Mendel was studying peas, and noticed patterns in the way different characteristics, like the height of plants or whether the pea pods were smooth or crinkled, were passed on from generation to generation. Whilst our knowledge has come on a long way since then, many of Mendel's fundamental principles of inheritance still apply.

Definitions

The specification has a nice list of definitions for you to know:

Term	Definition
Gene	a characteristic that can be inherited from parent to offspring
Allele	one of the two alternative forms of a gene that can be expressed, that are found at the same place in a chromosome
Dominant	an allele that is always expressed
Recessive	an allele that gets hidden if paired with a dominant allele
Heterozygous	where the two alleles of a gene are different
Homozygous	where the two alleles of a gene are the same
Phenotype	the displayed characteristics of a gene
Genotype	the genetic makeup of alleles in a gene
Chromosome	a long DNA molecule that carries the genetic information in the form of genes

Monohybrid Crosses

With an appreciation of those definitions, the next skill is to be able to use genetic diagrams to work out how genes can be inherited. This is best done using some examples, so let's start with Mendel's own peas. One characteristic he studied was whether pea pods were smooth or crinkled. He found that when he crossed smooth pea pods with crinkled pea pods, all the offspring had smooth pea pods. However, when he crossed those plants, he found that while most offspring had smooth pea pods, some had crinkled pods – and the ratio was almost exactly 3:1.

B4 – Inheritance

So why did this happen? Well, we can use monohybrid crosses to show the pattern of inheritance. The allele for smooth pea pods is dominant, and the allele for crinkled pea pods is recessive. We can record this using capital and little letters – so a capital S means smooth (and is dominant), and a small s means crinkled (and is recessive). Next, we can draw out a Punnet square. Remember, because chromosomes come in pairs, there's two alleles for every gene. In our first cross, we have homozygous dominant alleles (SS) crossed with homozygous recessive alleles (ss). Remember from meiosis, that each gamete contains one of the pair of chromosomes, which means it will only carry one allele. When two gametes fuse together during fertilisation, that will produce a zygote with two alleles – one from each parent. The Punnet Square allows us to see all the potential combinations of alleles, and we can use this to see the pattern of inheritance.

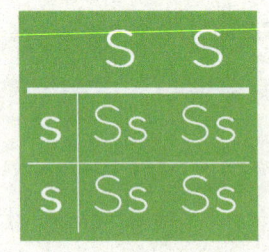

	S	S
s	Ss	Ss
s	Ss	Ss

So for our first cross, 100% of the offspring have the genotype Ss, and as S is dominant, then 100% off the offspring will have the phenotype smooth pea pods.

Now if we cross two of these offspring, let's make a Punnet square and see the result.

	S	s
S	SS	Ss
s	Ss	ss

There are three possible genotypes – SS, Ss, and ss – in a ratio of 1:2:1. However, there are only two possible phenotypes – smooth pea pods or crinkled pea pods – and they will appear in a ratio of 3:1.

The Complete BMAT Specification Explained

B4 – Inheritance

> **6Med Tip:** The BMAT could ask you to express Punnet squares using ratios, percentages, probabilities, or numbers. Practise converting between common examples (and this will help you in the Maths section as well)

Let's do another example, this time using sex determination from the previous chapter. As mentioned, females have two X chromosomes, and males have one X and one Y chromosome. If we put this into a Punnet square, we can see the ratio of sex in the offspring.

	X	X
X	XX	XX
Y	XY	XY

Here, you can see a nice 50:50 ratio for the sex of the offspring.

Of course, in reality things can be much more complicated, and usually many genes come together to produce a phenotype, which is why poor Mendel didn't get credit he deserved at the time, but he was eventually proved right and now his name lives on as one of the founders of inheritance!

Inherited Conditions

Punnet squares can be used for much more than studying peas. There are some diseases are caused by faulty genes. This means that these faulty genes can be passed on through families. It's important to understand how this happens, as then doctors can provide counselling or early interventions that can help families deal with these often life-limiting conditions.

These inherited conditions are also a good way for them to test you on interpreting family trees, like this one below:

The Complete BMAT Specification Explained

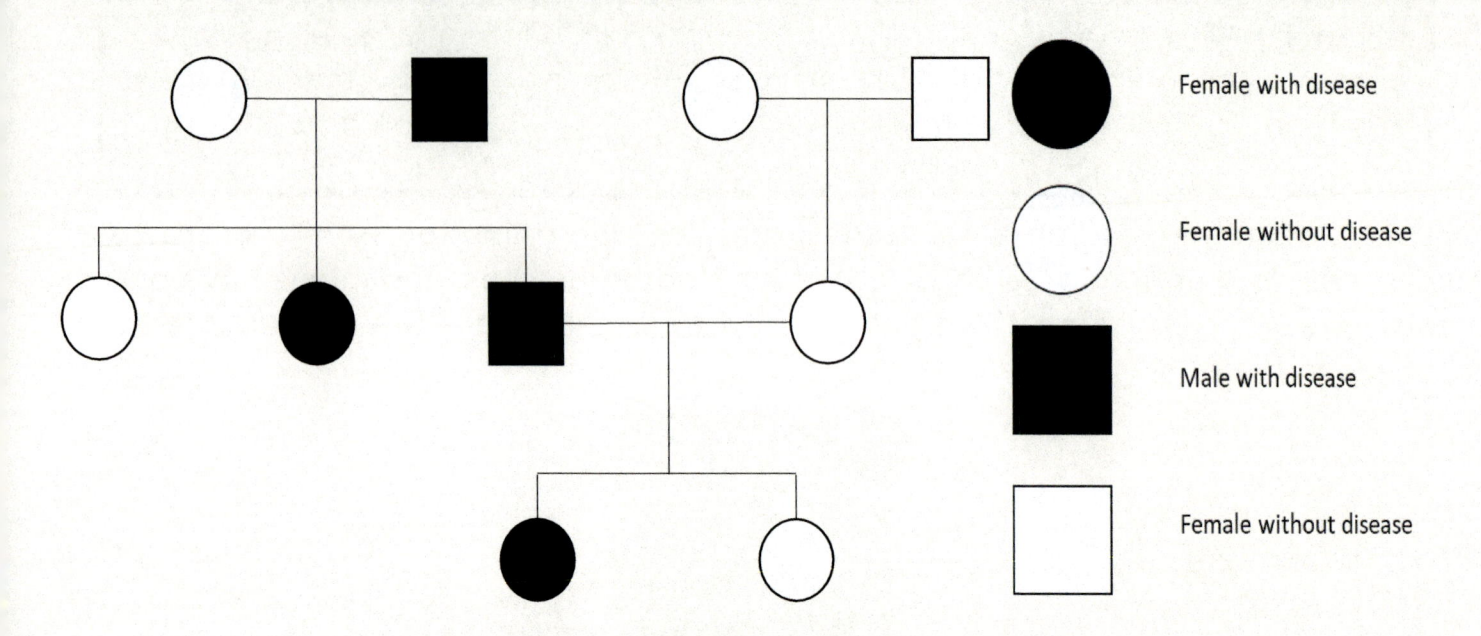

B4 – Inheritance

- ○ Female with disease (shown as ●)
- ○ Female without disease
- ■ Male with disease
- □ Female without disease

Each square or circle represents a family member, and whether the shape is filled or not shows whether that person has the disease you are investigating. By plotting out all the family members, it makes it easier to see any patterns of inheritance.

Some common inherited disorders

Disease	Pattern of inheritance
Cystic Fibrosis	Autosomal recessive
Huntingdon's Disease	Autosomal dominant
Duchenne Muscular dystrophy	X-linked recessive

6Med Tip: As a general rule of thumb, if there's an affected family member in every generation, then it's most likely a dominant disease. If the disease skips generations, then it's most likely a recessive disease. If mostly male members of the family are affected, then it's likely an X-linked recessive disease.

The Complete BMAT Specification Explained

B4 – Inheritance

Knowledge Check

1. Observe this family tree. Individual A is homozygous recessive and individual B is homozygous dominant for a particular feature

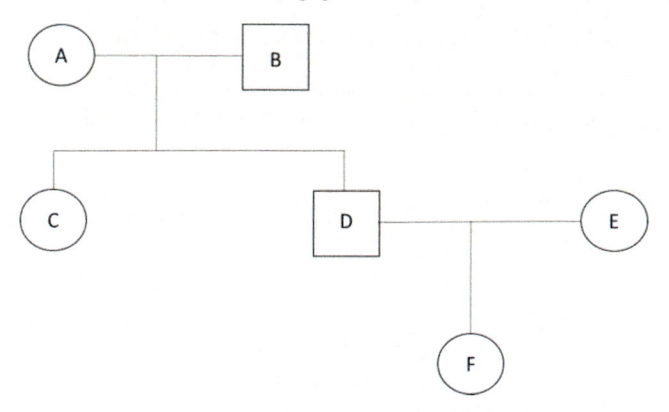

What is the percentage probability that individual F is homozygous recessive if:

E is homozygous recessive

E is heterozygous

2. Define the terms:

Genotype

Phenotype

Heterozygous

Homozygous

Answers 1: a = 50%, b = 25%;

2: genotype = the genetic makeup of alleles in a gene; phenotype = the displayed characteristics of a gene; heterozygous = where the two alleles of a gene are different; homozygous = where the two alleles of a gene are the same

B5 – DNA

One of the most famous scientific discoveries was the structure of DNA, which was unravelled in the early 1950's by James Watson and Francis Crick (and Rosalind Franklin, who didn't get the recognition she deserved). The double-helix shape is now an almost ubiquitous symbol for science. But what actually is DNA?

Structure of DNA

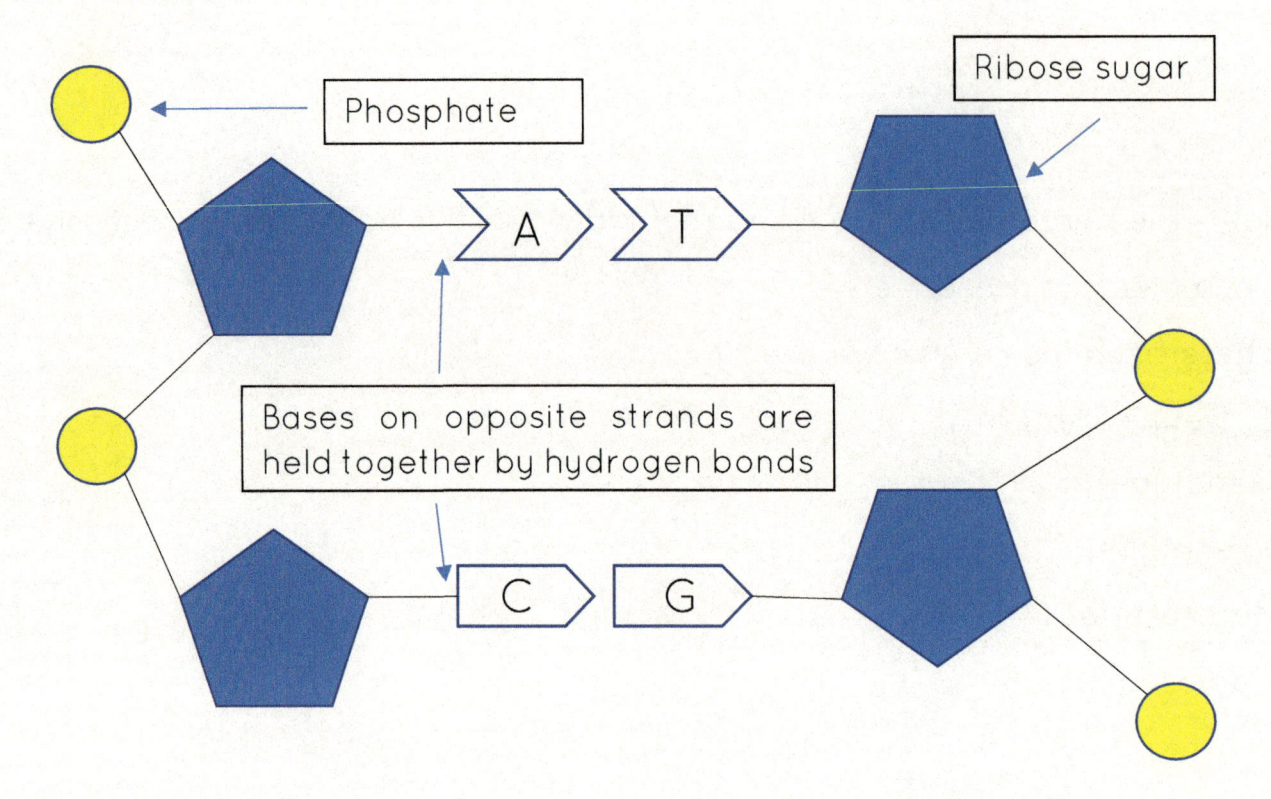

DNA is a polymer, made up of long chains of repeating monomers, called nucleotides. These nucleotides are made up of a sugar, a phosphate group, and a DNA base. There are 4 bases – A, C, G and T. These bases only pair in one way – A with T and C with G. The order of these bases forms our genetic code.

B6 – Gene Technologies

Protein Synthesis

So what good is the genetic code? Well, genes carry the codes for proteins, and it's these proteins that make up everything. The genetic code is read in triplets, and each amino acid has a triplet code. Proteins are made up of long chains of amino acids, so the order of the triplets in the gene will in turn produce a chain with the right amino acids, so in the end a nice whole protein will be made! There are also some codons – helpfully called START and STOP – that are needed to initiate protein synthesis, and then bring it to a close when the full protein has been made.

Gene mutations

During DNA replication, sometimes mistakes can be made, and a different nucleotide can be inserted. These changes to the gene are called mutations. However, some mutations might mean a different amino acid is selected, or even insert a STOP codon too early, which could have significant implications for the final protein that is produced.

> **6Med Tip:** Most mutations will have no effect on the phenotype, because each amino acid has several similar codons. This is called redundancy and means that even if there is a mutation that changes one base, most times the correct amino acid will still be selected.

Knowledge Check

1. There is a double stranded segment of DNA. Strand 1 of DNA contains 21% adenine (A), 26% thymine (T) and 33% guanine (G). What is the probability of any one base on strand 2 to be guanine (G)?
2. Define redundancy

Answers: 1 = 20% guanine, 2 = where several different codons code for the same amino acid

B6 – Gene Technologies

And once we had discovered the structure of DNA, science was complete, and we could rest happily ever after.

...

......

....

Of course not! Science never stops, and once we knew what DNA was, the next question was whether could we change it? Well, the answer to that, as you'll see, is yes!

Genetic Engineering

Genetic engineering is anything that involves changing an organism's DNA. For example, we can add genes that code for useful proteins, or we could remove genes that confer disadvantages. A fantastic example is how the insulin is produced as a drug. Insulin is a hormone produced naturally by the body to control blood sugar levels. However, people with type 1 diabetes are unable to make their own insulin, so must inject insulin every day. Much of this is produced using genetically engineered bacteria. The reason bacteria are so useful is they have plasmids, which as we saw earlier are extrachromosomal rings of DNA, that are easy to remove and manipulate.

First, we need to select and cut out the right gene. We do that with special enzymes called restriction enzymes. These are able to cut DNA in the right place because they will have a complementary base pair sequence to the bases either side of the target gene. The enzymes also cut each strand of DNA unequally, which produces 'sticky ends' that are necessary to insert the gene into the plasmid. By using the same restriction enzymes to open the plasmid, the sticky ends will have complementary base pairs to each other, so we can use DNA ligase to join the inserted gene and the plasmid together. The genetically modified plasmid is now reinserted into a bacterium, and this bacterium will now start producing insulin!

The Complete BMAT Specification Explained

B6 – Gene Technologies

Human Cell

Isolate the chromosome with insulin gene

Use restriction enzymes to cut out the insulin gene

Bacterial Cell

Take out the plasmid

Use restriction enzymes to open up the plasmid

Use DNA ligase to join the insulin gene into the plasmid

Reinsert the plasmid into the bacteria

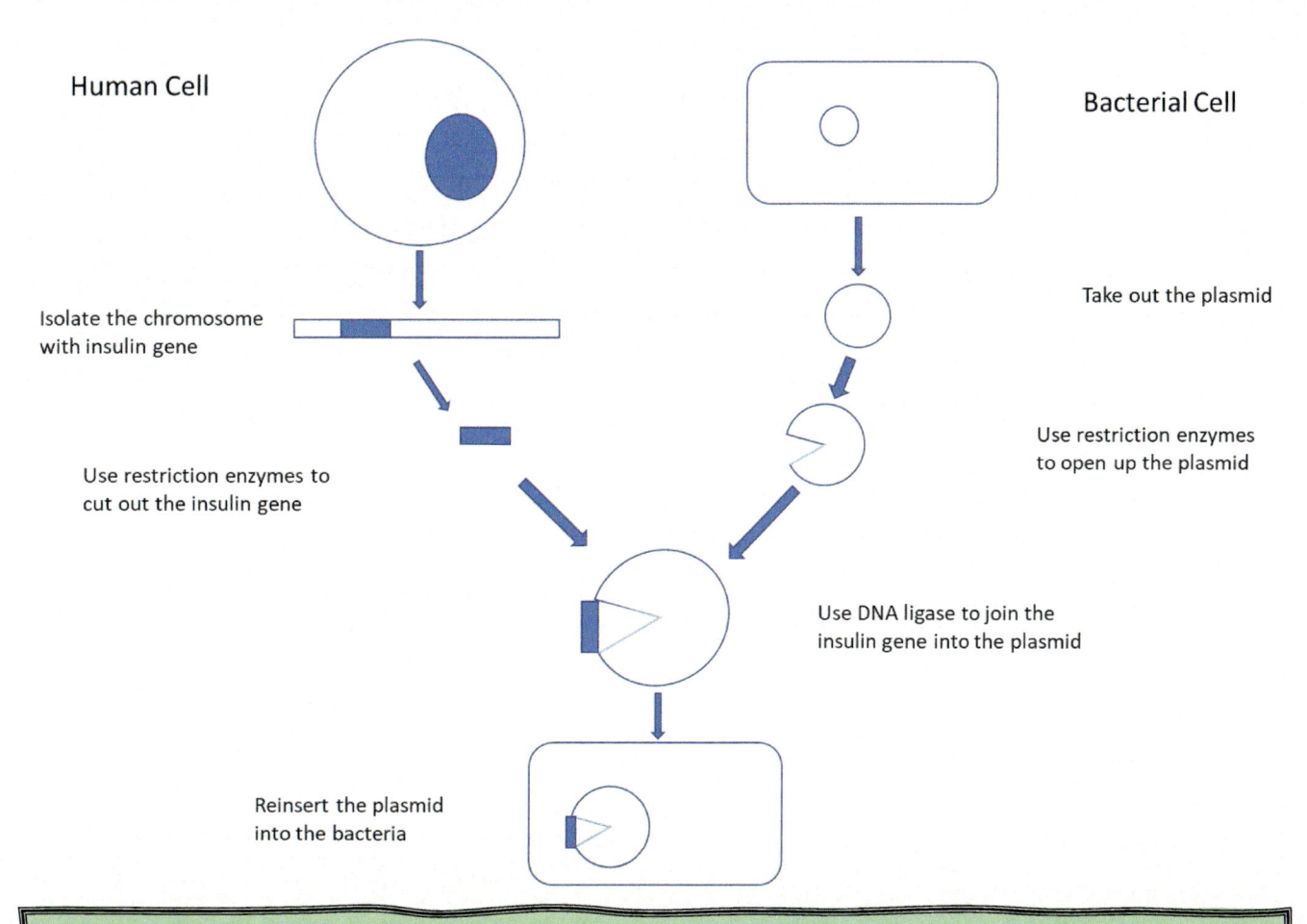

> **6Med Tip:** BMAT examiners love to give you diagrams of genetic engineering and ask you to pick which enzymes are used where. Remember, restriction enzymes cut up DNA, and DNA ligase puts it back together.

Stem Cells

Stem cells are one of medicine's exciting next great hopes, with huge potential but also some important ethical issues to understand (smells like a Section 3 essay...).

> **6Med Tip:** Generally, adult stem cells are found in places of the body where there is a high cell turnover

The Complete BMAT Specification Explained

B6 – Gene Technologies

Stem cells are cells that still have the potential to form a range of mature cells. When most people think of stem cells, they think of embryonic stem cells. These are the cells in the earliest embryonic stages (think under 100 cells) that have the potential to develop into every type of cell in the body. As the embryo continues to grow, these stem cells gradually specialise, so they have the potential to form fewer and fewer mature cells. Even in adults however, there are still stem cells. For example, in the bone marrow there are haemopoietic stem cells, which have the ability to form any type of blood cell. We have found adult stem cells all over the place now, even in the brain!

Selective Breeding

Whilst this might not be as sexy as tampering with DNA or stem cells, selective breeding is still a form of genetic engineering. By breeding animals together with particular characteristics that we want, that overall strengthens the characteristic. For example, if we wanted to make more muscular cows, to produce more beef per cow, we would breed the largest cows together, then off their offspring breed the largest cows again. Over many generations, the cows will become larger and larger.

> **6Med Tip:** Think of selective breeding like man-made evolution (which we will cover in the next chapter)

Knowledge Check

1. A scientist is deciding whether to use bone marrow or embryonic stem cells for research into a new treatment for heart disease. Which of the two statements are correct?
- Embryonic stem cells are able to differentiate into any type of specialised cell
- Bone marrow stem cells are easier to collect
- Bone marrow stem cells can differentiate into any type of specialised cell

2. Which of the following are needed to produce a bacteria that expresses the fluorescent protein from a jellyfish:
- Restriction enzymes
- Fluorescent protein from a jellyfish
- DNA ligase
- A plasmid or viral vector

Answers: 1 = a and b; 2 = a, c and d

B7 – Variation

The last few chapters have covered a lot of the nitty-gritty, molecular stuff around DNA and inheritance. Now let's step back a minute and take a wider view of how variation can lead to changes in a whole population – evolution, so to speak.

Natural Selection and Evolution

If you look around your classroom, you will see that everyone around you looks a bit different. There is usually huge genetic variation within a population, which means there will be a range of phenotypes. Now, in the classroom the short people are not ostracised and killed (well maybe if you aren't very nice!), but in the animal kingdom this range of phenotypes matter, as some organisms will be more adapted to the environment they are living in. These animals are more likely to survive and reproduce, so pass on their genes to the next generation. This process is called natural selection.

> **6Med Tip:** Bigger isn't always better. For example, if food becomes scarce then larger animals might become disadvantaged, because they will need more energy on a day to day basis.

Now over time (and we're talking many many many generations), natural selection will result in the inherited characteristics of a population changing. That is just a pretty wordy way of saying more and more members of a species will start to display the same phenotype that meant they stayed alive. This is evolution, as first thought of by Darwin when he observed finches and other animals on the Galapagos islands.

> **6Med Tip:** Eventually, evolution might lead to a new species being formed. What defines a different species is when two organisms cannot reproduce and produce fertile offspring.

B7 – Variation

Evolution usually takes thousands, if not millions of years, which makes it pretty hard to study. However, if we use organisms that reproduce much faster, like bacteria (some bacteria can double in population size in twenty minutes), then we can see natural selection and evolution in action. This is particularly pressing when it comes to modelling antibiotic resistance.

If a population of bacteria are exposed to an antibiotic, some of them will have genetic variants that make them more resistant to the antibiotic than the rest of the population. This could be for all sorts of reasons, like a small change in a structural protein that prevents the antibiotic binding, or they have an enzyme that is able to inactivate the antibiotic. These bacteria are more likely to survive because of natural selection, and the reduced competition for nutrients once all the other non-resistant bacteria have been killed. Over repeated exposures to antibiotics, eventually the population will evolve to develop total resistance to the antibiotic.

> **6Med Tip:** This is where the concept of antimicrobial stewardship comes into medicine. The theory goes that if we only prescribe antibiotics when necessary, use the most specific ones to the bacteria we are targeting, and take the full course of antibiotic, then fewer variants will be able to escape

Sources of variation

We've talked here mostly about genetic variation, which will produce a diverse range of phenotypes in a population. However, variation can also come from the environment. What this effectively means is variation not caused by genes. For example, environmental variation in humans could be having a tattoo or a scar, whilst in plants the soil they grow in can result in significant variation.

> **6Med Tip:** Of course, a lot of phenotypes will depend on both genes and the environment

Knowledge Check

1. Which two of the following statements about genetic variation are correct?
    a. The environment can cause genetic variation
    b. Genetic variation is necessary for natural selection
    c. Mutations can produce genetic variation
2. Define 'species'

Answers: 1 B, C; 2 organisms that can reproduce and produce fertile offspring

B8 – Enzymes

This is a pretty short chapter, and hopefully nice and straight forward. Every second, there's millions of chemical reactions happening inside your body, and enzymes are what makes them tick. They are biological catalysts, which means they speed up chemical reactions, so they work effectively at our body's temperature.

How do enzymes work?

One of the main reasons enzymes work so well is that they are specific – basically they have an active site (where the reaction happens) that can only fit one substrate. We also call this the 'lock and key' model – where the substrate is the key, and the enzyme's active site is the lock. If the substrate doesn't fit into the active site, then no reaction can take place.

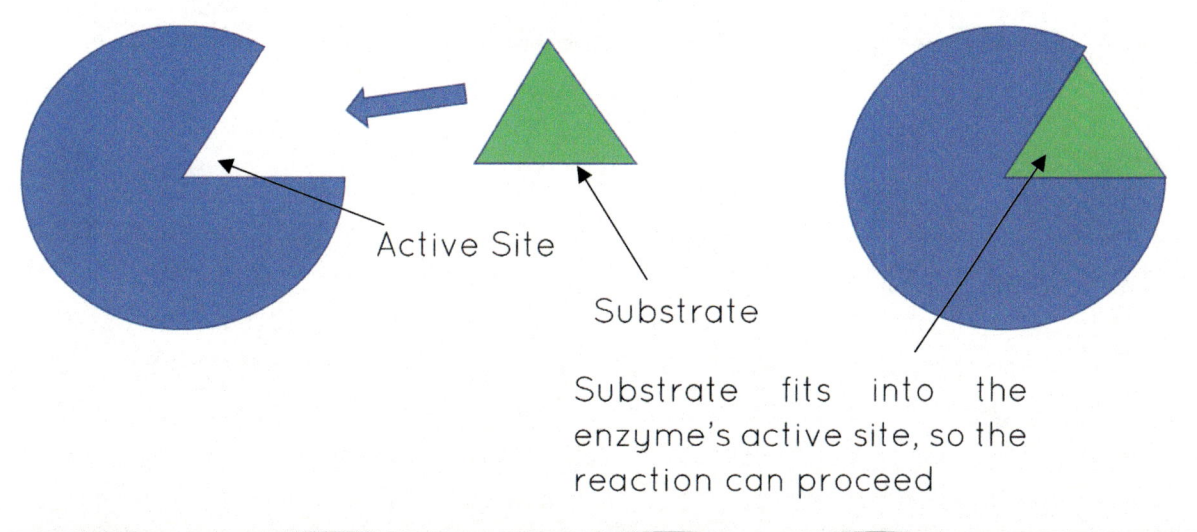

Active Site

Substrate

Substrate fits into the enzyme's active site, so the reaction can proceed

6Med Tip: Many enzymes contain a transition metal in their active site.

Temperature and pH

This leads nicely on to our next topic, because if something happens to the enzyme, and the active site changes shape, then naturally the enzyme won't function anymore. Using the lock and key model again, if you broke your lock then even though you have the right key, it won't turn. When this happens to an enzyme, we say it has been **denatured**. There are two things that can damage enzymes – heat and strong acids or alkalis (see the graph below).

The Complete BMAT Specification Explained

B8 – Enzymes

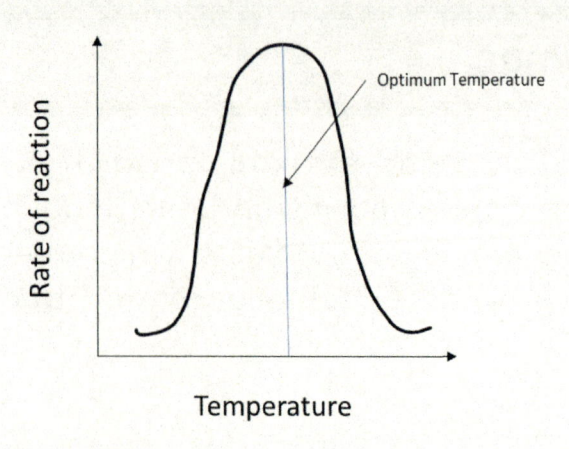

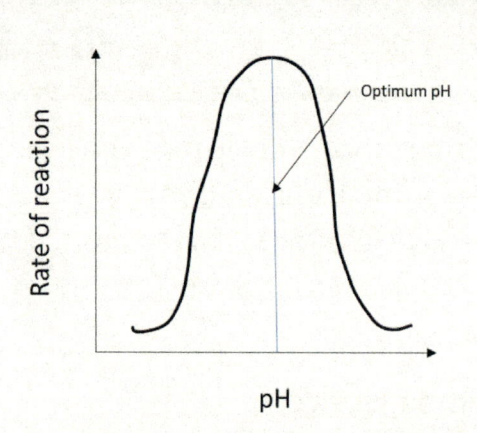

[Graph: Rate of reaction vs Temperature, showing bell curve with Optimum Temperature marked]

[Graph: Rate of reaction vs pH, showing bell curve with Optimum pH marked]

> **6Med Tip:** Cold temperatures don't denature enzymes, but remember there is still a chemical reaction that needs to take place, and at cold temperatures the particles involved have less energy, so are less likely to collide with each other to start the chemical reaction

Enzymes and digestion

As mentioned earlier, almost every chemical reaction in the body relies on an enzyme. There are huge dusty textbooks in the corners of university libraries with great long lists of them. Thankfully, at no point will you ever need to learn them all, but in the BMAT specification it does want you to know about some of the enzymes involved in digestion. And the reason for this is they demonstrate another great feature of enzymes, which is they are designed to work best at an optimum pH and temperature, depending on where in the body they are found. Below is a nice simple summary table of the three enzymes they want you to know:

Enzyme	Job	Where found	Optimum pH
Amylase	Break down carbohydrates	In the mouth	7
Proteases	Break down proteins	In the stomach	4
Lipases	Break down fats	In the small intestine	9

The Complete BMAT Specification Explained

B8 – Enzymes

Knowledge Check

1. Which two statements are correct about enzyme activity?
    a. Boiling an enzyme will reduce enzyme activity
    b. Treating the enzyme with a protease will have no effect on enzyme activity
    c. Placing an enzyme in strong acid will reduce enzyme activity
2. Fill in the table below

Enzyme	Function	Optimum pH
	Break down carbohydrates	
		4
Lipase		

Answers: 1: A,C, 2:

Enzyme	Function	Optimum pH
amylase	Break down carbohydrates	7
Protease	Break down proteins	4
Lipase	Break down lipids/fats	8

The Complete BMAT Specification Explained

B9 – Animal Physiology

B9 – Animal Physiology

Bit of a meaty chapter (we know you like them though, *really*), but whilst the specification looks quite intimidating, in practise they ask very few questions in the exam, and don't expect you to know it in too much depth. So what we'll do here is try and cover the essential stuff in a nice concise way.

> **6Med Tip:** Make sure you go through the BMAT past papers to get an understanding of the level of knowledge they want you to display in the exam

Respiration

This is what makes our cells tick. It is how they make ATP, which is the molecule that provides energy for all sorts of processes within cells. There are essentially two types of respiration, and it depends on whether or not there is sufficient oxygen available. When there is, cells can carry out aerobic respiration. The word equation for this (which you **need** to know) is:

Glucose + Oxygen -> Carbon Dioxide + Water (+ ATP)

> **6Med Tip:** ATP isn't made in the chemical reaction, but the energy released from the breakdown of glucose into carbon dioxide and water allows another phosphate group to be added to a molecule of ADP.

By contrast, anaerobic respiration happens when a cell doesn't have enough oxygen, for example a muscle cell after you've been sprinting hard. The word equation for this is:

Glucose -> Lactate (+ ATP)

Anaerobic respiration is much less efficient than aerobic respiration, as it produces less ATP per molecules of glucose. It also creates lactate (or lactic acid) as a waste product. Eventually, the amount of lactate produced will be a limiting factor, which is why you can't sprint forever.

Nervous System

All the BMAT really wants you to know about the nervous system is how the reflex arc works. Reflexes are **involuntary** actions that are usually protective, and by making them involuntary (that is, not having to involve the brain to think about doing them) they are faster. For example, if you put your hand on a hot stove, the reflex action is to pull your hand away. What is the mechanism behind this? The skin contains sensory receptors, that can detect the hot stove. An action potential will be sent through a sensory neuron, which synapses to a relay neuron in the spinal cord. A synapse is a specialised gap between two neurons. When an action potential reaches the end of one neuron, neurotransmitters are released into the synapse, which then diffuse across the gap, and then bind to receptors on the next neuron to trigger an action potential. The relay neuron synapses with a motor neuron, which will pass on the signal to the muscle, making the muscle contract and withdraw your hand from the heat source.

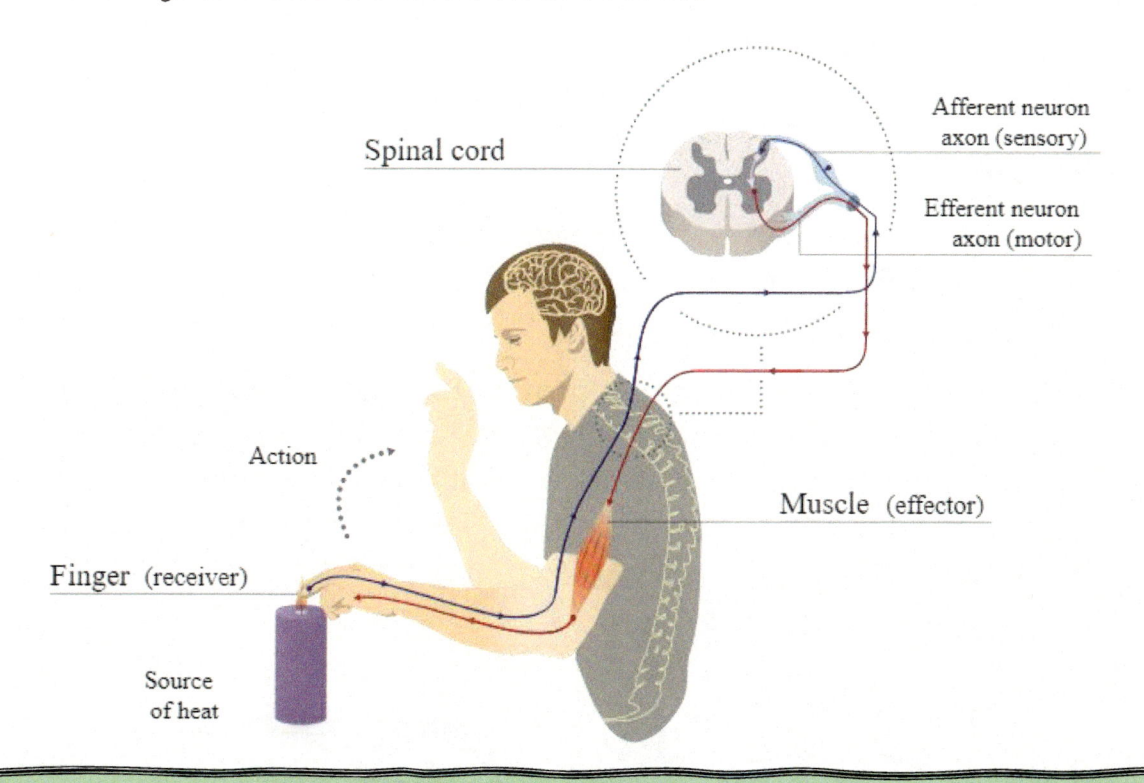

6Med Tip: Sometimes we want to overrule our reflexes, for example if we're picking up a hot plate of food. The brain can send signals down the spinal cord that affect how sensitive the reflex response is.

Respiratory System

The respiratory system is all about getting oxygen in and carbon dioxide out. There's two parts to consider. First is the mechanism of breathing. This is all about creating pressure differences between the outside air and within the lungs, so air will move in and out. The lungs sit within the thorax of the chest, and at the base is a large flat muscle called the diaphragm. When we want to breathe in, the diaphragm contracts and pulls downwards. This makes the thorax larger, which means the pressure within it falls so it's lower than the atmospheric pressure, so air moves into the lungs. When we breathe out, the opposite happens.

The second part is gas exchange. The body needs to get oxygen from the air into the blood, and carbon dioxide from the blood into the air. This happens across specialised cells called alveoli. They are found at the end of the airways, after they have branched off into bronchioles. They are thin, just one cell thick, and that means there's a very short distance for the gases to diffuse across. The second adaption is that there are lots of them, having the appearance of a load of grapes. This increases the surface area available for gas exchange.

Circulatory System

The circulatory system is made up of the heart and blood vessels, and it acts as a transport system to get important things, like oxygen and glucose, to cells and remove waste products, like carbon dioxide, for excretion.

Let's start with the heart itself. This is an organ made up of specialised myocytes (muscle cells), that are able to contract in a coordinated way to pump blood all around the body. A very clever system of electrical conduction enables this coordinated contraction, and that also means we can use something called an ECG to see how healthy the heart is.

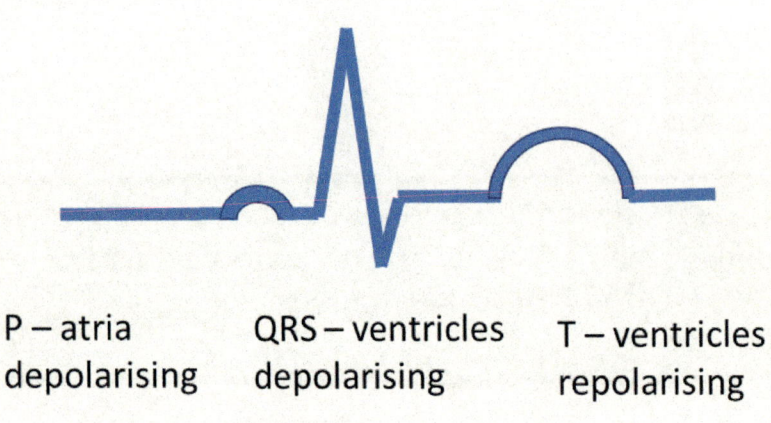

P – atria depolarising   QRS – ventricles depolarising   T – ventricles repolarising

B9 – Animal Physiology

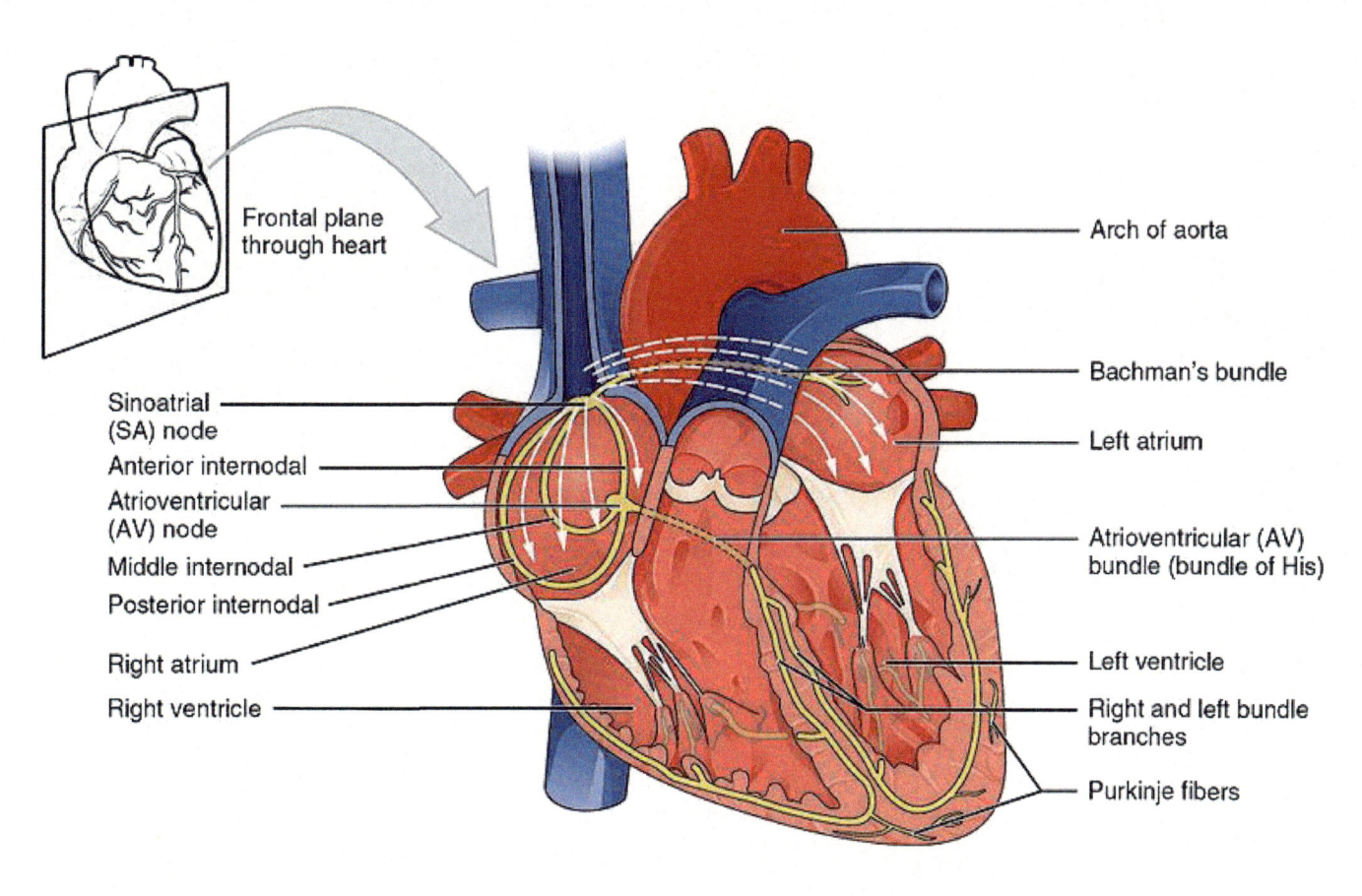

Anterior view of frontal section

Labels on diagram:
- Frontal plane through heart
- Sinoatrial (SA) node
- Anterior internodal
- Atrioventricular (AV) node
- Middle internodal
- Posterior internodal
- Right atrium
- Right ventricle
- Arch of aorta
- Bachman's bundle
- Left atrium
- Atrioventricular (AV) bundle (bundle of His)
- Left ventricle
- Right and left bundle branches
- Purkinje fibers

There are three types of blood vessels, and here's a summary table of the key facts:

Arteries	Veins	Capillaries
Carry blood away from heart	Carry blood back to heart	Between arteries and veins
Thick walls (blood at high pressure)	Thin walls & valves (stop backflow)	One cell thick (for exchange)

Carried within these vessels is blood. When a lot of people think of blood, they just see the red stuff and think red blood cells and oxygen. In reality, blood is much more complex.

- Red Blood Cells – carry oxygen
- White Blood Cells – fight infection
- Platelets – blood clotting (to stop bleeding)
- Plasma – a special liquid these cells are carried in, which also carries dissolved substances (like hormones, antibodies, urea, carbon dioxide) and is involved in temperature control

A circulatory system is necessary in multi-cellular organisms, because of the changing surface area to volume ratio. As an organism gets larger, it has less surface area relative to its volume for substances to diffuse across.

Digestive System

The digestive system runs from the mouth, down the oesophagus into the stomach, then through the small and large intestine, before finishing with the excretion of faeces from the anus. Its function is to break down food products, and absorb the nutrients within them, before excreting what the body cannot use.

In an earlier chapter, we touched on some of the key enzymes in the digestive system – amylases, proteases, and lipases – and the different optimum pHs they had. The digestive system is designed to maintain the correct pH for each of these enzymes. Amylase is predominantly found in saliva. Proteases are found in the stomach, and the stomach secretes hydrochloric acid, which lowers the pH in the stomach to allow the proteases to work. Lipases are found in the small intestine and need an alkaline solution to work. The gall bladder secretes bile salts, which have two functions – one to raise the pH in the small intestine to make it more alkaline, and second to emulsify the fats to increase the surface area for the lipases to act on.

Excretory System

The kidneys are (like most things in the body) pretty incredible. It is certainly under-selling them to say they just make urine. The kidneys are one of the centres for homeostasis, maintaining water and electrolyte levels in the blood, and even blood pressure. Nephrologists (the kidney doctors) are famously some of the smartest in medicine – and a good thing too, because when the kidneys go wrong things can get very complex. Again, we will try and keep things as simple as possible (you will have all of medical school to really get to grips with it).

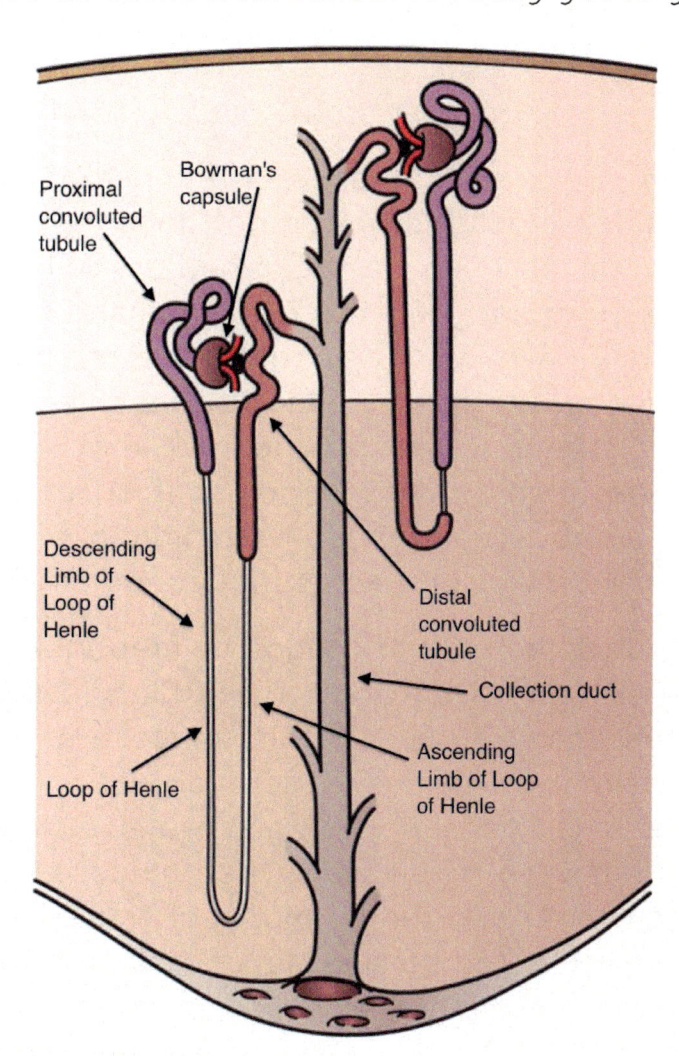

The kidney is made up of millions of nephrons. These are the functional units of the kidney. The nephron starts at the glomerulus. This is a network of tiny capillaries, which special cells called podocytes that crudely filter the blood. Small particles, like ions, urea, or water, get squeezed through special gaps between the podocytes, but larger proteins stay within the blood.

The filtrate then passes through the proximal convoluted tubule, where things the body wants to keep, like sodium and potassium, are returned to the blood via a mix of diffusion or active transport. The filtrate then passes into the loop of Henle. This is where water is pulled out of the filtrate and returned to the blood. This now really concentrated filtrate passes through the distal convoluted tubule, where again the kidney is able to carry out homeostasis and pull out or put in ions etc depending on what the body needs at that time. The final part of the tubule is the collecting duct, where multiple nephrons feed into. This is the final chance for the body to control how much water is lost in the urine, controlled by the release of ADH hormone.

Homeostasis

Homeostasis is defined as the maintenance of a constant internal environment. This rather bland definition hides the true importance of homeostasis. Our body is designed to work in an optimum range, whether that's temperature, blood glucose etc – you name it, our body wants it pretty constant otherwise things start to go wrong. Unfortunately, we live in the real world that throws up challenges. For example, on a hot day, the body needs to find ways to keep our internal temperature constant. Or when we eat a large meal, that will cause a spike in our blood glucose, which we need to keep under control (or the other way, if we cannot eat for a few hours, we still need to maintain blood glucose levels to provide energy for all the cellular processes that cannot stop).

Homeostasis relies on this principle of negative feedback loops. Simply, when something becomes too high in the body, these high levels are able to inhibit something back up the pathway. Let us take glucose as an example (as it is specifically mentioned in the syllabus). There are two hormones involved in regulating glucose. Insulin is released when glucose levels rise, and causes blood glucose levels to fall. Glucagon is released when glucose levels fall, and causes blood glucose levels to rise. After eating a big meal, there will be a spike in blood glucose. This will cause insulin to be released, and block the release of glucagon (there's already enough glucose in the blood, so no point wasting precious stores – this is negative feedback). Over the course of the day, the blood glucose levels will begin to fall. Eventually, they'll become low enough that the negative inhibition on glucagon production will cease, and the body will start producing glucagon – and the blood glucose levels will begin to rise. Concurrently, the falling blood glucose levels will mean less insulin is released, until eventually insulin is totally suppressed (negative feedback again)

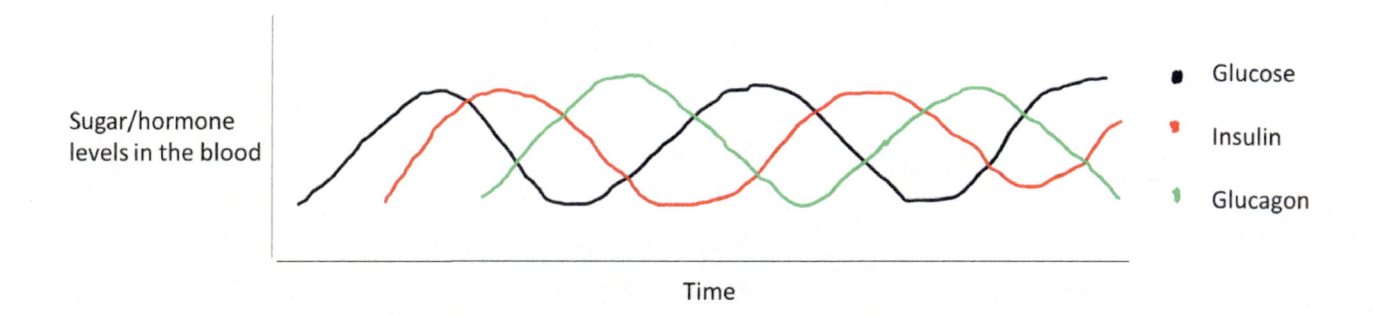

6Med Tip: Diabetes develops when blood glucose control goes wrong. In T1DM, body stops producing insulin. In T2DM, the body stops responding to insulin. This is why T1 can be treated simply by giving exogenous insulin, whereas for type 2 we have loads of different drugs that all try and make the body respond better to its own insulin

Hormones

Hormones are special proteins that are made by endocrine organs and secreted into the bloodstream to reach their target organs. What this means is they will have **systemic** effects across the whole body. It also means they will take longer to take effect, compared to the nervous system which is pretty much instantaneous. Hormones rely on negative feedback to control their release. There are several hormones mentioned by name in the syllabus, so the diagram below shows their negative feedback pathways.

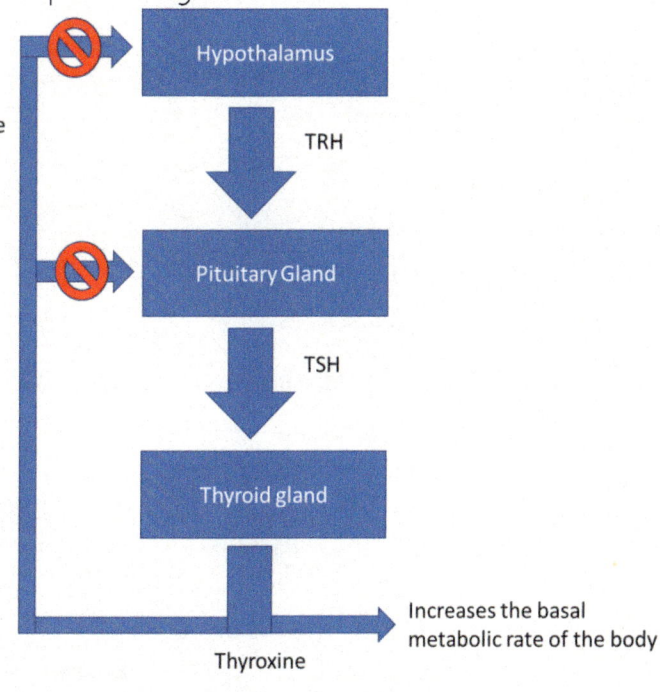

Negative feedback – thyroxine inhibits the release of the stimulating hormones from the hypothalamus and pituitary gland

Hypothalamus → TRH → Pituitary Gland → TSH → Thyroid gland → Thyroxine → Increases the basal metabolic rate of the body

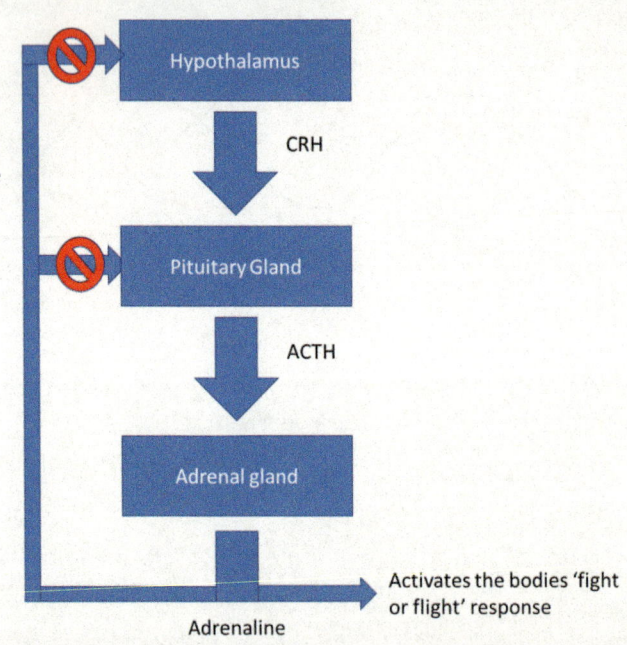

The Complete BMAT Specification Explained

B9 – Animal Physiology

Negative feedback – adrenaline inhibits the release of the stimulating hormones from the hypothalamus and pituitary gland

Hypothalamus → CRH → Pituitary Gland → ACTH → Adrenal gland → Adrenaline

Activates the bodies 'fight or flight' response

Hormones play a key role in the reproduction, in particular the menstrual cycle. There are two sets of hormones involved, LH and FSH released from the pituitary gland, and oestrogen and progesterone which are released from the ovaries. Oestrogen (or estrogen, for Americans) drives the growth of the follicle and the endometrium, preparing the uterus for implantation. LH and FSH trigger ovulation and the release of the oocyte. Progesterone maintains the lining of the uterus, however unless fertilisation occurs the levels of progesterone fall and the thickened endometrium is lost as a menses (or period).

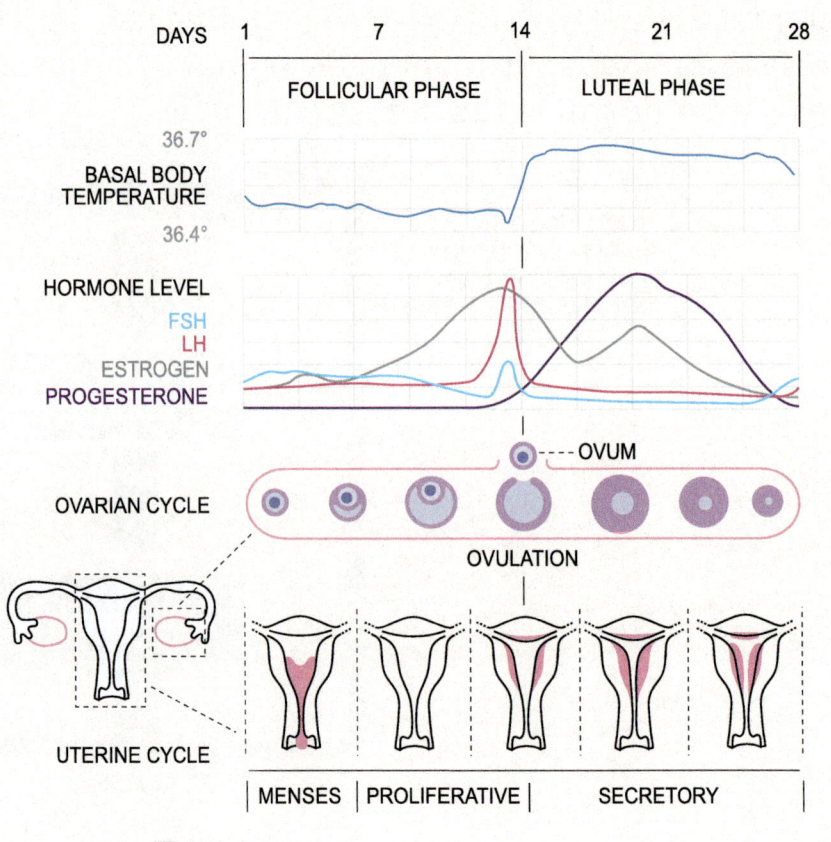

DAYS 1 — 7 — 14 — 21 — 28

FOLLICULAR PHASE | LUTEAL PHASE

BASAL BODY TEMPERATURE (36.4° – 36.7°)

HORMONE LEVEL
FSH
LH
ESTROGEN
PROGESTERONE

OVARIAN CYCLE — OVUM — OVULATION

UTERINE CYCLE: MENSES | PROLIFERATIVE | SECRETORY

> **6Med Tip:** Some forms of contraception, such as the pill or implant, contain hormones to interfere with the menstrual cycle and prevent ovulation. Contraception can also be non-hormonal, such as condoms or the coil.

Disease and Body Defence

Whilst the body is pretty nifty, it can go wrong. Sometimes, diseases are caused by other organisms – like bacteria, viruses protozoa and fungi. We call these communicable diseases, because they can also spread from person to person.

> **6Med Tip:** Not all bacteria cause disease. We have lots of 'healthy' bacteria in our digestive system that play crucial roles in digestion – in fact there are more bacterial cells in our body than our own cells!

Infections can be passed on in a huge variety of ways, such as through the food we eat, or the air we breathe. Some infections can also be transmitted by sex, such as HIV. HIV is a particularly difficult infection because the virus targets the body's own white blood cells – the CD4 T cells. Over many years, the virus will wipe out all the T cells, and the person will develop AIDS. At this point, because they're immune system simply isn't working, they are susceptible to lots of infections that someone with a healthy immune system would clear easily.

This is a nice lead in to talk about how the immune system works. It is a very complex and clever system, that needs to strike a balance between recognising threats, but also not being so sensitive that it starts to attack its own cells. Keeping things simple, there are cellular components (white blood cells) and antibodies (special circulating proteins). The role of T cells is to identify dangerous pathogens. When a pathogen is identified, they pass on the information to B cells, which destroy the pathogen. The B cells can either destroy the pathogen directly, or make antibodies specifically targeted against that pathogen. The antibodies travel round the body in the blood, and can bind to and destroy the pathogen wherever it is found. The immune system can also remember, and once a B cell makes a particular antibody, it turns into a memory B cell. These memory B cells lies dormant, until the same pathogen reinfects the person. Then, they are activated and start producing the right antibodies, and because the memory B cells are already ready to go, they mount a faster and stronger immune response.

Vaccines work by piggy-backing on this concept of immunity. We can use dead or inactivated pathogens, so they won't cause disease, but they will have the same surface markers so the T cell can recognise them as pathogens and start the production of antibodies. Then, if later in life the vaccinated person is infected, they will already have memory B cells, so can start producing antibodies straight away and hopefully clear the infection.

> **6Med Tip:** Drugs and vaccines usually take a long time to develop. First, they'll be tested in a lab, using petri dishes and fancy equipment – this is called pre-clinical testing. Once we are confident they might work and will be safe, then they can be tested on real people, to see if they are safe and effective – this is called clinical testing.

Sometimes however, an infection is too serious for the body's immune system to clear by itself. Then, a doctor might consider prescribing antibiotics. These are drugs that are designed to kill the bacteria, independent of the body's immune system. We have different classes of drugs that can kill fungi and viruses, and one of the most important jobs of a doctor is to choose the right drug, using clinical judgement and laboratory investigations. And of course, if we can not get infected in the first place, that's even better. For example, wearing condoms during sex massively reduces the risk of transmitted HIV infections.

Some diseases aren't caused by pathogens. These non-communicable diseases usually have a wide range of genetic and environmental factors that cause them. For example, cardiovascular disease or diabetes. Because they are multi-factorial, that means there are lots of potential treatment avenues. If we take cardiovascular disease (e.g. strokes and heart attacks) as an example, there are lots of drugs, such as statins (which lower cholesterol), anti-coagulants (which stop the body forming blood clots that block arteries) and anti-hypertensives (which lower the blood pressure), that can all reduce a person's chance of having a heart attack or stroke. We can also perform surgical procedures, such as putting in stents to keep clogged arteries open, or even replacing blocked arteries by harvesting a spare vessel from somewhere in the body. Finally, simple lifestyle changes, like eating a balanced diet and exercising regularly, can have a massive impact on a person's cardiovascular health.

The Complete BMAT Specification Explained

B9 – Animal Physiology

Knowledge Check

1. Which of the following statements about the reflex arc are correct?
    a. Neurotransmitters cross synapses by osmosis
    b. The release of neurotransmitters is triggered by the signal
    c. The reflex arc is involuntary
    d. A signal passing down the sensory neuron causes the muscle to contract

2. Which statements about the process of breathing in are correct?
    a. The pressure in the thorax rises
    b. The diaphragm contracts downwards
    c. The ribs swing up and outwards

Answers:
1 = c and d are correct
2 = b and c are correct

B10 – Ecosystems

Last chapter on biology, well done for getting this far. This one's hopefully pretty straightforward again, just got some definitions to understand and a cycle to learn.

Ecosystems

Ecosystems are the combination of all the organisms and the physical environment within which they interact. This can obviously be quite a broad definition, so ecosystems are organised into layers. The lowest layer is an individual member of a species. This is one animal, or one plant. The next level up is a population, which is all the members of the same species living in one physical area. When you have two or more populations (so two or more species), that is called a community. Now we've made it back to an ecosystem, which is the interaction of a community with its physical environment.

Individual → Population → Community → Ecosystem

If we take this definition of an ecosystem, then it makes sense that the communities in an ecosystem can be affected by changes to the populations in the community (such as the introduction of a new species), or by changes to the environment itself (such as a drought). These are formally called biotic and abiotic factors.

Within ecosystems, there is a lot of interdependence and competition, both of which are necessary for a healthy ecosystem. Interdependence can take the form of predation (where one organism kills another for food), mutualism (where both organisms benefit from the relationship without harming each other) and parasitism (where one organism gains but the other is negatively affected). Competition is important as a driver for natural selection, allowing the strongest and most well-adapted members of a species to survive. However, if a new species is introduced to an ecosystem, they can sometimes outcompete the incumbent species for the same niche – like grey squirrels being introduced and outcompeting red squirrels.

B10 – Ecosystems

> **6Med Tip:** A good parasite does not want to kill its host, otherwise it will not benefit from the parasitic relationship.

When we start to look at food chains and webs in an ecosystem, at the bottom is almost always a producer, which are plants or algae that can carry out photosynthesis. This means they can use sunlight to make glucose, and it is this biomass that will feed the whole rest of the food chain.

> **6Med Tip:** only about 10% of energy is transferred from one level to another in the food chain. This means that the producers make up most of the biomass, and the size of a population has to fall as you go further up the food chain.

Material Cycling

Material cycling is a fancy way of saying how does stuff change and move around an ecosystem. For the BMAT, they want you to know about the carbon cycle. This, unsurprisingly, is how carbon is recycled from organism to the environment, and vice versa.

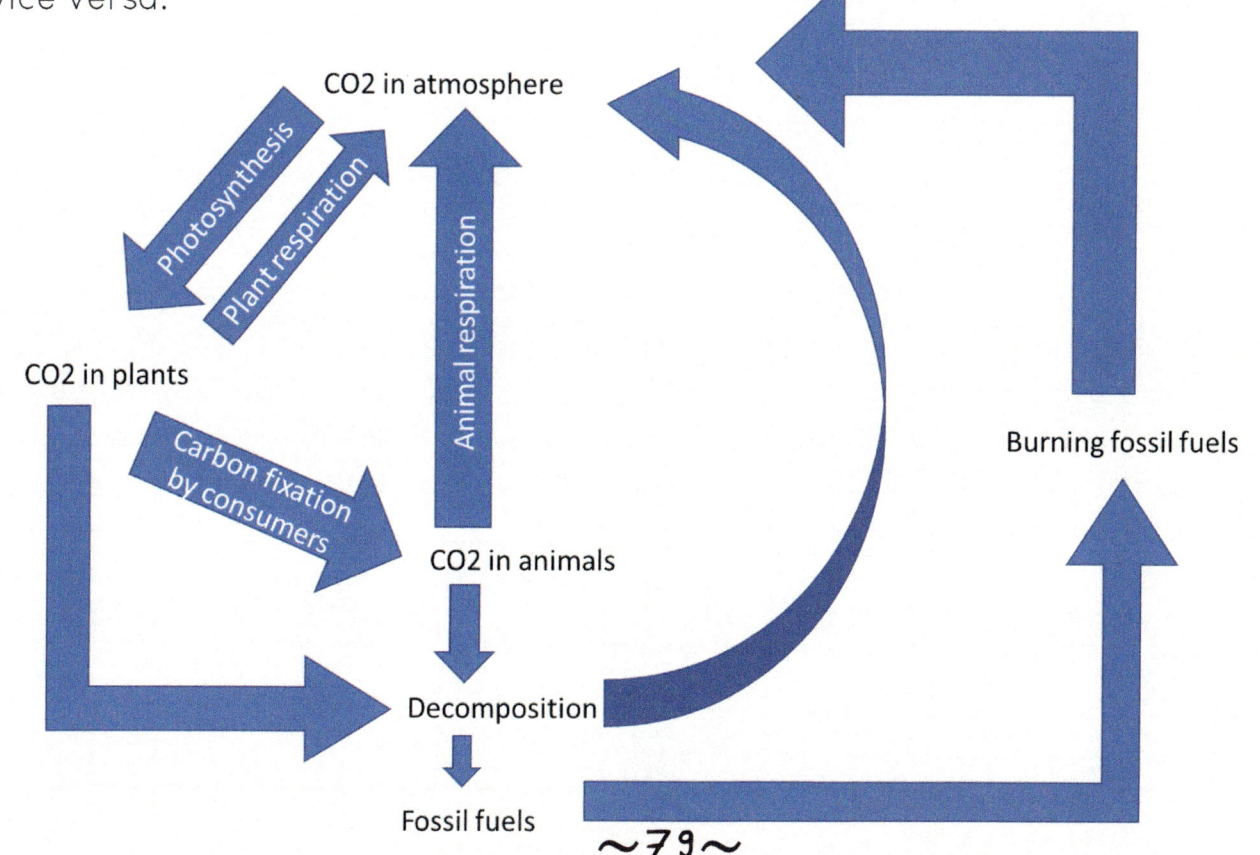

Carbon cycle diagram: CO_2 in atmosphere ↔ CO_2 in plants (Photosynthesis, Plant respiration); Carbon fixation by consumers → CO_2 in animals; Animal respiration → CO_2 in atmosphere; Decomposition → Fossil fuels; Burning fossil fuels → CO_2 in atmosphere.

The Complete BMAT Specification Explained

B10 – Ecosystems

> **6Med Tip:** as long as you can define the terms, no matter how the carbon cycle is presented in an exam question, you will be able to fill in the gaps

Knowledge Check

1. Fill in the gaps in the table

Adds carbon dioxide to the air	Removes carbon dioxide from the air	Adds oxygen to the air	Removes oxygen from the air

2. Define the following terms
    a. Competition
    b. Mutualism
    c. Predation

Answers:

1:

Adds carbon dioxide to the air	Removes carbon dioxide from the air	Adds oxygen to the air	Removes oxygen from the air
Respiration/combustion	photosynthesis	Photosynthesis	respiration

2: a = where two organisms compete for the same ecological niche; b = a relationship between two organisms where both benefit; c = where one species (predator) consumes another species (prey) for food

Section 2 Part 2: Chemistry.

C1 – Atomic Structure

Atoms are the smallest part of an element that can exist. They have no overall electrical charge. This section will cover all that you need to know about their structure.

Atomic Structure

Overview

Atoms are made up from 3 types of subatomic particle: protons, neutrons and electrons.

Each atom contains at nucleus at its centre, which consists of protons and neutrons. This nucleus is surrounded by the electrons, which are arranged in shells

(these shells are also known as energy levels). These electrons are constantly moving around within their shells.

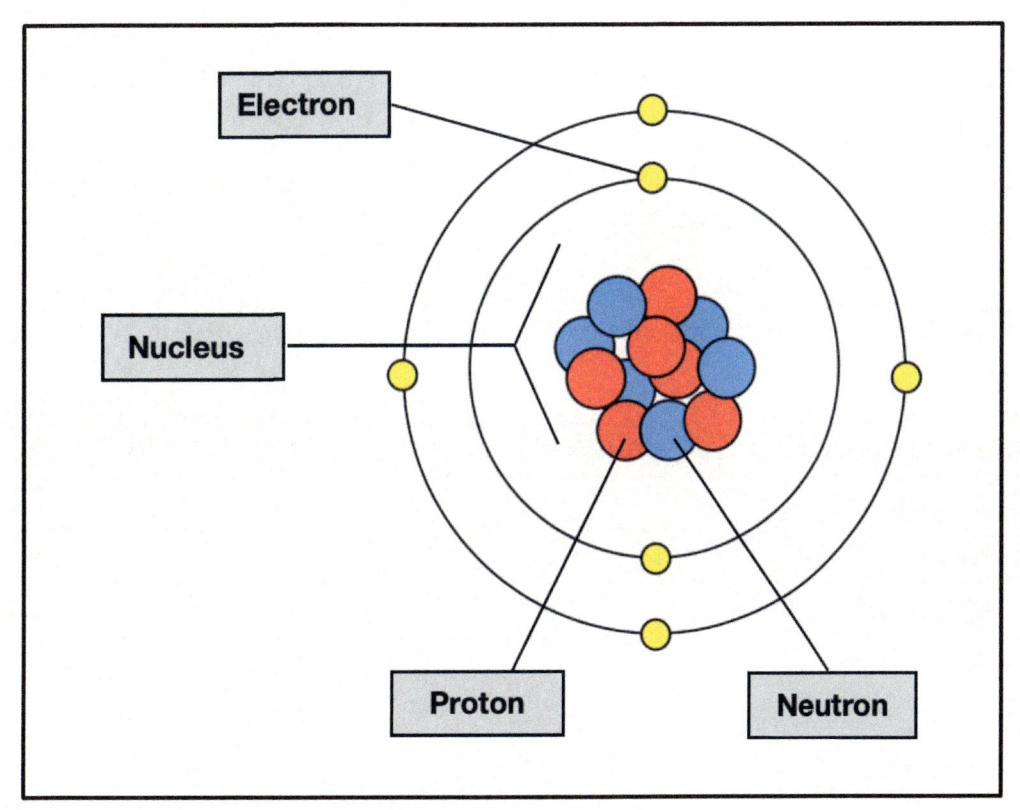

C1 - Atomic Structure

The diagram above represents an atom of carbon. This is not drawn to scale. In reality, the electron shells (shown here as black circles) are much larger in comparison to the nucleus.

Subatomic Particles

As mentioned above, there are 3 types of subatomic particle:

- Protons (positively charged)
- Neutrons
- Electrons (negatively charged)

Protons and electrons are electrically charged, whereas neutrons do not have a charge. The charges of protons and electrons are opposite and equal.

> **6Med Tip:** Atoms always contain an equal number of protons and electrons. This means that **atoms have no overall electrical charge!**

These particles each have a tiny mass, which is very difficult to think about and use if written in grams or kilograms. Because of this, we most commonly use their <u>relative masses</u>. This basically represents the amount of times heavier a particle is in comparison to another.

- E.g. if a particle has a relative mass of 1, any particle that is less heavy than it will have a relative mass smaller than 1.

The table below shows the relative charges and masses of each subatomic particle:

Subatomic Particle	Relative Charge	Relative Mass
Proton	+1	1
Neutron	0	1
Electron	-1	Very small

C1 – Atomic Structure

Atomic and Mass Numbers

An element's <u>atomic number</u> is the number of protons it has in each atom. All atoms of the same element have the same number of protons. Each element contains a different number of protons, and therefore has a different atomic number.

An element's <u>mass number</u> is the number of protons and neutrons found in an atom. This is usually different for each element, but can sometimes be the same.

We can calculate the number of each subatomic particle in an atom using these numbers:

- Number of protons = atomic number
- Number of neutrons = mass number – atomic number
- Number of electrons = atomic number

> **6Med Tip:** In an atom, the atomic number is also equal to the number of electrons. This is because atoms have no overall charge, so the number of protons = number of electrons.

In the periodic table, elements are written as their chemical symbol. The mass number is shown at the top, and the atomic number at the bottom.

- E.g. Fluorine (F) is shown here. It has an atomic number of 9 and a mass number of 19.

$$^{19}_{9}F$$

> **6Med Tip:** Remember, the mass number of an atom is the total number of protons and neutrons (it **doesn't include number of electrons!**)

Electron Configurations

The <u>electron configuration</u> of an atom shows how its electrons are arranged in their energy shell(s).

Electrons fill up each shell starting from the shell closest to the nucleus, and start to fill the next shell outwards once each becomes full. Each shell can hold a different maximum number of electrons:

- 1st shell: 2 electrons
- 2nd shell: 8 electrons
- 3rd shell: 8 electrons

For the BMAT, you need to be able to write the electron configurations of the first 20 elements only (atoms with up to 20 electrons). These can be deduced from the atomic number.

- E.g. for fluorine, its atomic number is 9, so each atom has 9 electrons. 2 electrons are in the 1st shell, and the other 7 occupy the 2nd shell. As the 2nd shell is not filled up, there are 0 electrons in the 3rd shell.

Electron configurations are most commonly written as the number of electrons in each shell, separated by commas.

- E.g. for fluorine, this would be: 2,7

Isotopes

<u>Isotopes</u> are atoms of the same element that have different numbers of neutrons. They have the same number of protons.

> **6Med Tip:** Isotopes of an element have the same atomic number but different mass numbers.

Isotopes are named by the element name, and its mass number.
- E.g. chlorine has two main isotopes: chlorine-35 and chlorine-37. These have mass numbers of 35 and 37 respectively.

Different samples of the same element can contain varying amounts of each isotope. This can be measured using mass spectrometry, and can be presented in multiple ways e.g. in a table, or on a mass spectrum itself:

Isotope	% Abundance in Sample
^{24}Mg	80
^{25}Mg	10
^{26}Mg	10

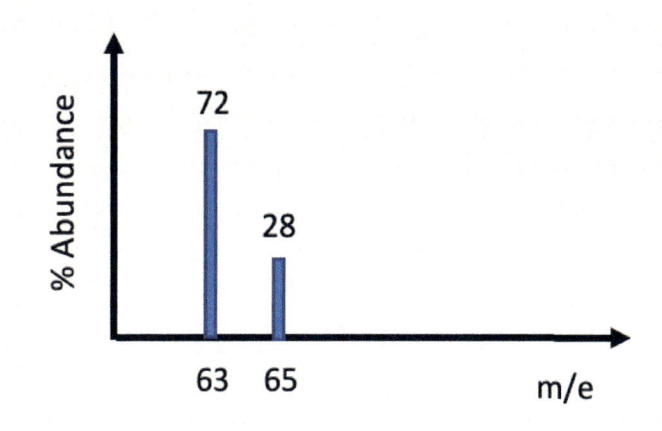

On the mass spectrum graph, each isotope is represented by a bar, and is labelled with its mass number. The height of each bar represents the **% abundance** of each isotope in the sample. The graph above shows the relative abundances of copper-63 (72%) and copper-65 (28%) in a particular sample.

Sometimes, you can be presented the actual amount of each isotope (e.g. in grams), rather than % abundance. To work out the % abundance of an isotope from this:

% abundance = (amount of isotope / total amount of all isotopes) x 100

> **6Med Tip:** '% abundance' just means what proportion of the sample is made up from that particular isotope.

Relative Atomic Mass

An element's **relative atomic mass** is the mean atomic mass of its various isotopes compared to 1/12 of the mass of a carbon-12 atom. In shorthand, relative atomic mass is represented as A_r.

> **6Med Tip:** Relative atomic mass can often be confused with mass numbers:
> - Relative atomic mass numbers are **not whole numbers**, as are a mean value of multiple isotope's mass numbers.
> - Mass numbers always **have to be a whole number**, as these represent the number of protons and neutrons (which can't be split up into partial particles!)

Calculating Relative Atomic Mass

We can calculate the relative atomic mass of an element using the % abundance of each isotope, and their mass numbers.

$$A_r = \frac{(\% \text{ abundance} \times \text{mass of isotope 1}) + (\% \text{ abundance} \times \text{mass of isotope 2}) \ldots}{100}$$

If using amounts of each isotope, this equation can be adapted:

$$A_r = \frac{(\text{amount} \times \text{mass of isotope 1}) + (\text{mount} \times \text{mass of isotope 2})}{\text{Total mass of sample}}$$

E.g. Chlorine consists of 75% chlorine-35 and 25% chlorine-37. What is the relative atomic mass of chlorine?

$$A_r = \frac{(75 \times 35) + (25 \times 37)}{100}$$

$$= \frac{2625 + 925}{100} = \frac{3350}{100}$$

$$= 35.5$$

C2 – The Periodic Table

The Periodic Table

Structure

The modern periodic table arranges elements by increasing atomic number (so each element has 1 more proton than the element before it).

Horizontal rows are called <u>periods</u>- these are numbered 1-7. The period number of an element shows the number of electron shells its atoms contain.

- E.g. aluminium (Al) is in period 3, so its atoms have 3 electron shells

Vertical columns are called <u>groups</u>- these are numbered 1-7, with group 0 following 7. The group number of an element shows how many electrons are in its outside shell of its atoms.

- E.g. magnesium (Mg) is in group 2, so there are 2 electrons in its outside shell

> **6Med Tip:** Group 0 was traditionally referred to as group 8 (in reference to 8 electrons in a full outer shell). However, this is more commonly referred to as group 0 to accommodate helium. As helium only has 1 electron shell, this is therefore filled with 2 electrons, as opposed to 8 electrons for the other elements in this group.

The diagram below shows a simplification of the structure of the modern periodic table. The symbols of the first 20 elements are shown. Periods are labelled in blue, groups are labelled in green.

The Complete BMAT Specification Explained

C2 – The Periodic Table

Metals and Non-Metals

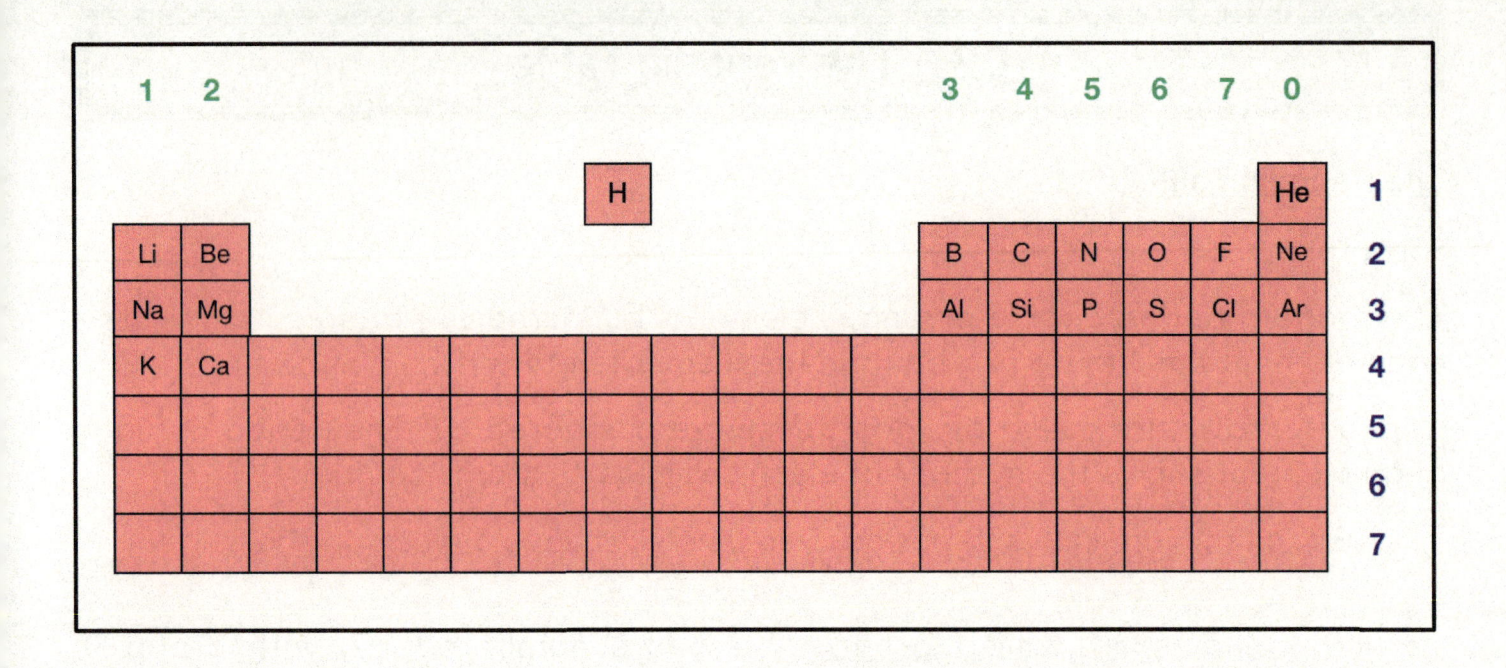

Metals and non-metals are separated on the periodic table by a stepped line. This is shown in the diagram below as a thickened black line. Elements to the left of this line are classed as metals (represented in blue), and elements to the right of this are classed as non-metals (represented in red).

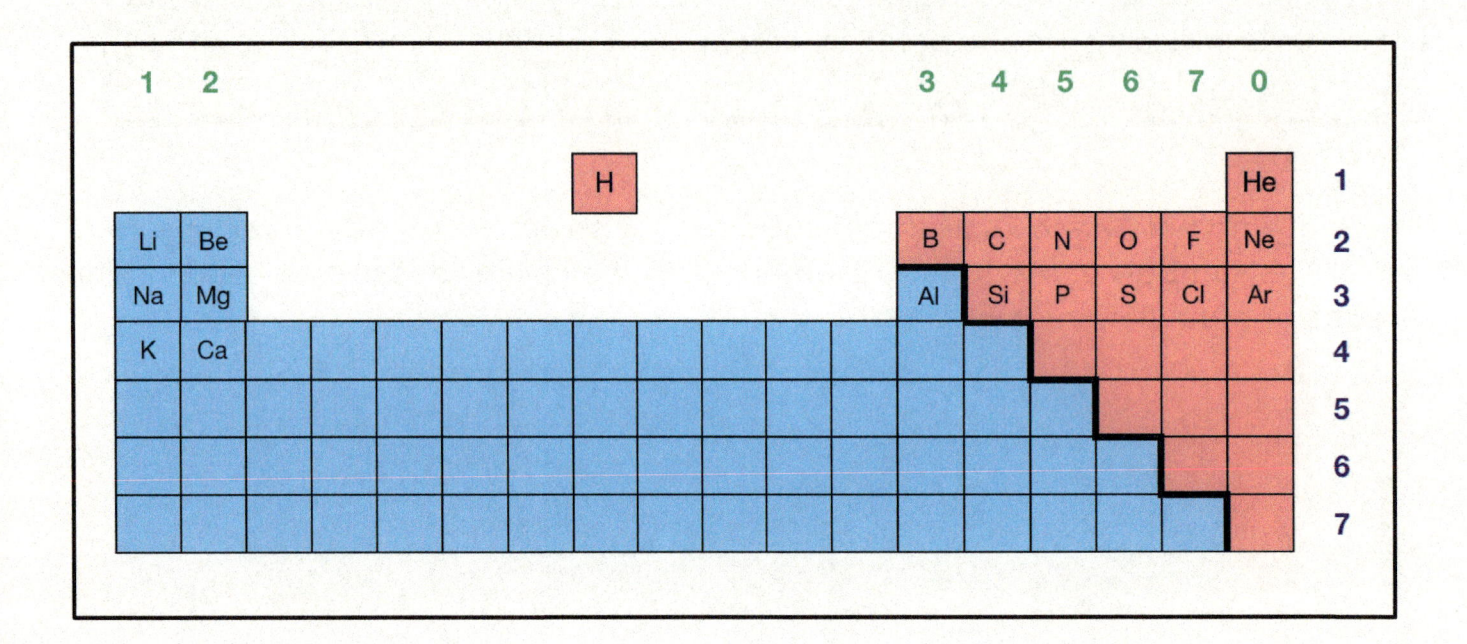

Named Groups

Some groups of elements have specific names. These include:

- Group 1- the alkali metals
- Group 2- the alkaline earth metals
- Group 6- the common non-metals
- Group 7- the halogens
- Group 0- the noble gases

The elements located in vertical columns between groups 2 and 3 are called the transition metals.

Properties

When atoms collide with each other during a chemical reaction, the electrons in their outer shell interact with the outermost electrons of the other atom involved. This means that elements in the same periodic group have similar chemical properties, as they have the same number of electrons in their outer shells.

Groups of elements show trends in their physical properties. The key one you need to know about is reactivity. Reactivity is used to describe how vigorously a substance will react with others- more reactive substances will react more vigorously.

In metal groups (groups 1 and 2), the reactivity of elements increases going down the group. In non-metal groups (groups 6 and 7), the reactivity of elements decreases going down the group.

The Complete BMAT Specification Explained

C2 – The Periodic Table

Knowledge Check

1. What is a 'period' in the context of the periodic table?
2. What is reactivity? What is the trend in reactivity seen in group 1?
3. Sodium is in group 1 and period 3 of the periodic table, what can be said about its electron configuration?

---

1. A period is a row of the periodic table. Although periods don't share properties the same way that groups (columns) do, there are certain trends that we see across periods. The period that an element is in is related to the number of electron shells it has, which can affect its reactivity.

2. Reactivity is the tendency of an element to gain, lose, or share electrons. In group 1, the elements need to lose their outer electron when they react. As it is easier to lose electrons which are further away from the nucleus, the larger elements at the bottom of group 1 are more reactive than the smaller elements at the top. In other words, reactivity increases down the group.

3. Period 3 means Sodium has 3 electron shells, and Group 1 means it has 1 electron in its outer shell. So the electron configuration of sodium is 2, 8, 1. (Note: you must be able to figure out that this is the configuration, without having to search for sodium's atomic number).

C3 – Chemical Reactions, Formulae and Equations

Chemical reactions can occur between elements and/or compounds. In a chemical reaction, the outermost electrons of each atom interact with each other and rearrange. This results in the formation of new substances. *No nuclei are created or destroyed* in a chemical reaction.

Chemical Formulae

Compounds are represented by chemical formulae. This shows the symbols for each element it contains, and the number of atoms of each of these in one molecule. If there is one atom of an element in the molecule, no number is written. If there are 2 or more atoms of an element in a molecule, the number of these is written subscript.

e.g. a water molecule contains 2 atoms of hydrogen and 1 atom of oxygen. The chemical formula of water is therefore H_2O.

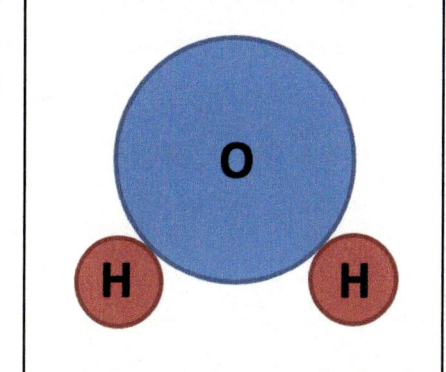

Shown below are some other common compounds, shown with their chemical formulae:

- Sodium chloride, $NaCl$
- Ammonia, NH_3
- Methane, CH_4
- Ethanol, C_2H_6O
- Carbon dioxide, CO_2

The Complete BMAT Specification Explained
C3 – Chemical Reactions, Formulae and Equations

> **6Med Tip:** The names of compounds containing only non-metal elements can give away their chemical formulae. The second word of the compound starts with a prefix that tells you the number of atoms of this element for each atom of the first element in the compound name.
>
> For example, 'mon' indicates 1, 'di' indicates 2 and 'tri' indicates 3. So carbon monoxide contains 1 oxygen for each carbon atom, and carbon dioxide contains 2 oxygens for each carbon atom.

State Symbols

Chemical reactions can be represented by <u>balanced chemical equations</u>. These show the chemical formulae of the reactants used and the products formed, and the number of units of each.

State symbols are used in chemical equations to show what physical state each reactant and product is in. They can be:

- Solid, (s)
- Liquid, (l)
- Gas, (g)
- Aqueous solution, formed when the substance is dissolved in water (aq)

Balancing Equations

You need to be able to construct and balance different forms of chemical equations.

The conservation of mass law means that no atoms are formed or lost in a reaction, meaning that the number of atoms of each element must be the same on the reactant side of the arrow (left hand side) as the product side of the arrow (right hand side). When balancing an equation, numbers are added in front of each chemical formula. This multiplies all of the atoms in that formula by the big number.

This is normally easiest to do in multiple steps, for example:

$$K + H_2O \rightarrow KOH + H_2$$
$$K + 2H_2O \rightarrow KOH + H_2$$
$$K + 2H_2O \rightarrow 2KOH + H_2$$
$$2K + 2H_2O \rightarrow 2KOH + H_2$$

> **6Med Tip:** When balancing equations, you can **only** change the big number in front of each chemical formula, not any small subscript ones (as no chemical formulae should be changed!)

Ionic Equations

Ionic equations are used to show the reactions of ions in a chemical reaction. For example, sodium ions react with chloride ions to form sodium chloride:

$$Na^+ + Cl^- \rightarrow NaCl$$

Half Equations

Half equations show the reaction of each ion in a reaction, in terms of their loss or gain of electrons. Using the example above, the two half equations occurring in this would be:

$$Na^+ + e^- \rightarrow Na$$
$$Cl^- \rightarrow Cl + e^-$$

> **6Med Tip:** Remember, in half equations, the number of atoms on each side of the equation must be equal! The charges on each side must also be equal!

C3 – Chemical Reactions, Formulae and Equations

Reversible Reactions

Many chemical reactions are irreversible, meaning that once the products are formed, they cannot easily be reversed back into the reactions. With reversible chemical reactions, the products can easily react to reform the reactants.

The equations of reversible reactions are shown with a reversible reaction arrow- this has two half arrows, one pointing right (representing the forward reaction) and one pointing right (representing the backward reaction):

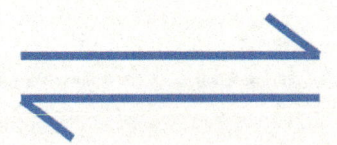

$$\rightleftharpoons$$

An example of a reversible reaction is the breakdown of ammonium chloride. This can be broken down into ammonia and hydrogen chloride, which can subsequently re-react to form ammonium chloride:

$$NH_4Cl \rightleftharpoons (s)\ NH_3(g) + HCl(g)$$

Reversible reactions can occur in a <u>closed system</u>. This means that none of the products or reactants can escape from the reaction mixture. In a closed system, not all of the reactants become products, but the mixture reaches a state of equilibrium. At the point of equilibrium:
- the concentrations of products and reactants stay the same
- the forward and backward reactions occur at the same rate as each other

Position of Equilibrium

The position of equilibrium measures the relative concentrations of substances in a mixture (whether there are more reactants or products).

The position of equilibrium can be changed by:

- different concentration of reactants or products
- temperature
- overall pressure of the reaction mixture

When a system in equilibrium undergoes a change, the position of equilibrium *moves to counteract the change.*

If the concentration of a reactant is increased, the equilibrium position moves to the right. The forward reaction increases in rate to use up the extra reactant, therefore producing more products.

In a reversible reaction, if one reaction is exothermic, it will be endothermic in the other direction. If the temperature is increased, the equilibrium position shifts in the *direction of the endothermic reaction*, to reduce the temperature of the reaction mixture.

If all the reactants and products are gases, increasing the pressure causes equilibrium to shift to the *side that produces fewer molecules*. For example, ammonia is produced from nitrogen and hydrogen in the Haber process:

$$N_2 \text{ (g)} + 3H_2 \rightleftharpoons \text{(g)} \; 2NH_3 \text{ (g)}$$

If the pressure is increased, equilibrium moves to the right (the rate of the forward reaction increases), as this produces less molecules (2 as opposed to 4).

> **6Med Tip:** It is important to know that catalysts don't change the position of equilibrium, they just decrease the time it takes to reach the point of equilibrium.

The Complete BMAT Specification Explained
C3 - Chemical Reactions, Formulae and Equations

Knowledge Check

1. Write the half equation for the formation of a calcium ion (Ca^{2+}) from calcium metal.
2. Balance the following equation: $ZnS + O_2 \rightarrow ZnO + SO_2$

Answers:
1. $Ca \rightarrow Ca^{2+} + 2e^-$
2. $2ZnS + 3O_2 \rightarrow 2ZnO + 2SO_2$

C4 – Quantitative Chemistry

Mass and Moles

In chemical calculations, we measure the amount of chemicals in <u>moles</u>. This is because the real mass of atoms, molecules and ions are so small that it becomes difficult to work with these numbers.

A mole is the amount of a substance that contains the same number of particles as 12 grams of carbon-12. If the substance is an element, 1 mole of it is equal to its relative atomic mass (A_r). If the substance is a compound, 1 mole of it is equal to its relative formula mass (M_r).

e.g.

- magnesium (Mg) has a relative atomic mass of 24. Therefore 1 mole of magnesium weighs 24g.
- calcium carbonate ($CaCO_3$) has a relative formula mass of $40 + 12 + (16 \times 3) = 100$. Therefore 1 mole of calcium carbonate weighs 100g.

1 mole of any substance contains the same number of particles as 1 mole of another substance. The number of particles in one mole of a substance is called the <u>Avogadro constant</u>, and it has a value of 6.02×10^{23}.

The number of particles in a substance can be calculated using the following equation:

Number of Particles = Avogadro Constant x Amount of Substance in Moles

We can also calculate the mass of a substance using the number of moles and vice versa. This is done according to the following equation:

Amount in Moles = Mass (g) / Relative Atomic or Relative Formula Mass

e.g.

- Calculate the number of moles in 3g of carbon.
    - Amount = mass/A_r, = 3/12, = 0.25 moles
- What is the mass of 0.5 moles of carbon dioxide?
    - Mass = moles x M_r, = 0.5 x 44, = 22g

The Complete BMAT Specification Explained

C4 – Quantitative Chemistry

You also need to be able to calculate the percentage composition by mass of a compound using given A_r values. To do this, you first need to calculate the relative formula mass of the compound, then use the following formula:

% of Element Y in Compound X = (Relative Amount of Y/M_r of X) x 100

> **6Med Tip:** The relative amount of an element in a compound is calculated by multiplying its A_r by the number of atoms of it present. In the BMAT, these A_r values will always be given to you.

Empirical Formulae

The <u>empirical formula</u> of a compound is the simplest whole number ratio of the atoms of each element in a compound. For example, compounds with the molecular formulae C_2H_4, C_3H_6 or C_4H_8 could all have the empirical formula CH_2.

We can deduce the empirical formula of a compound from different types of data, such as reacting masses, or the percentage composition by mass of its constituent elements.

e.g. If 2.4g of carbon reacts with oxygen to produce 8.8g of a carbon oxide. What is the formula of this oxide produced?

Step	C	O
Write the symbols of the elements involved and their masses	C, 2.4g	O, 8.8-2.4=6.4g
Find and write the Ar values	12	16
Divide the masses by the Ar values	2.4/12 = 0.2	6.4/16 = 0.4
Divide these by the smallest number	0.2/0.2 = 1	0.4/0.2 = 2

The ratio in this example is 1C:2O, so the formula is CO_2.

> **6Med Tip:** Sometimes the final step does not give the simplest whole number ratios (e.g. you could end up with 1.5 and 1). If this happens, you can't round up a half-number, but you simply **multiply all the values** by 2, so 1.5:1 becomes 3:2.

If you know the M_r of the compound you are calculating the empirical formula for, then you can calculate the molecular formula of the compound.

e.g. The empirical formula of a compound is CH_2 and its M_r is 56, what is the molecular formula of the compound?

- Firstly, calculate the mass of the atoms in the empirical formula: 12 + 1 + 1 = 14
- Divide the given M_r by this number: 56/14 = 4
- Multiple the empirical formula by this number: 4 x CH_2 = C_4H_8

Finding Masses from Chemical Equations

We can use balanced chemical equations to calculate either the mass of product formed using a given mass of reactant, or the mass of reactant needed to make a certain amount of product.

e.g. Magnesium reacts with oxygen in the following reaction:

$$2Mg(s) + O_2(g) \rightarrow 2MgO\ (s)$$

What mass of magnesium oxide can be made using 16g of oxygen? [M_r of MgO = 40, O_2 = 32]

- Calculate moles of oxygen: **mass/M_r** = 16/32 = 0.5 moles
- Look at the coefficients to find the **molar ratio** with magnesium oxide: 2 moles of MgO are produced for every mole of O_2, therefore 1 mole of MgO is produced here.
- **Mass = M_r x mol,** = 40 x 1 = 40g

> **6Med Tip:** Always remember to look at the **coefficients** to know what the ratios of moles are!

When one of the reactants is all used up, the other reactant(s) have nothing to react with, so the reaction finishes. The reactant left over is called the reactant **in excess**, and the reactant that has been used up is called the **limiting reactant**. The mass of product formed depends on the mass of the limiting reactant.

You also need to be able to construct balanced chemical equations from given masses or gas volumes.

e.g. If 16g of sulphur dioxide reacts with 4g of oxygen to produce sulphur trioxide, what is the balanced equation for this reaction? [M_r of SO_2 =64, O_2 = 32]

- Calculate the amounts of each reactant: mass/Mr (SO_2 = 16/64 = 0.25) (O_2 = 4/32 = 0.125)
- Divide both by the smaller amount to get the molar ratios: (SO_2 = 0.25/0.125 = 2) (O_2 = 0.125/0.125 = 1)
- Write out and balance the equation using these ratios: $2SO_2 + O_2 \rightarrow 2SO_3$

Moles of Gases

For a gas, one mole of it occupies a volume of **24dm³ (24,000cm³)** under room temperature and pressure conditions (rtp). The following equation can therefore be used:

Volume of Gas at rtp (dm³) = Number of Moles x 24

Solutions

A solution is the mixture formed when a solute dissolves in a solvent.

The concentration of a solution is a quantitative measure of how much solute is dissolved in a given volume of solvent, and can be measured using mass or moles. The units of concentration are therefore: g/dm^3 (or gdm^{-3}) if mass is used, and mol/dm^3 (or $moldm^{-3}$) if moles are used.

The concentration of a solution is calculated according to the following equation:

Concentration = Mass or Moles / Volume

A saturated solution is formed when no more solute can dissolve in a certain amount of liquid at a certain temperature. Solubility is the mass of solute needed to form a saturated solution in 100g of water at a given temperature. If a substance has a higher solubility, more of it can dissolve in the same amount of solvent.

e.g. If 10g of potassium chloride saturates 50g of water at 25°C, what is the solubility of potassium chloride at this temperature?

100g/50g = 2, so 2x10g=20g of potassium chloride would saturate 100g of water at 25°C. The solubility of potassium chloride is therefore written as 20g/100g water at 25°C.

Titration of Solutions

When two solutions of known volumes completely react, and we know the concentration of one solution, we can calculate the concentration of the other solution.

e.g. 25.0cm³ of 1.0mol/dm³ NaOH solution reacts completely with 20.0cm³ of HCl solution. What is the concentration of the HCl solution? [HCl + NaOH → NaCl + H_2O]

- Convert the volumes from cm³ to dm³: (volume NaOH = 25/1000 = 0.025dm³) (volume HCl = 20/1000 = 0.020dm³)
- Moles of NaOH = concentration x volume, 1 x 0.025 = 0.025 moles
- From the chemical equation of this reaction, we can see NaOH and HCl react in a 1:1 ratio, therefore 0.025 moles of HCl were also used.
- Concentration of HCl = moles/volume, = 0.025/0.020, = **1.25 moles**

Percentage Yield

The theoretical/predicted yield is the maximum possible mass of a product that can be formed in a chemical reaction. The actual yield is the actual mass of a product that is formed in a chemical reaction, and this is usually less than the theoretical yield.

We can calculate the percentage yield of a reaction using the following equation:

% Yield = (Actual Yield/Theoretical Yield) x 100

The percentage yield can range from 0%, where no product is formed, to 100%, where no product is lost.

The Complete BMAT Specification Explained

C4 – Quantitative Chemistry

Knowledge Check

1. At room temperature and pressure, a gas occupies $6dm^3$. How many moles of gas are present?
2. In a chemical reaction, the theoretical yield of a product is 12g, but only 8g of product was made. What was the percentage yield of this reaction?
3. What is the mass of 0.5 moles of $CaCO_3$? [A_r of Ca=40, C=12, O=16]

Answers:
1. 6/24 = 0.25mol
2. (8/12) x100 = 75%
3. 0.5 x 100 = 50g

C5 – Oxidation, Reduction and Redox

Oxidation and Reduction

Oxidation and reduction can be defined in terms of oxygen in a chemical reaction:

- <u>Oxidation</u> is the gain of oxygen
- <u>Reduction</u> is the loss of oxygen

e.g. Aluminium reacts with zinc oxide to produce aluminium oxide and zinc. In this reaction, aluminium is oxidised, and zinc is reduced.

However, not all chemical reactions involve oxygen. We therefore can use different definitions of oxidation and reduction:

- Oxidation is the **loss of electrons**
- Reduction is the **gain of electrons**

e.g. When magnesium chloride ($MgCl_2$) is formed, we can write this as 2 half equations. This makes it easier to see which substance has been oxidised, and which has been reduced:

- $Mg \rightarrow Mg^{2+} + 2e^-$, so the magnesium has been oxidised
- $Cl_2 + 2e^- \rightarrow 2Cl^-$, so the chlorine has been reduced

These alternative definitions can also be thought about in terms of oxidation state, whereby oxidation is an increase in oxidation state, and reduction is a decrease in oxidation state.

Redox Reactions

When oxidation and reduction happen in the same reaction, this is called a <u>redox reaction</u>. The examples given above are both redox reactions.

When the same substance is oxidised and reduced in the same reaction, this is called <u>disproportionation</u>.

e.g. $Cl_2 + H_2O \rightarrow HCl + HClO$

In this reaction, the chlorine is oxidised from oxidation state 0 (Cl_2) to +1 in HClO, and reduced to state -1 in HCl.

Oxidation State

The <u>oxidation state</u> is a number assigned to a substance which shows its degree of oxidation or reduction.

Oxidation states are written (+/-) followed by numbers. The oxidation number of an element or compound is always 0.

> **6Med Tip:** Be careful not to confuse oxidation numbers with charges! Charges are written as numbers followed by (+/-)

There are a few rules to remember when working out oxidation states:

- The charge of a substance must equal the sum of the oxidation states of its constituent species (e.g. OH- has an oxidation number of -1, because O is -2 and H is +1).
- The oxidation numbers of ions are the same as their charges (e.g. Na^+ is +1, Mg^{2+} is +2, Cl^- is -1).
- The oxidation number of hydrogen is usually +1, but when bound to a metal ion, hydrogen has an oxidation number of -1.
- The oxidation number of oxygen is usually -2, but this can sometimes change.

Oxidising and Reducing Agents

Oxidising agents are species that can oxidise others. These species undergo reduction themselves.

Reducing agents are species that can reduce others. These species undergo oxidation themselves.

The Complete BMAT Specification Explained
C5 – Oxidation, Reduction and Redox

Knowledge Check

1. Which species is oxidised in the following reaction:
   $CuO + H_2 \rightarrow Cu + H_2O$
2. Predict the oxidation state of sulphur in SO_2, SO_3 and SO_3^{2-}.
3. Which species is the reducing agent in the following reaction:
   $Zn + CuSO_4 \rightarrow ZnSO_4 + Cu$

Answers:
1. H_2
2. 4, 6 and 4 respectively
3. Zn

C6 – Chemical Bonding, Structure and Properties

Definitions

You need to know the differences between elements, compounds and mixtures.

An <u>element</u> is a substance which consists of all the same type of atom. Each of its atoms therefore contain the same number of protons.

There is only a certain number of elements, and these are each found on the periodic table. Elements are written as their chemical symbols, as are seen on the periodic table (e.g. He, Be, Na).

> **6Med Tip:** Some elements travel around as pairs of atoms. The symbols for these elements are therefore written with a subscript '2' (H_2, N_2, O_2, F_2, Cl_2, Br_2, I_2)

A <u>compound</u> is a pure substance containing 2 or more elements that are chemically combined. Each element in a compound cannot be separated by physical means and can be bonded to each other by various types of chemical bonds. Examples of commonly seen compounds are carbon dioxide (CO_2), water (H_2O), methane (CH_4) and table salt (NaCl).

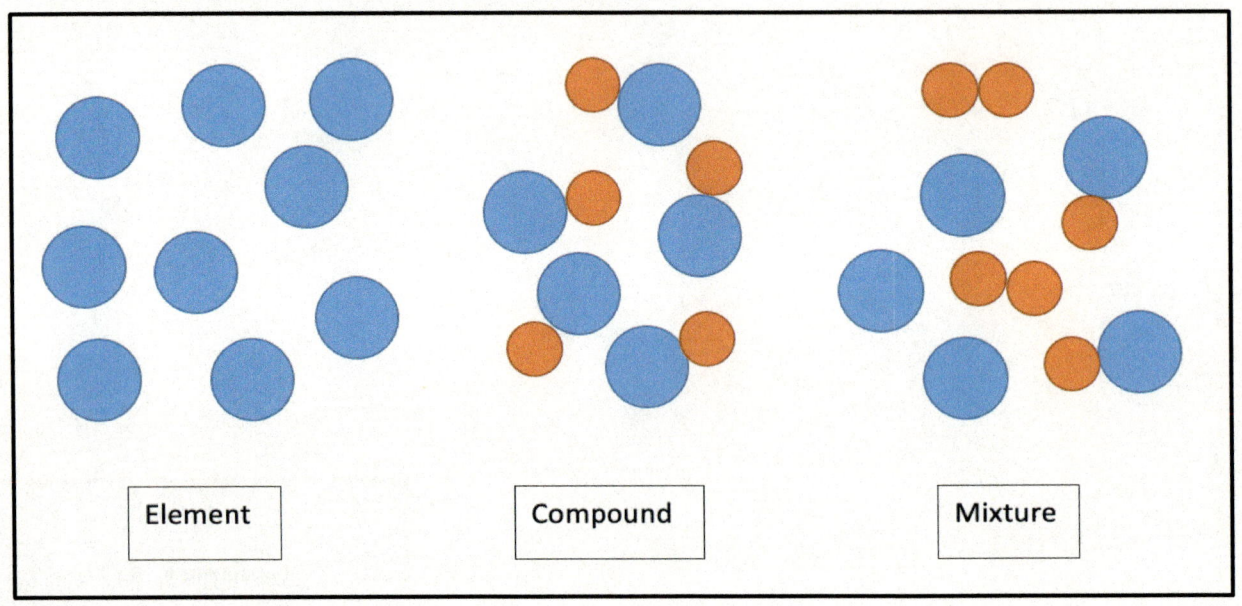

| Element | Compound | Mixture |

A <u>mixture</u> is a substance that contains 2 or more elements and/or compounds. The substances in a mixture are not chemically combined, and can therefore be separated by physical separation techniques. A commonly given example of a mixture is air- this contains both elements such as N_2 and O_2, and compounds such as CO_2.

Ionic Bonding

Ionic bonding occurs between metals and non-metals. This occurs due to electron transfer from metals to non-metals, forming oppositely charged ions that are have a strong electrostatic attraction to each other.

Metal atoms lose electrons from their outermost shells to form positive ions. Non-metal atoms gain electrons on their outermost shell to form negatively charged ions. Both of these types of ions are stable, as this electron loss or gain means that they have full outer shells (the electron structure of a noble gas).

Elements in groups 1, 2 and 3 lose 1, 2 or 3 electrons respectively to form ions with charges of 1^+, 2^+ or 3^+. Elements in groups 5, 6 and 7 gain 3, 2 or 1 electrons respectively to form ions with charges of 3^-, 2^- or 1^-. Some elements can form ions of different charges- this is shown by roman numerals. For example, iron (II) chloride has the formula $FeCl_2$, whereas iron (III) chloride has the formula $FeCl_3$.

Some ions are formed by multiple atoms- these are called <u>compound, or polyatomic, ions</u>. Some common examples of these include ammonium (NH_4^+), hydroxide (OH^-), nitrate (NO_3^-), carbonate (CO_3^{2-}) and sulphate (SO_4^{2-}).

You need to be able to determine the molecular formulae of ionic compounds based upon their constituent ions. Ionic compounds will always have an overall neutral charge. This means that you need to balance the amount of each ion so that there is the same amount of positive and negative charges present.

e.g. Magnesium chloride is formed from magnesium ions (Mg^{2+}) and chloride ions (Cl^-). Because there are 2 positive charges and 1 negative charge here, magnesium chloride contains 2 chloride ions for every magnesium ion: $MgCl_2$.

Structure of Ionic Compounds

Ionic compounds are arranged in a giant ionic lattice. This is a regular, 3D arrangement of ions where each ion is surrounded by inversely charged ions on all sides. This strongly holds the ions together due to strong electrostatic attraction acting on all sides of each ion. A 2D representation of part of a giant ionic lattice is shown in the diagram.

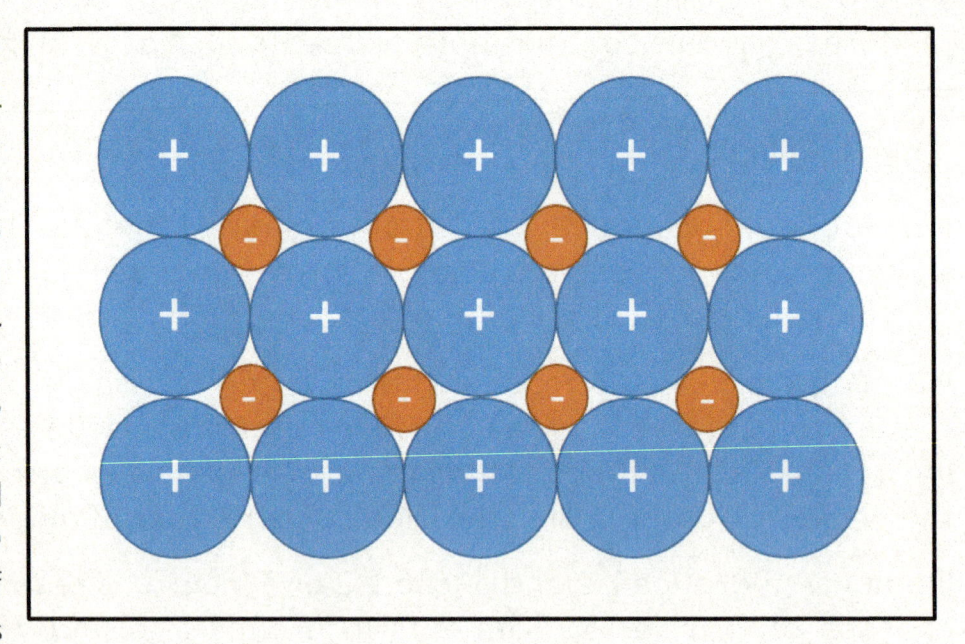

Properties of Ionic Compounds

Ionic compounds have **high melting and boiling points.** This is because the strong electrostatic attraction between oppositely charged ions requires a lot of energy to overcome.

The strength of ionic bonds increases with increasing charge of the ions. For example, magnesium oxide, formed from Mg^{2+} and O^{2-} ions, has a boiling point of 3,600ºC, whereas sodium chloride, formed from Na^+ and Cl^- ions, has a boiling point of 1,413ºC.

Ionic compounds can conduct electricity **when molten (melted) or in solution.** This is because, in these situations, the ions are free to move around and carry the electrical charge.

> **6Med Tip:** Remember- ionic compounds cannot conduct electricity when they are solid, as the ions cannot move around!

Covalent Bonding

Covalent bonding occurs between **non-metals**.

Covalent bonds are formed when atoms share a pair of electrons. Normally, one electron of this pair comes from each atom involved. Sometimes, 2 electron pairs can be shared, forming a double bond, or 3 pairs can be shared, forming a triple bond.

Structure of Covalent Compounds

Most covalent compounds form <u>small molecules</u>. Molecules of a compound always contain the same number of atoms of each element. Ions do not form molecules, so the atoms in a molecule will always be held together by covalent bonds. There are weak intermolecular forces holding these molecules together. Common small molecular compounds include carbon dioxide (CO_2), water (H_2O), methane (CH_4) and ammonia (NH_3).

On the other hand, some covalent compounds have <u>giant covalent structures</u>. These consist of lots of atoms joined together in a regular arrangement. Examples of giant covalent substances include diamond, graphite and silicon dioxide.

Properties of Covalent Compounds

Small molecular compounds have **low melting and boiling points** as it only takes a small amount of energy to overcome the weak intermolecular forces. In general, the larger the molecule, the higher its melting and boiling points, as there are stronger intermolecular forces between larger molecules.

> **6Med Tip:** The covalent bonds are not broken when melting or boiling a simple molecular compound- it is the intermolecular forces that have to be overcome! This is a common mistake to make, so be careful.

Small molecular compounds **cannot conduct electricity** because the molecules are not charged.

Giant covalent structures have **high melting and boiling points**. This is because lots of energy is needed to break the strong covalent bonds between atoms.

The Complete BMAT Specification Explained
C6 – Chemical Bonding, Structure and Properties

Most giant covalent substances **cannot conduct electricity** as they have no charged particles that are free to move and carry the electrical charge. An exception to this rule is **graphite**, which contains carbon atoms each bonded to 3 other carbon atoms. This structure means that graphite has 1 delocalised electron for every carbon atom, which can move through the structure to carry the electrical charge.

Metallic Bonding

Metals also form <u>giant lattice structures</u>. Within this lattice, the metal atoms lose their outermost electrons to become positively charged ions. These electrons become delocalised, so move throughout the structure. This sharing of electrons results in strong metallic bonding.

Properties of Metals

Metals have **high melting and boiling points** as large amounts of energy are needed to overcome the strong metallic bonds.

Metals are **good conductors of electricity**, as the delocalised electrons are free to move through the structure and carry the electrical charge. As well as this, delocalised electrons can also carry thermal energy, so metals are **good conductors of heat**.

Knowledge Check

1. Which of the following compounds will have a higher melting point, water (H_2O) or lithium metal (Li)?
2. What will be the molecular formula of the ionic compound formed from aluminium ions (Al^{3+}) and oxide ions (O^{2-})?
3. Can diamond conduct electricity? Why is this the case?

Answers:
1. Li, as it is held together by strong metallic bonds, unlike water, which only has weak intermolecular forces to be overcome
2. Al_2O_3
3. No - it has no free electrons to move and carry the charge

C7 – Group Chemistry

You need to know the physical and chemical properties of groups 1 (the alkali metals), group 7 (the halogens) and group 0 (the noble gases).

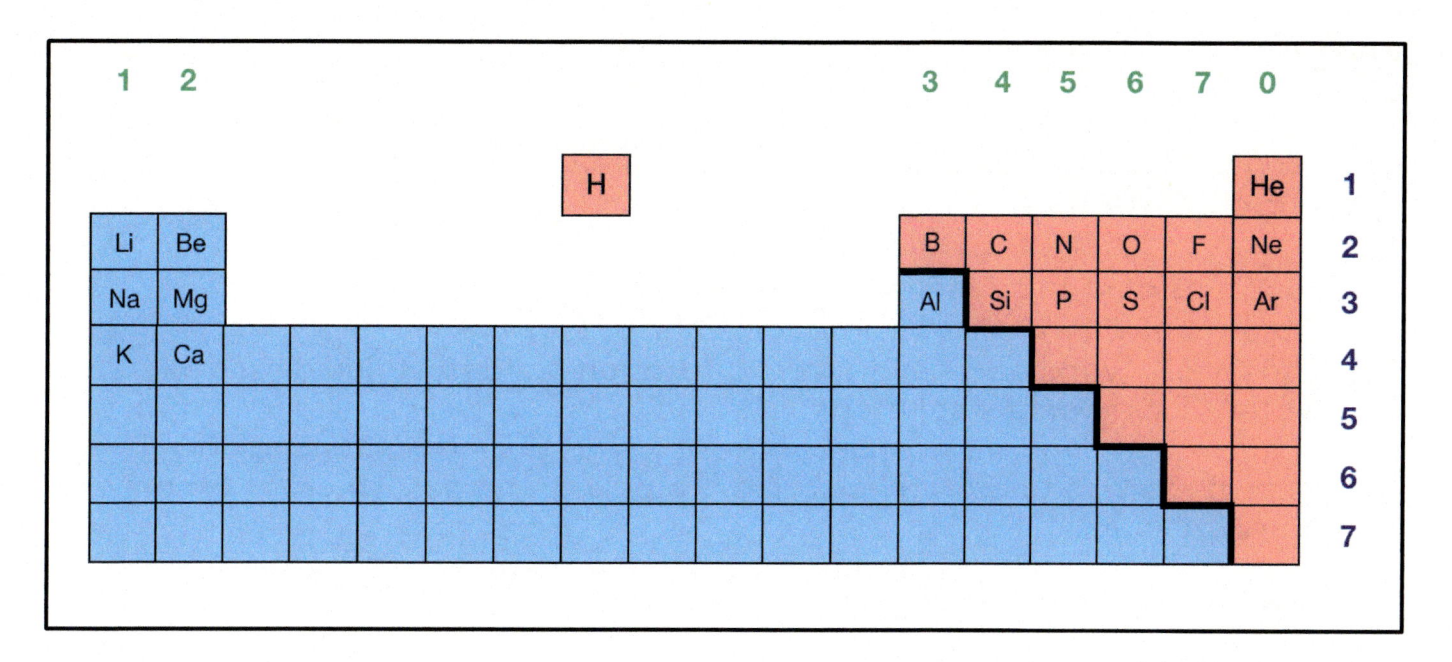

Group 1

Group 1, or the alkali metals, are found in the leftmost vertical column of the periodic table. They all have 1 electron in their outermost electron shell, so form ions with oxidation states of **+1**.

The properties of the group 1 elements are as follows:
- They react with water to form **alkalis** and hydrogen gas
- They are **soft silver solids** which are shiny when freshly cut, but quickly tarnish due to their reaction with the oxygen in air
- They have **low densities**
- They have relatively **low melting points**

There are trends seen in these properties:

- Their reactivity increases going down the group
- Density increases going down the group
- Melting and boiling points decrease going down the group

Group 7

Group 7, or the halogens, are found in a vertical column to the right hand side of the periodic table. They all have 7 electrons in their outer shell, and form ions with oxidation states of -1.

The properties of group 7 elements are as follows:
- They react with metals to produce **salts**
- They react with hydrogen to form **hydrogen halides**, which dissolve in water to form **acidic solutions**
- They vary in their physical properties such as boiling points and colours (e.g. at room temperature, chlorine is a pale green gas, whereas bromine is a brown liquid)

The following trends are seen in these properties:
- The reactivity of the halogens decreases going down the group
- The melting and boiling points increase going down the group

Group 0

The elements in group 0 are known as the noble gases. They exist as single atoms with full outer shells of electrons. These have **low boiling points**, as only a small amount of energy is needed to overcome the weak intermolecular forces between atoms.

The noble gases are **inert**, meaning that they are very unreactive and don't take part in chemical reactions.

The Complete BMAT Specification Explained
C7 – Group Chemistry

Displacement Reactions

Displacement reactions occur when one substance takes the place of another in a chemical reaction.

You should be aware of this in the context of halogens and halide ions. Here, more reactive halogens will displace less reactive ones.

e.g. adding chlorine gas to a solution of potassium iodide will displace the iodide ion from the potassium, producing potassium chloride and iodine:

$$Cl_2 \text{ (g)} + 2KI \text{ (aq)} \rightarrow 2KCl \text{ (aq)} + I_2 \text{ (aq)}$$

Knowledge Check

1. Write the balanced chemical equation for the reaction of sodium with water.
2. Will iodine displace chlorine from a solution of potassium chloride?

Answers:
1. $2Na \text{ (s)} + 2H_2O \text{ (l)} \rightarrow 2NaOH \text{ (aq)} + H_2 \text{ (g)}$
2. No - iodine is less reactive than chlorine

C8 – Separation Techniques

Chemical processes are needed to separate the different elements that make up a compound. However, separating mixtures can be done by physical processes, as the substances are not chemically combined.

Distillation

<u>Simple distillation</u> is used to separate a solvent from a solution. This works because the solute has a much higher boiling point than the solvent. The solution is heated, and so the solvent evaporates. This vapour is cooled and condensed.

<u>Fractional distillation</u> is used to separate a mixture of liquids. These are known as <u>miscible liquids</u>, as they dissolve in each other. This works because the liquids have different boiling points. The mixture is heated, causing the vapours to rise up the distillation column which is hot at the bottom and cool at the top. The vapours of each liquid in the mixture condense when they reach the section of the column which is just below the temperature of their boiling point, and are condensed and removed. A key example of when fractional distillation is used is the separation of crude oil.

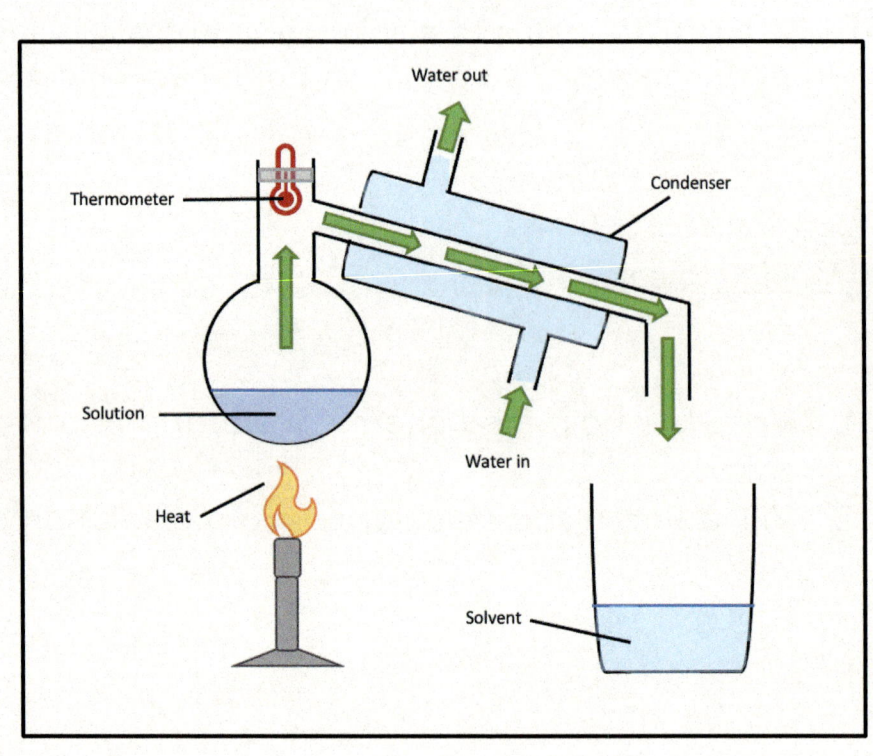

Separating Funnel

Separating funnels are used to separate immiscible liquids (liquids that do not mix). The mixture is placed into a separating funnel with a container for collection placed underneath. The liquid with a lower density floats on top of the liquid with a higher density. A tap at the bottom of the separating funnel can be opened, so the higher density flows through into the collecting container. The tap is closed just before the liquid with lower density flows through, separating the liquids.

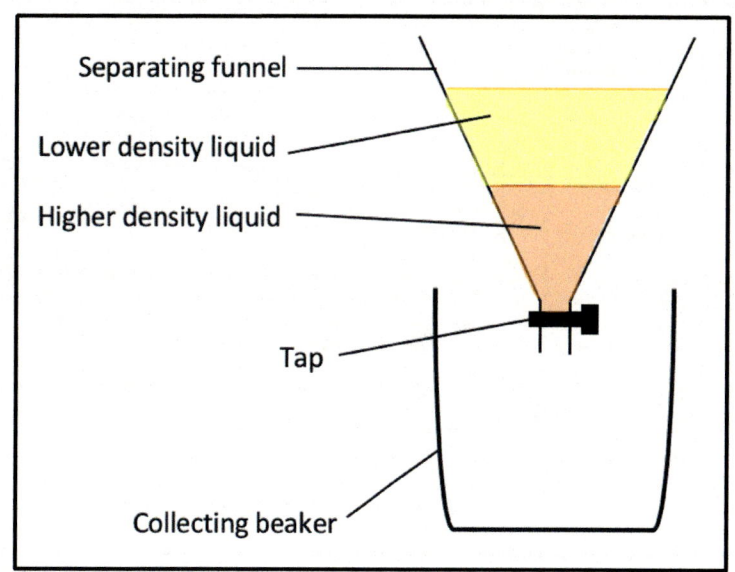

Paper Chromatography

Paper chromatography is used to separate a mixture of soluble substances.

A small amount of the substance(s) to be separated is placed onto the chromatography paper. The paper is lowered into a tray of solvent (making sure that the solvent stays below the level of the substance. The solvent travels up the paper, carrying the substance with it. The different components travel up the paper by different amounts, depending on their attraction to the paper and the solvent.

Paper chromatography produces a chromatogram, which can then be interpreted. Pure substances produce 1 spot on the chromatogram, whereas impure substances produce more than 1 spot. We can perform paper chromatography of multiple substances at once in order to compare them to each other, and to known substances.

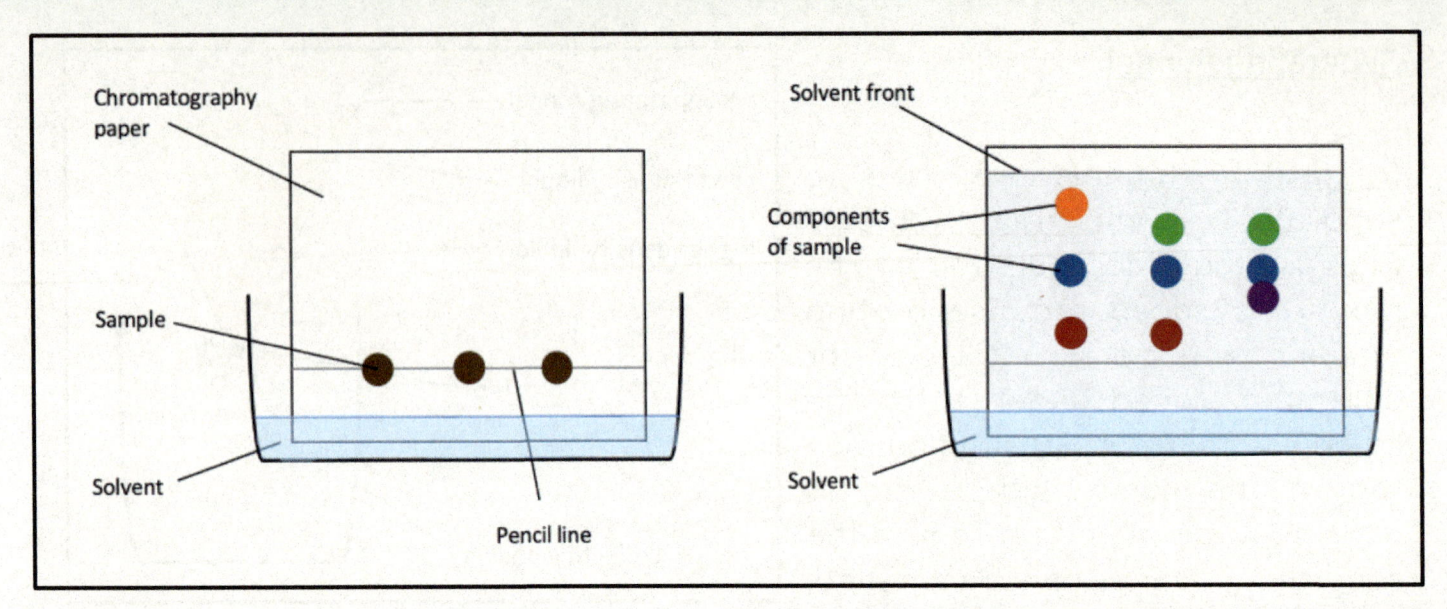

R_f **values** are used to identify unknown substances when compared to reference substances. The R_f value is always the same for a particular substance. R_f values are calculated using the following formula:

R_f = Distance travelled by Substance / Distance travelled by Solvent

In the example here, the Rf of the blue spot = A/B.

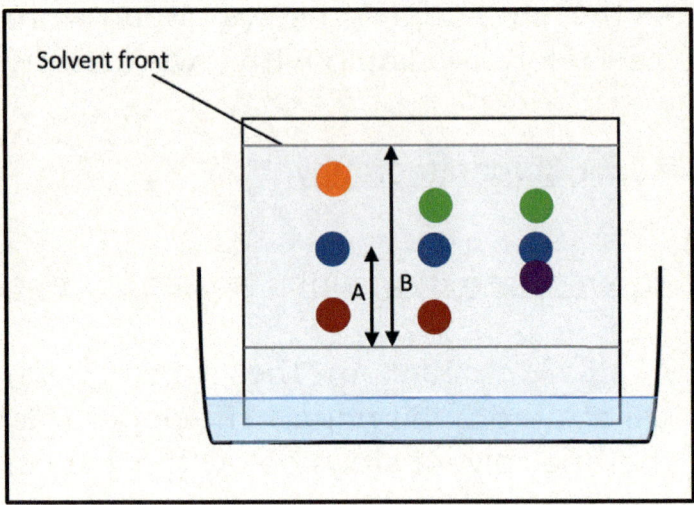

Centrifugation

Centrifugation is used to separate small amounts of solid that are suspended in a liquid. A centrifuge machine spins a test tube round at a high speed, causing solid to sink to the bottom of the tube. The liquid can then be removed from the top of the test tube.

Dissolving

Dissolving can be used to separate a mixture of solids. If 2 solids are mixed together and one is soluble in a particular solvent but the other is not, then the mixture can be dissolved in the solvent. For example, a mixture of salt and sand can be dissolved in water, forming a solution of salty water with suspended particle of sand. This can then be filtered and crystallised.

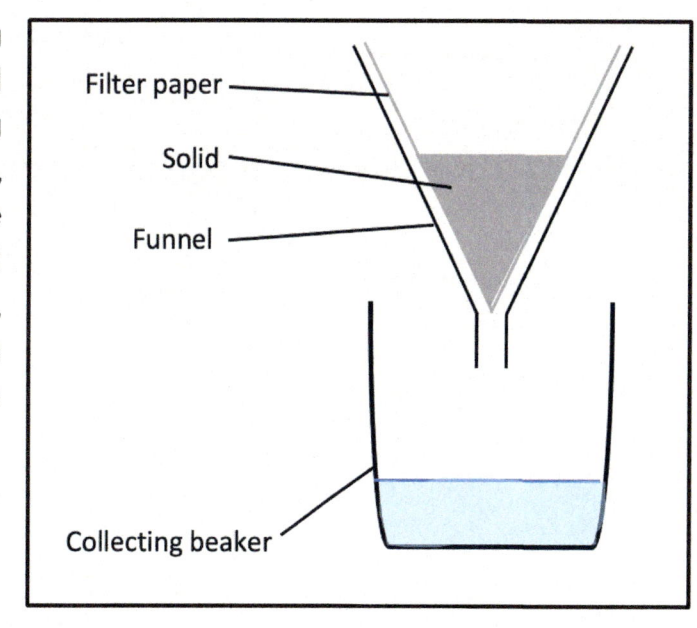

Filtration and Crystallisation

Filtration is used to separate an insoluble solid from a liquid. A beaker contains a funnel lined with filter paper. The solid and liquid mixture is poured into the funnel. The liquid drips through into the beaker, but the solid is trapped in the filter paper.

This works as the filter paper contains tiny pores, which let small molecules and dissolved ions through them, but not the pieces of undissolved solid.

We can use crystallisation to produce crystals from a solution. The solution is warmed in an evaporating basin, so the solvent evaporates and solid crystals of the solute form.

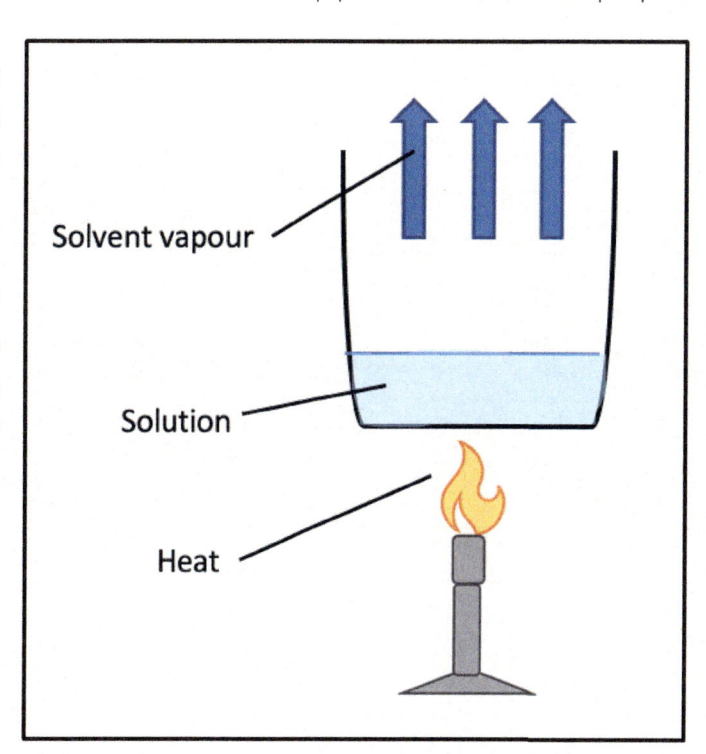

Knowledge Check

1. In a paper chromatography experiment, the solvent travelled 12cm up a piece of chromatography paper. Substance A travelled 6cm up and substance B travelled 8cm up the same paper. What are the R_f values of substances A and B?
2. What is the difference between miscible and immiscible liquids?

Answers:
1. A=0.5, B=0.67
2. Miscible liquids dissolve in each other/mix, whereas immiscible liquids do not.

C9 – Acids, Bases and Salts

Acids

<u>Acids</u> are substances that form H^+ ions in aqueous solution, or that act as H^+ donors.

You need to be able to describe the reactions of acids with the following substances:

1. Metals
   - Acid + metal → salt + hydrogen
   - The reaction of a metal with an acid is a redox reaction
     e.g. sulphuric acid + iron → iron (II) sulphate + hydrogen
     $$H_2SO_4 \text{ (aq)} + Fe(s) \rightarrow FeSO_4 \text{ (aq)} + H_2 \text{ (g)}$$
2. Carbonates
   - Acid + carbonate → salt + water + carbon dioxide
     e.g. hydrochloric acid + magnesium carbonate → magnesium chloride + water + carbon dioxide
     $$HCl \text{ (aq)} + MgCO_3 \text{ (s)} \rightarrow MgCl_2 \text{ (aq)} + H_2O \text{ (l)} + CO_2 \text{ (g)}$$

3. Metal hydroxides
   - Acid + metal hydroxide → salt + water
     e.g. hydrochloric acid + sodium hydroxide → sodium chloride + water
     $$HCl \text{ (aq)} + NaOH \text{ (aq)} \rightarrow NaCl \text{ (aq)} + H_2O \text{ (l)}$$

4. Metal oxides
   - Acid + metal oxide → salt + water
     e.g. sulphuric acid + copper oxide → copper sulphate + water
     $$H_2SO_4 \text{ (aq)} + CuO \text{ (s)} \rightarrow CuSO_4 \text{ (aq)} + H_2O \text{ (l)}$$

Some terms you need to know the differences between are as follows:
- <u>Strong acid</u>: an acid that fully dissociates into its constituent ions when in solution (e.g. HCl, HNO_3, H_2SO_4)
- <u>Weak acid</u>: an acid that only partially dissociates into its constituent ions when in solution (e.g. ethanoic acid). This is represented as a reversible reaction.

The **concentration** of a solution is the amount of solute dissolved in a given volume of solvent. A concentrated contains more particles in a given volume than a dilute solution.

> **6Med Tip:** Be careful! 'Strong' in the context of acids does not always mean concentrated! An acid can be strong, but dilute, for example if it is dissolved in a large volume of water!

The **pH** of a solution shows its concentration of H^+ ions. The higher the H^+ concentration, the lower the pH, and the solution is more acidic. This means that, for a given solution concentration, the stronger the acid, the lower the pH. Acids have pH values between 0 and 7. Neutral solutions always have a pH value of 7. Alkaline solutions have pH values between 7 and 14. A change of 1 on the pH scale corresponds to a change in H^+ concentration by a **factor of 10**. For example, an acid with a pH of 3 contains 10 times as many H^+ ions in a given volume than a solution of pH 4.

Acids can be **monoprotic**, **diprotic** or **triprotic**. This basically tells us how many moles of hydrogen ions are released by each mole of acid when in solution. HCl and HNO_3 are common examples of monoprotic acids. They release 1 mole of H^+ per mole of acid. H_2SO_4 is a common diprotic acid, releasing 2 moles of H^+ per mole of acid. H_3PO_4 is an example of a triprotic acid, releasing 3 moles of H^+ per mole of acid.

Bases

Bases are substances that form OH^- ions in aqueous solution, or that act as H^+ acceptors. Bases react with acids to form a salt and water only. Bases that are soluble in water are called **alkalis**- they dissolve to form alkaline solutions (pH > 7).

The terms strong, weak, dilute and concentrated (as explained above) can also be applied when talking about bases.

The Complete BMAT Specification Explained

C9 – Acids, Bases and Salts

Metals form oxides that are basic (e.g. MgO, CuO), whereas non-metals form oxides that are acidic (e.g. SO_2, CO_2).

When acids and bases react, a **neutralisation reaction** occurs. Neutralisation reactions are often **exothermic**, so give out heat energy. These produce a **salt and water**. Water is always produced as the H^+ ions from the acid react with the OH^- from the alkaline solution to produce neutral water:

$$H^+ (aq) + OH^- (aq) \rightarrow H_2O (l)$$

Knowledge Check

1. What products will be formed when sulphuric acid reacts with magnesium carbonate?
2. What can we say about the concentration of H+ in solutions with pH values of 8 and 10?

Answers:
1. Magnesium sulphate (salt), carbon dioxide and water
2. Solution with pH 8 has 100 times more H+ in a given volume than solution with pH 10.

C10 – Rates of Reaction

For a chemical reaction to occur, successful collisions between the particles of reactant are needed. This occurs when particles collide with each other with enough energy for them to react. The minimum amount of energy needed for collisions to be successful is known as the <u>activation energy (E_a)</u>, which is shown on a reaction profile as seen in the diagram.

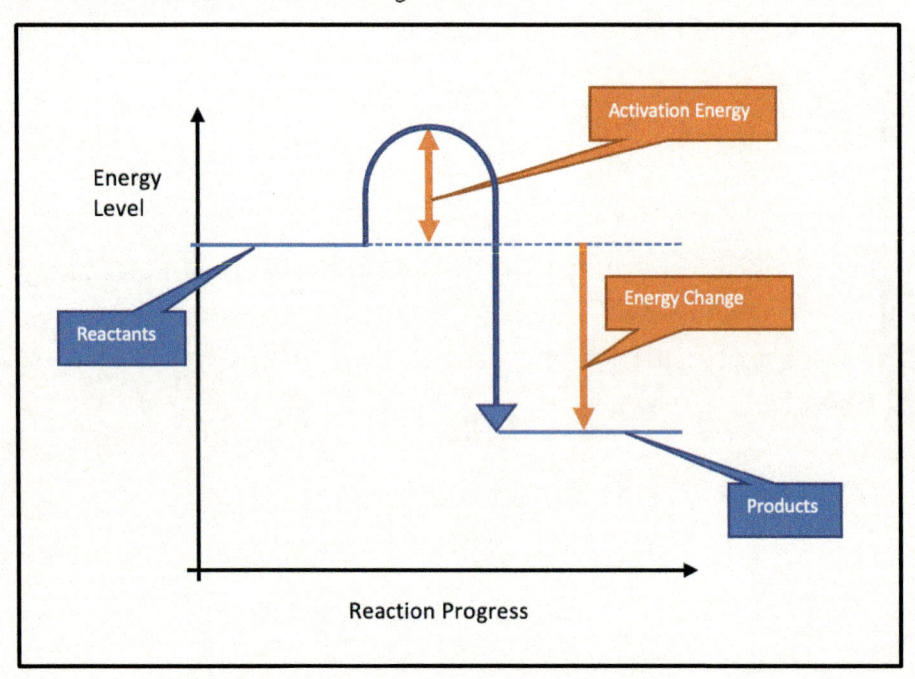

The rate, or speed, of a reaction is measured by the frequency of <u>successful collisions</u> between reactant particles.

We can work out the rate of a reaction by either of two equations:

Mean rate of reaction = Amount of reactant used / Time

Mean rate of reaction = Amount of product formed / Time

> **6Med Tip:** The units used for rate of reaction depend on the units used when making the measurements. For example, if we measure the amount of product formed in grams, and the time in seconds, the rate of reaction calculated will be in g/sec, or $g\,sec^{-1}$.

Using Graphs

We can plot a graph of the amount of product formed against time, and analyse this for different reactions.

The **gradient** of the graph is equal to the rate of reaction. This means that the steeper the line, the greater the rate of reaction. When the line becomes horizontal, the reaction is finished (as the gradient = 0). Faster reactions finish more quickly than slower reactions.

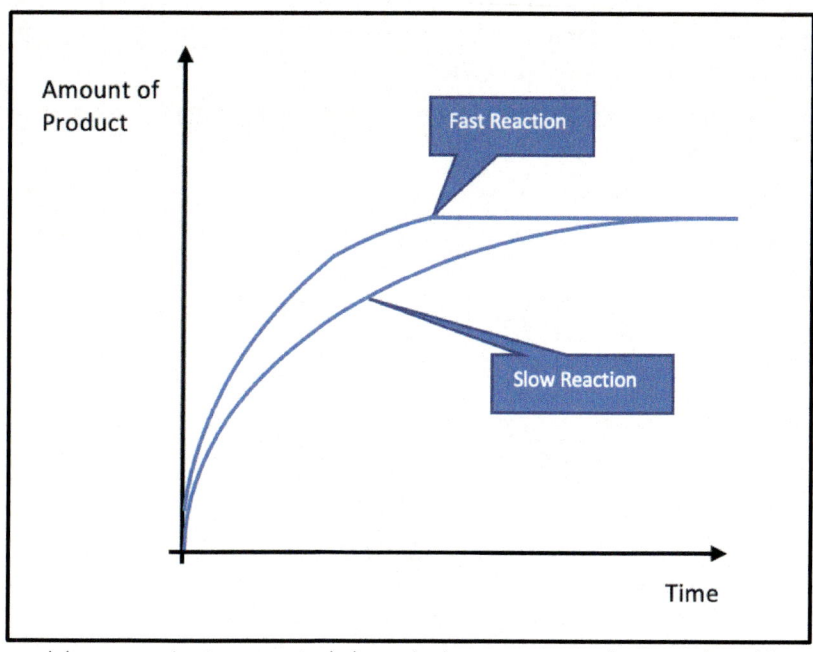

Changing the Rate of Reaction

The rate of reaction can be changed by certain variables. We can explain why this occurs by using the collision theory.

If the reaction is occurring in solution, **increasing the concentration** of the solution will increase the rate of reaction. If the reaction is between gases, **increasing the pressure** will increase the rate of reaction. This is because:
- The number of successful collisions is proportional to the number of reactant particles
- There are **more reactant particles in a given volume**
- The frequency of successful collisions increases

On a rate of reaction graph, increasing the concentration or pressure produces a steeper line that finishes sooner.

> **6Med Tip:** Be careful to remember that when increasing the concentration or pressure, the energy of the particles doesn't change. It is the frequency of collisions that increases the number of successful collisions.

C10 – Rates of Reaction

If a large lump of reactant is divided into smaller lumps, or into a powder, the **surface area to volume ratio** of reactant increases (its total volume stays the same, but the area of exposed surface increases). Grinding the reactant into a finer powder therefore increases the rate of reaction because:
- The number of successful collisions is proportional to the number of reactant particles
- There are **more reactant particles exposed** and therefore available to react
- The frequency of successful collisions increases

On a rate of reaction graph, increasing the surface area to volume ratio produces a steeper line that finishes sooner.

If the **temperature** of the reaction mixture is increased:
- The reactant particles have a **greater kinetic energy**, and therefore move around more quickly
- The frequency and proportion of successful collisions increases
- The rate of reaction increases

On a rate of reaction graph, increasing the temperature produces a steeper line that finishes sooner.

> **6Med Tip:** Increasing the temperature increases the rate of reaction by increasing 2 factors: frequency of collisions and energy of collisions.

A <u>catalyst</u> is a substance that increases the rate of reaction, without being chemically changed themselves. They do not alter the products formed in a reaction. Different catalysts are used for different reactions. Catalysts increase the rate of reaction by providing an **alternative reaction pathway with a lower activation energy**. This doesn't increase the frequency of collisions, but increases the proportion of successful collisions. Using a catalyst in a reversible reaction increases the rate of the forward and backward reactions equally, so the **position of equilibrium is unchanged**.

Knowledge Check

1. In a reaction, 120 cm³ of product were formed in 10 seconds. What was the mean rate of reaction?
2. What does the term 'successful collisions' mean in the context of rates of reaction?

Answers:
1. = 120/10 = 12 $cm^3 s^{-1}$
2. Successful collisions are collisions between reactant particles that have energy greater than activation energy, and therefore cause particles to react.

C11 – Energetics

Temperature Changes

During a chemical reaction, energy can be transferred to or from the surroundings. An <u>exothermic</u> reaction is when energy is transferred to the surroundings. This increases the temperature of the surroundings. An <u>endothermic</u> reaction is when energy is taken in from the surroundings to the reaction mixture, decreasing the temperature of the surroundings.

The <u>enthalpy change (ΔH)</u> of a reaction is a measure of the amount of energy given out or taken in. We calculate this using the following equation:

Enthalpy change (ΔH) = Energy taken in – Energy given out

ΔH is a negative value if the reaction is exothermic, and a positive value if the reaction is endothermic.

If a reversible reaction is exothermic in one direction, it is endothermic in the other direction.

Energy Level Diagrams

Energy level diagrams are used show the energy levels of the reactants and products of a reaction. We can use these diagrams to determine if a reaction is exothermic or endothermic.

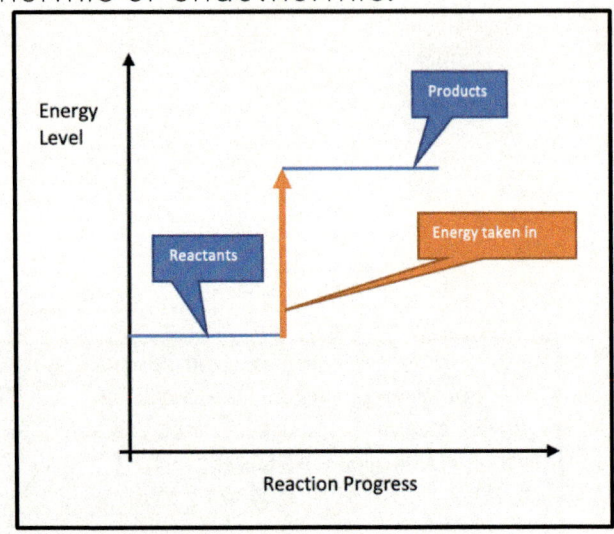

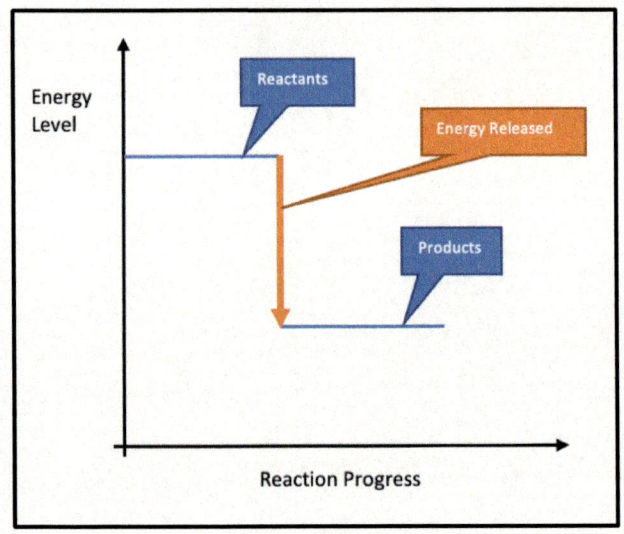

For an exothermic reaction, the energy level decreases from the reactants to products (ΔH is negative). For an endothermic reaction, the energy level increases from the reactants to the products (ΔH is positive).

Energy level diagrams importantly do not show the <u>activation energy</u> (the energy needed for the reaction to occur).

Calorimetry Experiments

Specific heat capacity can be used to calculate the change in heat energy undergone by a substance according to the following equation:

Change in energy (J) = Mass (kg) x Specific heat capacity (J/kg°C) x Temperature change (Δθ)

e.g. What is the change in energy occurring when 100g of water is heated from 25°C to 100°C? [The specific heat capacity of water is 4,200J/kg°C]
= mass in kg x specific heat capacity x temperature change
= (100/1000) x 4,200 x (100-25)
= 0.1 x 4,200 x 75
ΔH = 31,500J

> **6Med Tip:** When performing these calculations, always be wary of the units you are given, and the units you need! Often questions will require you to convert the values they give you into ones that can be substituted into the equation.

Chemical Bonds

The energy that is transferred in a reaction comes from either the **formation or breaking of chemical bonds.**

Breaking chemical bonds is an endothermic process, taking in energy. This occurs in the reactants. Forming chemical bonds is an exothermic process giving out energy. This occurs in the products. In an exothermic reaction, more energy is released in the formation of bonds than is taken in when the products are formed. In an endothermic reaction, less energy is released in the formation of bonds than is taken in when the products are formed.

C11 – Energetics

Knowledge Check

1. Using an energy change diagram, how can we tell if a reaction is exothermic or endothermic?
2. How much energy is given out when 1kg of water cools from 80ºC to 50ºC? [The specific heat capacity of water is 4,200J/kgºC]

Answers:
1. Exothermic reactions- the products have a lower energy level than the reactants. Vice versa is the case for endothermic reactions.
2. 1 x 4,200 x -30 = -126,000J

C12 – Electrolysis

We use the process of <u>electrolysis</u> to break down electrolytes into elements. This is done using electricity.

Process of Electrolysis

During electrolysis, an electric current is passed through a substance that is either molten or in solution (the <u>electrolyte</u>). In these conditions, the ions are free to move around, carry the electrical charge and therefore complete the electrical circuit.

In the electrolyte there are 2 electrodes:
- The positively charged electrode is called the <u>anode</u>
- The negatively charged electrode is called the <u>cathode</u>

The free moving ions of the electrolyte are attracted to the oppositely charged electrode. Ions gain or lose electrons at the electrode to form elements. Positively charged ions move to the cathode, gaining electrons (**they are reduced**). Negatively charged ions are attracted to the anode, where they lose electrons (**are oxidised**).

The electric current used in electrolysis is always a **direct current**. If an alternating current was used, each electrode would flicker very quickly between being positive and negative. This would mean that ions wouldn't be attracted to one particular electrode, so would not be able to form the desired atoms or molecules.

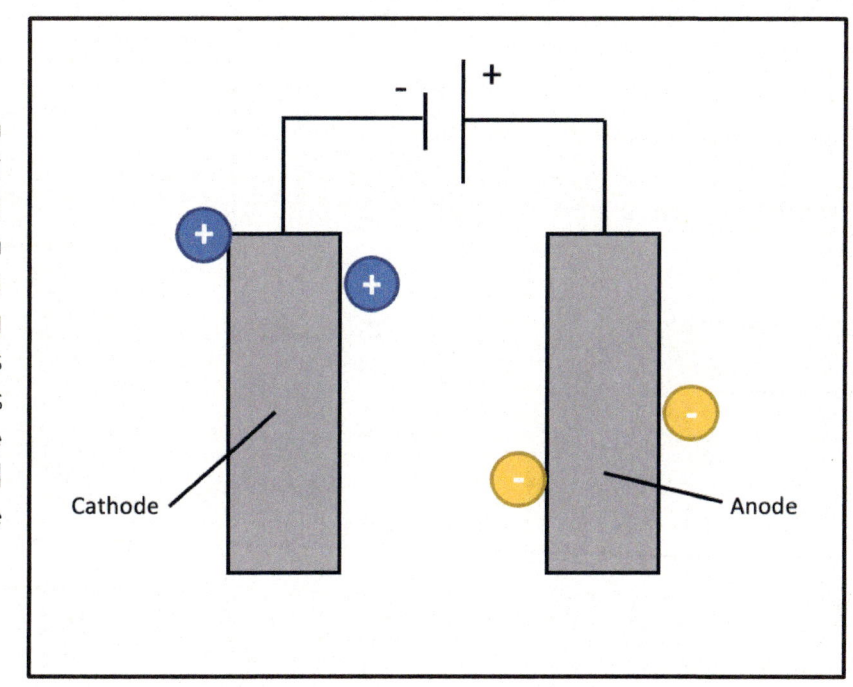

C12 – Electrolysis

Predicting the Products of Electrolysis

With a molten compound, there are only ions of the compound present. It can therefore be quite easily worked out as to which ions are attracted to which electrode, and therefore what substances are formed.

e.g. When molten sodium chloride, NaCl (l) is used as the electrolyte:
- Na^+ ions are attracted to the cathode. Here, they are reduced, gaining 1 electron each. This results in the formation of sodium metal (Na).
- Cl^- ions are attracted to the anode. Here, they are oxidised, losing 1 electron each. These atoms form diatomic molecules of chlorine (Cl_2).

This becomes slightly more complicated when using solutions as electrolytes, because the water used as a solvent contains ions itself (H^+ **and** OH^-). The positively charged ions from the substance compete with the H^+ at the cathode to gain electrons. The rule to remember here is that the **least reactive species** will be reduced to form the element.

> **6Med Tip:** As a general rule, copper, silver and gold are the only 3 metals less reactive than hydrogen (and so will be formed if contained in the electrolyte). With any other metal, hydrogen will be formed, as they are all more reactive than hydrogen.

At the anode, the rule to remember is that **oxygen** will be produced from the hydroxide ions of water, unless any halide ions are present (Cl^-, Br^-, I^-).

The electrolysis of sodium chloride solution is shown in the diagram.

e.g. If a solution of copper sulphate ($CuSO_4$) undergoes electrolysis, copper metal (Cu) and oxygen (O_2) will be formed.

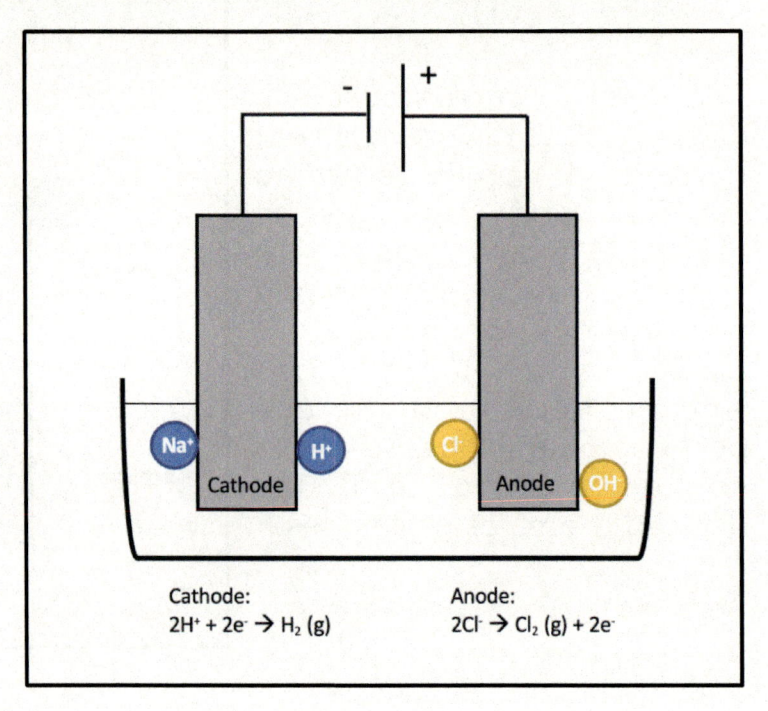

Cathode:
$2H^+ + 2e^- \rightarrow H_2 (g)$

Anode:
$2Cl^- \rightarrow Cl_2 (g) + 2e^-$

C12 – Electrolysis

We use half equations to show the reactions occurring at each electrode. In the example above:
- At the cathode: $Cu^{2+} + 2e^- \rightarrow Cu$
- At the anode: $4OH^- \rightarrow 2H_2O + O_2 + 4e^-$

Electroplating

We can use electrolysis in the context of <u>electroplating</u>, where one metal is coated with another. Here, the piece of metal to be coated is used as the cathode, and the coating metal is used as the anode. Ions of the coating metal are also present in the electrolyte. The coating ions are attracted to the cathode, where they are reduced to form a thin layer of metal on the outside of the cathode.

Knowledge Check

1. What will be the products formed at the anode and cathode when a solution of silver nitrate undergoes electrolysis.
2. If we want to electroplate a brass knife with silver metal, what substances do we need to use for the anode, cathode and electrolyte?

> Answers:
> 1. Anode: oxygen gas, cathode: silver metal
> 2. Anode: a piece of silver, cathode: the knife, electrolyte: a solution containing silver ions (e.g. silver nitrate)

C13 – Carbon/Organic Chemistry

Organic chemistry is the study of carbon containing compounds. This includes information about their structure, properties and reactions.

General Concepts

<u>Hydrocarbons</u> are compounds that contain only hydrogen and carbon atoms.

A key source of hydrocarbons is <u>crude oil</u>. This is a finite resource, containing a mixture of lots of different hydrocarbons. These hydrocarbons can be arranged as chains, rings or branches of joined carbon atoms.

We can use <u>fractional distillation</u> to separate the different hydrocarbons from each other according to their chain length. This forms fractions, mixtures of hydrocarbons with similar chain lengths. The hydrocarbons in each fraction differ in the following properties:

- **Boiling points:** hydrocarbons with longer carbon chains have higher boiling points
- **Viscosity:** hydrocarbons with longer chains are more viscous (they flow less easily)
- **Flammability:** hydrocarbons with shorter carbons chains are more flammable (they catch fire more easily)

You need to know what the following terms mean, and when to use each of them:

- <u>Molecular formula:</u> this is when the chemical symbols of each element in a molecule are written, followed by a subscript of the number of atoms of each element. This gives us no information about how the atoms are bonded together.
  e.g. the molecular formula of carbon dioxide is CO_2, the molecular formula of butane is C_4H_{10}

- <u>Full structural formula:</u> also known as displayed formula. This shows all the atoms in a molecule, written using their chemical symbols, and all bonds shown as lines (single bonds are 1 straight line and double/triple bonds are shown as groups of 2 or 3 parallel lines). These are useful in showing how the atoms in a molecule are bonded together.
  e.g. the full structural formulae of butane and butene are shown below

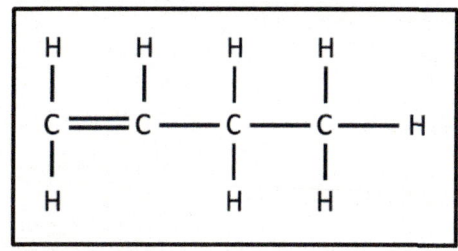

- **Condensed structural formula:** this is basically a list of how the atoms in a molecule are bonded to each carbon atom. Important bonds like double or triple bonds are shown. Identical groups are often written together in brackets (followed by the number of them that there are).
  e.g. the condensed structural formula of pentane can be written as $CH_2CH_3CH_3CH_3CH_2$ or $CH_2(CH_3)_3CH_2$

Another important general principle in organic chemistry is that of functional groups and homologous series.

- **Functional group:** an atom or atoms which cause a molecule to have certain physical or chemical properties
  e.g. the double bond joining together 2 carbon atoms in alkenes
- **Homologous series:** a group of compounds with the same functional group, but different numbers of carbon atoms. Compounds in the same homologous series have the same general formula. Examples of homologous series include alkanes, alkenes and alcohols.

Structural isomerism is when compounds have the same molecular formulae but different structural formulae. There are 3 types of structural isomerism:

- **Chain isomerism:** when 2 compounds of the same molecular formula have a different length of their longest chain of carbon atoms.
  e.g. butane and methylpropane both have the formula C_4H_{10}. Butane's longest carbon chain is 4 carbon atoms whereas methylpropane's longest carbon chain is 3 carbon atoms.

- **Position isomerism:** occurs when the functional group of a molecule is located on a different carbon atom. For example, the -OH group of an alcohol can be bonded to one of the end carbon atoms on a chain, or one of the middle carbon atoms.

- **Functional group isomerism:** when 2 molecules have the same molecular formula but different functional groups. For example, alkenes have the same general formula as cyclic alkanes (C_nH_{2n}) (so cyclopentane and pentene are functional group isomers).

Alkanes

Alkanes are saturated hydrocarbon molecules. This means that they only have single carbon-carbon bonds and no double bonds (all other bonds attach to hydrogen atoms).

Alkanes form a homologous series with the general formula C_nH_{2n+2}.

You need to be able to name straight chain alkanes with 1 to 6 carbon atoms. This is relatively easy, as you simply need the prefix for the particular number of carbon atoms, followed by the suffix -ane. The table below shows the first 6 prefixes:

Prefix	Number of Carbon Atoms
Meth-	1
Eth-	2
Prop-	3
But-	4
Pent-	5
Hex-	6

Combustion occurs when an organic substance reacts with oxygen. With an unlimited supply of oxygen, **complete combustion** occurs, whereby carbon dioxide and water are produced. With an unlimited oxygen supply, carbon monoxide and water are produced (this is called **incomplete combustion**). You should be able to balance these equations if given an unbalanced version.

$$e.g.\ C_3H_8 + 5O_2 \rightarrow 3CO_2 + 4H_2O$$

Alkanes with longer chains can be broken down into multiple, shorter chain molecules (these can be alkanes, alkenes or even just hydrogen) by a process known as **cracking**. You don't need to know how this is done, but you do need to be able to balance cracking equations. This is done the same as balancing other chemical equations, by counting the number of each atom on each side and balancing to make sure they are equal.

$$e.g.\ C_{16}H_{34} \rightarrow C_{10}H_{22} + C_6H_{12}$$

Alkenes

Alkenes are a homologous series containing the functional group of a C=C double bond. The general formula of alkenes is C_nH_{2n}.

The number of carbon atoms in the longest chain denotes the prefix given (these are the same as those for alkanes), and the suffix is -ene. The position of the double bond is shown by a number between the prefix and the suffix. This number shows, when counting from the end of the carbon chain closest to the double bond, the amount of carbon atoms until the double bond.

> **6Med Tip:** Ethene is the only alkene that never has a number in it, as there is only one possible position for the double bond to be!

We can test for alkenes by using **bromine water**. When bromine water is added to an alkene, this changes from orange to colourless. If bromine water is added to an alkane, it stays orange.

Alkenes can undergo addition reactions, due to their C=C. These reactions form 1 larger product:

1. Addition with **hydrogen**
   - This is called a hydrogenation reaction, and it requires a catalyst
   - The product formed is an alkane
   e.g. propene (CH2=CHCH3) + hydrogen (H2) → propane (CH3CH2CH3)

2. Addition with **halogens**
   - This forms a product form a halogenoalkane, with the prefix di-
   e.g. ethene (CH2=CH2) + chlorine (Cl2) → dichloroethane (CH2Cl)2

3. Addition with **hydrogen halides**
   - This reaction also forms a halogenoalkane, however this doesn't have the prefix di-, because there is only 1 atom of halogen added.
   e.g. ethene (CH2=CH2) + hydrogen chloride (HCl) → chloroethane (CH_2ClCH_3)

4. Addition with **steam**
   - This is called a hydration reaction, and its requires high temperatures and a catalyst.
   - The product formed is an alcohol
   e.g. propene (CH2=CHCH3) + water (H2O) → propan-1-ol (CHOHCH2CH3)

C13 - Carbon/Organic Chemistry

Alkenes (and other molecules with C=C double bonds) may react with each other to form long-chain saturated molecules called <u>polymers</u>. This is essentially another addition reaction, so is known as addition polymerisation. The individual unsaturated molecules that make up these polymers are called <u>monomers</u>.

When representing a polymer, we show the structure of its <u>repeating unit</u>, the part that is repeated over and over. The repeating unit can be deduced from the monomer by:

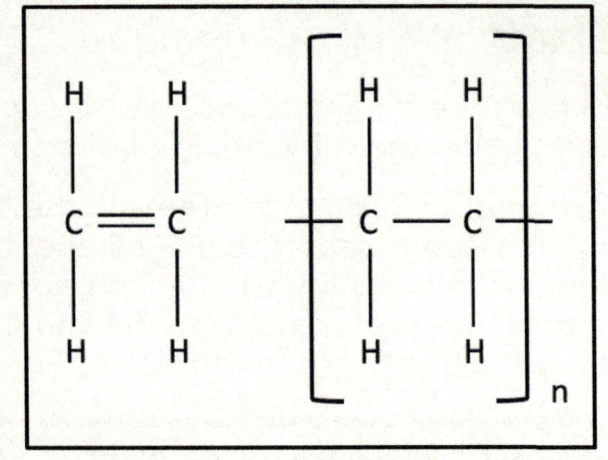

- Drawing the structure of the monomer, but replacing the C=C with a C-C
- Brackets are then drawn around this, with long horizontal bonds passing through each bracket
- A subscript 'n' shows that this unit repeats lots of times

Polymers

Another type of polymer that can be formed is a <u>condensation polymer</u>. This occurs when two monomers are joined together, causing a water molecule to be formed from the atoms that are no longer needed when the molecules join. The functional group of 1 monomer bonds to the functional group of the other, forming a polymer consisting of alternating monomers.

There are 2 types of polymers you need to be able to recognise from their repeating units: <u>polyesters</u> and <u>polyamides</u>:

Polyesters

Polyesters are formed from diols (alcohol molecules with an -OH group at either end) and dicarboxylic acids (carboxylic acids with -COOH at both ends). Each -COOH group reacts with an -OH group to form an ester bond, forming 1 water molecule per ester bond. The structure of an ester bond is shown in the diagram.

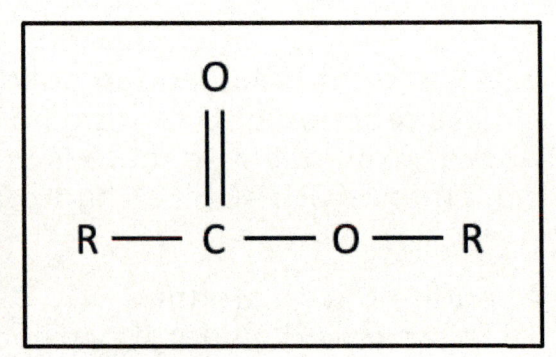

Polyamides

The important example of polyamides you should know is amino acids forming proteins.

There are 20 <u>amino acids</u>, all of which have a central carbon atom. This carbon is bonded to an amino group on one end ($-NH_2$), and a carboxylic acid group on the other end (-COOH). As well as these groups, there is another side group bound to the central carbon, which is different in each amino acid and often represented as 'R'.

<u>Polypeptides</u>, or proteins, are formed by the joining of multiple amino acids by **condensation polymerisation**. The amino group of 1 molecule reacts with the carboxylic acid group of another to form a peptide bond. 1 water molecule is lost per peptide bond formed.

In general, polymers can be either biodegradable or non-biodegradable:

- <u>Biodegradable</u> polymers can be broken down by a biological (living) agent such as bacteria. Natural polymers such as polypeptides are biodegradable, as are some types of polyester.
- <u>Non-biodegradable</u> polymers cannot be broken down by living agents. Most polymers, including common hydrocarbons like polyethene, are not biodegradable. Although this provides useful properties such as being able to safely store food, problems can arise as non-biodegradable polymers are difficult to dispose of.

Alcohols

The next homologous series you need to know about is alcohols. These have the functional group -OH, and the general formula $C_nH_{2n} + OH$.

You need to be able to name straight chain alcohols with chains of 1-6 carbon atoms. These have similar prefixes to those seen before (methan-, ethan-, propan- etc.), and the suffix -ol. The position of the functional group (which carbon atom it is bonded to) is shown by a number between the prefix and the suffix.

> **6Med Tip:** When thinking of which number to use to denote functional group position (e.g. 2 or 3 in the case of butanol), always use the lower of the 2!

Alcohols have properties of:

- They dissolve in water to form **neutral** solutions
- They are highly flammable, burning to produce CO_2 and H_2O
- They react with sodium metal to form **alkoxides** (these have the functional group -ONa)

Carboxylic Acids

The final homologous series on the specification is carboxylic acids. These have the functional group -COOH, and general formula C_nH_{2n} + COOH.

You need to be able to name straight chain carboxylic acids with chains of 1-6 carbon atoms. These have similar prefixes to those seen before (methan-, ethan-, propan- etc.), and the suffix -oic acid.

Carboxylic acids have the properties of:

- They react with metal carbonates to produce a salt, CO_2 and water
  e.g. sodium carbonate + propanoic acid → sodium propanoate + CO_2 + H_2O
- They dissolve in water to produce **weak acids**
- They react with alcohols in the presence of a strong acid catalyst to produce **esters**

Knowledge Check

1. What will be the product formed when pent-1-ene reacts with steam?
2. Hexane (C_6H_{14}) can be broken down by cracking to form butane (C_4H_{10}) and one other product. What is this other product?
3. Name a structural isomer of cyclohexane.

Answers:
1. Pentan-1-ol
2. Ethene C_2H_4
3. Hexene/hex-1-ene/hex-2-ene/hex-3-ene

C14- Metals

As previously covered, when metals undergo chemical reactions, the metal atoms lose electrons to form positively charged ions.

The Reactivity Series

The tendency of a metal to lose its outermost electrons and form positive ions determines its <u>reactivity</u>. The reactivity of a substance is essentially a measure of how vigorously it reacts with other substances. Metals can be ranked in order of reactivity in <u>the reactivity series</u>. A table summarising the reactivity series is shown below:

Metal	Reaction with H_2O	Reaction with dilute acids	Reactivity
Potassium	Violent	Violent	Most reactive
Sodium			
Lithium			
Calcium	Fast	Fast	
Magnesium	Slow		
Carbon			
Zinc	Usually no reaction	Slow	
Iron	Slow rusting		
Hydrogen			
Copper	No reaction	No reaction	
Silver			
Gold			Least reactive

We can use **displacement reactions** to deduce a reactivity series of metals. This is based on the fact that a more reactive metal will displace a less reactive metal from its compounds. A classic example of this is magnesium metal displacing copper sulphate from its solution: $Mg\ (s) + CuSO_4\ (aq) \rightarrow MgSO_4\ (aq) + Cu\ (s)$. In this reaction, the blue colour of the copper sulphate solution fades as colourless magnesium sulphate solution is produced. As well as this, copper metal coats the magnesium. A reaction would not occur between copper sulphate solution and silver, for example, as silver is less reactive than copper. When deducing a reactivity series, displacement reactions can be done with various combinations of metals and solutions to test if they react.

Extraction of Metals

The unreactive metals at the bottom of the reactivity series, such as gold, can be found in the Earth's crust in their pure form, as **uncombined elements**. Chemical reactions are still often needed when extracting these, to get rid of any other elements that may contaminate the desired metal.

Most other metals are found as ores in the Earth's crust. Ores are essentially rocks that contain enough of a metal, or its compounds, to make extraction of the metal worthwhile. Most commonly, metals are found in ores as **oxides**. You don't need to know the extraction processes used, but these differ depending on the position of the metal in the reactivity series.

Uses of Metals

Metals have a wide variety of uses, which are possible due to their physical and chemical properties. Some of these properties have been covered already in Chapter 6, but another key physical property of metals is that they are malleable and ductile.

Malleable describes the property of metals that allows them to be bent or hammered into different shapes without breaking. Ductility means that metals can be drawn out into thin wires. Both of these properties occur as the positive ions in the metal structure are arranged in layers, which can slide over each other. This movement doesn't disrupt the metallic bonds as the electrons are delocalised, so can move and still maintain the electrostatic attraction. In the diagram, the delocalised electrons have not been shown for simplicity.

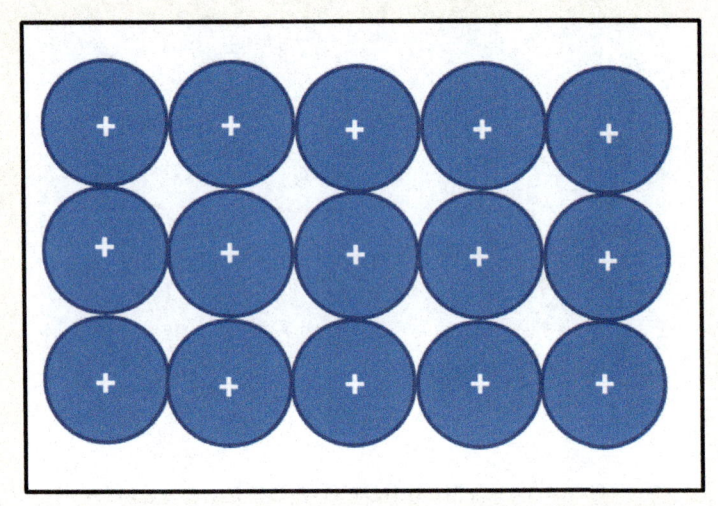

Some common examples of uses of metals are as follows:
- Aluminium is used in **aeroplane bodies** due to its high strength to weight ratio (it has a very low density)
- Aluminium is used in **power cables** as it is a good conductor of electricity
- Aluminium is used in **saucepans** as it is a good conductor of heat
- Copper is used in **electrical cables** as it is ductile and a good conductor
- Copper is used in **water pipes** as is malleable, non-toxic and unreactive

Alloys

Sometimes, these properties of pure metals mean that they are too soft for certain uses. This is overcome by mixing metals, or adding different elements to pure metals, forming an alloy.

In a pure metal, the amount of force needed to slide the layers of ions over each other is relatively small. With the mixture of elements in an alloy, there are ions of different sizes. This means that the layers of ions are distorted, requiring a larger force to slide over each other. Therefore alloys are harder and stronger than pure metals. The specific mixture of elements in an alloy determines its particular properties.

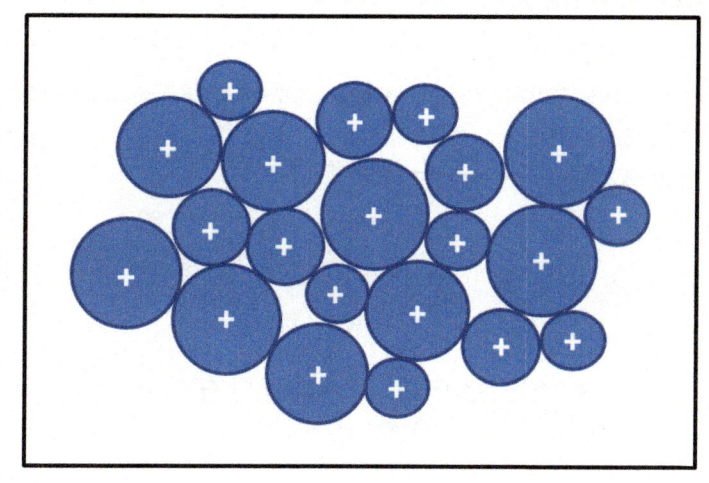

Transition Metals

Transition metals are those found in the middle of the periodic table, between groups 2 and 3. These include copper, zinc, iron, silver and gold. The important properties of transition metals you need to know are:
- They can exist in **more than 1 oxidation state** (e.g. iron can form Fe^{2+} or Fe^{3+} ions)
- They can act as **catalysts** (due to these variable oxidation states)
- They often form **coloured compounds**

Knowledge Check

1. If copper is added to a solution of calcium chloride, what will be seen?
2. Is it likely that sodium will be found in the Earth's crust as its pure metal form?

Answers:
1. No reaction, as copper is less reactive than calcium chloride
2. No, sodium is a reactive metal, so will be found in compounds.

C15- Kinetic/Particle Theory

Kinetic theory basically describes the arrangement of particles (atoms, ions or molecules) within the 3 states of matter: <u>solids, liquids and gases</u>.

Solids

- The particles in a solid are packed **closely together** in a **regular pattern**
- Particles **vibrate**, but their position remains fixed
- The particles have a low energy level

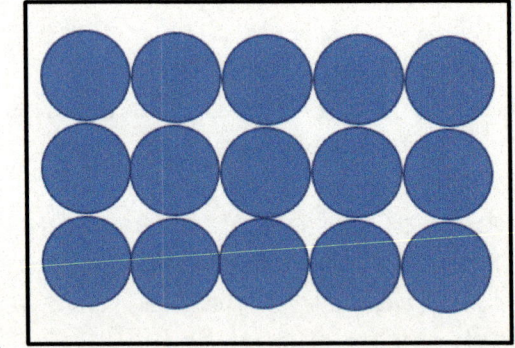

These properties mean that solids have a set shape, and **cannot flow or be compressed**. This is because their particles are very close together and cannot move around each other.

Liquids

- The particles in a liquid are closely packed, but not as close as that in solids
- Particles are **randomly arranged**
- Particles can **move around** each other
- Particles have a **greater energy** than in solids, but lower than in gases

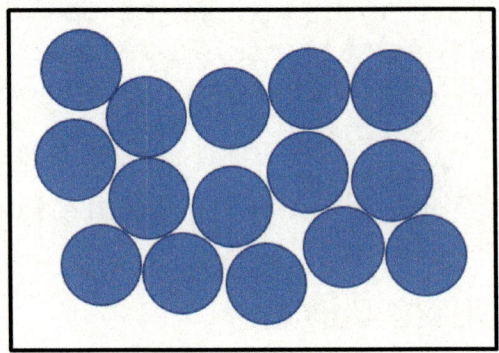

These properties mean that liquids can **flow**, and **take the shape of the container** they occupy, as their particles can move around each other. Liquids also **cannot be compressed**, as there is no space for particles to move into when squashed.

Gases

- The particles in a gas are **spaced apart**, and randomly arranged
- Particles move around **quickly** in all directions
- The particles have the **highest energy** of all the states of matter

These properties mean that gases can **flow**, and **completely fill** the container they occupy, as gas particles move quickly in all directions. Gases **can be compressed**, as their far apart particles have space to move closer together.

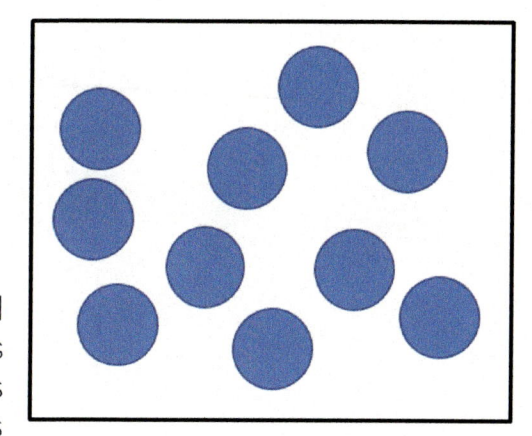

Changes of State

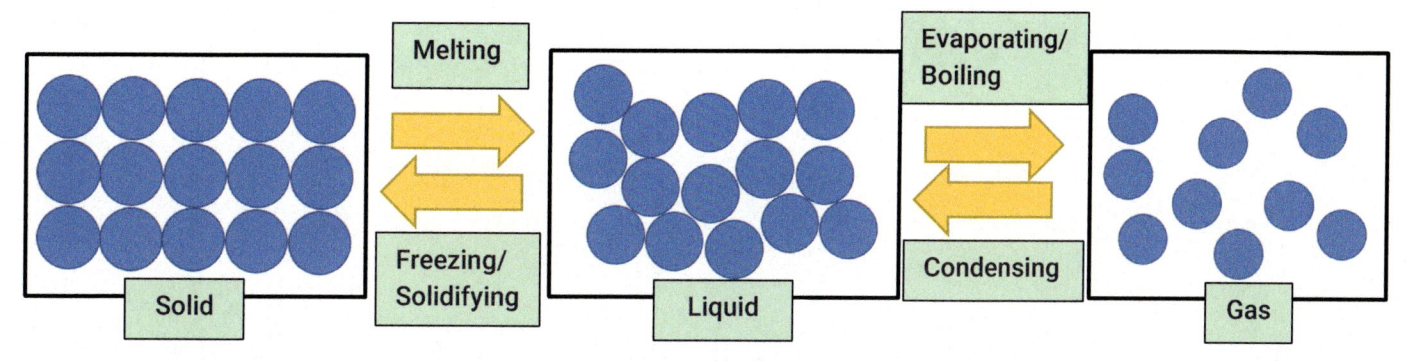

Solid → (Melting / Freezing/Solidifying) → Liquid → (Evaporating/Boiling / Condensing) → Gas

Solids <u>melt</u> to form liquids. When liquids <u>evaporate</u> or <u>boil</u>, they form gases. Gases can <u>condense</u> to reform liquids. Liquids form solids by <u>solidifying</u> or <u>freezing</u>. Less commonly, solids can directly turn to gases and vice versa by <u>sublimation</u>.

These physical state changes occur due to **energy transfer by heating**. The energy gained by solid particles during melting can break some of the bonds between particles. When evaporating or boiling, the remaining attracting forces between particles are overcome.

The amount of energy needed to change the state of a substance from solid to liquid to gas depends on how strong the forces of attraction between its particles are. This amount of energy determines the melting and boiling points of the substance. This is explained in more detail in chapter 6.

When condensing or freezing occurs, heat energy is transferred from a substance to its surroundings.

C15 – Kinetic/Particle Theory

Knowledge Check

1. Why can a solid substance not flow?
2. Which of the following processes are exothermic, and which are endothermic? Freezing, melting, boiling.

Answers:
1. The regular, tightly packed particles in a solid cannot move over each other to allow the solid to flow
2. Melting and boiling are endothermic processes, freezing is exothermic

C16 – Chemical Tests

Chemical tests are used to identify and analyse substances in samples.

Testing for Gases

There are 4 gases that you need to recognise the various tests and results for:

1. **Hydrogen (H_2):** when a lighted splint is held at the open end of a test tube containing hydrogen gas, a '**squeaky pop**' sound is heard.

2. **Oxygen (O_2):** if a test tube contains oxygen gas, a glowing splint put into the test tube will **relight**.

3. **Carbon Dioxide (CO_2):** if we bubble carbon dioxide gas through **limewater** (a solution of calcium hydroxide), the limewater turns milky.

4. **Chlorine (Cl_2):** chlorine gas causes **damp litmus paper** to turn from blue to red, and then bleaches it white.

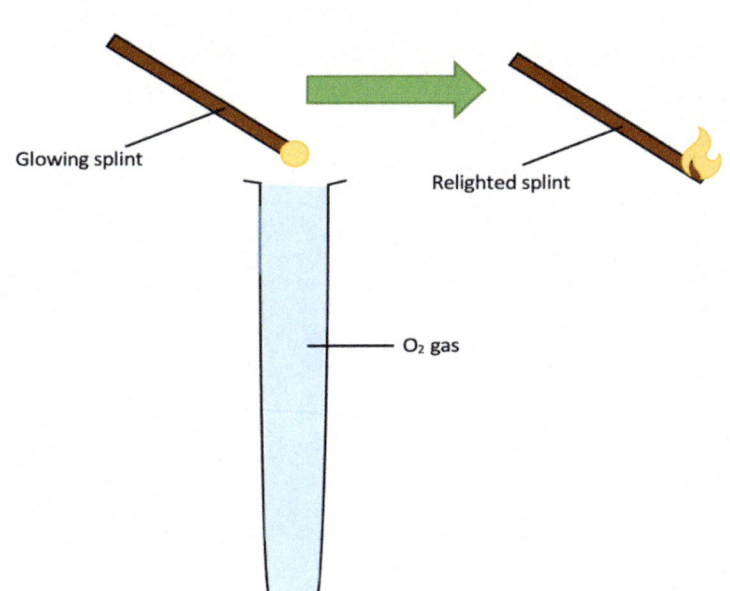

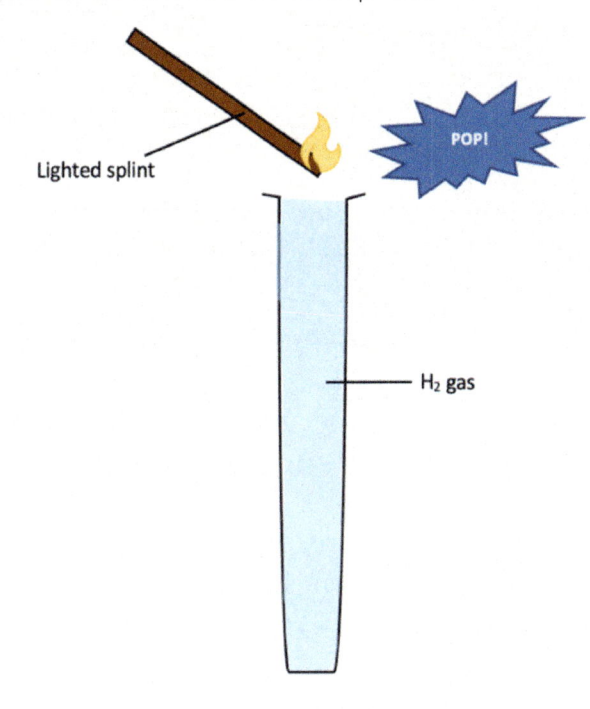

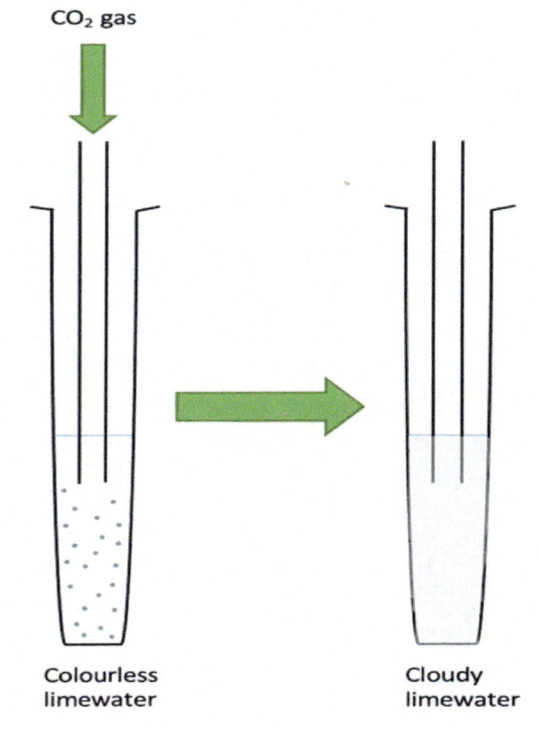

Testing for Anions

There are 3 anions for which you need to know the tests and positive results:

1. **Carbonate ions (CO_3^{2-}):** when an **acid** is added to a substance containing carbonate ions, bubbles of **carbon dioxide gas** are produced. We can test for carbon dioxide by bubbling the gas through limewater, as described above.

> **6Med Tip:** It doesn't matter what acid is used when testing for carbonate ions- they will all produce CO_2 gas!

2. **Halides (Cl^-, Br^-, I^-):** halide ions react with silver ions to produce precipitates. We add **dilute nitric acid** to the sample, followed by a few drops of **silver nitrate** solution.

   - Chloride ions form a **white precipitate**: $Ag^+ (aq) + Cl^- (aq) \rightarrow AgCl (s)$
   - Bromide ions form a **cream precipitate**: $Ag^+ (aq) + Br^- (aq) \rightarrow AgBr (s)$
   - Iodide ions form a **yellow precipitate**: $Ag^+ (aq) + I^- (aq) \rightarrow AgI (s)$

We add the nitric acid to the sample first in order to react with any carbonate ions in the sample. This is because carbonate ions also produce a white precipitate with silver nitrate solution, so would give a **false positive result** for chloride ions.

3. **Sulfates (SO_4^{2-}):** to test for sulfate ions, we add a few drops of **dilute hydrochloric acid** to the sample, followed by a few drops of **dilute barium chloride solution**. If sulfate ions are present, then a **white precipitate** is formed. This is because the barium ions react with sulfate ions to produce insoluble barium sulfate:

$$Ba^{2+} (aq) + SO_4^{2-} (aq) \rightarrow BaSO_4 (s)$$

We add the hydrochloric acid in order to react with any carbonate ions in the sample. If carbonate ions were present, this would produce a **false positive result**, as carbonate ions also react with barium ions to produce a white precipitate.

Testing for Metal Cations

We can use **sodium hydroxide solution** to test for some metal ions that form insoluble metal hydroxides. An example chemical equation for this is:

magnesium sulfate + sodium hydroxide → sodium sulfate + magnesium hydroxide

$MgSO_4$ (aq) + NaOH (aq) → Na_2SO_4 (aq) + $Mg(OH)_2$ (s)

The metal hydroxides produced appear as precipitates of various colours:

- Calcium (Ca^{2+}): white
- Magnesium (Mg^{2+}): white
- Aluminium (Al^{3+}): white
- Copper (II) (Cu^{2+}): blue
- Iron (II) (Fe^{2+}): green
- Iron (III) (Fe^{3+}): brown

As calcium, magnesium and aluminium ions all form white precipitates, we need to run a further test to distinguish between these. To do this, we add an **excess of sodium chloride solution**. With aluminium hydroxide, the **white precipitate redissolves**. With both calcium and magnesium hydroxide, the precipitate remains white.

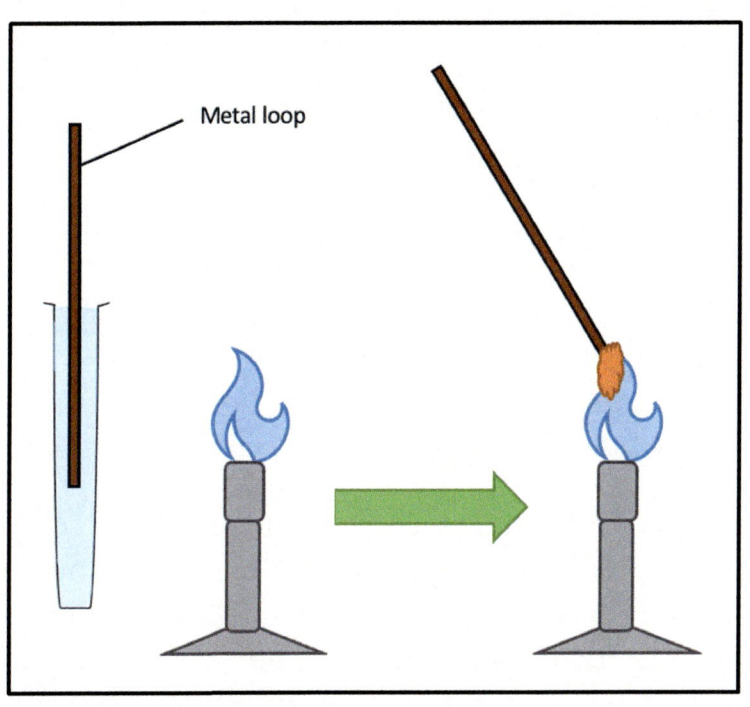

Ions of metals from group 1 form soluble hydroxides. These are identified by using **flame tests** instead of precipitation with sodium hydroxide solution. We can also use these to distinguish between calcium and magnesium ions.

Each metal ion produces a different flame test result, producing a different colour. The flame test is carried out as follows:

- Dip a clean wire loop into a sample to be tested
- Place the loop with the sample on into the side of a Bunsen burner flame
- Look for the colour produced, and use this to identify the metal cation present

The 5 metal ion flame test colours you should know are:

- Lithium (Li^+): crimson
- Sodium (Na^+): yellow
- Potassium (K^+): lilac
- Calcium (Ca^{2+}): orange-red
- Copper (Cu^{2+}): green

> **6Med Tip:** The flame test has the disadvantage that if multiple ions are present, some of the colours may be hard to identify (especially the lighter colours like lilac).

Testing for Water

We can test for water (H_2O) by adding a few drops of a sample to **anhydrous copper (II) sulfate**. This is a white substance, usually a powder, that **changes to blue** when hydrated by water molecules. Other colourless liquids, for example ethanol, will not produce this change.

Knowledge Check

1. Sodium hydroxide was added to a sample, producing a green precipitate. The same sample produced a white precipitate upon the addition of dilute hydrochloric acid and barium chloride solution. What is the molecular formula of this sample?
2. A sample produced a white precipitate upon the addition of dilute nitric acid and silver nitrate. The flame test for this sample produced a lilac flame. What is the molecular formula of this sample?

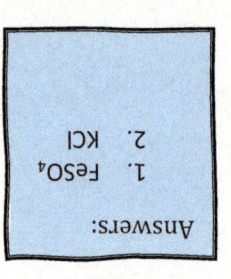

Answers:
1. $FeSO_4$
2. KCl

C17- Air and Water

Gases in Air

The air of the atmosphere is a **mixture of gases**- some elements and some compounds. We usually describe the amount of each of these in '<u>dry air</u>', which doesn't take into account water vapour.

> **6Med Tip:** We often discount water vapour from air, as the proportion of this varies greatly between locations, and at different times.

You should remember a broad percentage breakdown of the main substances in air:
- 78% Nitrogen (N_2)
- 21% Oxygen (O_2)
- 0.9% Argon (Ar)
- 0.04% Carbon Dioxide (CO_2)

We can separate these components of air by **fractional distillation** as they have different boiling points. This process is done as follows:

- Liquify the air by cooling it to -200ºC
- Water vapour condenses and carbon dioxide freezes, and are both removed
- Oxygen liquifies at -183ºC. The bottom of the fractionating column is around -185ºC, so liquid oxygen can be removed from here.
- Nitrogen liquifies at -196ºC. The top of the fractionating column is around -190ºC, so gaseous nitrogen is removed from here.

Greenhouse Gases

<u>Greenhouse gases</u> are gases that absorb heat energy radiated from the Earth. They cause this heat energy to be released in all directions, keeping the Earth and its atmosphere warm. The three major greenhouse gases are water vapour (H_2O), carbon dioxide (CO_2) and methane (CH_4).

The amount of these greenhouse gases in the atmosphere can be increased by various human activities. For example:

- **Burning fossil fuels**, such as in power stations and by motor vehicles, releases carbon dioxide
- **Cattle farming**, and farming **rice in paddy fields** releases methane
- **Deforestation** increases the amount of carbon dioxide in the atmosphere by its release, as well as by reducing carbon dioxide absorption in photosynthesis

Pollutants

The burning of fuels, especially fossil fuels, produces a number of other pollutant substances. A <u>pollutant</u> is essentially a toxic object or chemical that causes damage to the land, air or water. The table below describes the major pollutants, their sources and their effects:

Pollutant	Source	Effects
Carbon dioxide (CO_2)	Complete combustion of fuels which have carbon atoms	Greenhouse gas
Carbon monoxide (CO)	Incomplete combustion of fuels which have carbon atoms	Poisonous gas
Carbon particulates (C)	Incomplete combustion of fuels which have carbon atoms	Health problems for humans such as asthma, global dimming
Various unburned hydrocarbons	When hydrocarbon molecules are not oxidised at all	Many hydrocarbons are toxic and carcinogenic
Sulfur dioxide (SO_2)	Combustion of a fuel with sulfur impurities	Further oxidised and dissolved in rainwater to make acid rain
Nitrogen oxides (NO_x)	Oxidation of atmospheric nitrogen due to high temperatures inside an engine	Can react with other pollutants to cause photochemical smog, can cause acid rain

6Med Tip: Multiple different compounds can be formed from the reaction of nitrogen with oxygen, such as NO and NO_2. These are grouped together and referred to as NO_x.

C17 – Air/Water

Treatment of Drinking Water

To allow water to be safe for consumption, it needs to contain:
- A sufficiently low amount of dissolved salts, as high levels of these can be harmful. For example, if we use sea water to produce drinking water, it needs to go through a process called <u>desalination</u> to be safe to drink
- A sufficiently low amount of microorganisms, as ingestion of microorganisms can make us ill. This is achieved by a process called <u>sterilisation</u>.

<u>Chlorine gas (Cl_2)</u> is used in the sterilisation process, during which it is bubbled through the water in order to **kill any microorganisms.**

In some areas of the UK, small amounts of <u>fluoride ions (F^-)</u> are added to drinking water. This is done to help **prevent tooth decay.**

Knowledge Check

1. Name 2 factors that contribute to an increased amount of carbon dioxide in the atmosphere.
2. What is a pollutant? Give 3 examples of pollutants.

Answers:
1. Released during deforestation, burning of fossil fuels
2. A pollutant is a toxic object or chemical that causes damage to the land, air or water. Examples of pollutants include carbon dioxide, carbon monoxide, carbon particulates, nitrous oxides, sulfur dioxide and unburnt hydrocarbons.

Section 2 Part 3: Physics.

P1 Electricity

Electrostatics

- Conductors are materials in which electric charges can flow through easily.
- An insulator is a material through which electric charges do **not move** easily

You can charge insulators by **rubbing them together** exerting friction.

- One insulator will **lose electrons** and one will **gain them**
- Therefore the one that loses the electrons will become positively charged
- The one that gains the electrons will be negatively charged.
- These will now have **opposing charges** and be **attracted to each other**!

> **6Med Tip:** An example of this in every day life is when you rub a balloon on your hair
> - Electrons move from atoms in your hair into the balloon
> - Therefore your hair becomes positively charged
> - The balloon becomes negatively charged
> - This is why the balloon will stick to your hair!

Another example where this is used in industry is in **spray paints**.

- The paint droplets and the object have **opposing charges**
- Therefore the paint is attracted to the object and **sticks tightly**

As static energy builds all that charge is looking for an escape. This is dangerous as it may jump and cause sparks which can lead to fires. Therefore certain objects that build up lots of static may need to be earthed.

The Complete BMAT Specification Explained

P1 - Electricity

- When you earth and object you **physically connect** it to the ground via a **wire or other metal object**.
- This provides a path for the electrons to the ground.
- This means the charge can **dissipate** from the object.

Circuits and Circuit Diagrams

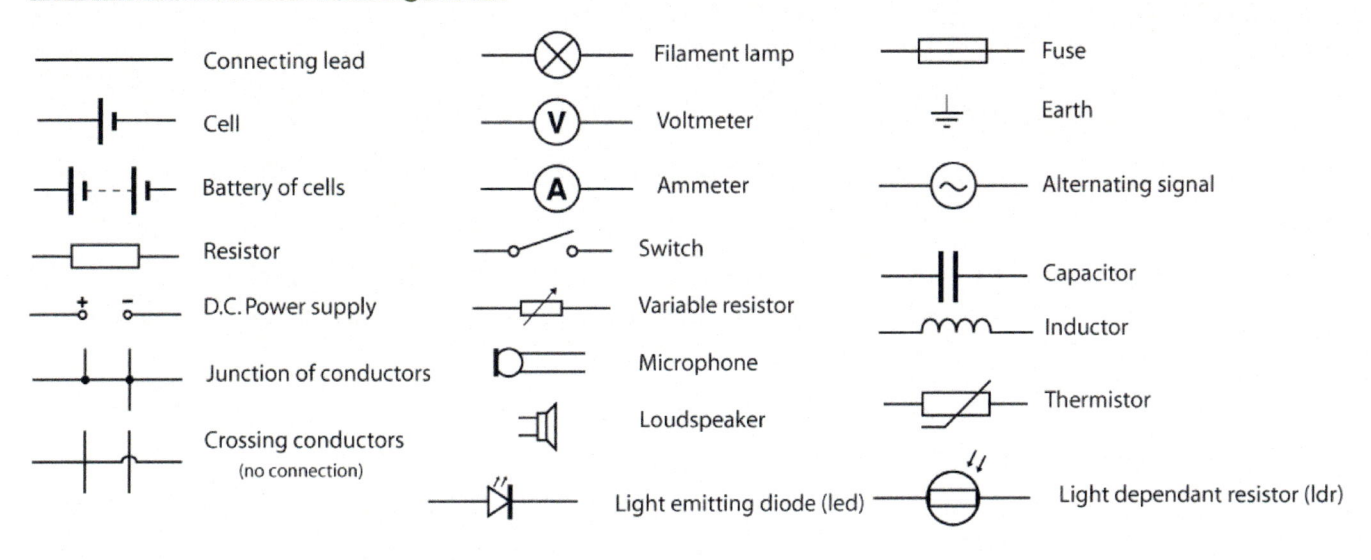

Symbol	Name
—	Connecting lead
—|I—	Cell
—|I--I—	Battery of cells
—▭—	Resistor
—⊕ ⊖—	D.C. Power supply
—•—	Junction of conductors
—┼—	Crossing conductors (no connection)
—⊗—	Filament lamp
—Ⓥ—	Voltmeter
—Ⓐ—	Ammeter
—o o—	Switch
—⌇—	Variable resistor
⊃	Microphone
◁	Loudspeaker
—▷|—	Light emitting diode (led)
—▯—	Fuse
—⏚	Earth
—∼—	Alternating signal
—||—	Capacitor
—mmm—	Inductor
—⌇—	Thermistor
—⊖—	Light dependant resistor (ldr)

Drawing Circuit Diagrams

Being able to interpret circuit diagrams and draw them is a key skill for interpreting basic circuits. Below we outline a few key rules.

- All circuits require an **energy source** and a **closed path/complete circuit** for the electrons to flow round.
    o The exception to this is an **open switch** as this when closed will complete the loop
- Direction of current flow is always from **positive** to **negative**
- An **ammeter** is always connected in **series**
- A **voltmeter** is always connected in **parallel**

> **6Med Tip:** Always draw the with **straight lines** making sure the diagram is **neat** as possible.

~153~

P1 - Electricity

Voltage/Potential Difference

Voltage and potential difference both mean the same thing and are interchangeable terms.

- A circuit has a positive end and a negative end
- We push charge units from one end to the other
- This creates a potential difference across the circuit

The definition of potential difference is:

Potential difference is the difference in the amount of energy that charge carriers have between two points in a circuit

We can think of potential difference as the amount of **push** in a circuit. If the circuit was a river the potential difference would be the **pressure of flow** behind the river.

The equation for voltage is

$$V = \frac{E}{Q}$$

- V = potential difference, measured in **volts** (V)
- E = energy transferred, measured in **joules** (J)
- Q = charge moved, measured in **coulombs** (C)

Measuring Potential Difference in a circuit

We measure potential difference using a **voltmeter**

- We set this up in parallel.
- If we wanted to set it up to measure the voltage across a component we would set it up in parallel around the component
  - This way we are assessing the voltage before and after the component

P1 - Electricity

Charge and Current

Current

Current is defined as *'the rate of flow of charge'*

- This can be thought of as the **amount of charge** passing through a component
- If we go back to our river analogy it would be **amount** of water flowing **past a certain point over a certain time**
- Current flows from positive to negative

Charge

In circuits the actual flow comes from **negatively charged electrons** moving through **metal wires.**

We can relate current and charge using the following equation.

$$Q = It$$

Where:

- Q = charge in Coulombs
- I = current in amps
- t = time in seconds

Conductors will **allow** the flow of electrons whereas insulators will **inhibit** the flow of electrons.

Resistance

Resistance is the **opposition to current.** It quite literally resists the current getting to where it wants to go.

- Every electrical component in a circuit will have a resistance
- A **good conductor** will have a **low resistance**
- A **poor conductor** will have a **high resistance**

In our river analogy the resistance is like a **bridge with arches.** The water is now forced to flow through the arches and a **smaller gap.** This **reduces the current** and holds the river up.

Linking Current Resistance and Potential Difference

The equation that links all three together is as below:

$$V = IR$$

Where:
- V is potential difference measures in V
- I is current measured in A
- R is resistance measured in Ω

If we rearrange this we have the below:

$$I = V/R$$

From this we can see how current is effected by resistance. Assuming a constant voltage:
- When resistance is **increased** the current will **drop**
- And vice versa when resistance **falls** current will **increase**

Series vs Parallel Circuits

- In a series circuit all components are connected **end to end** in a chain leading to a **single path** for current to flow
- In a parallel circuit all components are **connected across each other**. This leads to **another branch** for the current to **split** and take two paths.

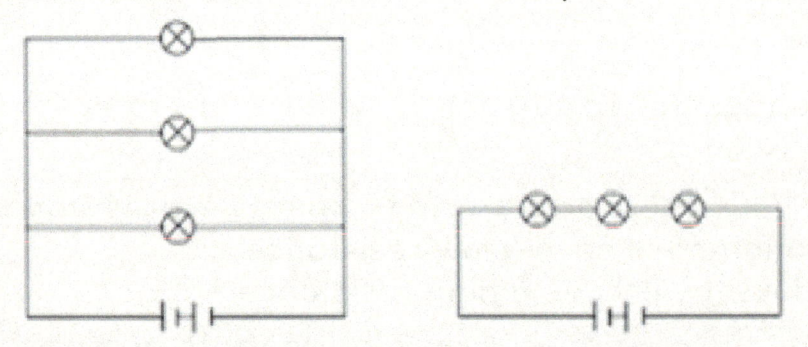

On the left we can see a parallel circuit and the right a series circuit

Current

In a series circuit the current will be the same at any one point on the circuit. Whereas in a parallel circuit once there has been a new branch the current will halve.

> **6Med Tip:** In our river analogy imagine an island in the river.
> - The current will divide and flow either side of the island
> - If you added up the current on wither side of the island it would be the same as that before the island.

Potential Difference

- In a series circuit the potential difference of the power supply is **shared** by the components in the circuit
- Whereas in a parallel circuit the voltage from the power supply will be **the same** as across each component.

Resistors

Remember earlier we said that each component creates resistance? Well this resistance has different effects in parallel and series circuits.

- In a series circuit the **sum of all the resistances** from the varying components added together will give you the **overall resistance.**
    o This is as the charge has to go through each resistor
- In a parallel circuit the **total resistance** will actually be **less** than the sum of the resistances of the individual components
    o This may seem odd but actually makes good sense
    o In a parallel circuit the current splits and some will go through te resistor and some won't
    o As you increase components and therefore pathways the amount of charge in each pathway will be less
    o Therefore the resistance will be less

Components and Their Effect I-V Graphs

By using the equation V = IR we can visualise resistance on a I-V graph. When we take the gradient of an I-V graph we are looking at the change in current over change in voltage which shows us that resistance is equivalent to 1/gradient of the line.

Your BMAT specification requires you to know and be able to recall the *V-I* graphs for the following:

A fixed resistor

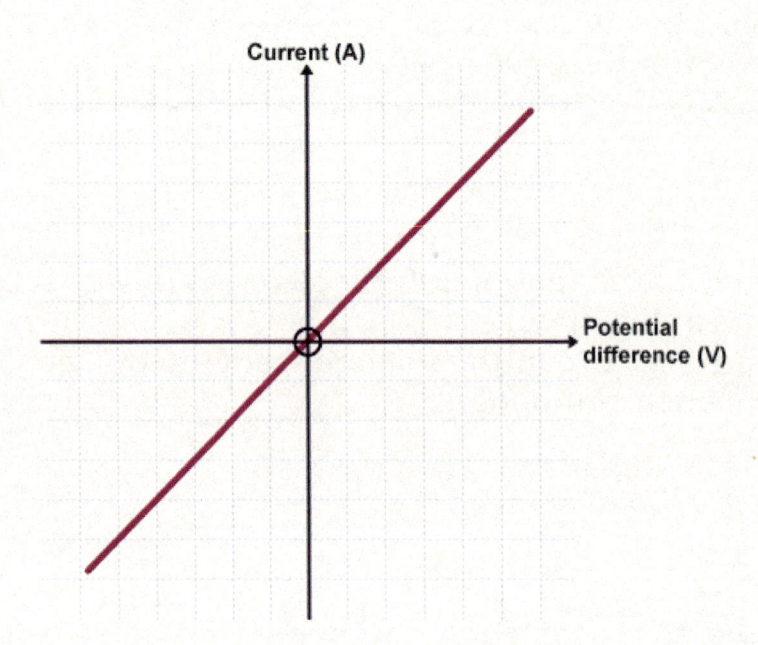

A filament lamp

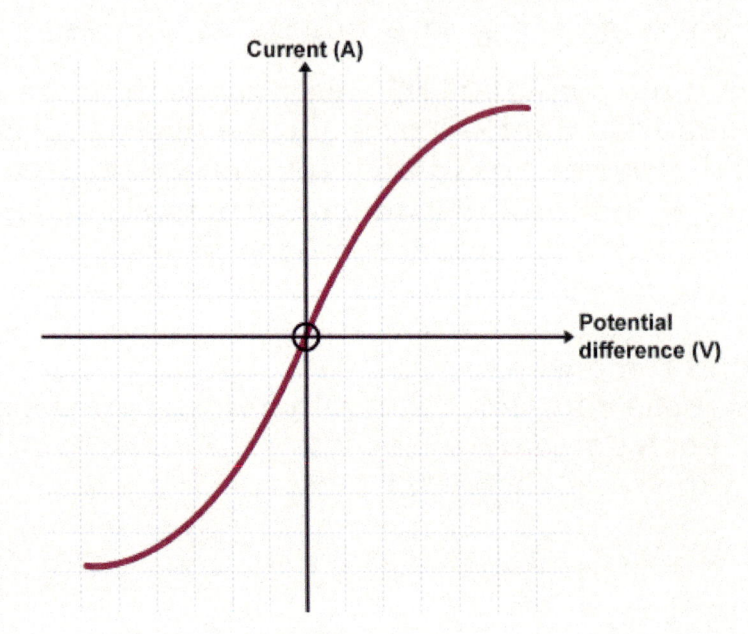

Negative Temperature Coefficient Thermistors

- These are components whose resistance is **dependent on temperature**
- As temperature **increases** the resistance **decreases**

Light Dependent Resistors

- As the name suggests these are components where the **resistance** depends on the **light**
- With **increasing light intensity** the resistance will **decrease**

Ideal Diodes

Ideal diodes are components which allow current to only flow in one direction

- This direction is marked by an arrow on the circuit symbol.
- When a current is applied in the intended direction the diode will act as a **perfect conductor**
- When it acts in the **opposing** direction the diode will act as a **perfect insulator**

Power

Power just refers to the rate of energy transfer. The power of electrical transfer can be calculated using the equation:

$$Power\ (W) = Voltage\ (V) \times Current\ (I)$$

To calculate the transfer of electrical power we use:

$$E = VIt$$

E = Energy transfer

V = Voltage

I = Current

t = Time

You need to be aware and comfortable with both these equations for the BMAT.

The Complete BMAT Specification Explained

P1 - Electricity

Knowledge Check

1) In a negative temperature coefficient thermistor what effect does an increase in temperature have on current?
2) What is charging in terms of electrostatics?
3) Recall the equation for energy transfer

Answers

1) It will decrease
2) The addition/loss of electrons
3) $E = VIt$

E = Energy transfer
V = Voltage
I = Current
t = Time

P2 Magnetism

Magnets have two ends, a north and a south pole. The law of magnetism states that there will be an **attractive** or **repulsive force** as below:

Opposites attract, likes repel.

Magnetic material is material that is **attracted to a magnet**. It will **only be attracted** and not repelled. This is different from magnets which will have **one end** which will **repel**, and one **attract**.

To test if a material is magnetic or if itself is a magnet bring the material close to a known magnet

- If one end can be **repelled**, then it itself is a **magnet**
- If it can only be **attracted**, then it is a **magnetic material**

Induced vs Permanent Magnets

A permanent magnet is as the name suggests. It is made from **permanent magnetic materials** and will always produce its **own** **magnetic field**.

An induced magnet is made up of magnetic material however is not usually magnetic.

- It **becomes magnetic** when placed in **another magnetic field**
- The magnetism is therefore **induced**
- The material will then become **polar**
- The pole will be **opposite** to the magnet
    - If you introduced a magnetic material to a south pole then the part of the material closest to the magnet will become a north pole and the part furthest away will be a south pole.

The Complete BMAT Specification Explained

P2 – Magnetism

This is only **temporary**. As soon as the magnetic material is removed the magnetic field it will **lose its magnetism**.

Magnetic Fields

All magnets produce a magnetic field that surrounds the magnet.

- This is why magnets don't need to touch to exert a force
- It is their fields interacting that is causing a force

The definition of a magnetic field is:

"The region around a magnet where a force acts on another magnet or on a magnetic material"

A magnetic field diagram can be read somewhat like a map

- The arrows show the **direction** that the force is being applied
    - This originates at the north pole and travels to the south
- The **closer together** the lines the **stronger the field** at that point
- As you move further away from a magnet the lines become further apart

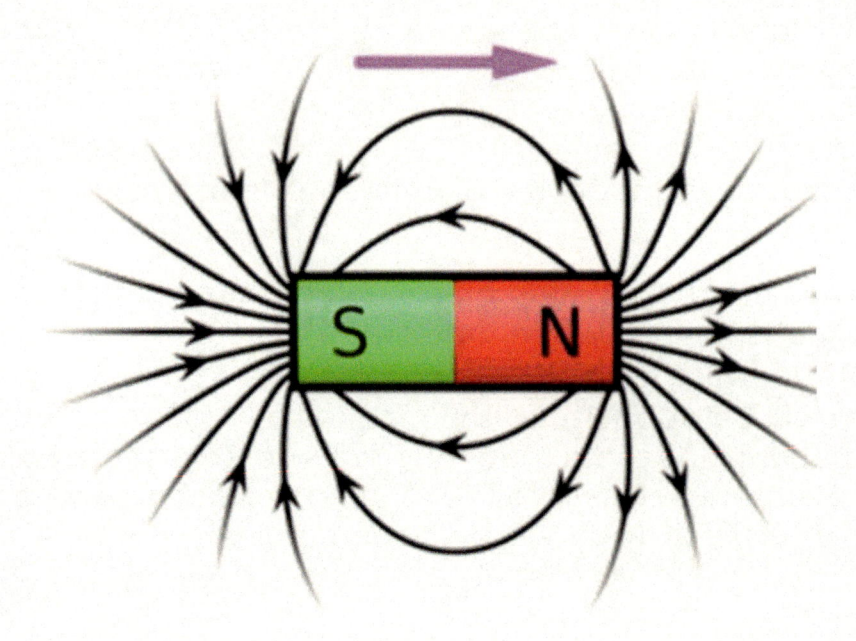

A **uniform field** is a **direct attraction** between a north and south pole of two magnets.

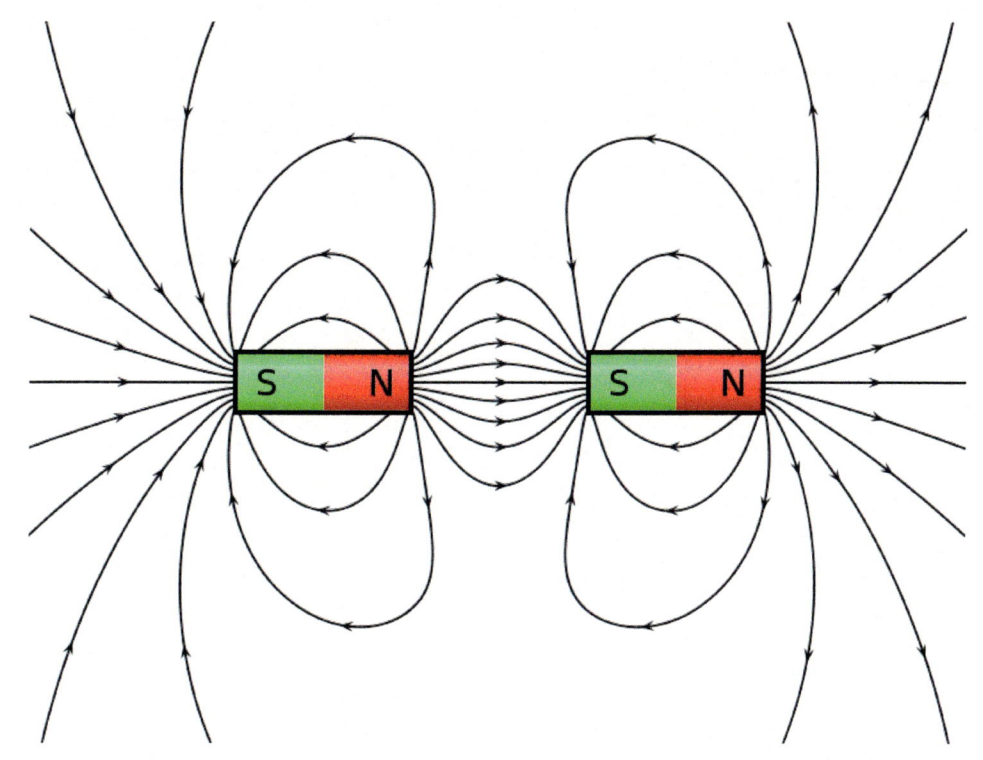

Remember if two forces are acting in **opposing directions** they will **oppose**! This can be shown in magnetic field diagrams as below. The two north poles will **repel** each other.

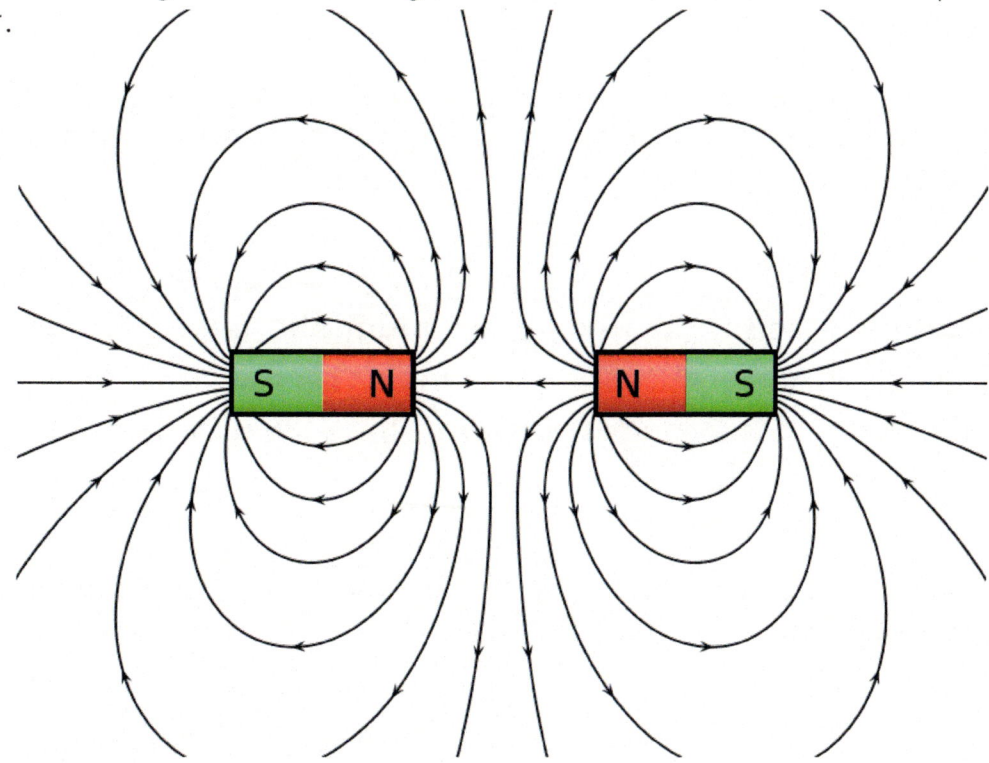

The Earth's Magnetic Field

When we think about in the earth is just one giant magnet

- It has a north and south pole
- Therefore a magnetic field exists between these poles and round the world.

For years we have used this **magnetic field** to help us navigate in the form of **compasses!**

- A compass is a **tiny magnet** suspended so it can rotate freely
- The point on the magnet is the **north pole**.
- This points to the earth's **geographical north**.

However surely this is a contradiction? If same poles repel, how is it that the north of a compass is attracted to the geographical north pole?

- This is as the **geographical** north pole is actually the **magnetic south**
- Vice versa the geographical south is the magnetic north
- In practice no one ever asks where magnetic north is, however, it is worth bearing in mind.

Electromagnetism

Electromagnetism allows us to use electricity to create a **magnetic effect.** Using the electricity, we can **turn the magnet on/off** and **change the intensity.**

Wires and Magnetic Fields

When a **current** is passed through a **wire** a **magnetic field** is produced **around the wire.**

- This magnetic field is **strongest** closer to the wire and **weaker** further away
- There will only be a magnetic field produced **when current flows through the wire**
    - This is useful as it allows you to turn the magnetic properties on/off...
- The **direction** the current flows will determine the direction of the field

P2 – Magnetism

If asked to draw a magnetic field around a wire think remember these two things:
1. The field becomes **weaker** as you move from the wire
    a. Therefore your circles will have to become gradually further apart!
2. The direction of the current will be perpendicular and have a direction.
    a. Have a look at the diagram below. It shows a wire cross section.
    b. If the wire is coming out the page and current flowing towards us then the field will be **anticlockwise**
    c. This would be opposite if the current was flowing in the opposite direction into the page.

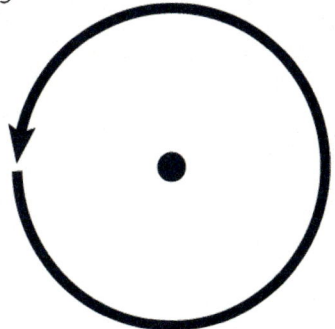

The Thumb Rule

A nifty way to remember this and other parts later is using the thumb rule. It requires the following. (Have a go as you read...)

1. Make a thumbs up with your right hand
2. Imagine the wire is passing through your fist. Your thumb shows the direction of the current.
3. Now if you point the thumb towards you you will have the current coming towards you. (As in the diagram above.)
4. Look where your fingers point. They will be wrapped around anti clockwise just like the magnetic field!
5. Now if you point your thumb in the opposing direction the magnetic field changes. This is as you have changed the direction of the current!

All you must remember is that you need your **right hand**! (It will be the opposite on the left...)

Using Wires to Induce a Magnetic Field

As mentioned above we now can generate a magnetic field around any point in a wire. Another property of wires is that they are malleable. This means we can bend them.

Using the above properties we can coil a wire. When we do this:

- We bring all the fields **close together**
- This concentrates the **forces** of each individual field
- So we get **one large field**
- This acts much like a **bar magnet would**

When we coil the wire together like this we make something called a **solenoid**.

The definition of a solenoid is

"A long cylindrical coil of wire that acts as a magnet when carrying current"

A solenoid is an example of an **electromagnet**. We can change the strength of the magnetic force the following ways:

1. We can turn an electromagnet on/off.
   - We do this by **stopping/starting** the current through the coil
2. We can increase the strength of the magnet. This can be done two ways
   - We can **increase the current**. This will **increase** the **magnetic force**.
   - We can **increase the number of coils**. This is called **increasing the number of turns**. This will also **increase** the **magnetic effect**.
3. We can add an iron core.
   - The iron acts as an **induced magnet**
   - Therefore, when current runs through the solenoid the **iron** will be **induced** to produce a **magnetic field**

The magnetic field inside the coils will be strongest. This is where the fields are most concentrated as they pass through the coils. We can describe the field inside the coils as **strong** and **uniform**.

The Complete BMAT Specification Explained

P2 – Magnetism

- **Strong** as this is the most **concentrated point** of the fields
- **Uniform** as the field will have the same **strength** and **direction** through the field.

Working out the Poles of a Solenoid

Like all magnets a solenoid will have a north and a south pole

To work out the polarity we need to view the coil from the end on.

- At the **north pole** the current will flow in am **anticlockwise direction**
- At the **south pole** it will run in a **clockwise direction**

If we **change the direction** of **current**, we will **reverse the poles** so be aware!

The Motor Effect

We know from above that a wire carrying a current will produce a **magnetic field**. We can use this magnetic field and by interacting it with another magnetic field we can generate a **force**. This is known as the **motor effect**. This follows some rules:

- The force produced will be **perpendicular** to both the direction of current and the magnetic field you are introducing the current to.
    - Think about it in 3D with the magnetic field and the current in the same plane and the force coming in or out of the page
- If the magnetic field and current are **parallel** then **no force** will be exerted
- If the magnetic field and current are **perpendicular** to each other the force exerted will be at its **greatest**

> **6Med Tip:** You may be asked to predict the direction of force generated when a current interacts with a magnetic field. To remember this in the exam you can bring something in to cheat! (Your left hand...)

Flemings Left Hand Rule

The Flemings left hand rule allows you to work out the direction of any of the components of force, current and magnetic field when given the other two. Set your fingers out like the image below the fingers correspond to:

- Thumb – The force generated
- Index finger – Magnetic field
- Middle finger – The Current

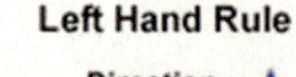

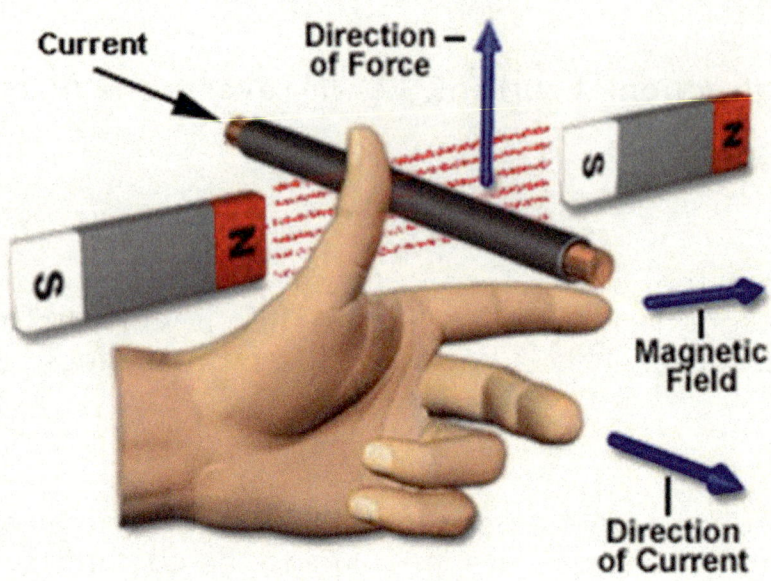

> **6Med Tip:** You may see the notation 'B' used in other diagrams of the left-hand rule. This just is the notation for magnetic field!

Factors Effecting Strength of the Motor Effect

The force generated by the motor effect is determined by the following factors:

1. **Angle** between the magnetic field and current.
    a. When this is at 90 degrees it will be greatest
    b. When at 0 degrees (parallel) no force will be generated.
2. **Length of the wire** – Increasing the length will increase the force

3. **Magnetic field strength** – increasing this will increase the force generated from the field and current interacting.
4. **Current** – increasing the current increases the strength of magnetic field produced by the wire. This therefore will have a stronger interaction with the external magnetic field and increase the force generated.

> **6med tip:** We only include the length of wire that is **perpendicular** to the field. If the wire changes direction this will **not be included**.

We can show this by using the equation below:

$$F = BIL$$

F = Force generated in (N)

B = Magnetic field strength in (T)

I = Current in (A)

L = the length of wire in (M)

> **6Med Tip:** If you change the direction of either the current or the magnetic field you will get a change in the direction of force. However if you change both you will get no change in direction of force! Have a go at trying it with your hand now. See that the force will rotate round a full 360 degrees back to the original position.

DC Motors

We are able to use the above properties to create a **simple motor**. In the case above we will use **DC (Direct Current)** to create a motor.

For this we will need the following components

- A **uniform magnetic field**
- A **coil of wire**, we arrange this in a rectangle so that the sections interacting with the magnetic field are **perpendicular** the whole way along to get **maximum force**
- A split ring commutator (we will come onto this later)

The Complete BMAT Specification Explained

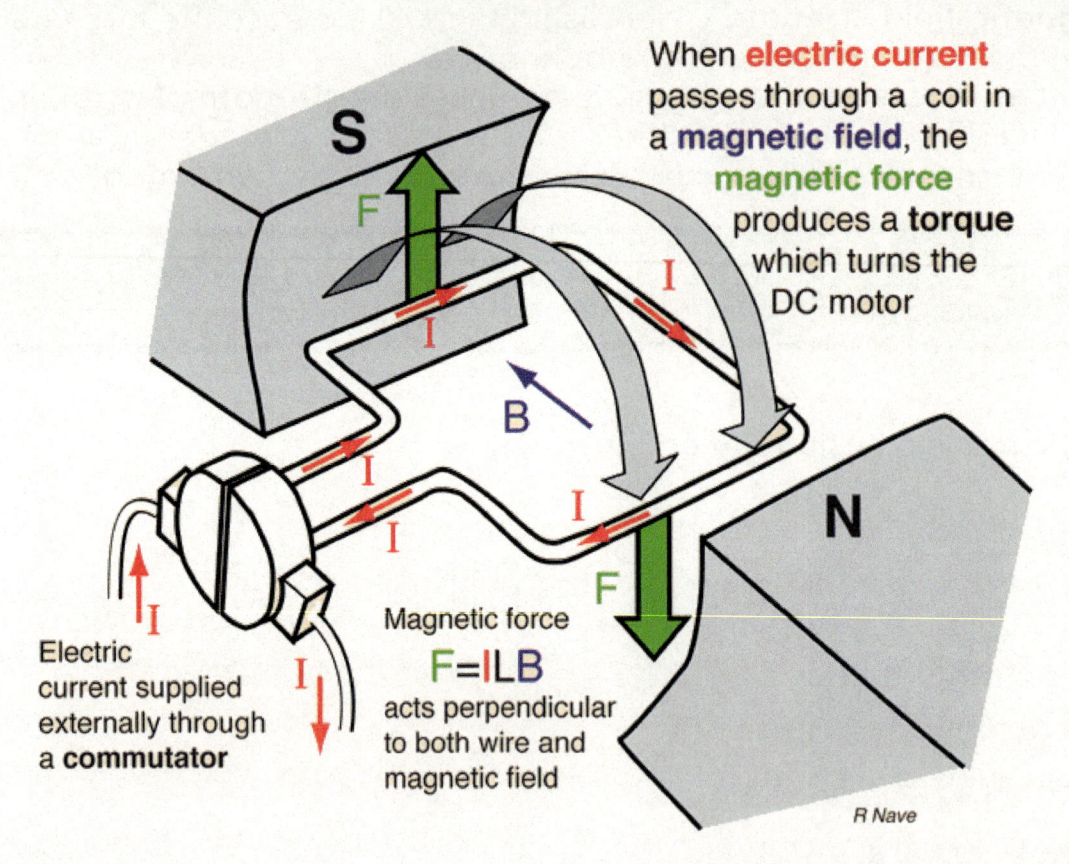

P2 – Magnetism

When **electric current** passes through a coil in a **magnetic field**, the **magnetic force** produces a **torque** which turns the DC motor

Electric current supplied externally through a **commutator**

Magnetic force
$F = ILB$
acts perpendicular to both wire and magnetic field

R Nave

- The coil will have **current** running in **two directions** as in the diagram.
    - As it goes from the power source round the coil then back to the source
- Therefore it will pass through magnetic field twice in **opposing directions**
- This means the **force** will be in **opposing directions** on each side of the coil.
- This will cause the coil to **spin**! We now have the beginnings of a motor.

However quickly the coil will rotate to a point where it is **parallel** to the **magnetic fields** and will **not** go any further as the forces are now acting against each other. This is where the split ring commuter comes in!

- The split ring commuter **reverses** the current every time the current passes **vertical**
- As per our rules above the forces will therefore **reverse direction** and now allow the coil to rotate again till it is **vertical**
- Then the split ring commuter kicks back in reversing the current and so on!

The strength of the force generated is determined by a few factors:

- The coil – a few factors can be changed in the coil to increase the force
    - The **current** going through the coil
    - The **size** of the coil – greater the area greater the wire length
    - **Number** of turns – greater the number of turns greater the force
    - Adding a **soft iron core** to the coil
- **Angle of the coil** – As the coil passes through the perpendicular plane to the magnetic field the greatest force is applied to it.
- **Magnetic field strength** – Increasing this increases the force exerted on the coil

Electromagnetic Induction

Electromagnetic induction is defined as:

"A change in magnetic field around a conductor that can give rise to an induced potential difference across the ends of the conductor. This can in turn drive a current which generates its own magnetic field"

Electromagnetic induction can be thought of as the **opposite** of the motor effect. When we start there is **no current** going through the wire.

- We use **force** to move a wire through a magnetic field
- This in turn induces a **potential difference** in the wire
- This potential difference will then produce a **current** if the circuit is closed.

This also works if you move a **magnet** through a **fixed wire coil**.

This is used every day to convert **kinetic energy** into **electrical energy**.

- Generators are petrol powered
- These use **combustion engines** to burn the fuel and power pistons
- The pistons via levers can **move** the **coil** or **magnet** across each other.
- This then allows a current to be **induced** and electricity can be provided
- This is useful in remote areas where there is no mains electricity as generators can be small and portable

Factors affecting the magnitude of induced potential difference (PD)
- **The area of the coils** – Increasing these will increase the PD induced
- **The number of coils** – Increasing this increases the PD induced
    - This is as there are more segments of wire to cut through the magnetic field
    - Therefore, the cumulative effect is greater
- **The speed** at which the wire or magnet is **moved**
    - Faster speed will induce a greater PD
- **The strength of the magnetic field**
    - A stronger magnetic field will induce a greater PD

Factors affecting the direction of an induced voltage
- The potential difference generated will always **oppose** the change that produces it
- When you introduce a magnet to the coil the PD induced will create a **dipole** in the coil
    - We will get a **positive reading** on the ammeter
    - This dipole will **repel the magnet** and try force it out
- As we remove the magnet the reverse happens
    - We will get a **negative reading** on the ammeter as direction of current reverses
    - The coil will now try to attract the magnet and pull it in

Using this principle we can predict the direction of current in the coil.

Alternating Current Generators

We can us the generator principle to generate an **alternating current**

- By constantly **rotating** a coil in a magnetic field
- The coil is **cutting** the magnetic field **many times over** inducing a PD and therefore a **current**
- However the current that is induced **alternates** as the coil rotates and cuts through the magnetic field in the **opposite direction.**
- Therefore you get a current that **switches direction** constantly
- This is known as **alternating current**

The Complete BMAT Specification Explained

P2 – Magnetism

Factors affecting output voltage for AC generators follow the same factors above for the generator effect these are:

- **Rotate** the coil more rapidly
- Increase the **area** of the coil
- Increase the **number** of turns
- Increase the **magnetic field strength**

Transformers

Transformers can **increase** or **decrease** the potential difference of an alternating current.

Step-up transformers **increase** the voltage. Step-down transformers **decrease** the voltage.

They do this using the generator effect and two coils.

- Two coils with **differing number of turns** are placed around an iron core
- One coil will have the original voltage passed through it in AC current
    - As this is AC current it will be constantly changing direction
    - This will cause it to generate a **magnetic field** that is constantly changing
- This changing magnetic field passes **through the magnetic core**
- It will now reach the **second core** and induce a current in this core using the generator effect
    - This is as the magnetic field is constantly changing and cutting through the secondary coil
- Therefore, the secondary coil will now have a PD and current flowing through it

So how does this change voltage?

- Well as we said above we can change factors to **increase or decrease** our induced PD
- If the coils were identical the primary coil would induce the **same** PD in the secondary coil
- However if the secondary coil had a different number of coils the wire would cut the magnetic field **less/more** and the induced PD would be **less/more**

This is how transformers work; they **change the number of coils** on the secondary coil relative to the **first coil** depending on if they want to **increase or decrease the voltage**.

7

The Complete BMAT Specification Explained
P2 – Magnetism

We can predict how this will affect voltage using the below equation:

$$\frac{V_p}{V_s} = \frac{n_p}{n_s}$$

- V_p = potential difference (voltage) across the primary coil in volts (V)
- V_s = potential difference (voltage) across the secondary coil in volts (V)
- n_p = number of turns on primary coil
- n_s = number of turns on secondary coil

Knowledge Check

1) Which hand would you sue for the motor and generator effect?
2) How does an induced magnet differ from a permanent magnet?
3) Name the factors that can increase the PD in the generator effect?

Answers

1) Motor is right. Generator is left.
2) An induced magnet will only become magnetic when introduced to another magnetic field. A permanent magnet will always produce a magnetic field.
3) The area of the coils – Increasing these will increase the PD induced
   The number of coils – Increasing this increases the PD induced
   a. This is as there are more segments of wire to cut through the magnetic field
   b. Therefore, the cumulative effect is greater
   The speed at which the wire or magnet is moved
   c. Faster speed will induce a greater PD
   The strength of the magnetic field
   d. A stronger magnetic field will induce a greater PD

P3 Mechanics

Kinematics

When we describe a quantity we can either describe it using just the **magnitude** or we can also add a **direction** to that quantity. For example:

- A car travels at 50 mph
- A car travels at 50 mph in a southerly direction

If you see above, one shows just the speed whereas the second shows both speed and direction. We call these scalars and vectors.

> Scalar – quantities that only have a magnitude
>
> Vector – quantities that have both a magnitude and direction

Some examples:

Speed is a **scalar** whereas **velocity** is a **vector** as it has a direction

Mass is a **scalar** whereas **weight** is a **vector**

- Weight is a force therefore it has a direction

All **forces** are **vectors**. This is as all forces act in a **direction**

> **6med tip:** If you are ever stuck in deciding if something is a vector or a scalar think can it **go negative**. For example you **can't** have a **negative speed** however you can have a **negative** velocity (reverse.)

Distance is a **scalar quantity** whereas displacement is a **vector**.

- Distance tells us the **amount of ground** between two objects
- Whereas displacement refers to how far out an object is **from the other**
    - One way will be positive and the opposing direction negative

Your BMAT requires you to know the following equations.
1) Speed (m/s) = Distance (m)/ Time (s)
2) Velocity (m/s) = Displacement (m)/ Time (s)

- Velocity is a vector and therefore can be negative whereas speed can't as there is no direction.
    o Displacement has a **direction** whereas distance **doesn't**

3) Acceleration (m/s^2) = change in velocity (m/s)/ Time (s)

Graphs for Distance and Velocity

Distance/Displacement Time Graphs

Distance is a **scalar** whereas displacement is a **vector**

- Distance time graphs the value for distance (Y axis) can **only increase**
- Displacement time graphs the value of **displacement** (Y) axis can **decrease** and become **negative.**

If we think of the above in terms of leaving your house and going to the shop and back. You take the same route there and back.

- Your distance will only increase. Think of this like miles on a car, the odometer doesn't distinguish if you are going to or from the house, it will still **increase in miles**
- However your displacement will increase to the point you reach the shop
    o When you then return from the shop your displacement will decrease until eventually reaching zero again when you get home.

There are some important take aways when distance time graphs and velocity time graphs.

- Gradient of the graph
    o In a distance time graph this will give you **speed**
    o In a displacement time graph this will give you **velocity**
    o If the gradient is changing (e.g the line is curved) then you will be **accelerating/decelerating**
- A horizontal line shows a **stationary object**
- To read distance/displacement you will read this off the **Y axis**

The Complete BMAT Specification Explained

P3 – Mechanics

Velocity Time Graphs

The take aways form velocity time graph are as below

- A straight horizontal line now shows a velocity
    - Therefore the object is still moving but at a constant speed
- A diagonal line will show an accelerating object
    - You can tell the acceleration by taking the **gradient**
    - This is as it shows the change in velocity over time which is **acceleration**
- By looking at the area under the graph we can determine the **displacement**.

> **6Med Tip:** You need to be aware of what the gradient shows in each graph and you need to be able to calculate the displacement in a velocity time graph
>
> To do this try to split the area under the graph up into rectangles and triangles to find the area easily. To find the total area just add them all together.

Equations To Know

You need to be aware of the following equations and be able to apply them. They can be derived from the graphs above however it is easier to learn them!

$$v = u + at$$

$$s = 0.5(u+v)t$$

$$v^2 = u^2 + 2as$$

v = final velocity (m/s)

u = initial velocity (m/s)

a = acceleration (m/s^2)

t = time (s)

Forces

A force in general can be defined by:

"A push or pull that can change the velocity of an object"

When a force is **exerted** on an object, unless an **equal** force is exerted in the **opposite** direction an **action** will happen. This can take shape in many ways. Some examples are:

- Change in speed of an object, for example breaks slowing a car
- Change in shape, for example moulding clay
- Changing direction, for example a tennis racket returning a tennis ball

As we saw in the previous chapter a force can be exerted **with** or **without** contact. Therefore we can categorise forces into **contact** and **non-contact forces**.

Contact Force

A contact force can be defined as:

"A force which acts at a point of contact between two objects"

Examples of contact forces include:

You on the earth

- It is down to balancing contact forces that you are not driven down through the earth or off into space
- The contact force of your weight is equal to the **reactionary** force the floor is exerting in the **opposing direction**

Friction

- Another common contact force
- Exists in the **opposing direction** to motion
- Only exists when two objects are touching

P3 – Mechanics

Mechanical
- A car engine creates a force
- This force is delivered through gears and shafts to the wheels
- Here it causes the wheels to turn and the car to move

Some less obvious contact forces also exist

Air Resistance
- Although it may not seem like it air resistance is actually a **contact force**
- The air particles are exerting a **force** when they **hit** the moving object

Tension
- If a rope between two objects becomes taught then a contact force is being applied to those objects
- Even though the objects aren't directly touching the point of contact is the rope between

Non-Contact Forces

We can define non-contact forces as

"A force that acts at a distance, without any contact due to the action of a field"

Vector Diagrams

We now know that forces have both a direction and a magnitude.
- Some of these will have **opposing directions** working **against** each other
- Some will have the **same directions** working **with** each other
- The combination of these is known as the **resultant force**

P3 – Mechanics

Splitting forces into two planes

- To work out the resultant force we need to split the forces into the horizontal and vertical plane
- We then decide which two directions are our positive (e.g up and right.)

An example below:

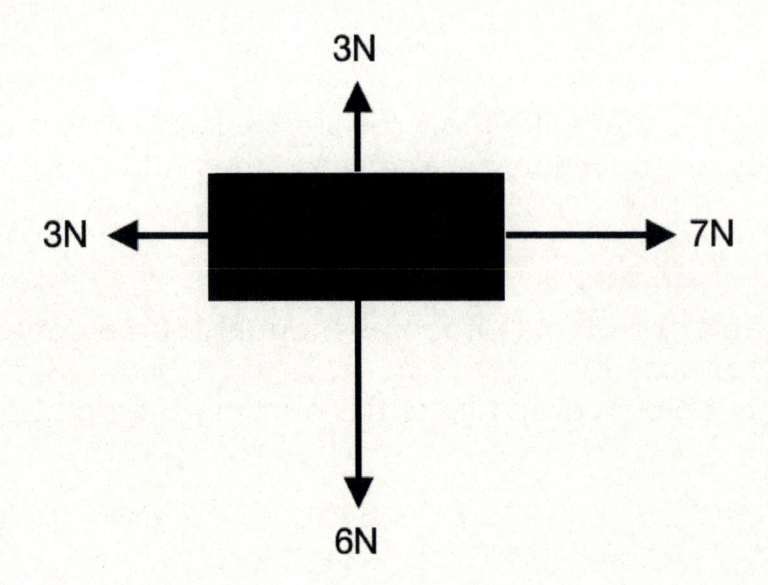

```
            3N
            ↑
    3N ← [████] → 7N
            ↓
            6N
```

In this example we will define right and up as our positives. The resultant forces will be:

$$7N - 3N = 4N \text{ to the right}$$

$$3N - 6N = -3N \text{ Upwards}$$

Resultant forces and movement

Taking the above example. We now know the net forces in two planes, However if we are to decide how this will effect the object we need to find the overall **resultant force**.

To do this we need to construct a **vector** diagram. Place both vectors head to tail as below. We have some rules:

- The vectors must be to scale.
    - Their length has to be proportional to the magnitude of force
- The vector must be in the correct orientation
    - The angle the force is drawn in must be the same angle as the force is acting.
    - In horizontal and vertical planes this is at 90 degrees to each other.

So carrying on with our example above we end with a diagram like this:

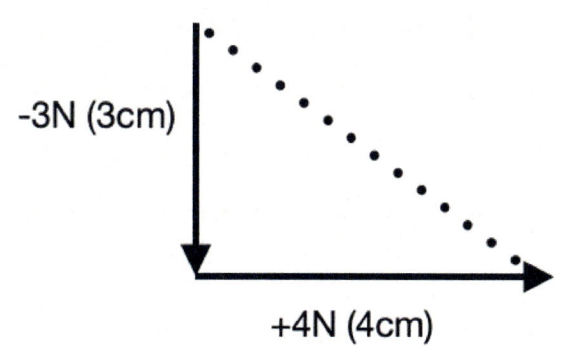

-3N (3cm)

+4N (4cm)

To work out the resultant force we can either

1. Physically measure the dotted line and angle. This will only work if the drawing is to scale!
2. As we know the planes are at right angles to each other we can use Pythagoras theorem

$$3^2 + 4^2 = 25$$

Therefore our resultant force is 5N in the direction of 45 degrees from either vertical or horizontal as shown on the arrow.

Balanced and Unbalanced Forces

As we have seen above forces can act in all directions and cause a resultant force. This is described as a **net force**.

Net forces can either be **balanced or unbalanced**

- A balanced net force is where the forces all cancel each other out
- An unbalanced net force will lead to a resultant force on the object
    - This will lead to an action (the object will move or change shape etc.)

Stationary objects are **still experiencing forces** it is just their forces are **balanced** and therefore there is **no resultant force.**

- Think about how you are now reading this
- Assuming you are stationary in a chair there are still forces acting
    - Your weight is pushing down into the chair
    - The chair is pushing back up against you with an equal force
- This why you are stationary and not falling through the chair!
- You have a net resultant force of 0.
- Should you get to a point where your weight exceeds that of the force the chair can exert back it will break and you will fall through.
- This is as you now have a resultant force.

Force and Extension

When you pull a spring a force is **acting against you** to bring the spring back to its original shape. As you apply **more force** the spring **extends** and so too does the pull you feel working against you. When we pull this spring it is being subject to a **tension force.**

Therefore we can say that in general the greater the **tension force** the greater the extension. When the object returns to normal after the force is removed we call this elastic extension.

We can model this using **Hooke's Law** which states:

$$F = Kx$$

F = force in (N)

K = spring constant (N/m)

x = extension in (m)

P3 – Mechanics

Force Extension Graphs

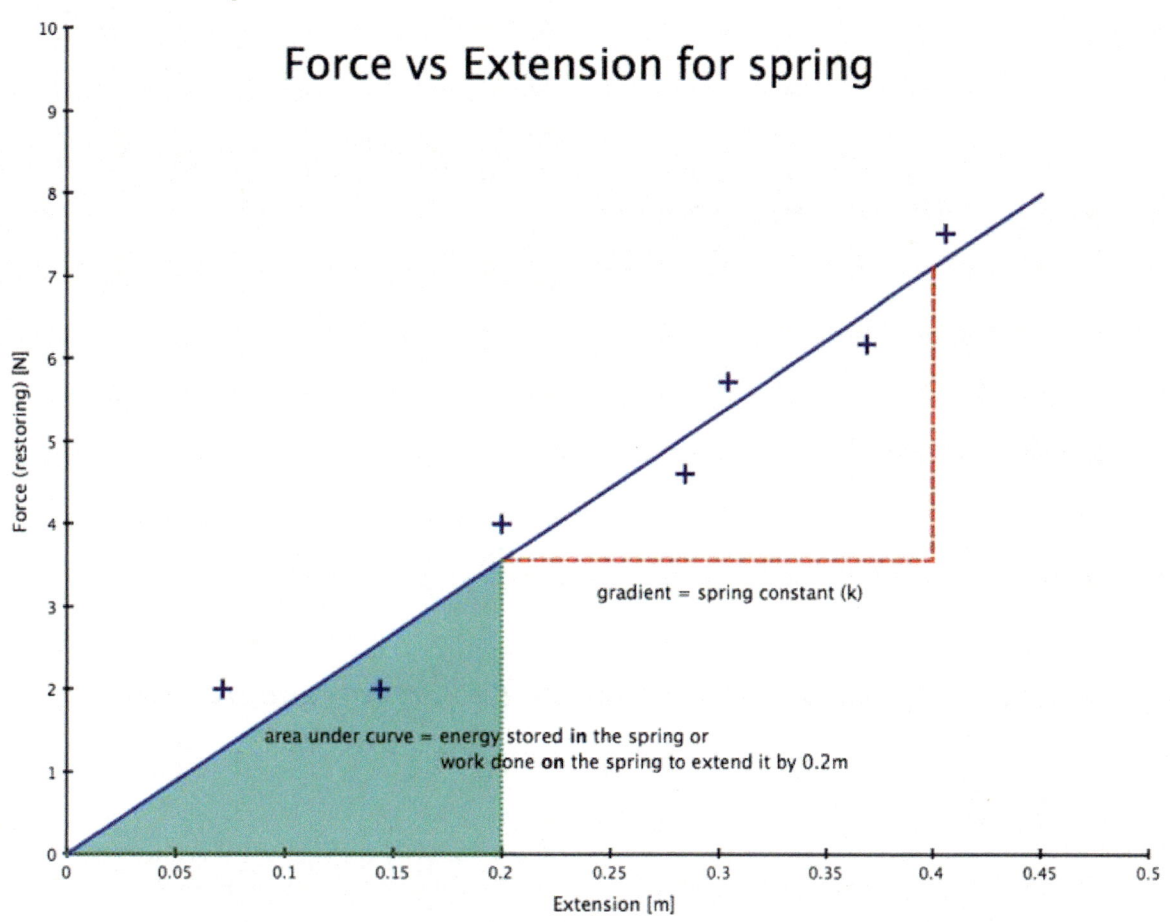

Force vs Extension for spring

gradient = spring constant (k)

area under curve = energy stored in the spring or work done on the spring to extend it by 0.2m

When we stretch a spring we are storing energy in the spring as **elastic potential energy**. We can find out the quantity of energy by looking at the **area under the graph** as shown above.

We can also find this out using the following two equations

$$E = \tfrac{1}{2} F x = \tfrac{1}{2} k x^2$$

However have you ever pulled a spring to the point that it permanently changes shape?

- We would now say the object has passed its **elastic limit**
- This is called **plastic deformation** and the **limit of proportionality** has been reached
- Hooke's law would **no longer apply** from this point on
- The energy stored also becomes **irretrievable** beyond this point

Newton's Laws

Newton's first law states that:

"a body will remain at rest or in a state of uniform motion in a straight line unless acted on by a resultant external force"

Newton's second law states that:

Force = mass x acceleration

Newton's third law states:

"If body A exerts a force on body B then body B exerts an equal and opposite force of the same type on body A"

Momentum is the quantity of motion of a moving body. Simply we can consider it a combination of the mass and velocity.

It is calculated by:

$$\text{Momentum} = \text{Mass} \times \text{Velocity}$$

- In a **closed system** momentum will be **conserved** in a collision
- Therefore in a closed system if object A knocks into object B the combined momentum of the two objects before will **equal** that after the collision.

Force generated in a collision is represented by

$$\text{Force} = \text{Change in momentum} / \text{Change in time.}$$

This makes sense if you think about it. If you are travelling in a car at 30 mph and break suddenly returning to stationary in 2 seconds the force exerted on you is much greater than slowing the car from 30 to 0 over 10 seconds!

> **6Med Tip:** You need to know and be able to apply both these equations. They may also be shown in symbols. We represent momentum with the letter p

Mass and Weight

Mass is the **quantity of matter** within a physical body. This does not change regardless of volume or external forces actin on it.

- We measure mass using Kg

Weight is the **force** exerted on a physical body by **gravity**. It is measured using Newtons (N)

We can relate mass and weight by using the following equation.

Weight = mass x acceleration due to gravity

- For the purposes of BMAT the acceleration due to gravity is constant at $10 m/s^2$

Free Fall Acceleration

- When an object falls from height two forces are acting on it
    - Gravity is pulling it towards the earth
    - Air resistance is **resisting** this as the object moves towards earth.
- We know that when an object starts falling it's **weight exceeds** the air resistance
    - If this was not true then the **object would not fall**
    - As to accelerate downwards the object has to have a **resultant force** in this direction.

The Complete BMAT Specification Explained
P3 – Mechanics

- As the object accelerates towards the earth the air resistance (drag) acting on it **will increase**
    - The object is hitting the air particles at **greater speed** with more force
    - More over the object encounters **more air particles/second** when it moves at a greater speed
    - These both act to **increase air resistance**.
- Eventually we will get to a point where the air resistance is **equal** to the force of weight
- Now the forces acting on each other are **balanced** and there is **no resultant force** acting on the object
- It will therefore continue moving at a **constant velocity** in the same direction until a new force is introduced.
- This final velocity is called **terminal velocity**

Factors Affecting Air Resistance

- Air resistance is caused by **loads of tiny collisions** between air particles and the moving object.
- So to reduce the air resistance on an object we can change a few factors
    - We can reduce the surface area that meets the air
        - It is for this reason rockets are **thin and cone shaped**
        - The section that comes into the air first is the **tiny top of the cone**
        - Parachutes have a large surface area in order to **increase the air resistance** and slow the sky diver down.
    - You can reduce the **density of the air**
        - As airplanes climb higher their drag actually decreases
        - This is as the air higher up is **less dense**
        - Therefore less air particles to hit the plane and slow it down.

Energy

Your BMAT requires you to know the following equations:

Work done (J) = Force (N) x distance (M)

- Work done simply means the **net change in kinetic energy**
    - I.e the amount of energy transferred to the moving object

Power (W) = Energy (J)/Time (s)

- This equation helps show us the definition of power
- It is simply the **rate of energy transfer**

Change in GPE = Mass (Kg) x Acceleration due to gravity (m/s^2) x change in height (m)

- GPE is Gravitational Potential Energy
- It is effectively how much energy we have stored up in an object due to the effect of the earths gravitational field
- As earlier we use 10 m/s^2 for g
- The equation may appear as GPE = *mgh*

The law of energy conservation states that:

"Energy can neither be created nor destroyed"

- Therefore in a closed system energy must be **transferred**
- This is useful as we can use this rule in **equations**
- For example with momentum
  - We know the **total momentum before** will equal **that after the collision**
- Energy may be transferred to useful forms or may be lost as waste products
- For example heat is a common waste product in electrical systems
- We use the proportion of useful energy to wasted energy to calculate our efficiency as below:

Percentage efficiency = (Useful energy output/Total energy input) x 100

The Complete BMAT Specification Explained

P3 - Mechanics

Extra Reading – NB This is not on the BMAT Specification. An understanding of this however is useful for vector diagrams.

Moments.

When two forces of the **same magnitude** pass through the same point on an object they will have no effect. This is as the **resultant force** will be 0.

However if these forces don't go through the **same point** they will lead the object to **move.** See below:

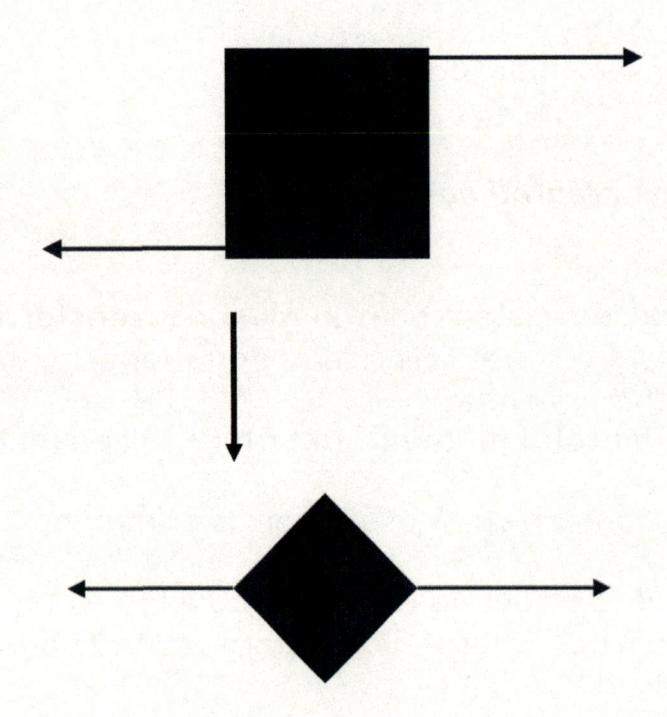

As above we can see that originally the forces aren't acting through the same point.

- This leads to the object to **rotate**
- It **pivots** around the centre
- It **rotates** until the **forces align** and **cancel** each other out.

Moments are defined as:

"The turning effect of a force about a pivot"

A moment is a force. We can define a moment by the equation

$$M = Fd$$

M = Moment (in Newton metres Nm)

F = Force

d = perpendicular distance of force to pivot in m.

This equation shows some **key properties** of moments

- The turning force can be increased by **increasing the perpendicular distance**
- This is the basis of spanners
- They allow us to exert force at the end of a long rod
- This increases the **perpendicular distance** to the nut
- Thus increasing the **turning force** through the nut
- Therefore you can undo nuts with spanners you couldn't do by hand!

When referring to moments we label the direction as **clockwise** or **anticlockwise**

Moments are still **forces**. Therefore we still need to take into account if they are **balanced or not**. Going back to our spanner example

- When loosening you will rotate the spanner anticlockwise
- If you apply light pressure the nut won't move
- This is as the moment you are applying through the spanner equals that of the friction on the nut.
- Therefore the forces are **balanced**.

The Complete BMAT Specification Explained

P3 – Mechanics

Knowledge Check

1) What distance must B be for the moments to be balanced?

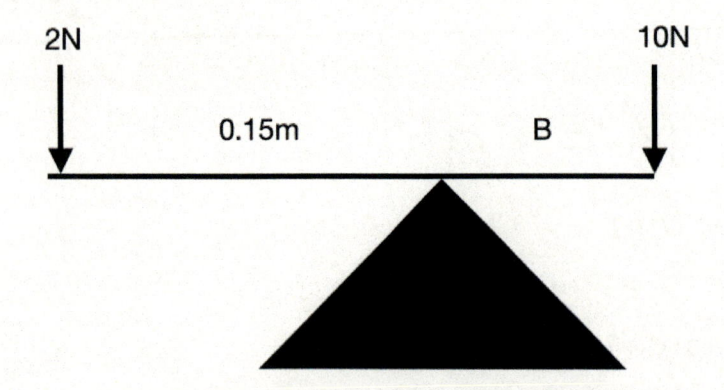

[Diagram: A seesaw on a triangular pivot. On the left, a 2N force points down at 0.15m from the pivot. On the right, a 10N force points down at distance B from the pivot.]

2) John cycles up a hill. Identify the main forces acting on him and split them into contact and non-contact forces

---

Answers

1)
1. First let's work out the anticlockwise force = 2×0.15 = 0.3Nm
2. We know they are balanced so the clockwise moment must equal this as well
3. Let's plug this in to what we know so far into M=Fd
   a. 0.3 = 10 × B
   b. Therefore B = 0.3/10 = 0.03m

2)

Contact Force	Non-Contact Force
Friction – each time the wheel makes contact with the road friction is acting. (This stops him sliding down the hill!)	**Gravity** - will be trying to pull him down the hill back to earth!
Air Resistance – The air particles hitting John will act in the opposite direction to his motion slowing him down	
Thrust – As John pushes down on the pedal that energy is transferred through the chain and exerts a force turning the wheel	

P4 Thermal Physics

Conduction

- As you heat a substance the particles gain kinetic energy
- This means they move **faster**
- The higher you heat the object the higher the kinetic energy of the individual particles that make up that object

Conduction is the transfer of heat energy through the transfer of kinetic energy.

- As the particles gain kinetic energy they vibrate at a **higher rate**
- They will then knock into the next particle with **greater force**
- This particle will now **vibrate** with **greater force**. It has gained **kinetic energy**
- This goes on as the energy dissipates through the whole structure

Certain materials lend themselves to being **better conductors** than others.

- Solids are the best conductors, their particles are **closely packed together**
- Gasses are poor conductors as the particles are **very far apart**
- Metals are good conductors as they have free electrons which allow the transfer of **kinetic energy** more efficiently than the fixed ions

Insulators use the fact that some materials are poor conductors to their advantage

- Puffer jackets have lots of air between their fillings
- Air, a gas, is a poor conductor
- Thus by placing gas between you and the surrounding cold air you reduce the heat lost through conduction from your body

Convection

When you heat a fluid you are causing the particles to gain kinetic energy.

- The particles now move round at a greater speed
- This causes the atoms to become slightly less closely packed
- This means the atoms now occupy a larger area and the liquid has become less dense

So as we heat a liquid the liquid becomes less dense.

If you are heating a container of fluid from the bottom, then the fluid at the bottom will warm up quickest

- As we have just discussed the fluid will then become less dense than the colder fluid above it
- Therefore this warmer less dense fluid will swap places with the cooler denser fluid and rise to the top of the container.
- The cooler fluid is now closest to the heat source and will begin to heat

This cycle repeats itself and forms a current. We call this a convection current.

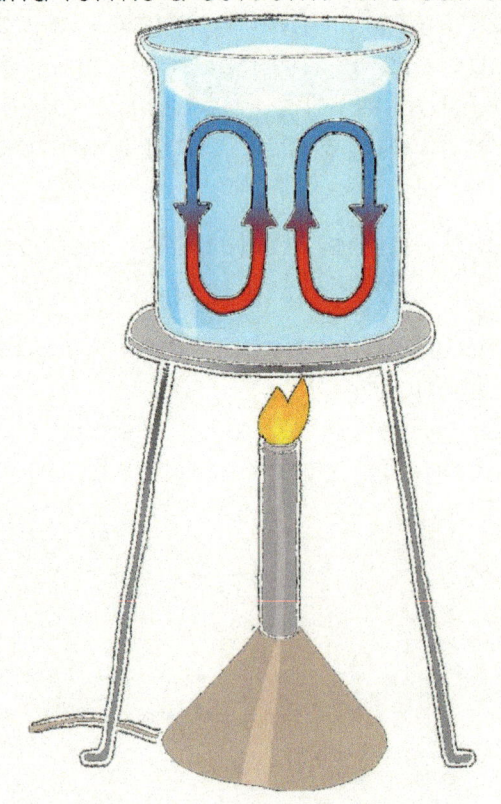

Thermal Radiation

Thermal radiation is electromagnetic radiation that is emitted from an object due to the heat of the material.

- All materials will emit this **thermal radiation**
- It will be emitted across the **whole electromagnetic spectrum**
- However the majority will lie in the **infrared** region at room temperature
- The **hotter** something is the **greater** the **radiation emitted**

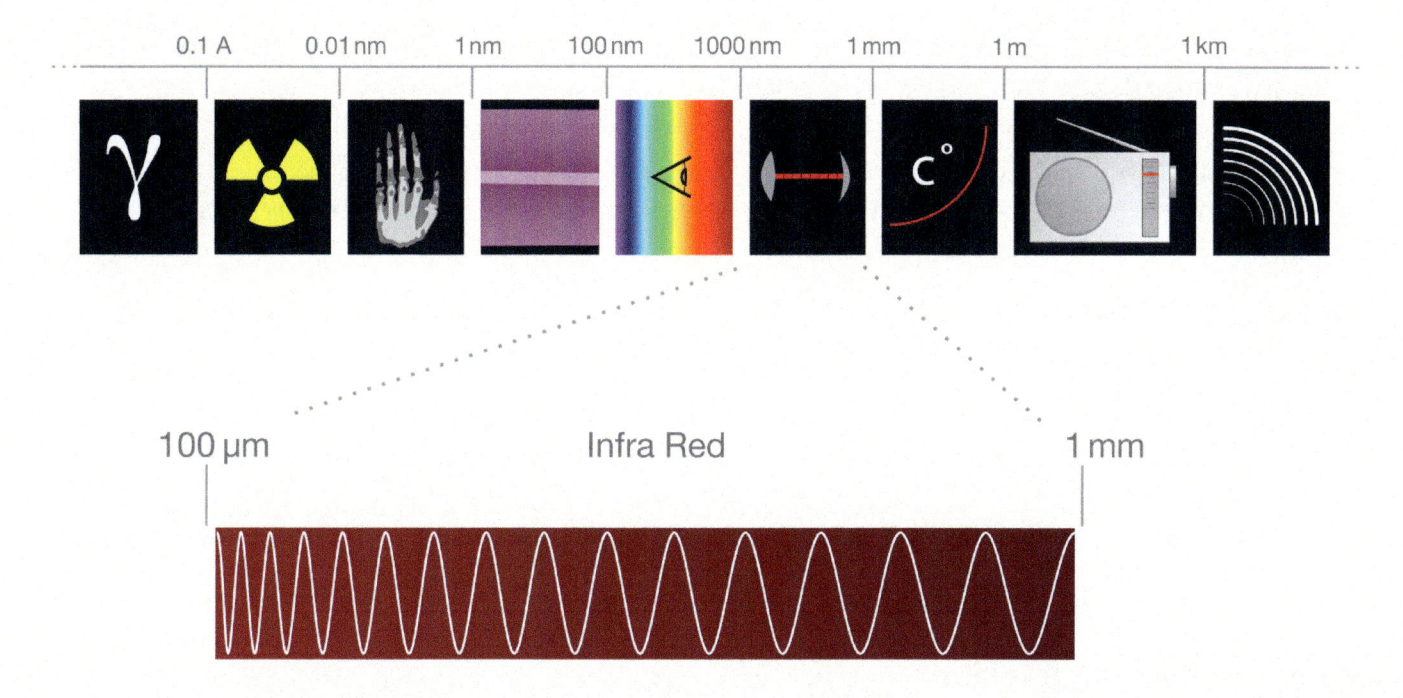

As above generally at room temperature most of the thermal radiation released is released in the form of **infrared radiation**. However, as objects change temperature so too does the following:

- Waves with a **smaller wavelength** have a **higher energy**
- As objects get hotter, they emit **more thermal energy**
- Therefore, they emit waves with **higher intensity** and **smaller wave lengths**
- This means waves emitted are in the visible light region or even in the UV region.

Search and rescue use this to search for people who are lost in forests
- Both the background forest and the lost person will emit IR radiation
- However the human will be **hotter than the surroundings**
- Therefore will emit **more IR** and at a **slightly higher wavelength.**
- Using a special camera that picks up IR radiation they can see the difference and the human will show up as a bright red spot on the camera.

Thermal Equilibrium

- Now we have said above that object are constantly losing heat in the form of IR radiation
- However if this is true and nothing else happens eventually objects would lose all their heat energy
- Therefore the object must also be simultaneously absorbing radiation.

Thermal Equilibrium is where an object is absorbing radiation at the same rate it is losing it.

- If this is the case, then the object will stay at a constant temperature
- If it loses radiation quicker than it absorbs it will lose temperature until the rates equalise
- Vice-versa if it is absorbing radiation at a rate quicker than it is losing it it will heat up.

Surfaces that Affect Radiation

Certain surfaces will absorb/emit more radiation than others

- Shiny silver surfaces will reflect radiation away reducing absorption
- Dull black surfaces will absorb/emit radiation best

Have you ever stepped on a tarmacked road after a hot day?

- You will notice the road is much hotter than the surroundings
- This is dull black and a good absorber of thermal radiation
- During the day it has absorbed all this energy heating it up
- It is now emitting this as thermal energy as it cools down

The Complete BMAT Specification Explained

P4 – Thermal Physics

Noticed how the roast turkey is wrapped in foil to keep it warm?

- Shiny foil reflects most the radiation
- Therefore, it absorbs/emits less radiation
- All that radiation being emitted from the hot turkey is leading it to cool down
- The foil reflects this back towards the turkey
- If the foil was dull and black the lost radiation would be absorbed and some emitted away from the turkey being lost
- This would lead to turkey to cool down at a faster rate

> **6Med Tip:** Next time you are out have a look at certain objects and think why are they the colour/texture they are? Is this due to wanting to gain/lose heat? What could they do different to improve this? This will reinforce your understanding of thermal radiation without even thinking actively revising!

Specific Heat Capacity

Specific heat capacity is defined as:

"The amount of energy required to raise the temperature of 1kg of substance by one degree Celsius"

Different substances have different heat capacities. A substance with a low heat capacity will heat up and cool down quickly.

The equation for specific heat capacity is:

$$\Delta Q = mc\Delta\theta$$

ΔQ = change in thermal energy, in joules (J)

m = mass, in kilograms (kg)

c = specific heat capacity, in joules per kilogram per degree Celsius (J/kg °C)

$\Delta\theta$ = change in temperature, in degrees Celsius (°C)

The Complete BMAT Specification Explained
P4 – Thermal Physics

We are looking to at the amount of energy needed to change the temperature of a substance in a constant state.

Knowledge Check

1) What material is the best conductor?
2) What region on the electromagnetic spectrum is thermal radiation emitted at?
3) What is the definition for specific heat capacity?

Answers
1) Solids, in particular metals.
2) Infrared.
3) "The amount of energy required to raise the temperature of 1kg of substance by 1°C."

P5 Matter

Explaining the Atom

Through history many people have tried to explain how the atom exists. As we have gone on we have got a greater understanding of the true structure of an atom until we arrive where we are today....

The Nuclear Model of an atom suggests the following:

- Nearly all mass of an atom is **concentrated** in **the centre** of an atom in what we call the **nucleus**
- The nucleus is **positively charged**
- This nucleus is **orbited** by **electrons**

In the 20th century this model was further refined by Danish Physicist Niels Bohr to give us the classic energy levels model we see below:

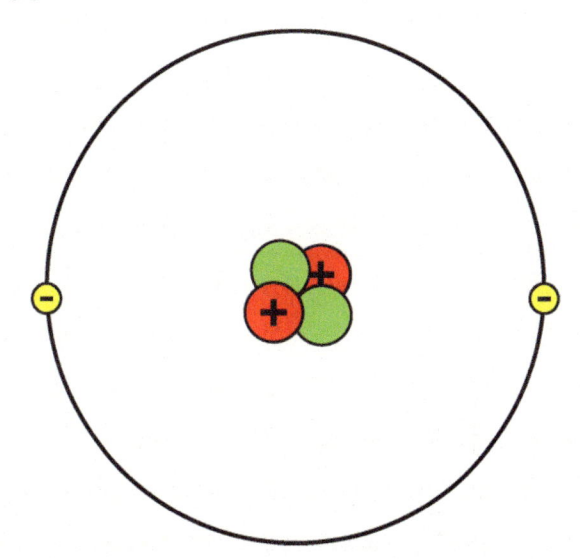

This suggests that electrons orbit the nucleus at **set distances**

- As we move out in distance (shell) we get an **increase in energy level**
- This is as it moves further away from the positive nucleus

Today this is the model that we commonly accept.

Density

The definition of density is:

"The mass of a substance per unit of volume"

The equation for density is:

$$p = \frac{m}{V}$$

p = Density (Kg/m³)
m = Mass (Kg)
V = Volume (m³)

> **6Med Tip:** As well as remembering the equations make sure you note the units! They can some times be sneaky and change Kg to g. Make sure you know how to change between units.

You may be required to calculate the density of Spheres and Cylinders. Learn the below equations for their volume:

$$\text{Sphere} = \frac{4}{3}\pi r^3$$

$$\text{Cylinder} = \pi r^2 \times l$$

Density and State

- As substances change state the atoms **increase in kinetic energy** vibrating more and more
- Eventually they escape their **intermolecular bonds** and break free
- It is for this reason that gas has a **much lower density** than solids and liquids
- There is **much more space** between particles and literally less mass/volume!

Liquids and solids have generally the **same density**

- In a solid the molecules are unable to slip past each other
- In a fluid some of these bonds that hold atoms together have broken
- This allows molecules to slip past each other whilst still in close proximity
- However intermolecular forces still exist packing the molecules together
- This means that although the properties are different the densities are similar.

Changes of State

There are six changes of state that can occur.

1. **Melting** – solid to liquid
2. **Evaporating** – liquid to gas
3. **Condensing** – gas to liquid
4. **Freezing** – liquid to solid
5. **Sublimation** – solid to gas
6. **Deposition** – gas to solid

Solids

- Molecules vibrate lightly in fixed positions
- Molecules are still close together

Liquids

- Molecules can slide past each other
- Still close together

Gas

- Molecules are widely separated (about 10x more than solid)
- Molecules have lots of kinetic energy
    - Move rapidly in random directions

Heat Energy and Intermolecular Forces

As you add heat energy to a substance this is converted to kinetic energy in the molecules.

- Bonds between molecules **keep them in place**
- It causes the molecules to **vibrate**
- As they vibrate it takes **more force** to **keep them in one place**
- When you increase the kinetic energy to a certain point some of these intermolecular **forces break**
- We then see a **change in state**

As a solid increases in temperature the molecules vibrate with greater intensity in their fixed positions

- Eventually they can **break free** from their fixed position and slide past each other
- However they do not have enough energy to escape completely
- They now exist as a fluid
- Adding this heat energy has caused the solid to **melt**.

If you keep applying heat energy to this liquid molecules will gain more kinetic energy

- They will eventually gain enough to break free from each other
- Now they will **rapidly spread** out
- They now exist as a gas
- You have **evaporated** the liquid

Specific Latent Heat

Specific latent heat is defined as:

"The amount of thermal energy required to change the state of 1 kg of a substance with no change in temperature"

This is subtly different from specific heat capacity. In this example we are specifically looking at the energy needed **to break those intermolecular bonds** and **change the state** of the substance whilst keeping temperature constant.

We look at the specific latent heat in two ways

- Fusion – solid to liquid
- Vaporisation – liquid to gas

These are both true for their backward directions (e.g liquid to solid.)

Ideal Gasses

Gasses are lots of identical particles all whizzing around at **high speed** in **different directions**. They are constantly bouncing off each other and the walls of the container they are held within.

They exert a **force** on the container which we can model using the ideal gas equation. However for this equation we have to assume some **constants**:

- Temperature is constant
- Volume of the container is constant

If we were to increase the temperature the particles in the gas would have more kinetic energy

- Therefore they would have more momentum when they collided with the walls of the container
- This would exert a greater force!

You can identify the pressure a gas exerts using the following equation:

$$\frac{Pressure \times Volume}{Temperature} = a\ constant$$

Pressure

Pressure is the force exerted over a certain area. It can be calculated using the following equation

$$pressure = \frac{force}{area}$$

The Complete BMAT Specification Explained

P5 - Matter

The pressure of fluids is **variable** and varies with **depth**. It also acts in all directions. If asked to calculate the hydrostatic pressure exerted by a fluid you can use the equation:

$$\text{hydrostatic pressure} = h\rho g,$$

h = Depth (m)

p = Fluid density (kg/m³)

g = Gravitational field strength (N/Kg)

Knowledge Check

1) Define latent heat of vaporisation
2) Which two states have roughly the same density?
3) What is the equation to find the pressure a gas exerts?

Answers

1) The amount of energy required to turn one 1kg of a liquid to a gas
2) Liquid and Solid
3) $\dfrac{Pressure \times Volume}{Temperature} = a\ constant$

P6 Waves

Some Wave Definitions

The BMAT requires you to know the following definitions when it comes to waves:

- **Amplitude** – *"The distance from the undisturbed position to the peak or trough of a wave"*
- **Wavelength** – *"The distance from one point on the wave to the same point on the next wave"*
- **Frequency** – *"The number of waves passing a point in a second"*
- **Period** – *"The time taken for one full cycle of a wave"*
- **Peak** – *"The point at which a wave is at its highest displacement"*
- **Trough** – *"The point in a wave where displacement is at its lowest"*
- **Compression** – *"Areas in a longitudinal wave where particles are closes together"*
- **Rarefraction** – *"Areas in a longitudinal wave where particles are furthest apart"*

Describing Wave Motion

Think of a wave coming into shore from a beach. It can be easy to think that the water particles themselves are moving with the wave and into the beach. However this is not the case...

In fact the water particles **don't** move any closer to the beach at all. They move **perpendicular** to the beach.

Think of a buoy floating in the water.

- As a wave passes under the buoy the buoy goes **up** and then **down**
- However the buoy itself **doesn't move** any **closer** to the beach
- This is a good example of how waves transfer **energy** and **not matter**

Waves transfer energy and not matter.

- The actual particles involved in the waves remain stationary
- By **bumping into each other** they **transfer the energy** onto the next particle

Transverse and Longitudinal Waves

We can split waves into two types
- Longitudinal
- Transverse

Transverse Waves

The definition of a **transverse wave** is:

"A wave where the particles vibrate at 90° to the direction of energy transfer"

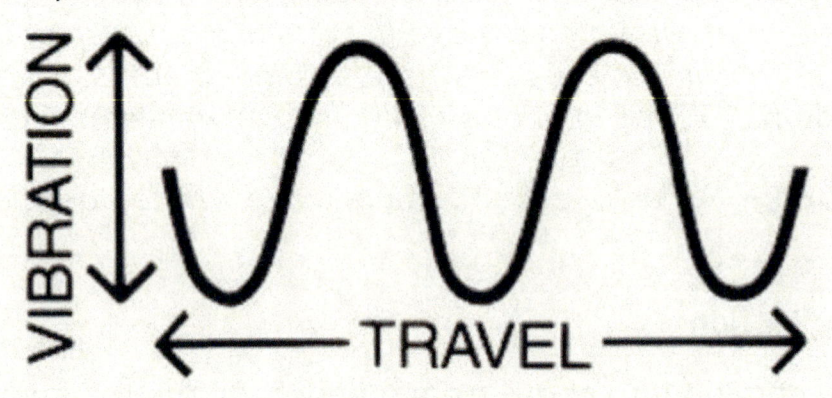

Some examples of transverse waves include:
- Ripples on water
- Electromagnetic waves
- Even a Mexican wave!

Longitudinal Waves

The definition of a longitudinal wave is:

"A wave where particles vibrate parallel to the direction of energy transfer"

Some examples of longitudinal waves include:
- Sound waves
- Seismic P waves (used to detect earth quakes)
- Slinky waves!

P6 – Waves

Transverse Wave

Longitudinal Wave

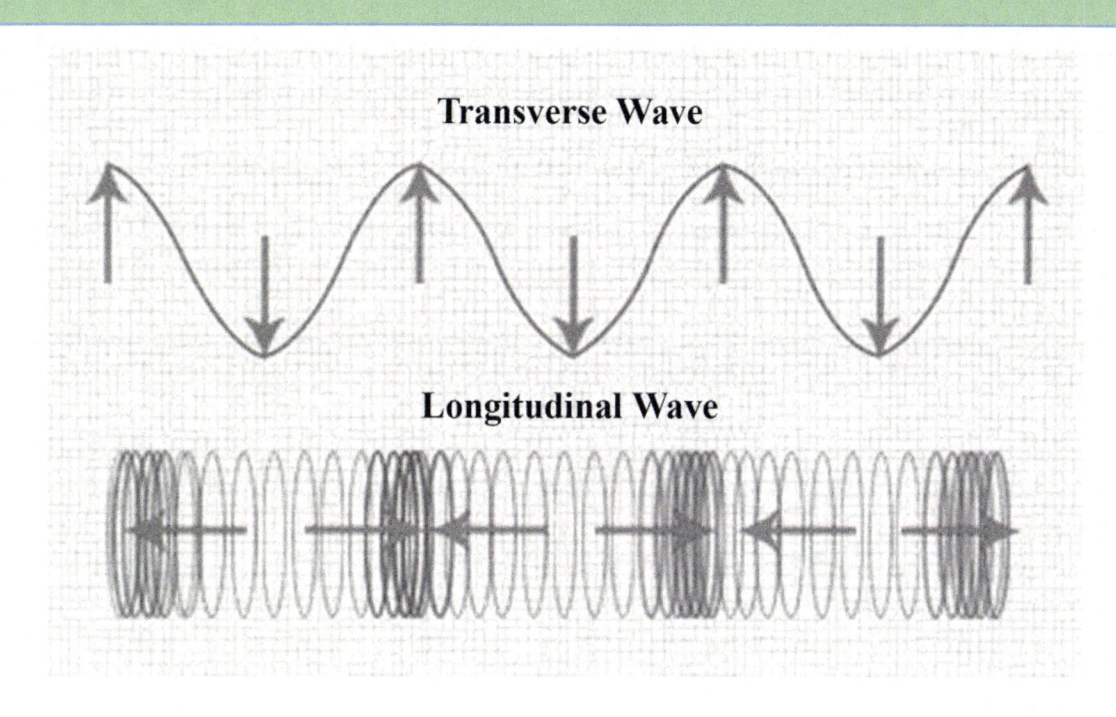

Equations in Waves

The BMAT requires you to be aware of the following equations:

1)
$$\text{frequency} = \frac{1}{\text{period}}, \quad f = \frac{1}{T}$$

2)
$$\text{wave speed} = \frac{\text{distance}}{\text{time}}$$

3)
$$\text{wave speed} = \text{frequency} \times \text{wavelength}, \quad v = f\lambda$$

> **6Med Tip:** Learn these equations off by heart
> - Also have a go at rearranging them in order to make them relate to each other
> - If you are presented with a question/concept you are unsure of you can usually fall back on to these equations.

o Fill in as many gaps as possible with information you are given in the question
o Then see how you can relate the equations to get down to a single unknown!

Wave Behaviour

If a wave meets a boundary between two media that it does not pass through then it will be **reflected**.

- We are able to predict the direction of this reflected wave using the law of reflection.

The law of reflection states that the **angle of incidence** is equal to that of the **angle of reflection**.

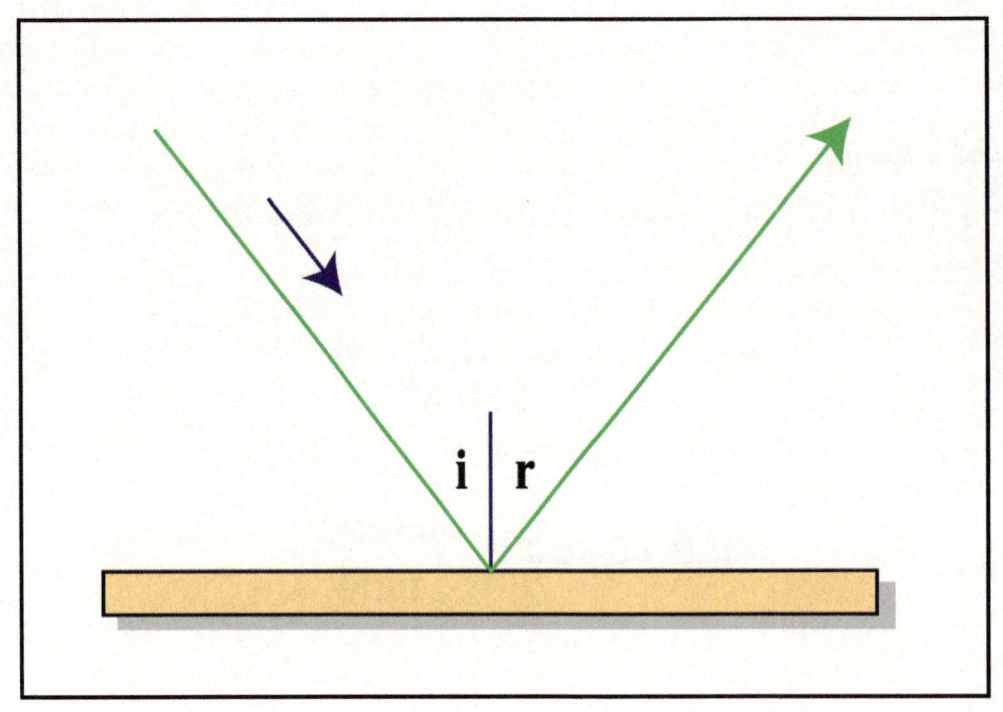

In this example i is the angle of incidence and r is the angle of the reflected ray.

Certain surfaces will reflect better than others.

- Some waves may be absorbed by the surface.
- Flat surfaces are the best reflectors
- Matted/rough surfaces will cause the wave to scatter and not reflect cleanly
    o This is as at a microscopic level the surface isn't flat and has lots of ridges that reflect the wave in many different angles

If the wave passes through the medium and comes out the other side then **transmission** has occurred

If transmission occurs then the wave coming out may have a **lower amplitude**

- This is as some of the waves energy will be absorbed by the medium
- Think of sound travelling through a thin wall
- You can still hear the sound however it will be **quieter**
- A sound wave of lower amplitude will be quieter

So as we have seen above as a wave passes through a medium some of the energy is lost to the medium. This is known as **absorption.**

- Waves can be **partially** absorbed or **completely** absorbed
- A partially absorbed sound wave you may still be able to hear the other side of a medium
- However a completely absorbed sound wave you will not be able to hear
- This is as all the energy from the wave was absorbed by the medium and nothing is transmitted the other side

Colour is another example of absorption.

- Take green grass
- When the spectrum of white light hits this grass all but the frequencies that produce green light will be **absorbed**
- The green light is the only light that is reflected and meets your eye
- Therefore due to the other colour frequencies being absorbed the grass appears green!

Refraction

As we have seen above waves may be able to pass through a change in medium. However when they do this the waves undergo a change in direction. This change in direction is known as **refraction.**

This change of direction is down to the waves changing speed

- As they pass through a **denser medium** they **slow down**

When we want to represent refraction, we can do this using **ray diagrams**. There are a few important angles to be aware of in ray diagrams

- Both angles are taken from the **normal**
    o This is a line **perpendicular** to the medium
- The angle of incidence is the angle between the **normal** and the ray **before** it is refracted
- The angle of refraction is angle from the normal **after** the ray has been refracted

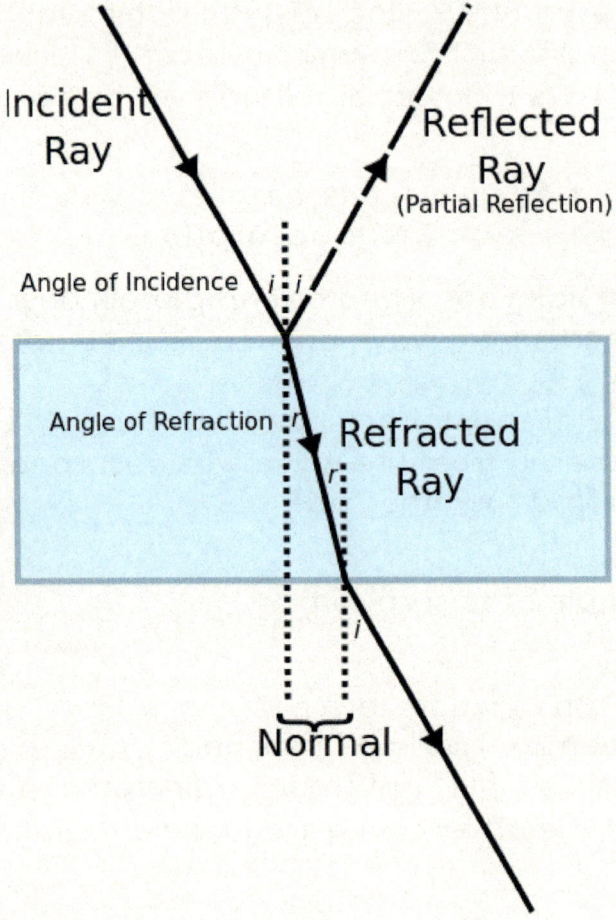

We can predict the change in direction of light using some rules below

- From a less dense medium to a more dense medium the light will bend towards the normal
- From a more dense medium to a less dense it will bend away from the normal
- If the light hit the medium along the normal (i.e perpendicular to the medium) it will not bend at all

Sound Waves

When we hear sounds this is our brain detecting **changes of pressure** at our ear drum. The energy from the sound wave is converted to **kinetic energy** and our ear drum will move back and forth.

We are only able to interpret certain frequencies of sound waves. These are between **20Hz to 20kHz**.

- The sound waves themselves are produced when an object **vibrates**
- If you think of a speaker you can sometimes see the speaker cone itself vibrating
- These vibrations are **transmitted** through the air as a **sound wave** until they reach a source.

For sound to be transmitted there needs to be **particles** in between the source and the receptor.

- For sound to spread it relies on **vibrations**
- These vibrations need to be passed on by particles knocking into each other
- If there are no particles between a source and receptor then the vibrations can't spread
- It is for this reason sound can't be transmitted through a **vacuum**

The particles in-between source and receptor are referred to as the **medium**.

- The medium **dictates** the **speed** at which the sound can go
- The denser the medium the closer the particles
- Therefore the quicker they knock into each other and **transmit** the sound at a **greater speed**

In sound waves the amplitude relates to the loudness of the sound.

- The amplitude is determined by the source
- The more energy the source emits the greater the vibrations
- Therefore the greater the amplitude

Sound waves also reflect in the same way as light waves. They follow the law of reflection.

- The angle of **incidence equals** the angle of **reflection**

The reflection of soundwaves is also why you hear an echo.

- As a source emits a sound wave the wave hits you and another object
- You initially hear the wave coming **direct** from the source
- Meanwhile the wave also **reflects** off the other object
- This **reflected** wave now hits you shortly after the first wave
- This is why you hear the **echo** shortly after!

Ultrasound are waves with a frequency greater than 20kHz. Ultrasound beams are regularly used in sonar to detect depth. For example finding the depth of water beneath a boat.

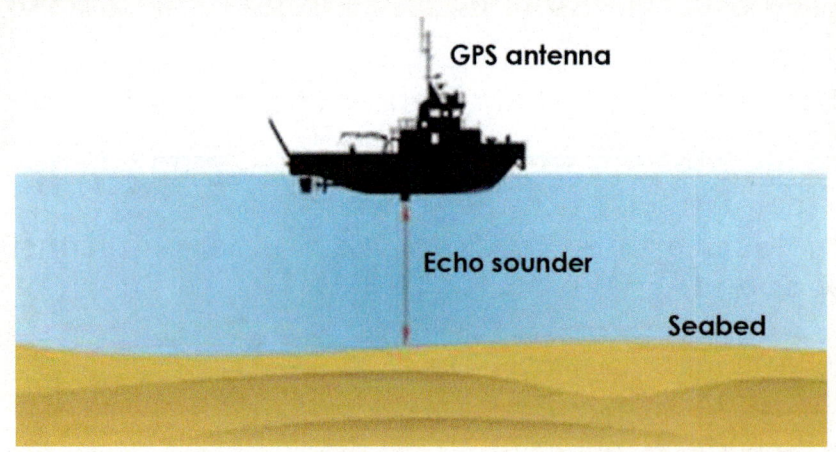

The beams will be emitted by the probe where they travel down to the bottom of the ocean before reflecting up and being detected by the probe as well.

Here using the equation below we can fill in the gaps to get our distance.

Distance (m) = [velocity (m/s) x time (s)]/2

P6 – Waves

> **6Med Tip:** If presented with a question asking you to use the distance = velocity x time in to find a distance in an ultrasound make sure to divide your answer by two!
> - This is as the time you will be given is the time for the wave to hit the bottom and be reflected back to the probe
> - Therefore the distance will also be double the distance as the wave travels to the bottom and back.

We are also able to use ultrasound in medical devices.

- Different tissues in the body will reflect ultrasound waves in different quantities
- By detecting the difference in waves being reflected the ultrasound machine can interpret this and present it as an image
- This image shoes the different structures in the body beneath the skin.

The Doppler Effect

When an object emits a sound, the sound is emitted equally and symmetrically from the object.

However when an object is moving we get a slightly different effect.

- The waves emitted in the same direction as the object is moving will become squashed
- The waves travelling in the opposing direction from the object will appear to spread out more
- When a wave becomes squashed the wave length becomes smaller
- When a wave is elongated the wavelength also increases

The pitch of a sound is determined by the frequency.

- Using the equations from earlier we can see that:

$$\text{wave speed} = \text{frequency} \times \text{wavelength}, \quad v = f\lambda$$

- The wave speed in this case is constant (the speed of sound)
- Therefore we can deduce that frequency and wave length are inversely proportional
- Therefore higher the wave length the lower the frequency and pitch!

The Complete BMAT Specification Explained

P6 – Waves

As we have seen the doppler effect has the ability to alter the pitch of sound.
- Therefore when this sound hits our ears it will be of a different pitch
- However as the object passes you it will go from a high pitch to a low pitch
  - This is as the waves in front are compressed and the waves behind are stretched!
- This can be heard every day with sirens on emergency vehicles!

Electromagnetic Spectrum

What are electromagnetic waves?
- Electromagnetic waves are a spectrum of waves that share the same properties
- They are divided into categories depending on their wavelength.
  - Radio waves have the greatest wave length and gamma rays the smallest
  - They are all transverse waves
  - In a vacuum they all travel at the speed of light

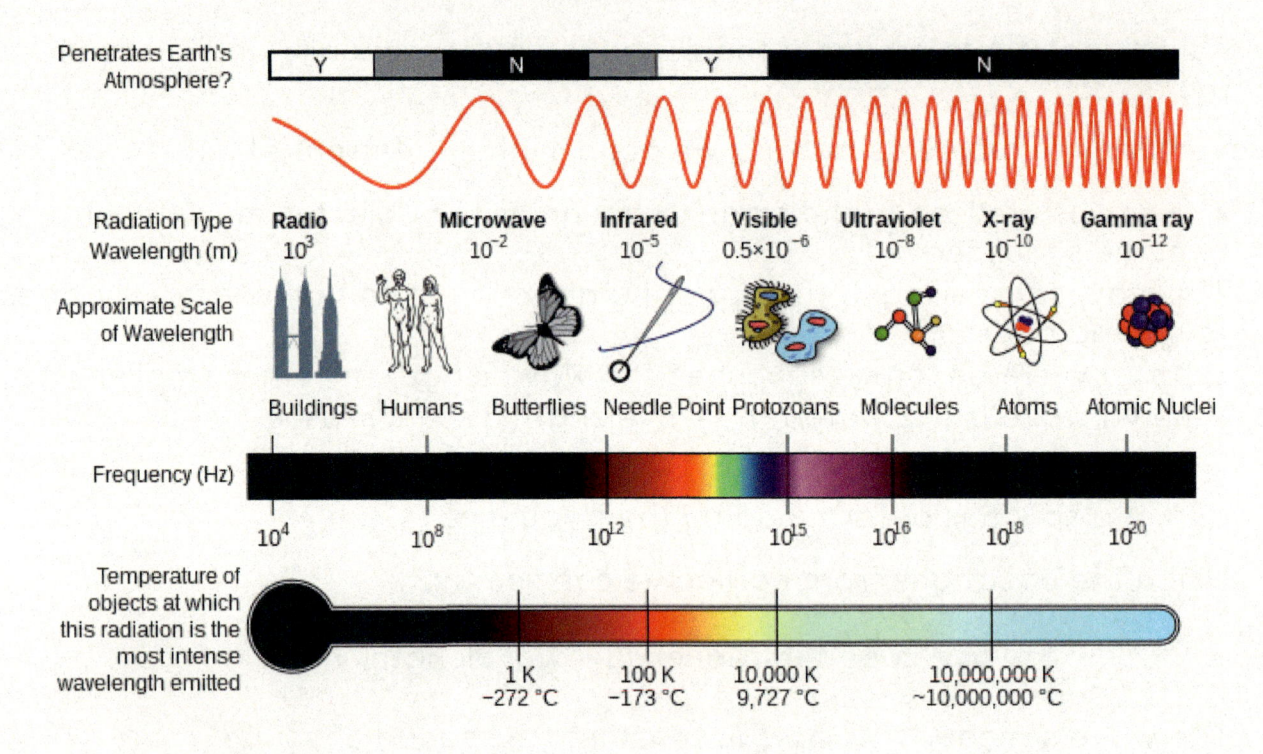

Penetrates Earth's Atmosphere?	Y	N	Y	N

Radiation Type	Radio	Microwave	Infrared	Visible	Ultraviolet	X-ray	Gamma ray
Wavelength (m)	10^3	10^{-2}	10^{-5}	0.5×10^{-6}	10^{-8}	10^{-10}	10^{-12}
Approximate Scale of Wavelength	Buildings	Humans / Butterflies	Needle Point	Protozoans	Molecules	Atoms	Atomic Nuclei
Frequency (Hz)	10^4	10^8	10^{12}	10^{15}	10^{16}	10^{18}	10^{20}
Temperature of objects at which this radiation is the most intense wavelength emitted		1 K / −272 °C	100 K / −173 °C	10,000 K / 9,727 °C		10,000,000 K / ~10,000,000 °C	

The electromagnetic spectrum and their properties.

The Complete BMAT Specification Explained

P6 – Waves

> **6Med Tip:** For your exam you need to be able to recall the order of the EM spectrum. A nifty tip I find is to use the mnemonic
>
> Raging Martians Invaded Venus Using X-ray Guns

Applications and Hazards of the EM spectrum

We utilise the EM spectrum every day

- Visible light allows us to see
- Radio waves allow us to transmit information.
- The shorter the wave length the greater the energy it carries

These high energy waves can become dangerous though as they become **ionising**

- Ionising waves have the enough energy to break chemical bonds and strip electrons from atoms
- This can have issues in the human body
- It can disrupt the DNA and increase risk of these cells mutating into cancer cells.
- It is for this reason X-Rays in hospital are only used when absolutely necessary. As well as this the dose of radiation is kept as low as possible.

Knowledge Check

1) Which category of wave has the third largest wavelength on the EM spectrum?
2) Which way would light bend when passing from a less dense to a denser medium?
3) What frequencies can humans hear?

Answers
1) Infrared
2) Towards the normal
3) 20Hz to 20kHz

P7 Radioactivity

Atomic Structure

An atom is the **smallest unit** of ordinary matter that exists. Every element is made up of **atoms**. We define the structure of an atom using the nuclear atomic model. The structure of atoms is as follows:

- A **dense nucleus** that contains **protons and neutrons**
  - This nucleus makes up about 1/100,000 the atoms size
  - Yet it accounts for 99.9% of the mass!
- **Electrons** that **orbit** this nucleus in clouds

For the BMAT exam you are asked to learn the relative properties of the constituent parts of an atom. These are as follows:

Types of particle	Relative mass	Relative charge
Proton	1	+1
Neutron	1	0
Electron	1/2000	-1

Some Definitions

Atomic number is the number of **protons** in a nucleus

- In electronically neutral atoms this is equivalent to the number of electrons

The atomic mass number is the number of **protons and neutrons** in the nucleus

Isotopes are two or more atoms of the **same element** that have **the same number of neutrons** but **differencing numbers of protons.**

Nuclides are simply a form of atom characterised by the **specific** number of protons and neutrons

Ionisation is the creation of ions by changing the number of **electrons**

- Ions have a charge
- To create this charge we need to **remove** or **add** an electron to the atom
- Adding a **negative electron** to a neutral atom will give a -1 charge
- **Removing** a negative electron from a neutral atom will give us a **+1 charge**

P7 - Radioactivity

Radioactive Decay

Most atoms have nuclei which are stable. However some atoms have nuclei which are unstable, due to an imbalance of forces in the nucleus. These begin to decay. This can be for a few different reasons:

- The nucleus can be **too large**
- The nucleus may have lots of energy making it **unstable**
- Some atoms and their isotopes may **vastly different** numbers of **neutrons and protons**

Unstable nuclei will emit radiation to become stable. For BMAT you need to know about the following forms of radiation:

- Alpha
- Beta
- Gamma

We will go into each of these in more depth below.

When an atom emits a form of radiation it is known as radioactive decay. Radioactive decay is a **completely random** process. It cannot be predicted when a nucleus will decay.

Types of Radioactive Decay

There are three types of radioactive decay you need to know about. They all have different characteristics however all will produce **ionising radiation**.

- This means all three forms of radiation can ionise atoms that they collide with

Alpha Decay – decay that occurs from the nucleus

- An alpha particle is made up of **two protons** and **two neutrons**
    - You might sometimes see this referred to as a helium nucleus as they both have the same structure
- It is a **large** and **slow moving**
- It is unable to **penetrate** very far
    - This means it is **easily stopped**
    - In reality it can be stopped by a few cm of air

- When an alpha particle is emitted, the following will happen
    - The atomic mass will **drop by four**
    - The atomic number will **drop by two**
    - This will mean a **new element** will be **formed**

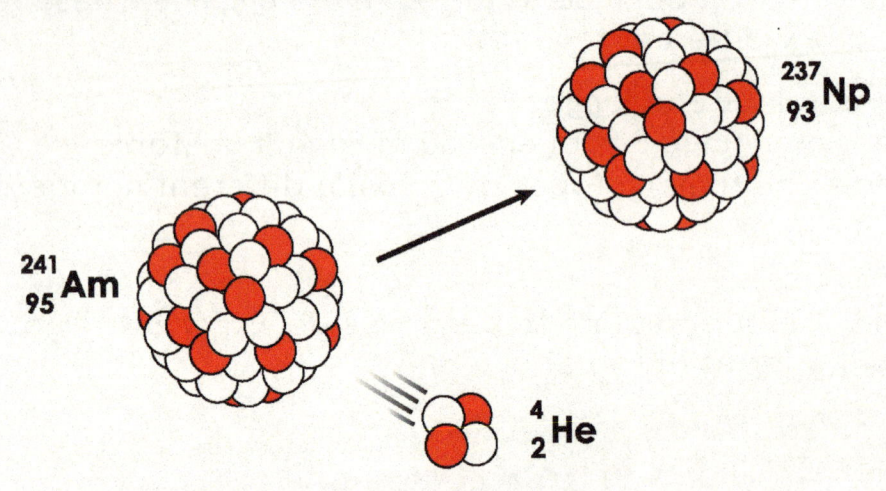

An example of alpha decay

Beta Decay - Also emitted from the nucleus

- Beta decay is a high energy electron emitted from the nucleus
    - This may seem contradictory as we said above electrons exist outside the nucleus
    - However what actually happens is a neutron changes into a proton and an electron as below
- Beta particles are smaller than alpha particles
    - They are more moderately more ionising. Less than alpha however more than gamma decay
    - They are fast moving
    - They have a greater penetrance than alpha particles but less than that of gamma particles

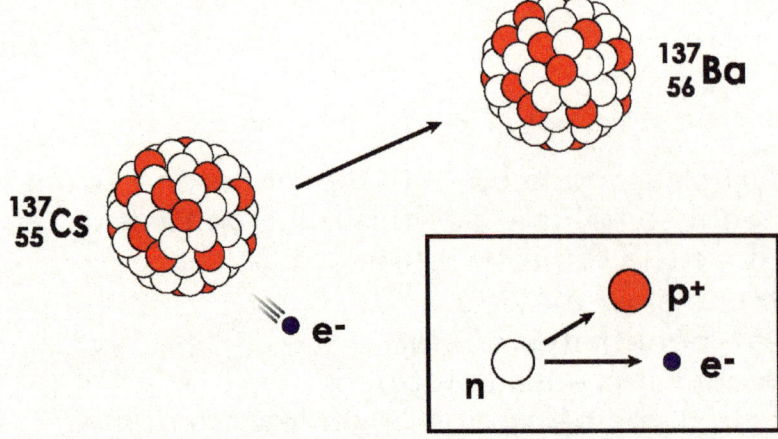

An example of beta decay. The insert shows the splitting of a neutron.

- The electron given off will have a mass of zero
- Therefore when an atom emits beta decay
    - The atomic number will increase
    - The atomic mass will stay the same (both protons and neutrons have the same relative mass)
- Beta decay will occur where atoms are unstable due to having more neutrons than protons.

Gamma Decay – A high energy photon.

- A photon is a high energy EM wave.
- In the form of gamma decay this takes the form of a gamma wave
- The process does not change the atomic number or mass
    - This is as only energy is emitted
- Therefore the element remains unchanged in structure
- Gamma rays are weakly ionising but highly penetrating

Deflection

When the different forms of decay pass through a magnetic field they all react differently. Some change direction, we call this deflection.

Alpha particles

- These are heavy particles (require more force to deflect)
- They are also positively charged (as they have two protons and no electrons)
- Overall they will be slightly deflected in one direction

Beta particles

- These particles are relatively very light compared to alpha particles (Require little force to deflect)
- They also have a negative charge
- Therefore on balance they are heavily deflected in the opposite direction to the alpha particles

Gamma rays

- They have no mass or charge
- Therefore they are not deflected in a magnetic field

P7 – Radioactivity

The properties of alpha, beta and gamma decay can be summarised below.

Radiation	Penetration	Ionising Power	Deflection in a Magnetic Field
Alpha	Weak	Strong	Moderately deflected
Beta	Moderate	Moderate	Strongly deflected in the opposing direction of alpha
Gamma	Strong	Weak	Not affected

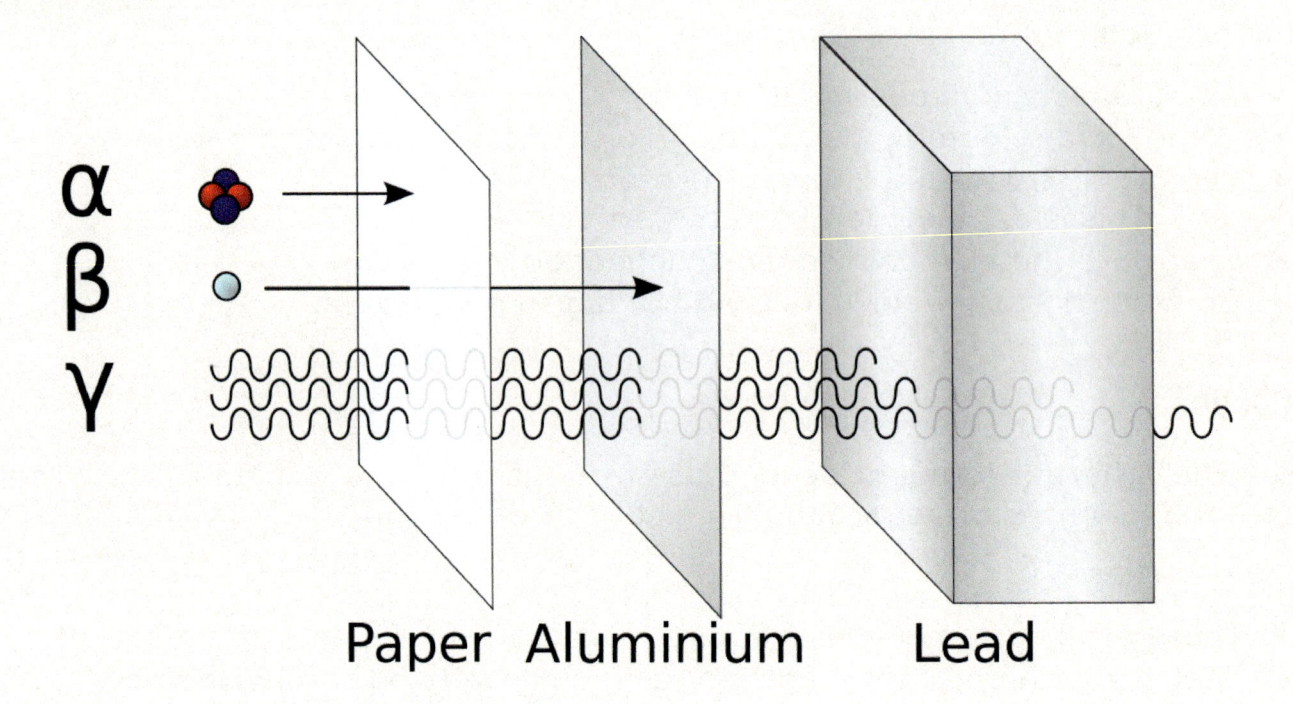

This diagram shoes the **penetrating power** of the various forms of radiation.

Radiation in Every Day Life

Radiation when used in the correct way can be very useful. Your BMAT specification requires you to understand some uses of radiation. Below I have outlines some common examples along with the risk and how this can be mitigated.

P7 – Radioactivity

Radiation Type	Beneficial Uses	Risks
Alpha Particles	Alpha particles are regularly used in smoke detectors. A tiny amount of decaying material (usually americium-241) is used. These ionised air molecules can carry current and complete a circuit. When smoke enters the alarm it prevents the air being ionised thus interrupting the circuit and triggering the alarm!	Alpha particles are highly ionising. If these are able to get close to tissue they can cause extensive damage to the DNA of the cells. However they also have a low penetrance. Therefore to get close enough to cause damage they usually need to be ingested or inhaled.
Beta Particles	Beta particles have a moderate penetrating power. Therefore they will be able to pass through materials of certain thickness. This property is used in manufacturing the asses the thickness of certain materials in quality control.	The fact that beta particles have a higher penetrating power means they pose a risk at greater distances than alpha particles. Therefore they need to be properly shielded from humans. However relative to alpha particles they are less ionising.
Gamma Rays	Gamma rays are used in medical radiotherapy. Due to their damaging nature gamma rays can be used to target and kill cancer cells. They do this by concentrating high doses on the cancer whilst trying to keep radiation doses to a minimum for healthy tissue.	Gamma rays have a high penetrance. Therefore we need thick barriers to avoid unintentional exposure (lead for example.) However it is weakly ionising so we are able to expose tissues to small amounts without large damage being done.

P7 - Radioactivity

Half Life

We define half life of radioactive material as:

"The time taken for 50% of a sample of radioactive material to decay"

Although radioactive decay is random we can average out the time taken for a nucleus to decay to get the half life. Although this does not mean we can predict exactly when the nucleus will decay.

Calculating the half life should be done as follows:

1. Find a level on the Y axis that can be easily halved. Record the corresponding time at this point
2. Take the half of your first Y axis reading and record the corresponding time.
3. The difference in time is your half life!
    a. Quite literally the time it taken for half the matter to decay

> 6Med Tip: Background radiation in calculations
>
> - You may see a reference to background radiation
>   o This is just radiation that the meter is picking up that does not come from the material you are trying to measure
> - We need to take account for this in our measurements.
> - Take the background radiation off any readings before calculating half life!

Knowledge Check

1) Which form of radiation is the most ionising? Which has the greatest penetrance?
2) What is the relative mass of an electron?
3) What is a beneficial use of alpha particles?

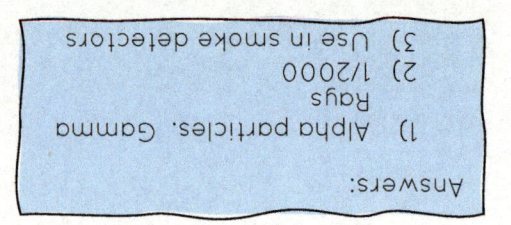

Answers:
1) Alpha particles, Gamma Rays
2) 1/2000
3) Use in smoke detectors

Section 2 Part 4: Mathematics.

M1 - Units

Most of this should be obvious! Review the following tables and make sure you are confident converting between related units:

Mass

Unit	Value
Milligram (mg)	$1000mg = 1g$
Gram (g)	$1g$
Kilogram (kg)	$1000g = 1kg$
Tonne (t)	$1000kg = 1t$

Length

Unit	Value
Millimetre (mm)	$1mm = 0.1cm$
Centimetre (cm)	$10mm = 1cm$
Metre (m)	$100cm = 1m$
Kilometre (km)	$1000m = 1km$

Area

Unit	Value
Square millimetres (mm^2)	$1mm^2 = 0.01cm^2$
Square centimetres (cm^2)	$1cm^2 = 100mm^2$
Square metres (m^2)	$1m^2 = 10,000cm^2$
Square kilometres (km^2)	$1km^2 = 1,000,000m^2$

Volume

Unit	Value
Millilitre (ml)	$1ml = 0.001L$
Litres (L)	$1L = 1000ml$
Cubic millimetres (mm^3)	$1mm^3 = 0.001ml$
Cubic centimetres (cm^3)	$1cm^3 = 1ml, 1cm^3 = 1000mm^3$
Cubic metres (m^3)	$1m^3 = 1000L, \ 1m^3 = 1,000,000cm^3$

Time

Unit	Value
Seconds	$1\ second$
Minutes	$1\ minte = 60\ seconds$
Hours	$1\ hour = 60\ minutes$
Days	$1\ day = 24\ hours$
Weeks	$1\ week = 7\ days$
Months	$28, 29, 30\ or\ 31\ days$
Years	$1\ year = 12\ months = 365\ days$ $Leap\ year = 366\ days$

Compound Units

- This refers to units that are the combination of more than one unit. They can be determined by the formula for the given unit. Examples include:
    - Speed
        - Formula: $speed = \frac{distance}{time}$
        - Standard unit $= ms^{-1} = \frac{m}{s}$
    - Density
        - Formula: $density = \frac{mass}{volume}$
        - Standard unit $= kgm^{-3} = \frac{kg}{m^3}$
    - Pressure
        - Formula: $pressure = \frac{force}{area}$
        - Standard unit = pascal $Nm^{-2} = \frac{N}{m^2}$
- To convert between different compound units, you need to **convert each unit separately**:

- Express $20 gcm^{-3}$ in the units kgm^{-3}
    1. We need to apply conversion factors for g to kg and cm^3 to m^3. If we multiply by these conversion factors, we will reach our desired unit:
    2. $20 \frac{g}{cm^3} \left(\frac{kg}{g}\right) \left(\frac{cm}{m}\right)^3$
    3. $\frac{kg}{g} = \frac{1}{1000}$
    4. $\frac{cm^3}{m^3} = \frac{1000000}{1}$
    5. $\frac{20g}{cm^3} \left(\frac{1kg}{1000g}\right) \left(\frac{1000000 cm^3}{1 m^3}\right) = \frac{20000 kg}{m^3}$
    6. Therefore, the answer is $20,000 kgm^{-3}$

6Med Tip: Learn this table to convert between different units with the given prefixes:

Prefix	Meaning	Scientific notation
Tera-	1,000,000,000,000	10^{12}
Giga-	1,000,000,000	10^{9}
Mega-	1,000,000	10^{6}
Kilo-	1,000	10^{3}
Hecto-	100	10^{2}
Deka-	10	10^{1}
	1	10^{0}
Deci-	0.1	10^{-1}
Centi-	0.01	10^{-2}
Milli-	0.001	10^{-3}
Micro	0.000001	10^{-6}
Nano-	0.000000001	10^{-9}
Pico-	0.000000000001	10^{-12}

M2 - Number

Order of operations

Remember that the order you perform operations in a calculation is important:

$$3 \times 4 + 4^2 \div 2 + 5 \times 2 - 1 = ???$$

You probably know that this kind of calculation becomes much more understandable if it contains brackets:

$$(3 \times 4) + (4^2 \div 2) + (5 \times 2) - 1 =$$

But *where* the brackets are placed also makes a difference:

$$3 \times (4 + 4^2) \div 2 + 5 \times (2 - 1) =$$

Be sure to remember **BIDMAS** to make sure that you follow the normal convention for priority in calculations:

B – Brackets	Any calculation involving terms in brackets should be performed first! (Remember to use BIDMAS rules within each set of brackets)
I – Indices	Then calculate any terms involving indices (use index rules below)
D – Division	Division and multiplication have the same priority and should be performed next, work from left to right for calculations involving both multiplication and division
M – Multiplication	
A – Addition	Addition and subtraction also have the same priority. Perform any remaining addition/subtraction from left to right.
S – Subtraction	

Review the above examples and write an answer for each.

Answers: 1. 29 2. 29 3. 35

M2 - Number

Fractions:

You need to be comfortable using fractions – not just in the maths section but they come up all over Section 2 in the other science questions. Check you can perform these fraction operations:

1. Simplify $\frac{45}{125}$
2. $\frac{2}{5} + \frac{3}{7} =$
3. $\frac{1}{4} \div \frac{5}{6} =$
4. $\frac{3}{8} \times \frac{1}{9} =$
5. $\frac{5}{4} - \frac{5}{12} =$
6. Find $\frac{7}{20}$ of £120
7. Express $5\frac{3}{4}$ as an improper fraction
8. Express $\frac{65}{7}$ as a mixed number

Answers: 1. $\frac{9}{25}$ 2. $\frac{29}{35}$ 3. $\frac{3}{10}$ 4. $\frac{1}{24}$ 5. $\frac{5}{6}$ 6. £42 7. $\frac{23}{4}$ 8. $9\frac{2}{7}$

You also need to be able to convert between decimals and fractions – converting from fractions to decimals is important when writing numbers in standard form (see below) but fractions are normally much easier to work with! Remember that fractions can be converted from *terminating* or *recurring* decimals:

- to convert a terminating decimal to a fraction express the decimal as a fraction over a power of 10 then cancel down:
    - $0.4 = \frac{4}{10} = \frac{2}{5}$
    - $0.44 = \frac{44}{100} = \frac{11}{25}$

- to covert a recurring decimal to a fraction:
    o Find the length of the repeating sequence, multiply by a power of 10 to move 1 repeating sequence past the decimal point, subtract the original decimal from the multiple of 10 and divide:
        - $x = 4.7777777777777...$
        - $10x = 47.7777777777...$
        - $10x - x = 47.777777777... - 4.777777777...$
        - $9x = 43$
        - $x = \frac{43}{9} = 4\frac{7}{9}$

Alternatively you could find $0.7777777..$ as a fraction ($\frac{7}{9}$) and replace the 4 to express as a mixed number: $4\frac{7}{9}$

6Med Tip: You can determine whether a fraction will give a terminating or recurring decimal by checking the denominator – if the denominator has prime factors (see below!) of *only* 2 or 5 it will give a terminating decimal, all others will give a recurring decimal.

Prime numbers

Prime numbers are numbers greater than one whose only factors are one and itself.

- The first 4 prime numbers are 2, 3, 5 and 7 (1 is not a prime number!)
- All prime numbers (apart from 2 and 5) end in a 1, 3, 7 or 9

> **6Med Tip:** To work out whether a number is a prime number:
> - it must end in 1, 3, 7, or 9
> - find an approximation for the square root
> - the number will not divide by any of the prime numbers below the value of the square root

Any number can be expressed as a product of its prime factors, e.g.:

- $36 = 2 \times 2 \times 3 \times 3 = 2^2 \times 3^2$
- $124 = 2 \times 2 \times 31 = 2^2 \times 31$

This is helpful when you need to find the highest common factor or the lowest common multiple.

Highest common factor and lowest common multiple

Being able to quickly find a highest common factor or lowest common multiple is really important in the BMAT – not just for the maths section but for any question where you may be dealing with pattern recognition, for example in section 1 problem solving questions.

There are two principal techniques which can help you with this, we've broken them down into a handy table on the next page. We recommend you take the time to study and learn both of these, as they can really help across multiple sections of the BMAT:

The Complete BMAT Specification Explained

M2 – Number

Highest common factor	Lowest common multiple
1. Express the numbers as a product of their prime factors: - $140 = 2 \times 2 \times 5 \times 7 = 2^2 \times 5 \times 7$ - $84 = 2 \times 2 \times 3 \times 7 = 2^2 \times 3 \times 7$ 2. Find the lowest power for *each common* prime factor - common prime factors are **2** and **7** - lowest power of **2** is 2^2 - lowest power of **7** is **7** 3. Multiply the lowest power for each prime factor to find the highest common factor: - $2^2 \times 7 = 28$ - Therefore, the highest common factor for 140 and 84 is 28	1. Express the numbers as a product of their prime factors: - $15 = 3 \times 5$ - $24 = 2 \times 2 \times 2 \times 3 = 2^3 \times 3$ 2. Find the highest power for *every* prime factor: - prime factors are: 2, 3, and 5 - highest power of 2 is 2^3 - highest power of 3 is 3 - highest power of 5 is 5 3. Multiply the highest power of each prime factor to find the lowest common multiple: - $2^3 \times 3 \times 5 = 120$ - Therefore, the lowest common multiple for 15 and 24 is 120

Index laws

It is typical for a BMAT maths question to try and overwhelm you with positive, negative and fractional powers. Practise these index rules to stay on top of it:

Operation	Rule
Any number^0 is always **1**	$x^0 = 1$
1 to any power is **1**!	$1^x = 1$
Multiplication	$x^a \times x^b = x^{a+b}$
Division	$x^a \div x^b = x^{a-b}$
Raising one power to another	$(x^a)^b = x^{a \times b}$
Raising fractions to a power	$\left(\dfrac{x}{y}\right)^a = \dfrac{x^a}{y^a}$
Negative powers	$x^{-a} = \dfrac{1}{x^a}$ $x^{-1} = \dfrac{1}{x}$ is known as the 'reciprocal' of x. Any number multiplied by its reciprocal = 1.
Fractional powers	$x^{\frac{a}{b}} = (x^a)^{\frac{1}{b}} = \left(x^{\frac{1}{b}}\right)^a = \sqrt[b]{x^a} = \left(\sqrt[b]{x}\right)^a$ $x^{\frac{1}{2}} = \sqrt{x}$ $x^{\frac{1}{3}} = \sqrt[3]{x}$

The Complete BMAT Specification Explained

M2 - Number

Standard Index Form

Writing numbers in standard form is a practical way of dealing with very large or small numbers. Any number can be expressed in the form $A \times 10^n$ where $1 \leq A < 10$ and n is an integer.

Express the following numbers in standard form:

1. 68000000
2. 0.000000073
3. $\frac{1}{250}$
4. $\frac{9}{150}$

Answers: 1. 6.8×10^7 2. 7.3×10^{-8} 3. $\frac{1}{250} = 0.004 = 4 \times 10^{-3}$ 4. $\frac{9}{150} = 0.06 = 6 \times 10^{-2}$

You need to be able to perform operations using numbers in standard form. Remember these rules:

Operation	Rule
Addition & Subtraction	You can add/subtract numbers in standard form if they are expressed to the same power of 10, i.e.: n is the same: $$5.1 \times 10^4 + 3.0 \times 10^2$$ $$= 5.1 \times 10^4 + 0.03 \times 10^4$$ $$= 5.13 \times 10^4$$ $$1.43 \times 10^7 - 5.2 \times 10^6$$ $$= 1.43 \times 10^7 - 0.52 \times 10^7$$ $$= 0.91 \times 10^7$$ $$= 9.1 \times 10^6$$
Multiplication	With multiplication, simply multiply the two numbers together and the two powers together using the multiplication index rule: $$(3.5 \times 10^4) \times (1.2 \times 10^6)$$ $$= (3.5 \times 1.2) \times (10^4 \times 10^6)$$ $$= 4.2 \times 10^{10}$$
Division	Similar to multiplication, divide the two numbers and use the division index rule for the powers: $$(5.6 \times 10^4) \div (2.5 \times 10^7)$$ $$= (5.6 \div 2.5) \times (10^4 \div 10^7)$$ $$= 2.24 \times 10^{-3}$$
Powers	The power distributes to the number and the power: $$(3.0 \times 10^{-2})^2$$ $$= (3.0)^2 \times (10^{-2})^2$$ $$= 9.0 \times 10^{-4}$$

The Complete BMAT Specification Explained

M2 – Number

Irrational numbers

Square roots and cube roots commonly result in irrational numbers – i.e. never ending, non-repeating decimals that cannot be expressed as fractions.

Surds are expressions using irrational square roots which allow you to perform calculations involving irrational numbers to express an exact number.

Once again, there are some important rules to remember when performing calculations involving surds:

Operation	Rule
Multiplication	$\sqrt{x} \times \sqrt{y} = \sqrt{x \times y}$
Division	$\dfrac{\sqrt{x}}{\sqrt{y}} = \sqrt{\dfrac{x}{y}}$
Addition/Subtraction	You can only add surds when the number inside the root is the same: $$a\sqrt{x} + b\sqrt{x} = (a+b)\sqrt{x}$$ You CANNOT add surds when the numbers inside the roots are different: $$\sqrt{x} + \sqrt{y} \neq \sqrt{x+y}$$
Simplification	This involves recognising when the number inside the root can be expressed as a square number multiplied by another factor: $$\sqrt{12} = \sqrt{4 \times 3} = \sqrt{4} \times \sqrt{3} = 2\sqrt{3}$$

The Complete BMAT Specification Explained

M2 – Number

Rationalising the denominator	Another common BMAT question! When a surd is present in the denominator, *rationalising* the denominator involves multiplying both the numerator and the denominator by that surd: $$\frac{3}{\sqrt{7}} = \frac{3 \times \sqrt{7}}{\sqrt{7} \times \sqrt{7}} = \frac{3\sqrt{7}}{7}$$ This becomes more complicated when the denominator involves more than one term. Notice that the sign before the surd between the terms is the opposite to the original to ensure that the surd is cancelled out when the brackets are expanded: $$\frac{6}{5+\sqrt{3}} = \frac{6(5-\sqrt{3})}{(5+\sqrt{3})(5-\sqrt{3})} = \frac{30-6\sqrt{3}}{25-3} = \frac{15-3\sqrt{3}}{11}$$ $$\frac{1}{\sqrt{15}-\sqrt{7}} = \frac{(\sqrt{15}+\sqrt{7})}{(\sqrt{15}-\sqrt{7})(\sqrt{15}+\sqrt{7})} = \frac{\sqrt{15}+\sqrt{7}}{15-7} = \frac{\sqrt{15}+\sqrt{7}}{8}$$ Experiment with what would happen if you did not change the sign before the surd in each example. If you are unsure how to expand brackets turn to the algebra section!

π is also an irrational number which comes up a lot in geometry and almost always is much better left expressed as 'π' rather than its decimal form (**3.14159265359 ....**). Find the exact answer to the following questions:

1. Find the exact area of a circle with radius **3cm** (review geometry section if you need a reminder on circle formulae)
2. $\frac{15\pi \times 2\pi}{4\pi^2} + \frac{2}{\pi}$

Answers: 1. 9π 2. $\frac{15\pi+4}{2\pi}$

M2 – Number

Approximation and rounding

- When rounding to a specified number of decimal points or significant figures, simply identify the position of the last digit:
  - If the digit to the right of the last digit is 5 or more, round up the last digit
  - If the digit to the right of the last digit is 4 or less leave the last digit as it is

> **6Med Tip:** For significant figures:
>
> 1. The first significant figure is the leftmost number which is not a zero
> 2. All other significant figures follow immediately after the first
> 3. If your rounding involved changing a number to a zero, make sure you still give the answer to the required number of significant figures:
>   - 0.000269847 rounded to 3 significant figures = 0.000270

Practice questions

1. Round 4.36718 to 3 decimal places
2. Express 54.758 to 1 decimal place
3. Round 0.012857 to 3 significant figures
4. Round 100.0178 to 4 significant figures
5. Round 0.00462 to 3 decimal places

Answers: 1. 4.367 2. 54.8 3. 0.0129 4. 100.0 5. 0.005

Sometimes you are given a rounded number and are required to find the **upper and lower bounds**. The upper and lower bounds can be determined by finding half the value of the rounded unit, for example:

- A wooden plank is cut to $2.3m$ to the nearest $0.1m$
- The rounded unit is $0.1m$ and half the rounded unit is $0.05m$
- The real length of the plank could be $0.05m$ above or below $2.3m$
- $2.25 \leq l < 2.35$
- Think about a square made from 4 of these planks of length l where $l = 2.3m$ to the nearest $0.1m$. The perimeter of the square could be between $4 \times 2.25 = 9m$ and $4 \times 2.35 = 9.4m$

The Complete BMAT Specification Explained

M2 – Number

Knowledge Check

Question 1: Find the highest common factor and lowest common multiple of $27, 45$ and 126

Question 2: Evaluate: $\sqrt{\dfrac{6\times 10^4}{(3\times 10^{-2})^2}} + \sqrt{1.6 \times 10^3}$

Question 3: If $x = 3.4 \times 10^5$ and $y = 8.5 \times 10^{-2}$, what is the value of $\dfrac{x}{2y}$

Answers:

1. HCF = 9, LCM = 1890. As product of primes: $27 = 3 \times 3 \times 3$, $45 = 3 \times 3 \times 5$, $126 = 2 \times 3 \times 3 \times 7$. HCF = $3^2 = 9$, LCM = $2 \times 3^3 \times 5 \times 7 = 1890$

2. $\sqrt{\dfrac{6\times 10^4}{9\times 10^{-4}}} + \sqrt{16 \times 10^2} = \sqrt{\dfrac{2}{3}} \times 4 \times 10^4 + \dfrac{\sqrt{6}}{3} = 40 + \dfrac{\sqrt{6}}{3} = \dfrac{1}{3}(\sqrt{6} + 120)$; $\dfrac{\sqrt{6}+120}{3}$

3. 2×10^6 ; $\dfrac{3.4\times 10^5}{(2)(8.5\times 10^{-2})} = \dfrac{3.4\times 10^5}{1.7\times 10^{-1}} = 2 \times 10^6$

M3 - Ratio and Proportion

Ratio

- Ratios let you express how one quantity relates to another.

Example: If a jar contains x red pens and y blue pens, the ratio of red to blue pens is $x:y$.

- Like fractions, ratios can be cancelled down to their simplest form – just remember to divide both sides by the same number.

Example: If there are 9 red and 12 blue pens the ratio of red to blue pens is $9:12 = 3:4$.

- You can also express ratios as fractions (see **Proportion** section below)

Example: The ratio of $3:4$ ($x:y$) tells you there are $\frac{3}{4}\left(\frac{x}{y}\right)$ as many red pens in the jar as blue pens. If there were 20 blue pens in the jar, there would be $20 \times \frac{3}{4} = 15$ red pens.

> **6Med Tip:** It is often most useful to reduce a ratio to the form $1:n$ or $n:1$.

- You might be given a question which tells you how a quantity is divided into two or more parts by a ratio.
- If a total quantity Q, is divided by the ratio $x:y$, then $\frac{Q}{x+y}$ tells you the value of 'one unit'. Therefore, $\frac{Q}{x+y}(x)$ will give you the value of the x component and $\frac{Q}{x+y}(y)$ will give you the value of the y component.

Example: A recipe requires $1kg$ flour to be split between three bowls in the ratio $8:5:3$.

(turn over...)

1. Sum the parts: $8 + 5 + 3 = 16$
2. Divide the total: $\frac{1000}{16} = \frac{125}{2}$ (= value of one unit)
3. Multiply each part by one unit:
   - $8 \times \frac{125}{2} = 500g$
   - $5 \times \frac{125}{2} = \frac{625}{2}g = 312.5g$
   - $3 \times \frac{125}{2} = \frac{375}{2}g = 187.5g$

You can check you have the right result by making sure that the three parts sum to give the original quantity.

- Alternatively, you might be given one part of the ratio and asked to find the other:

Example: A fruit juice is made by mixing water and concentrate in the ratio $7:2$. If $1.4L$ of water is used, how much concentrate is needed?

- For these questions, you again must recognise that the total quantity (in this case the total volume) is made up by the sum of the ratio's parts ($7 + 2 = 9$).
- Here, $1.4L$ represents $\frac{7}{9}$ of the total volume and the concentrate makes up the remaining $\frac{2}{9}$.
- The quantity of concentrate required is therefore $\frac{1400ml}{7} \times 2 = 400ml$

- Ratios are useful in geometry to describe the relationship between *similar* shapes:
    - If a triangle is similar to another triangle (all the angles are the same) but the sides are a different length by scale factor x, then the area of the triangle will be x^2 times the area of the smaller triangle.

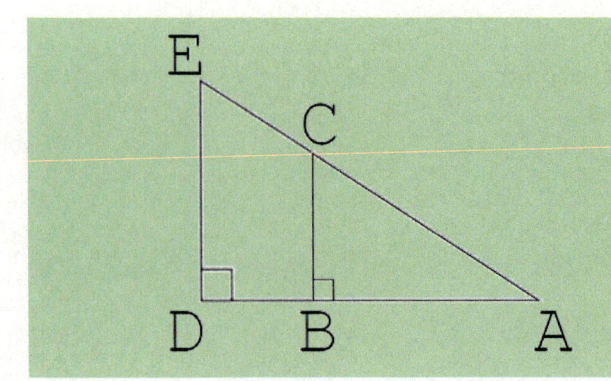

Importantly, for right-angled triangles:

$$\sin(A) = \frac{CB}{CA} = \frac{ED}{EA}$$

$$\cos(A) = \frac{BA}{CA} = \frac{DA}{EA}$$

$$\tan(A) = \frac{CB}{BA} = \frac{ED}{DA}$$

The Complete BMAT Specification Explained
M3 – Ratio and Proportion

- If a shape, A, has sides larger than another shape, B, by a magnitude of scale factor x (given the shapes are similar):
    - The surface area of A will be x^2 times larger than B
    - The volume of A will be x^3 times larger than B

Percentage

- 'Percentage' means 'number of parts per hundred'.
    - 50% means 50 parts per 100 which is equivalent to $\frac{50}{100} = \frac{1}{2} = 0.5$

> **6Med Tip:** To convert between percentages, fractions, and decimals:
>
> Percentages are be written as fractions by writing the percentage over 100 and cancelling down: $48\% = \frac{48}{100} = \frac{12}{25}$
>
> Percentages are written as decimals by dividing by 100: $37.5\% = 0.375$

- To express one quantity as a percentage of another:
    - Divide that quantity by the other and multiply by 100
    - *Example:* Give 3cm as a percentage of 1.2m: $\frac{3}{120} \times 100 = 2.5\%$

- To find a given percentage of a quantity:
    - Divide the percentage by 100 and multiply by the quantity:
    - *Example:* Find 20% of £4.50: $0.2 \times £4.50 = £0.90$.
    - *Example:* Find 130% of £60: $1.3 \times £60 = £78$.

- To give a change in a quantity as a percentage: *percentage change* = $\frac{change}{original} \times 100$
    - *Example:* A car decreases in value from £5,000 to £4,250. What is the percentage change in the value of the car? Change = £5000 − £4250 = £750. Percentage change = $\frac{£750}{£5000} \times 100 = 15\%$ decrease.

- You might be given a question where you need to work out the *original value* following a percentage change:
    - *Example:* A house increases in value by 20% to £288,000. Find the value of the house before the rise: £288,000 represents 120% of the original value, therefore the original value is $\frac{£288,000}{120} \times 100 = £240,000$.

Growth and decay

Simple interest is where the interest added (% increase) is calculated on the initial amount and that amount added is the same each year. When interest is *compounded*, that means that the interest added (% increase) is calculated on the latest year. Therefore, the amount added changes each year. Simple and compound interest can confuse a lot of people – but it is simple(!) if you remember these 2 formulae:

For simple interest: $N = N_0(1 + \left(\frac{r}{100}\right)t)$

For compound interest: $N = N_0\left(1 + \left(\frac{r}{100}\right)\right)^t$

N = final amount

N_0 = initial amount

r = % change per unit time

Examples:

1. A bank offers **1.5%** simple interest on a savings account. If you deposit £3,000, how much interest will you earn in 3 years?
- $N = (£3000)\left(1 + \left(\frac{1.5}{100}\right)(3)\right) = £3,135$, therefore **£135** earned in interest.

2. Another bank offers **1%** compound interest on a savings account. If you deposit £3,000, how much interest will you earn in 3 years?
- $N = (£3000)\left(1 + \left(\frac{1}{100}\right)\right)^3 = £3,090.90$, therefore **£90.90** earned in interest

The formulae above do not just apply to 'interest' in financial context but also can be applied for any situations with simple or compound growth:

Example: A microbiologist counts 100 cells in a sample of bacteria. They increase in number by 20% each day. How many bacteria cells will there be after 4 days?

- Using the compound formula: $N = 100\left(1 + \left(\frac{20}{100}\right)\right)^4 = 207$ cells (3 *sig. fig.*)

Proportion

A proportion is an equality of two ratios. They are helpful when you need to calculate unknown quantities.

> **6Med Tip:** the relationship between equivalent ratios and proportion is given by:
>
> $$a:b = c:d \qquad \frac{a}{b} = \frac{c}{d}$$

The Complete BMAT Specification Explained

M3 – Ratio and Proportion

Example: There are 36 dogs at an animal care centre. If the ratio of *dogs: cats* is 9:5, how many cats are there?

$$9:5 = 36:x \qquad \frac{9}{5} = \frac{36}{x} \qquad x = 5 \times \frac{36}{9} = 20 \text{ cats.}$$

You need to understand the difference between *direct* proportion and *inverse* proportion. The relationship between 2 variables, x and y, can be described algebraically depending on the nature of the relationship. Compare the formulae in the table below (a numerical constant is represented by the letter k).

	Direct proportion	Inverse proportion
Formula	$y = kx$	$y = \dfrac{k}{x}$
Explanation	As one variable (y or x) increases, the other increases. The ratio $\dfrac{x}{y}$ is the same for all pairs of values x and y.	As one variable increases, the other decreases. The product xy is the same for all pairs of values x and y.
Graph	(linear increasing graph)	(inverse decay graph)

Check your knowledge!

Question 1: Which one of the following equations shows inverse variation?

a. $x = 4y$
b. $y = \dfrac{x}{7}$
c. $y = 4 + x$
d. $x \times y = 6$
e. $\dfrac{1}{y} = \dfrac{1}{4} \times \dfrac{1}{x}$
f. $\dfrac{1}{4}y = x$

Question 2: Andrew invests £3000 at 2% rate of return compounded annually. How much interest will he have earned after 2 years?

a. £3120.00
b. £3121.20
c. £121.20
d. £120.00
e. £60

The Complete BMAT Specification Explained

M3 – Ratio and Proportion

Question 3: Simon is planning a walk around a lake. On his map, the area of the lake is $20cm^2$. If the map is drawn to a scale of 1:25000, calculate the area of the real lake.

a. $1.25km^2$
b. $125km^2$
c. $0.625km^2$
d. $5km^2$
e. $1.25m^2$
f. $500m^2$

Question 4: Julie and Leah share some money in the ratio $3:8$. Leah gets £35 more than Julie. How much did Julie receive?

a. £56
b. £7
c. £77
d. £21
e. £14

Question 5: I buy a new phone in a sale. The original price of the phone was reduced by **10%** before the sale, and then this price was reduced **15%** during the sale. By what percentage has the original price of the phone been reduced when I buy it?

a. 25%
b. 20%
c. 23.5%
d. 15%
e. 17.5

Answers:

1. D. – the product of xy is constant and the equation rearranges to $y = 6/x$
2. C £121.20 - a = total amount after 2 years simple interest, b = total amount after 2 years compound, d= total simple interest after 2 years, e=total simpe interest after 1 year
3. A – 1cm:25000cm = 1cm:0.25km, finding area so $1cm^2 : 0.0625km^2$, area on map = $20cm^2$ so $20cm^2$: $1.25km^2$
4. D - $\frac{J}{3} = \frac{J+35}{7}$, $7J = 3J + 35$, $\frac{J+35}{7} = \frac{J}{3}$, $8J = 3J + 105, 5J = 105, J = 21$
5. 23.5% - Let n = original price. After first reduction: price = $0.9n$. After further reduction in sale: price = $(0.85)(0.9n) = 0.765n$. Therefore change = $n - 0.765n = 0.235n$. Percentage change = $\frac{0.235n}{n} \times 100 = 23.5\%$

M4 - Algebra

Basic algebra:

Algebraic expressions follow all the same rules as numerical expressions – review the Numbers section if you need to refresh your knowledge on order of operations, index rules or irrational numbers. However, algebraic expressions involve variables rather than representing a fixed definite value.

> **6Med Tip:** Understand the difference between an *equation* and an *identity*:
> - An equation is conditionally true for *specific* values of a variable:
>   - $x + 5 = 8$ is true *only* for $x = 3$ but not true for any other values of x
>   - $y = 2x + 5$ is an equation true for all points on the line, but not true for any value outside the line (e.g., $x = 3, y = 2$)
> - An identity is an expression which is always true for *all* values of a variable
>   - $3x + 15 = 3(x + 5)$, or $(x + 1)^2 = x^2 + 2x + 1$

Make sure you can use the following rules which apply to algebraic notation:

Rule	Explanation
Commutative law	For addition and multiplication, terms can be reordered: $x + y = y + x$ $x \times y = y \times x$ Note: you cannot reorder expressions that involve a mixture of addition and multiplication (like $x + y \times z$) you must use BIDMAS.
Associative law	For addition and multiplication, terms can associate differently: $(x + y) + z = x + (y + z)$ $(x \times y) \times z = x \times (y \times z)$
Distributive law	When a sum $(y + z)$ is multiplied by a factor x, the factor is distributed to each part of the sum: $x(y + z) = (x \times y) + (x \times z)$
Multiplication	$x \times y = xy$
Addition	$x + x + x + x = 4x$
Division	$x \div y = \dfrac{x}{y}$
Powers	$x \times x \times x = x^3$

The Complete BMAT Specification Explained

M4 – Algebra

Review the following algebraic procedures then use the practice questions to make sure you have it!

Procedure	Example
Collect like terms	Applying the commutative law: $$5x + 3y + 7x - 5y = 5x + 7x + 3y - 5y$$ $$= 12x - 2y$$
Take out common factors	Using the above example, recognise that 12 and 2 both divide by 2: $$12x - 2y = 2 \times (6x) + 2 \times (-y))$$ $$= 2(6x - y)$$
Expanding brackets	When a single term is multiplied across a bracket remember the distributive law (This is the reverse of taking out common factors!): $$3(21 - xz) = 63 - 3xz$$ When you need to expand the product of two or more binomials remember that *each* term must be distributed across the brackets: $$(w + x)(y + z) = wy + wz + xy + xz$$ This is particularly important when dealing with quadratic expressions (see below): $$(x + 4)(x + 2) = x^2 + 6x + 8$$

> 6Med Tip: Use the 'FOIL' or 'crab' techniques to make sure you expand binomials correctly $(w + x)(y + x)$:
>
> - FOIL = first, outside, inside, last
>   o Take the sum of the products of the first term of each bracket, the outside terms, the inside terms and finally the last terms
> - CRAB = drawing out the FOIL mnemonic leaves you with a diagram looking like a crab pincer:
>
> $$(w+x)(y+z)$$

The Complete BMAT Specification Explained

M4 – Algebra

Practice questions:

1. Which of the following is the correct expansion of $(12x - y)(2x + 3)$?
    a. $12x^2 + 3y + 2xy + 36x$
    b. $24x^2 - 3y$
    c. $24x^2 + 36x - 2xy - 3y$
    d. $24x^2 + 34x - 3$
    e. $24x + 36xy - 2y + 3y^2$
2. Find the value of $x^3 + 3y^{\frac{1}{2}}$ for $x = 3$ and $y = 4$.
3. If $15x + 20y = 10$, what is the value of $6x + 8y$?
4. Solve for x: $\sqrt{\frac{106}{11} - \frac{x+4}{2x+5}} = 3$

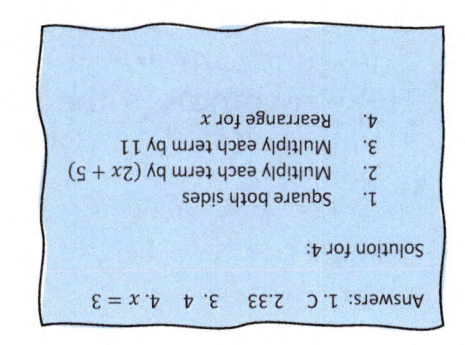

Solution for 4:
1. Square both sides
2. Multiply each term by $(2x + 5)$
3. Multiply each term by 11
4. Rearrange for x

Answers: 1. C 2. 33 3. 4 4. $x = 3$

Formulae

Formulae are algebraic expressions involving more than one variable. They describe relationships between variables. For example, the formula for the area, A, of a rectangle with height h and length l can be written:

$$A = hl$$

You need to be able to rearrange formulae to change the *subject* of the formula. **Remember that whatever you do to one side of the equals sign you must do the same to the other side.** For example, to make h the subject of the formula for the area of a rectangle you can divide both sides of the expression by l:

$$\frac{A}{l} = h$$

Practise rearranging these formulae:

1. Make I the subject of the formula: $P = I^2R$
2. Make m the subject of the formula $KE = \frac{1}{2}mv^2$
3. Make S the subject of the formula $L = 4 + \sqrt{5(5-S)^2 + 2}$

Answers: 1. $I = \sqrt{\frac{P}{R}}$ 2. $m = \frac{2KE}{v^2}$ 3. $S = 5 - \sqrt{\frac{(L-4)^2 - 2}{5}}$

Solution for 3: $L - 4 = \sqrt{5(5-S)^2 + 2}$, $(L-4)^2 = 5(5-S)^2 + 2$, $\frac{(L-4)^2 - 2}{5} = (5-S)^2$, $\sqrt{\frac{(L-4)^2 - 2}{5}} = 5 - S$, $S = 5 - \sqrt{\frac{(L-4)^2 - 2}{5}}$

M4 – Algebra

Quadratic equations

The standard format for quadratic equations is $ax^2 + bx + c = 0$. There are several methods for solving quadratic equations. You need to know:

- How to **factorise** quadratic equations.
- The **quadratic formula** and how to use it.
- How to **complete the square**.

Factorising quadratic expressions means rewriting them as a product of 2 brackets:

- Aways make sure the equation is written in the standard format above.
- When $a = 1$:
    o Write 2 brackets with x as the first term: $(x \quad)(x \quad)$
    o Find 2 numbers which multiply to give c and sum to give b.
    o Arrange the numbers in the brackets and check they expand to give the original equation.
- When $a \neq 1$:
    o You need to be more careful to make sure the brackets expand correctly to give the original equation.
    o You can either work by trial and error, factor out the a, or use the quadratic formula (see below).
- When the factorised equation $= 0$, to solve for x find the value of x for each bracket to $= 0$:
    o $x^2 + 5x + 6 = 0$
    o $(x + 2)(x + 3) = 0$
    o Therefore, $x = -2$, or $x = -3$.

The quadratic formula

The solutions for any quadratic equation in the form $ax^2 + bx + c = 0$ are given by the quadratic formula:

$$x = \frac{-b \pm \sqrt{b^2 - 4ac}}{2a}$$

6Med Tip: make sure you can use the quadratic formula from memory and practise using it to solve quadratic equations

Completing the square

- Always rearrange the equation into the form $ax^2 + bx + c = 0$ where $a = 1$.
- Write out a bracket $\left(x + \frac{b}{2}\right)^2$.
- Multiply out the bracket and compare with the original equation to make them equivalent.

- *Example:*
$$3x^2 + 6x - 18 = 0$$
$$x^2 + 2x - 6 = 0$$
$$(x + 1)^2 - 7 = 0$$
$$(x + 1)^2 = 7$$
$$(x + 1) = \pm\sqrt{7}$$
$$x = -1 \pm \sqrt{7}$$

Expanding $(x + 1)^2$ gives $x^2 + 2x + 1$, so we need to add a -7 to make this equivalent to $x^2 + 2x - 6$

Check this result gives the same result as using the quadratic formula

Difference of two squares

Every polynomial that is the difference of two squares, i.e., $x^2 - y^2$, is factorised in the following way: $x^2 - y^2 = (x + y)(x - y)$. When you expand $(x + y)(x - y)$ you will see that the result is $x^2 - y^2$. Be careful not to not to apply this principle to expressions like $x^2 + 25$. It must be the *difference* of two squares. This principle is useful when rationalising a denominator with a surd (see our section on the Number part of the BMAT spec).

Graphs

Try and match the following graphs with the correct equation:

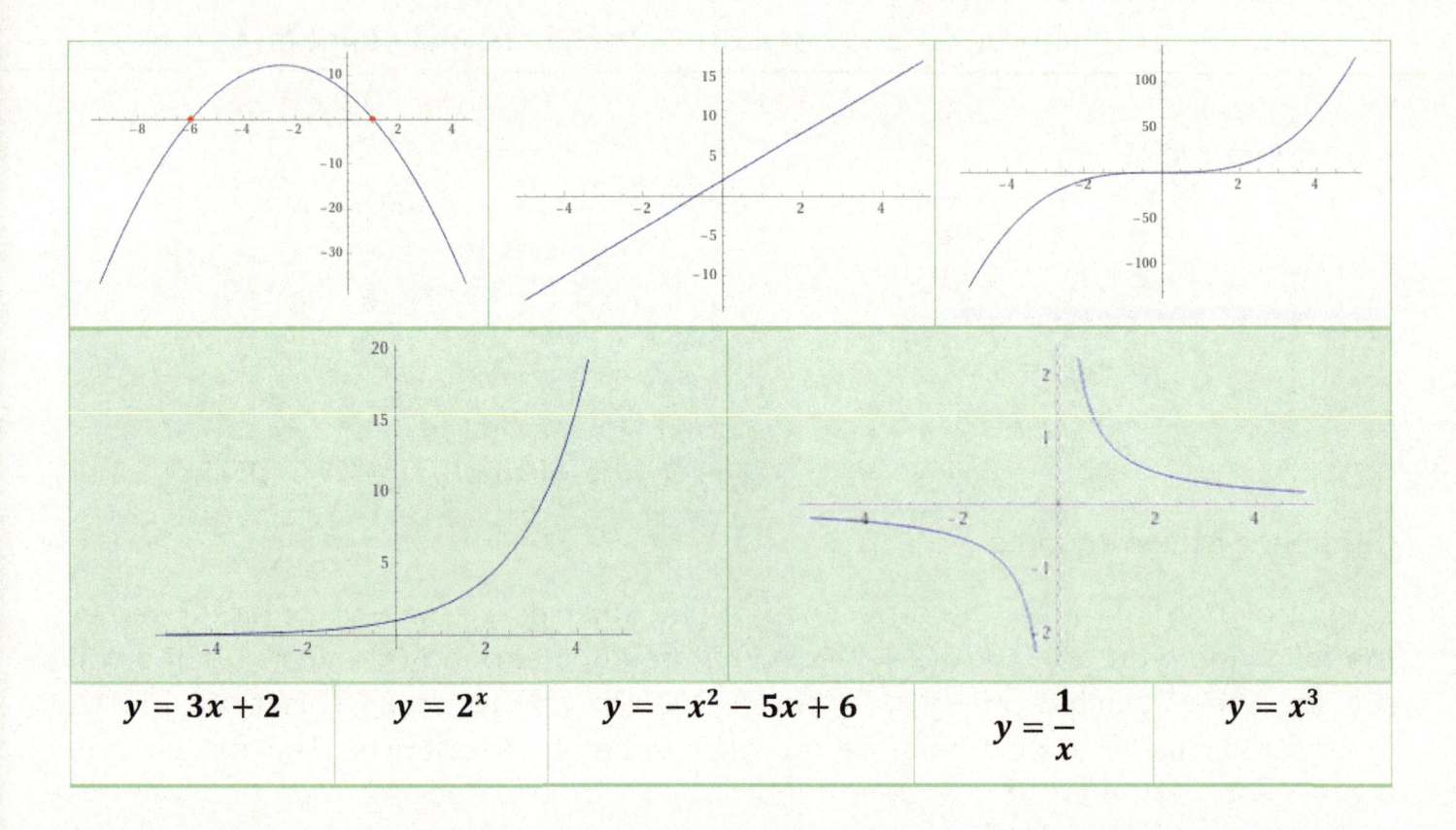

$y = 3x + 2$	$y = 2^x$	$y = -x^2 - 5x + 6$	$y = \dfrac{1}{x}$	$y = x^3$

Graphs of linear functions

Straight line graphs can be written in the format $y = mx + c$:

- m represents the gradient of the line
- c represents the y-intercept

Important points to remember:

- **Parallel lines** have the same gradient, i.e., m is the same for both lines.
- The gradients of two **perpendicular lines** multiply to give -1. i.e., for a straight line $y = mx + c$, a perpendicular line will have a gradient of $-\dfrac{1}{m}$ (the negative reciprocal of m).
- If you are given two points of a straight line you can determine the formula:

The Complete BMAT Specification Explained

M4 - Algebra

- o The gradient, m, is the $\frac{change\ in\ y}{change\ in\ x}$. For example, a line passing through the points (1,3) and (6,9) has a gradient of $\frac{9-3}{6-1} = \frac{6}{5}$
- o You now know that $y = \frac{6}{5}x + c$ and just need to find c.
- o To find c, substitute one of the coordinates back into the equation: for example, using (1,3): $3 = \frac{6}{5}(1) + c$, $c = 3 - \frac{6}{5} = \frac{9}{5}$
- o The formula for the line passing through (1,3) and (6,9) is therefore:
$$y = \frac{6}{5}x + \frac{9}{5}$$
- o The y-intercept is $\left(0, \frac{9}{5}\right)$ and the x-intercept is $\left(-\frac{3}{2}, 0\right)$

- You can also find the formula for a line if you are given one point and the gradient:
  - o This is even easier as you already know m.
  - o Just substitute the coordinate you are given back into the equation to find c.

Graphs of quadratic functions

You can plot quadratic equations in the form $y = ax^2 + bx + c$. Quadratic graphs are symmetrical 'bucket' shaped graphs (or inverted buckets in the case of negative a values).

You can use a quadratic graph to find approximate solutions to quadratic equations:

- The *roots* of a quadratic are the x-intercepts i.e., the values for x when $y = 0$.
- You can determine the exact roots by solving the quadratic equation for $y = 0$, but you can also draw a sketch of the equation to approximate the roots. For example: $y = x^2 + 3x + 2$
- If you plug in a few values for x you can determine some coordinates of the graph:

x	−4	−3	−2	−1	0	1
y	6	2	0	0	2	5

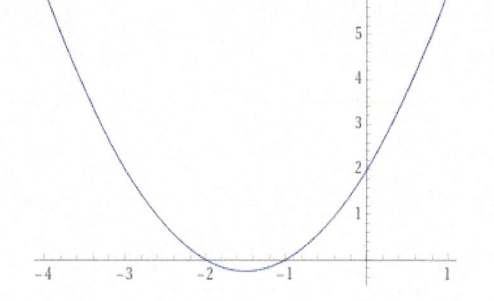

- Plotting these coordinates, you to draw a sketch of the graph:
- Note that the roots of the graph are −2 and −1 which can also be determined from the factorised form $y = (x + 1)(x + 2)$.
-

You can write quadratic equations in the completed square form to determine the **turning point** and **line of symmetry** of a quadratic graph:

- The quadratic expression $y = x^2 + 2x - 5$ can be written in the form $y = (x + 1)^2 - 6$.
- In this form you can see that the lowest value for y will occur when $(x + 1) = 0$, i.e., when $x = -1$. (Any other value for x will result in a larger y value since the $(x + 1)$ term is squared so will always be positive).
- When $x = -1$, $y = -6$. The turning point for this graph is therefore at the point $(-1, -6)$ and the graph will have a line of symmetry at $x = -1$.

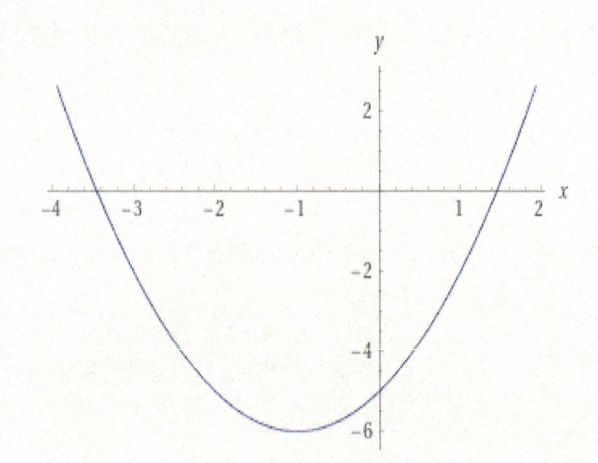

Gradient

You should know that the gradient of a straight-line graph is constant and is represented by m in the equation $y = mx + c$. The gradient of a curved line, however, is constantly changing and can be *approximated* at any one point by drawing a tangent to the line at that point (a tangent is a straight line which touches the curve at one point only). By finding the gradient of the tangent you can approximate the gradient of the curve:

- Shown is a plot of the curve:
  $$y = x^2 - 2x - 3$$
- At the point $x = 2, y = -3$
- If you draw a tangent to the curve at $(2, -3)$ you will notive that it passes through the point $(3.5, 0)$
- With two points of a straight line you can work out the gradient of that line $= \frac{3}{1.5} = 2$ to approximate the gradient of the curve at $(2, -3)$

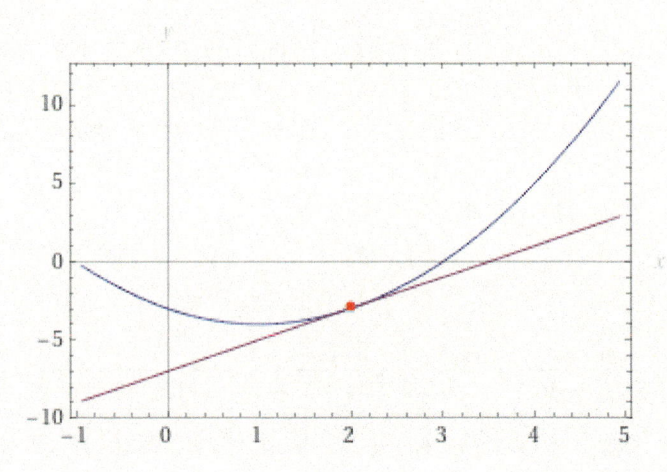

Other graphs:

- Review the graphs from the graph matching exercise and note that:
    - $+x^3$ graphs move from the bottom left quadrant to the top right
    - $-x^3$ graphs would plot from the top left quadrant to the bottom right
    - Graphs of the reciprocal function $y = \frac{1}{x}$ contain lines that do not touch and are symmetrical about the lines $y = x$ and $x = y$
    - **When k is positive:** graphs of the exponential function $y = k^x$ are always above the x-axis, always go through the point **(0,1)** (any number raised to the power **0 = 1**) and curve upwards for values $k > 1$.
    - The graph $y = \left(\frac{1}{k}\right)^x$ is a mirror image of $y = k^x$ about the y-axis.
    - Don't worry about graphs of $y = k^x$ for negative values of k

Certain characteristics of graphs can be used to solve problems:

> **6Med Tip:** the gradient of any graph tells you the **rate** of y-axis units **per** x-axis units

- the gradient of a distance-time graph tells you the speed (m/s)
- the gradient of a speed-time graph tells you the acceleration (m/s^2)
- if you plotted a graph for dollars, $, against the pound, £, the gradient would tell you the exchange rate, i.e., dollars/pound

- If the units of the y-axis are *something*/variable, with that variable plotted on the x-axis, the area under a graph tells you the total *something*. E.g.:
    - the area under a speed-time tells you the total distance travelled (y-axis = m/s, x-axis = s)
    - Use geometric formulae to calculate the area under a graph

M4 - Algebra

Graphs of trigonometric functions

From geometry you will be familiar with the functions $y = \sin(x)$, $y = \cos(x)$, and $y = \tan(x)$. You need to be able to recognise each of these graphs and know the key differences between them:

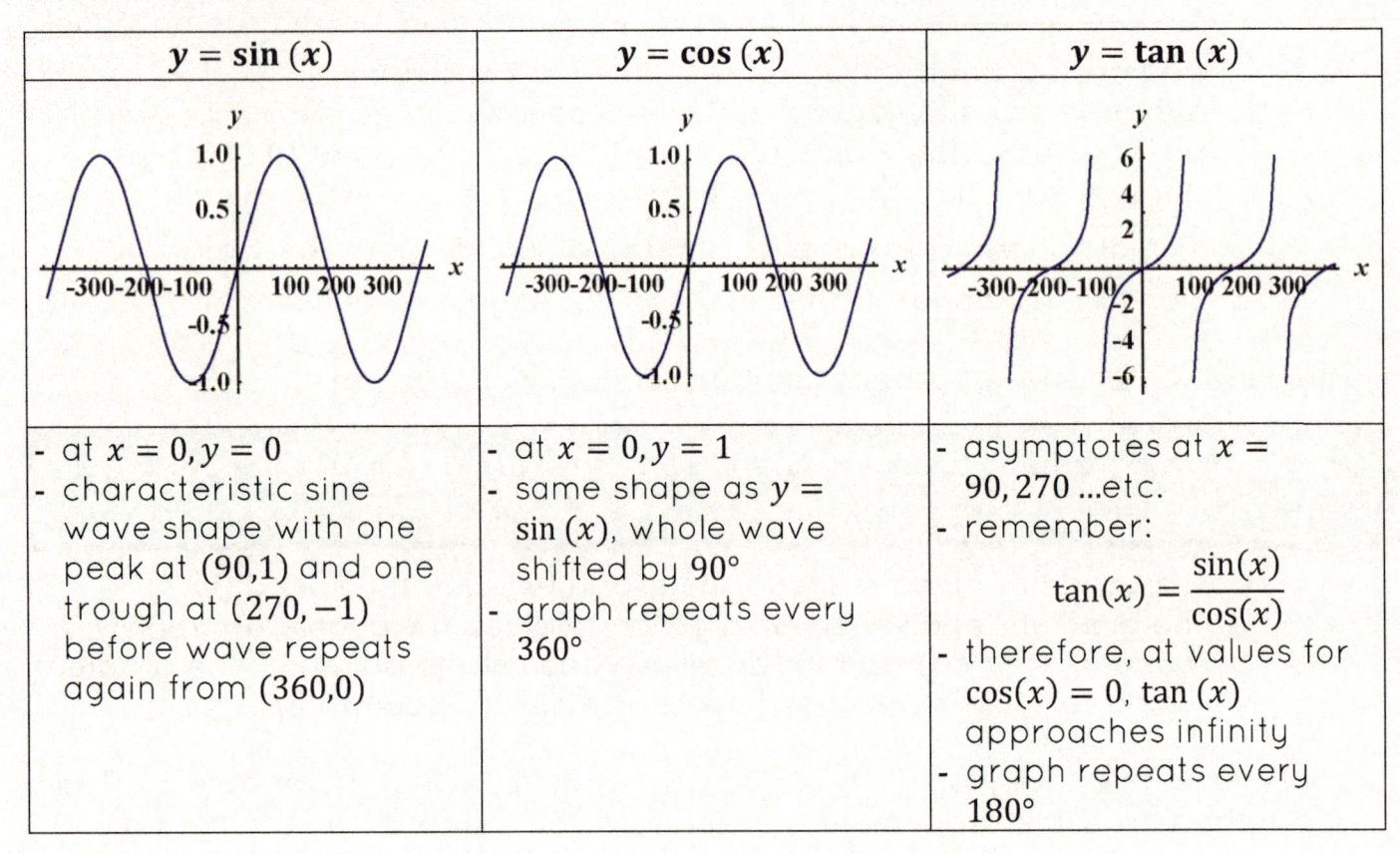

$y = \sin(x)$	$y = \cos(x)$	$y = \tan(x)$
(graph of sine wave from -300 to 300, amplitude 1)	(graph of cosine wave from -300 to 300, amplitude 1)	(graph of tangent from -300 to 300, with asymptotes)
- at $x = 0, y = 0$ - characteristic sine wave shape with one peak at $(90,1)$ and one trough at $(270, -1)$ before wave repeats again from $(360,0)$	- at $x = 0, y = 1$ - same shape as $y = \sin(x)$, whole wave shifted by 90° - graph repeats every 360°	- asymptotes at $x = 90, 270$ ...etc. - remember: $$\tan(x) = \frac{\sin(x)}{\cos(x)}$$ - therefore, at values for $\cos(x) = 0$, $\tan(x)$ approaches infinity - graph repeats every 180°

Simultaneous equations

It is important to be able to construct equations for interpreting and solving problems.

A Hibiscus flower has 5 petals, and a Red Lily has 6 petals. In a box containing Hibiscus and Red Lily flowers I count 40 stems and 230 leaves. Given that each type of flower has one stem, how many of each flower are in the box?

Let number of hibiscus flowers = H and number of Red Lily flowers = R

For stems: $H + R = 40$

For leaves: $5H + 6R = 230$

These equations can be solved *simultaneously*: $R = 40 - H$, so $5H + 6(40 - H) = 230$

$5H + 240 - 6H = 230$, therefore $H = 10$. Since $R = 40 - H$, $R = 30$.

You may be asked to solve simultaneous equations where one of the equations is a quadratic expression:

1. $x + y = 1$
2. $y = x^2 - 7x + 9$

Substituting #2. into #1.:

$$x + (x^2 - 7x + 9) = 1$$

$$x^2 - 6x + 8 = 0$$

$$(x - 4)(x - 2) = 0$$

$$x = 4, x = 2$$

Substituting these values into the first equation you can find the corresponding y values:

When $x = 4, y = -3$, and when $x = 2, y = -1$.

You can also solve simultaneous equations using a graph. The solution to the equations is the point where the graphs *intersect*.

For the equations above, the graphs of $y = -x + 1$ and $y = x^2 - 7x + 9$ are:

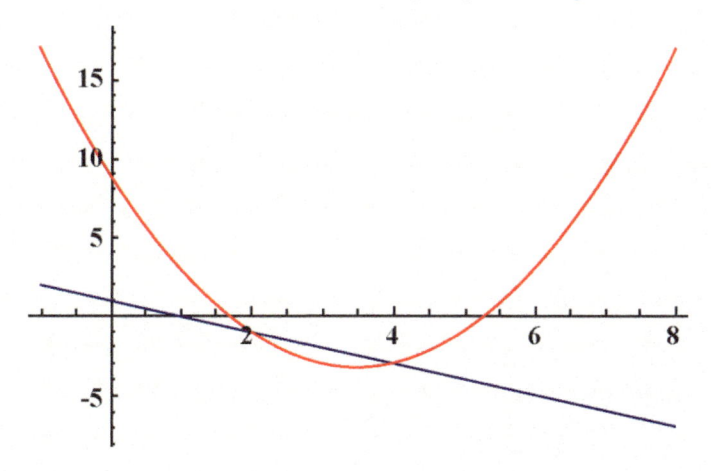

Note that the graphs intersect at $(4, -3)$ and $(2, -1)$: the solutions to the simultaneous equations

Inequalities

Inequalities are used to represent sets of numbers:

>	greater than	≥	greater than or equal to
<	less than	≤	less than or equal to

When solving equations involving inequalities, you can treat the inequalities like an 'equals' sign except on one occasion: **if you multiply by a negative number, you must flip the inequality sign.**

- $7x + 3 < 5x$
- $2x < -3$
- $x < -\frac{3}{2}$
- $-x < -5 \quad x > 5$
- Integer values of x when $6 < x \leq 9$ are 7, 8 and 9.

- The range of values for x when: $x^2 \leq 36$ are $x \leq 6$ and $x \geq -6$ which can be written: $-6 \leq x \leq 6$
- For the range of values when $x^2 \geq 36$, $x \geq 6$ or $x \leq -6$

You can also represent inequalities on graphs. Simply draw the line represented by each inequality as an equation (with an '=' sign instead of the inequality) and then shade the region for the area represented by the inequality. This can help visualise the sets of numbers which satisfy a particular inequality or group of inequalities:

- 'Shade the region represented by $x > -4$, $y > 1$, $y > 2x + 1$ and $x + 2y < 6$'

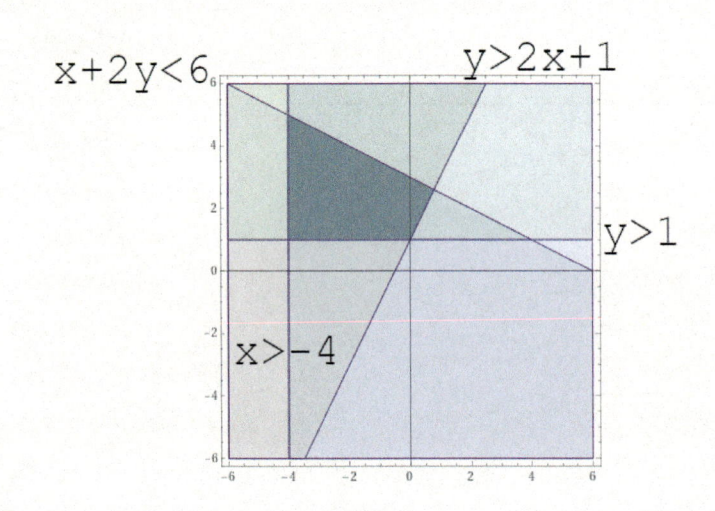

The Complete BMAT Specification Explained

M4 – Algebra

Sequences and calculating the *n*th term

	Linear sequences	Quadratic sequences
Example	2, 5, 8, 11, 14, 17, 20 …	1, 5, 11, 19, 29, 41, 55, 71 …
Explanation	There is a common difference between each value. In the example above, the common difference is +3.	The difference between each term changes each time, but the *amount* the difference changes by each time (the 'second difference') is the same. In the example above, the second difference is +2.
Formula for the nth term	$a_n = a + (n-1)d$ where a is the first term and d is the common difference.	$a_n = an^2 + bn + c$ $a + b + c$ = the first term, $3a + b$ = the first difference (difference between the first two numbers) $2a$ = the second difference.
Worked example	The common difference is 3, so: $a_n = 2 + (n-1)(3)$ $a_n = 3n - 1$	the first difference is +4, the second difference is +1, so: $2a = 2, \quad a = 1$ $3a + b = 4, \quad 3 + b = 4, \quad b = 1$ $a + b + c = 1, \quad 1 + 1 + c = 1, \quad c = -1$ $a_n = n^2 + n - 1$

> **6Med Tip:** Remember these formulae for linear and quadratic sequences and how to use them! It means you will be able to deal with sequence questions

Check your knowledge!

Question 1: Which graphs intersect? Select all that apply

a. $x + y = -3$
b. $y = x^2 + 3x + 2$
c. $y = -x^2 - 2$
d. $y = \frac{x}{2} - 4$

1. A and B
2. B and C
3. C and D
4. B and C
5. A and C
6. B and D
7. A and D
8. A, C and D
9. A, B and D

M4 - Algebra

Question 2: Two non-zero numbers, x and y satisfy $\frac{x+2y}{2} = 5(x-y)$

- What is the value of $\frac{4y}{\sqrt{x^2+y^2}}$

Question 3: A straight line passes through point $A(a,b)$ and point $B(2, b-2)$. The line $y = \frac{3}{2}x + 6$ is perpendicular to this line. Given that $a = 2b$, find the value of a and b and the equation of the line passing through A and B.

Question 4: A football season consists of 38 games. Football teams receive 3 points for a win, 1 point for a draw and no points for a loss. A team ended the season with 58 points having lost 12 games. How many games did they win and how many games did they draw?

Question 5: Here are the first three patterns in a sequence of tiles:

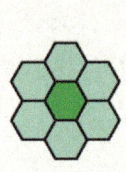

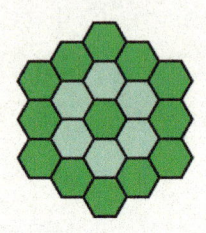

- How many tiles are needed to make the 12th pattern in the sequence?

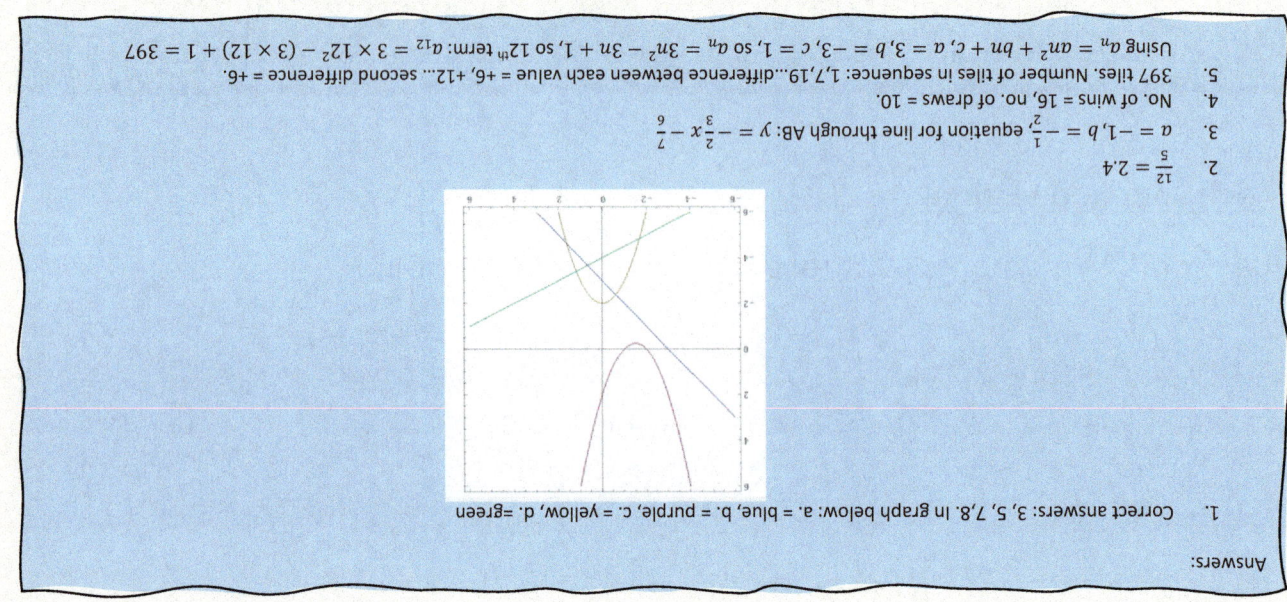

Answers:

1. Correct answers: 3, 5, 7, 8. In graph below, a. = blue, b. = purple, c. = yellow, d. = green
2. $\frac{12}{5} = 2.4$
3. $a = -1, b = -\frac{1}{2}$, equation for line through AB: $y = -\frac{2}{3}x - \frac{7}{6}$
4. No. of wins = 16, no. of draws = 10.
5. 397 tiles. Number of tiles in sequence: 1, 7, 19...difference between each value = +6, +12...second difference = +6.
Using $a_n = an^2 + bn + c$, $a = 3, b = -3, c = 1$, so $a_n = 3n^2 - 3n + 1$, so 12th term: $a_{12} = 3 \times 12^2 - (3 \times 12) + 1 = 397$.

M5 - Geometry

Angles recap:

Angles! Hopefully, you're pretty familiar with the absolute fundamentals of Geometry, but some of us had bad teachers (or new kinds of stethoscope to doodle) and may have missed some of the basics:

- angles around a point add up to 360°
- angles on a straight-line add up to 180°
- angles in a triangle add up to 180°
- The exterior angle of a triangle is the sum of the opposite interior angles
- angles in a quadrilateral add up to 360°

6Med Tip:

- *sum of interior angles for any polygon* $= (n-2) \times 180°$
$(n = number\ of\ sides)$

Parallel lines

Look at the diagram on the right and remind yourself of alternate and corresponding angles:

- $x + y = 180°$
- when a line intersects two parallel lines, the angles, x, formed by a 'Z' shape are the same and called alternate angles
- the angles, y, formed by an 'F' shape are the same and called corresponding angles

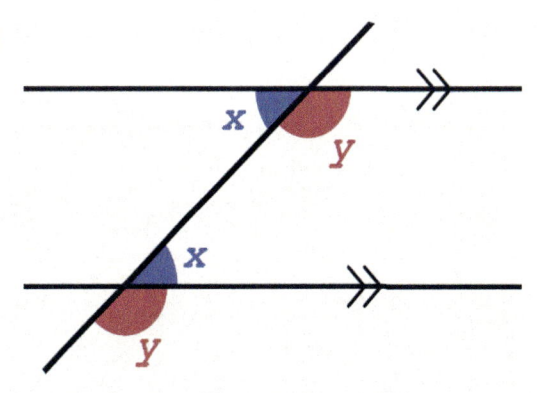

The Complete BMAT Specification Explained

M5 – Geometry

Congruence and similarity

- If two shapes are *congruent*, they are simply the same size and the same shape. They can also be mirror images of each other.
- If two shapes are *similar*, they are only the same shape and are different sizes.

Look at these two triangles and determine whether they are congruent:

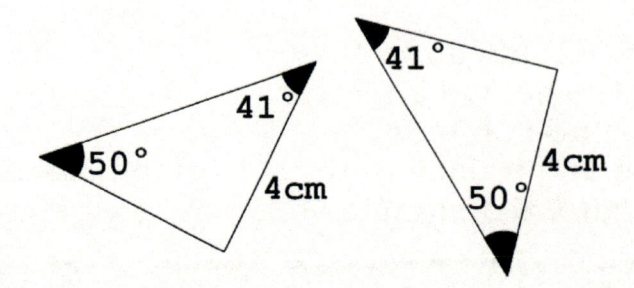

Answer: these triangles aren't congruent. Draw them in the same orientation and check the criteria in the green box

6Med Tip: Remember the 4 criteria for triangle congruence:

1. SSS – three sides are the same
2. AAS – two angles and a side match
3. SAS – two sides and the angle between them match
4. RHS – a right angle, the hypotenuse and on other side all match

If at least one is true, the triangles are congruent; if none are true, the triangles are not congruent.

Transformations

You need to be familiar using the four transformations on the next page:

The Complete BMAT Specification Explained

M5 – Geometry

Translation - translations are 2-dimensional vectors – they have an x-component and a y-component - all that changes is the position of the shape - the image is congruent of the original shape	Blue to green is a translation of $\begin{pmatrix} 8 \\ -2 \end{pmatrix}$

Rotation
 - the object is turned:
     o a specified angle
     o in a given direction – clockwise/anticlockwise
     o around a centre of rotation
 - the position and orientation change
 - the image is congruent of the original shape
	The shape is rotated clockwise twice 90° around the origin

Reflection - an object can be reflected over a specified mirror line - the position and the orientation change - the image is congruent of the original shape	The yellow shape is a reflection of the blue shape in the line $x = 1$

Enlargement
 - an object can be enlarged:
     o by a defined scale factor
     o around a centre of enlargement
 - the angles of the object remain the same
 - the ratios of the lengths remain the same
 - only negative scale factors alter orientation.
 - the image is similar to the original shape – not congruent
	Purple to red is an enlargement of scale factor 2 and centre (0,0)
	 Purple to green is an enlargement of scale factor $-\frac{1}{2}$ and centre (0,0)

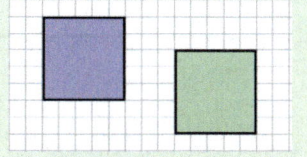

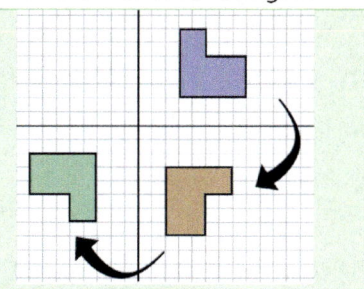

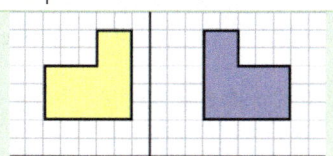

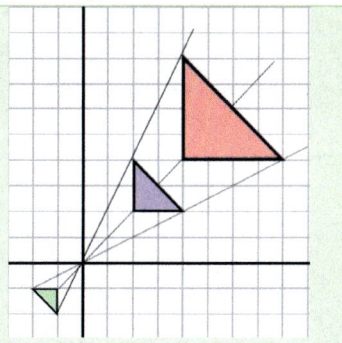

The Complete BMAT Specification Explained

M5 – Geometry

> **6Med Tip:** Enlargements take place in one, two and three dimensions.
>
> Remember for an enlargement of scale factor n:
>
> - sides are n times bigger
> - areas are n^2 times bigger
> - volumes are n^3 times bigger
>
> Look back at the enlargement example in the table above and notice how the area change is related to the scale factor

Triangles

Remember that the area of a triangle is $\frac{1}{2} b \times h$, where h is the vertical height:

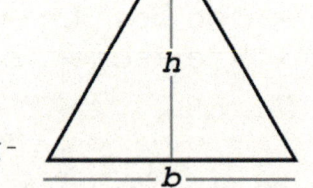

You should be familiar with Pythagoras' theorem for right-angled triangles:

$$a^2 + b^2 = c^2$$

Pythagoras' theorem can be used to solve problems in 2 and 3 dimensions:

Practice questions:

1. Find the exact length of the missing side, x, in the triangle shown
2. Find the exact height of the square based pyramid in the diagram shown

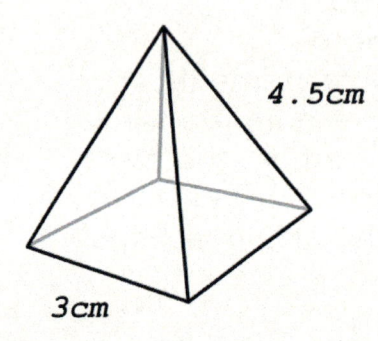

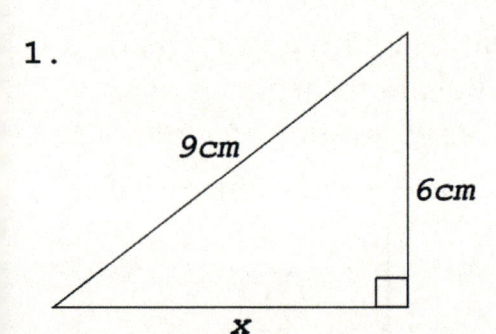

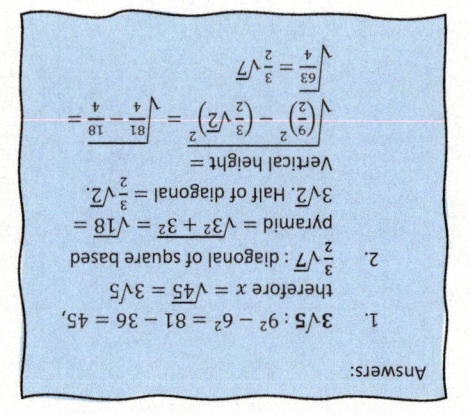

Answers:

1. $3\sqrt{5}$: $9^2 - 6^2 = 81 - 36 = 45$, therefore $x = \sqrt{45} = 3\sqrt{5}$
2. $\frac{3}{2}\sqrt{7}$: diagonal of square based pyramid $= \sqrt{3^2 + 3^2} = \sqrt{18} = 3\sqrt{2}$. Half of diagonal $= \frac{3}{2}\sqrt{2}$.

Vertical height $= \sqrt{\left(\frac{9}{2}\right)^2 - \left(\frac{3}{2}\sqrt{2}\right)^2} = \sqrt{\frac{81}{4} - \frac{18}{4}} = \sqrt{\frac{63}{4}} = \frac{3}{2}\sqrt{7}$

You also need to know how to use basic trigonometric ratios for right-angled triangles:

$$\sin(\theta) = \frac{opposite}{hypotenuse}$$

$$\cos(\theta) = \frac{adjacent}{hypotenuse}$$

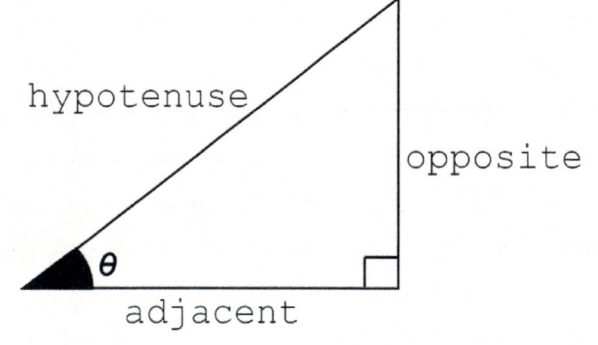

$$\tan(\theta) = \frac{opposite}{adjacent} = \frac{\sin(\theta)}{\cos(\theta)}$$

$\theta =$	$\sin(\theta)$	$\cos(\theta)$	$\tan(\theta)$
0°	0	1	0
30°	$\frac{1}{2}$	$\frac{\sqrt{3}}{2}$	$\frac{\sqrt{3}}{3}$
45°	$\frac{\sqrt{2}}{2}$	$\frac{\sqrt{2}}{2}$	1
60°	$\frac{\sqrt{3}}{2}$	$\frac{1}{2}$	$\sqrt{3}$
90°	1	0	–

6Med Tip: Cover up the table and test yourself on values of $\sin(\theta)$, $\cos(\theta)$ and $\tan(\theta)$ for all values of $\theta°$ until you know them off by heart

Using $sin(\theta) = \frac{opposite}{hypotenuse}$, the following formula can be used to find the area of any triangle when you know two sides and the angle between them:

$$area\ of\ the\ triangle = \frac{1}{2} ab \sin(C)$$

The Complete BMAT Specification Explained

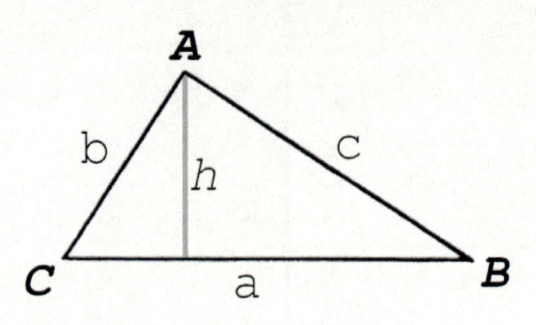

M5 – Geometry

From the right-angled triangle with hypotenuse b and height h we can write the expression:

$$\sin(C) = \frac{h}{b}, \qquad h = b\sin(C)$$

Substituting this value for h into the basic triangle formula ($area = \frac{1}{2}a \times h$)

Circles

Exercise: match the following terms onto the two circles:

centre, radius, chord, diameter, circumference, tangent, minor arc, major arc, minor sector, major sector, minor segment, major segment

Learn these important circle formulae:

$$circumference = 2\pi r = \pi d$$

$$area = \pi r^2$$

You can use these formulae to calculate area of a sector and the length of an arc if you know the angle (*x* in green circle above) creating the sector/arc:

6Med Tip:

- Area of sector = $\frac{x}{360} \times$ area of full circle (πr^2)
- Length of an arc = $\frac{x}{360} \times$ circumference of full circle (πd)

Make sure you understand the circle geometry rules on the next page:

M5 – Geometry

The angle subtended at the centre is twice the angle subtended at the circumference		For angles at the circumference in the major segment of a chord
The angle in a semicircle is 90°		Always 90°, no matter the orientation of the diameter
The angles in the same segment are equal		All angles from 2 ends of the same chord are the same within each segment. Angles in opposite segments sum to 180°, i.e.: $x + y = 180°$
The angle between a radius and a tangent is 90°		Wherever the radius meets a tangent the angle is always 90°
The angle between a tangent and a chord is equal to the angle in the opposite segment of the chord		This rule can be a bit harder to remember – remember it is the *opposite* segment (this is called *the alternate segment theory*)
Opposite angles in a cyclic quadrilateral sum to 180°		$w + x = 180°$ $y + z = 180°$ $w + x + y + z = 360°$

Area and volume for other shapes

The area of a parallelogram is $b \times h$:

The area of a trapezium is $\frac{1}{2}(a+b) \times h$:

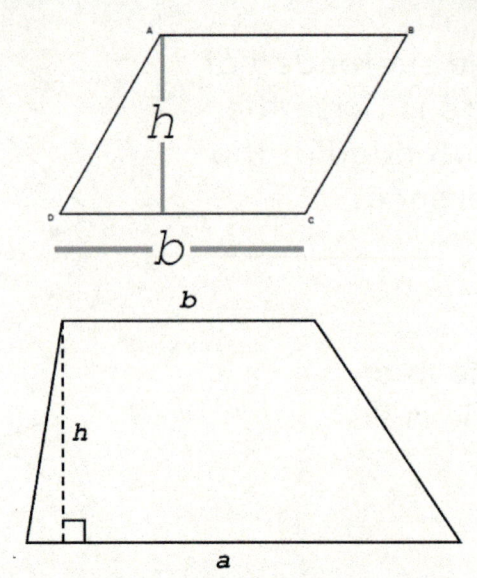

Volume

> **6Med Tip:**
>
> $Volume\ for\ any\ prism = cross-sectional\ area \times length$

A prism is a solid object with a constant cross-section: it's two ends are the same shape.

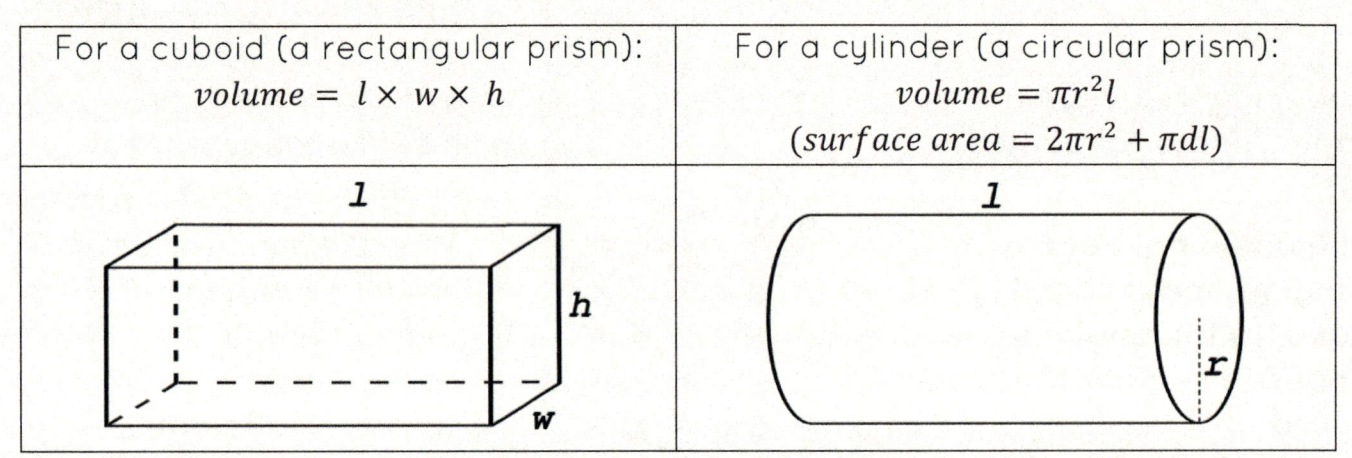

For a cuboid (a rectangular prism):	For a cylinder (a circular prism):
$volume = l \times w \times h$	$volume = \pi r^2 l$
	$(surface\ area = 2\pi r^2 + \pi d l)$

You should also know how to use formulae to calculate the volume of spheres, pyramids, cones, and composite solids, but these formulae will be given to you – memorise all the other formulae in this section.

The Complete BMAT Specification Explained

M5 – Geometry

Three figure bearings

Bearings tell you the angle from north and are really easy to use if you remember these key points:

- make sure you know which point the bearing is from
- draw a north line at this point
- the bearing is always given in three figures and is the angle clockwise from north

Example: Find the bearing from A to B, and the bearing from B to A:

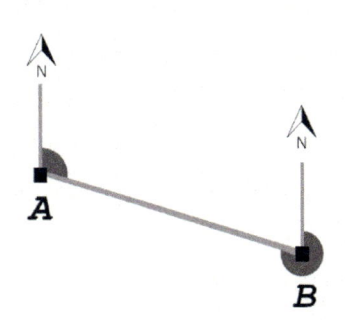

> The bearing from A to B is 110° (approx.)
>
> The bearing from B to A is 290° (approx.)
>
> For angles less than 100°, write a 0 before the angle, e.g.: 090°, 045°.

Check your knowledge!

Question 1:

A triangle ABC is drawn inside a larger triangle ADE:

AB = x

BC = $x - 1$

BD = 6

DE = $x + 3$

Find the length of AD

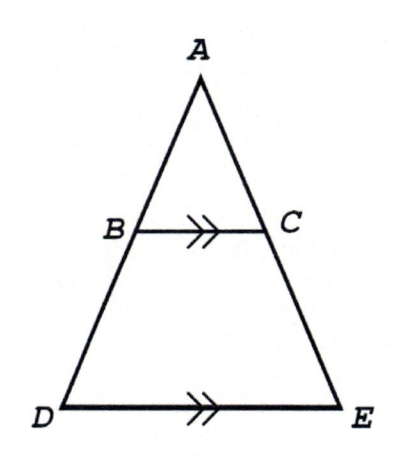

The Complete BMAT Specification Explained

M5 – Geometry

Question 2:

A prism of depth 1 cm is made from a square with 2cm sides

Calculate the length of the line shown joining the vertex to the midpoint of one of the opposite faces.

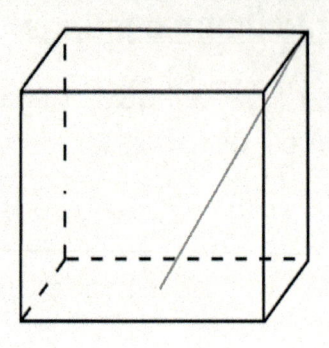

Question 3:

Three circles of radius **2cm** overlap to form the following shape with an area of $30cm^2$.

Given that the shape is symmetrical, find the exact area of a single overlapping region.

Answers:

1. 9cm: $\frac{x+6}{x} = \frac{x+3}{x+1}$, $x^2 + 5x - 6 = x^2 + 3x$, $2x = 6$, $x = 3$, $AD = x + 6 = 9cm$

2. $\frac{\sqrt{21}}{2}$: length of diagonal of base 2×1 rectangle = $\sqrt{2^2 + 1^2} = \sqrt{5}$, halfway along diagonal = $\frac{\sqrt{5}}{2}$, length of line shown = $\sqrt{\left(\frac{\sqrt{5}}{2}\right)^2 + 2^2} = \sqrt{\left(\frac{5}{4} + 4\right)} = \frac{\sqrt{21}}{2}$

3. $6\pi - 15$: x = area of overlapping region, total area = $3\pi(2)^2 - 2x = 30$, $12\pi - 30 = 2x$, $x = 6\pi - 15$

M6 - Statistics

Understanding the basics of statistics helps us to interpret data and make comparisons between groups.

Data can be described as 'discrete' or 'continuous' depending on how it is measured. Generally speaking:

- discrete data describes values that can be counted or assigned to a group, for example:
  - the number of coffees a café sells in an hour might be 20, 30 or any number depending on how busy it is (but not 23.46!).
  - an individual's blood group can be A, B, AB or O
- continuous data describes values that can be measured to a specific value, for example:
  - the amount of milk a café uses in an hour could be 1L or 10L or (theoretically) an infinite number of values between 1L and 10L
  - a group of individuals' height or weight

An 'average' is a way of communicating general characteristics of a data set. You should be familiar with these 4 concepts:

- Mode = the most common value
- Median = the middle item value, position found using: $\frac{\text{number of values}+1}{2}$
- Mean = the numerical average calculated by: $\frac{\text{sum of all values}}{\text{number of values}}$
- Range = the difference between the highest and lowest values

> 6Med Tip: Always remember to order data into ascending order to determine the middle position when calculating the median

Graphs and tables are used to present data and make it easier to interpret.

Frequency tables are a helpful way of organising data groups and you can use them to calculate the mean, median, mode and range:

The Complete BMAT Specification Explained

M6 - Statistics

Respondents were asked the question 'how many cups of coffee do you drink a day?':

No. of coffees	0	1	2	3	4	5	6	7	Totals
Frequency	12	53	45	16	15	5	4	0	150
No. x Frequency	0	53	90	48	60	25	24	0	300

The data in rows 1 and 2 is represents the responses from the survey. The 3rd row is made by multiplying rows 1 and 2 together to give the total number of coffees.

This is useful when you need to calculate the mean:

- The **mean** is $\frac{\text{sum of all values (overall total)}}{\text{number of values (frequency total)}} = \frac{300}{150}$
- mean = 2 coffees/day

- The **median** is the value that corresponds to the middle position in row 2: the middle position is $\frac{150+1}{2}$ = 75.5 which means the middle value falls between the 75th and 76th position.
- The 75th and 76th values both fall within group 2 so the **median = 2 coffees/day**

- The **mode** is just the group with the greatest frequency which from the table is group 1, so the **mode = 1 coffee/day**
- The table shows that there were respondents who answered anything from 0 to 6 coffees/day (no one responded with 7), so the **range is** $6 - 0 = 6$

Frequency tables can also be used to present grouped continuous data, for example, the distribution of height in a class:

Height (cm)	130 ≤ h < 140	140 ≤ h < 150	150 ≤ h < 160	160 ≤ h < 170	170 ≤ h < 180	Totals
Frequency	4	5	6	4	1	20
Mid-Interval value	135	145	155	165	175	-
No. x Mid-Interval value	540	725	930	660	175	3030

It is important to add a row representing the mid-interval value of each group as this lets us to calculate an estimate for the mean:

- Mean (estimate) = $\frac{\text{sum of all values (overall total)}}{\text{number of values (frequency total)}}$, = $\frac{3030}{20}$ = 151.5
- The median is the value at the middle position which is $\frac{20+1}{2}$ = 10.5 so is found in between the 10th and 11th position. We can't give an exact value, but we can say the **median is in the 150 ≤ h < 160 group.**
- **The modal group is 150 ≤ h < 160.**
- To estimate the range, we take the highest possible value (180cm*) and the lowest possible value (130cm) and find the difference, so the **range = 50cm**
- *Technically, 180 falls just outside the range of the last group (170 ≤ h < 180) but as we are calculating an *estimate* from grouped continuous data, it is more practical to use 180 than 179.99...

> **6Med Tip:** The mean will be an estimate given that we do not know the exact position of each value within each group.

Using the same example of heights in a class, you can add a row with cumulative frequency (cum. freq.):

Height (cm)	130 ≤ h < 140	140 ≤ h < 150	150 ≤ h < 160	160 ≤ h < 170	170 ≤ h < 180	Totals
Frequency	4	5	6	4	1	20
Cum. freq.	4	9	15	19	20	-

A cumulative frequency graph can be used to estimate the median and interquartile range:

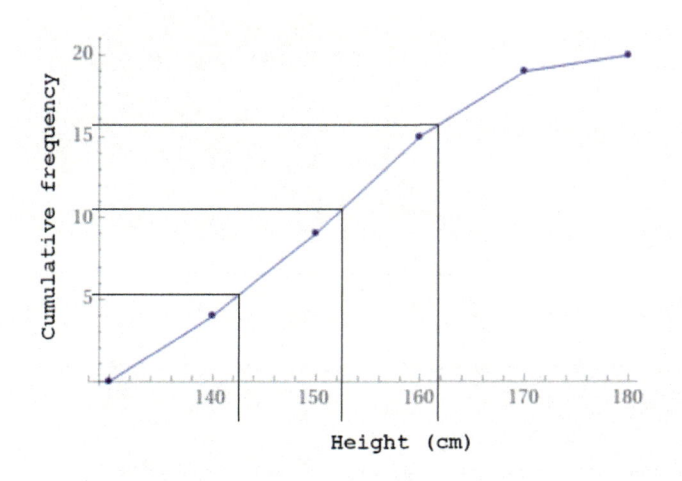

From marking the median, and upper and lower quartiles we can read estimates off the x-axis:

- median = 152cm
- lower quartile = 142cm
- upper quartile = 162cm
- interquartile range = 20cm

The Complete BMAT Specification Explained

M6 - Statistics

A box plot can also be used to present these summary statistics:

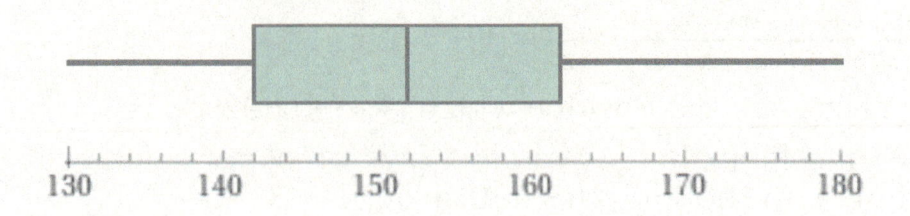

The whiskers represent the range, and the lines within the box represent the lower quartile, median and upper quartile

Histograms

Histograms are like bar charts but use frequency density (y-axis) to represent data. With histograms, it is the area of each bar that represents the frequency rather than the height. Note that the width of each class can differ!

This histogram shows the age distribution of people owning a mobile phone in a remote village:

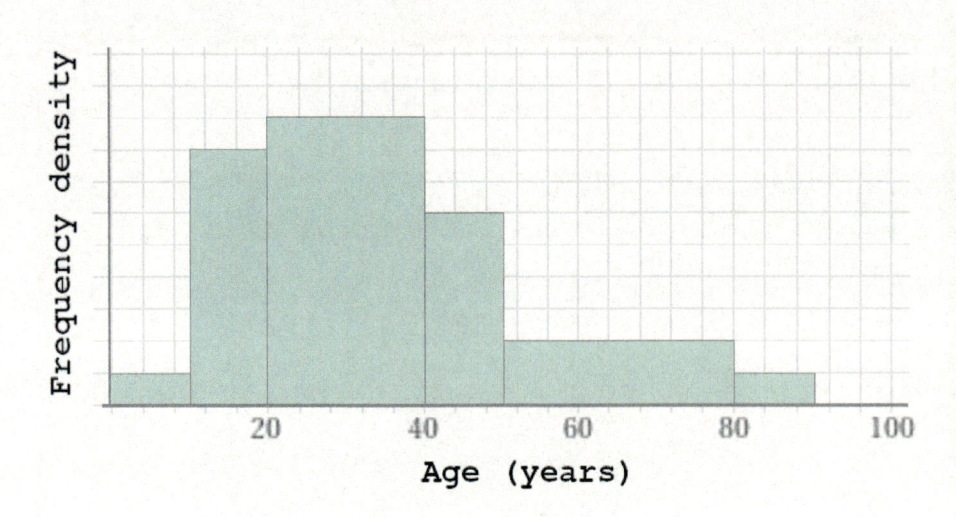

If you are told that the 20-40 age group represents 90 people, you can work out the frequency of the other age groups.

The 20-40 group is 5 squares wide and 9 squares tall. Given that the area represents 90 people, each square must represent 2 people.

There are therefore 5 people in the 80-90 group etc.

Scatter graphs show how closely related two data sets are. A line of best fit can be drawn onto a scatter graph to demonstrate the direction of the correlation. If the line has a positive gradient, there is a positive correlation, if it has a negative gradient, there is a negative correlation.

6Med Tip: Frequency density = $\frac{\text{frequency}}{\text{class width}}$

For example, if the heights and weights of a group of individuals were to be plotted, you might get a graph like this:

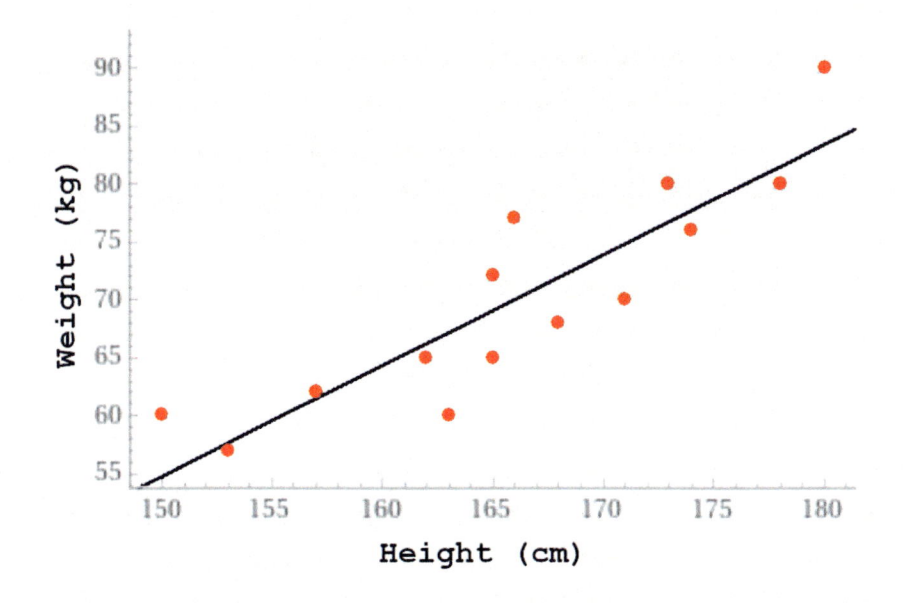

The line of best fit drawn between the points shows a positive correlation between height and weight

6Med Tip: Remember that correlation does not mean causation! For example:

- Over the past 20 years there has been an increase in the number medical school applicants in the UK.
- Over the past 20 years UK household pizza consumption has increased.
- Whilst there is a correlation between these two variables, one does not *cause* the other! They are likely both explained by a general population increase.

Two-way tables:

Two-way tables are like frequency tables, but they show two variables rather than just one:

	Oxford	Cambridge	Total
Blue eyes	310	290	600
Brown eyes	240	160	400
Total	550	450	1000

The Complete BMAT Specification Explained

M6 - Statistics

Knowledge check

Household income (£/year)	Frequency
$0 \leq y < 16{,}000$	5
$16{,}000 \leq y < 50{,}000$	60
$50{,}000 \leq y < 55{,}000$	25
$55{,}000 \leq y < 60{,}000$	10

1. Find an estimate for the mean household income
2. Complete a cumulative frequency table
3. Draw a cumulative frequency graph to find an estimate for the interquartile range

Answers:
1. £39,075
2. Add a column with 5, 65, 90, 100
3. Appropriate graph with approximate UQ = 52000, LQ = 27000, IQR = 25000

The Complete BMAT Specification Explained

M7 - Probability

The probability of a probability question coming up in the BMAT exam is almost 1! – you need to be comfortable using fractions, percentages, and ratios for interpreting questions to calculate probabilities.

Think about the following problem:

A (heavy!) rucksack contains 6 mathematics textbooks, 2 physics textbooks and 1 geography textbook. 2 books are chosen at random from the bag. What is the probability of picking exactly 2 books of the same subject?

Before working through this question let's recap a few key principles:
- All probabilities are between 0 and 1 – a probability of 0 means something will *never* happen and a probability of 1 means it *always* will – e.g. the probability of picking a History textbook from the rucksack is 0 (given we know there are only mathematics, physics and geography books in the bag).
- Probabilities always add up to 1 for a given scenario – e.g. there is a 6 in 9 chance ($\frac{6}{9} = \frac{2}{3}$) that a mathematics book will be picked from the rucksack, a $\frac{2}{9}$ chance that a physics book will be picked and a $\frac{1}{9}$ chance that a geography book will be picked.. These probabilities sum to 1: $\frac{6}{9} + \frac{2}{9} + \frac{1}{9} = 1$

Relative frequency:

We have just shown that the *theoretical probability* of picking a mathematics textbook from the rucksack is $\frac{2}{3}$. However, the universe doesn't always behave as we expect! If we imagine an experiment where we pick a book from the rucksack and then replace it and then keep picking and replacing a book over and over again whilst recording the subject of the book we picked, we could produce a table like this:

Number of times a book was picked	5	20	50
Number of times the book was a mathematics book	2	9	25
Relative frequency	$\frac{2}{5} = 0.4$	$\frac{9}{20} = 0.45$	$\frac{25}{50} = \frac{1}{2} = 0.5$

Looking at the probability table, a few things might strike you:

> **6Med Tip:** For relative frequency,
>
> $$Probability\ of\ something\ happening = \frac{number\ of\ times\ that\ thing\ happened}{number\ of\ attempts}$$

- the relative frequency changes depending on the number of times the experiment is repeated
- The relative frequency appears to get closer to the theoretical probability (0.666) as the number of times the experiment is repeated increases: as a general rule, *the more times an experiment is repeated the more accurate the probability will be.*
- In this example, even after 50 repeats, the relative frequency (0.5) is still quite different to the *expected frequency* (0.666). This could tell us something about the *fairness* of the experiment – perhaps the mathematics books are smaller than the other books, or further from the opening of the bag so less likely to be picked. This means the arrangement of the books may be *biased*, resulting in the relative frequency being different to the expected frequency.

When 2 events are performed consecutively it is vital to think about:

a) the relationship between the 2 events, i.e. whether the 2 events are *independent or dependent* and whether one event is conditional on the outcome of the other
b) whether the question is an 'AND' question or an 'OR' question.

> **6Med Tip:**
> - for 'AND' questions, probabilities are multiplied together
> - for 'OR' questions, probabilities are summed

M7 - Probability

Practice question

From a normal 52 card deck of playing cards, what is the probability of picking (assuming the cards are not replaced after being picked)
a) 3 kings
b) 110 and the ace of spades
c) a pair of Jacks, Queens or Kings

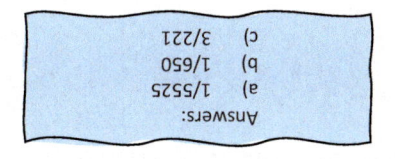

Answers:
a) 1/5525
b) 1/650
c) 3/221

Probability Tree Diagrams

Back to the rucksack problem: imagine a scenario where two books are picked consecutively (and not replaced) and consider:

A) the probability of picking a mathematics book and a physics book
B) the probability of picking exactly two books of the same subject

You can use a tree diagram to illustrate the probabilities of each event (mathematics = blue, physics = green, geography = yellow):

> **6Med Tip:** Tree diagram rules:
> 1. Fill out all the branches with the respective probabilities
> 2. select the branches relevant to the problem
> 3. multiply *along* the branches
> 4. sum *down* the final column
> - note: the final column always sums to 1 if you sum the result for each branch
> - watch out for conditional probabilities: when the action of each branch depends on the previous branch, the denominator will change

A) The tree shows there are 2 ways of picking a mathematics book and a physics book. By multiplying along the relevant branches, you can see that the overall probability is a sum of each branch, in this case: $\frac{1}{6} + \frac{1}{6} = \frac{1}{3}$

B) The only way to pick 2 books of the same subject is to pick 2 maths books or 2 physics books (there is only one geography book in the bag!). By multiplying along the relevant branches and summing down the final column this gives an overall probability of: $\frac{5}{12} + \frac{1}{36} = \frac{16}{36} = \frac{4}{9}$

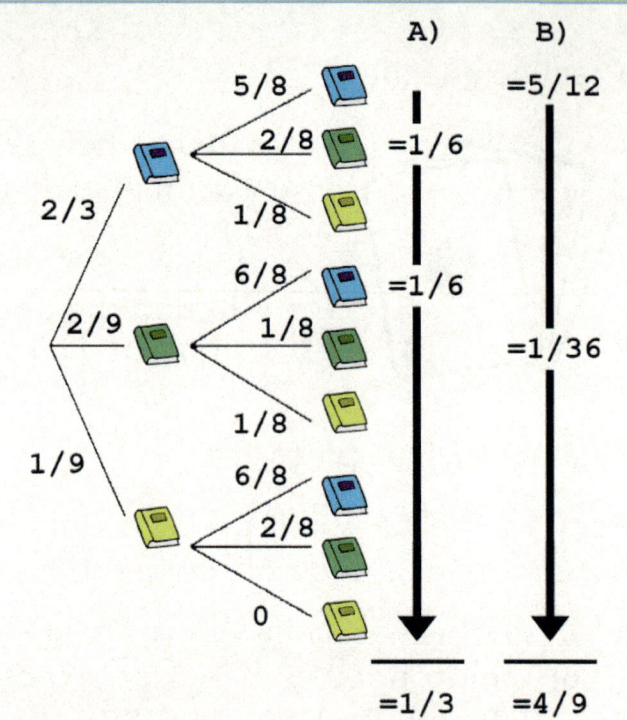

Venn diagrams:

Think about this question:

150 students were asked whether they owned a mobile phone or a tablet device.

- *112 said they owned a mobile phone*
- *40 said they owned both a mobile phone and a tablet*
- *30 said they did not own a mobile phone or a tablet*

Find the probability that a random pupil owns a mobile phone, given that they own a tablet.

For this question it is easiest to organise the data with a Venn diagram to visualise the number of students in each category:

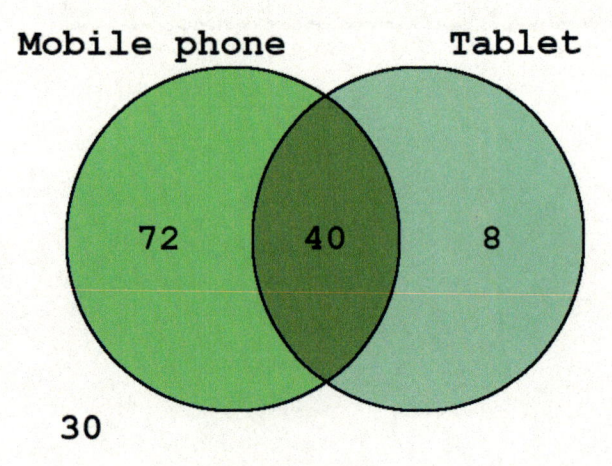

Mobile phone 72 | 40 | 8 **Tablet**

30

By filling in the diagram with the data given in the question you can work out that there are 8 students who only own a tablet

Now you have all the information to work out the question. The Venn diagram shows there are 48 students who own a tablet, so this becomes the denominator, and out of those 48 students, 40 own a mobile phone, so this becomes the numerator, and the probability of a student with a tablet owning a mobile phone is: $\frac{40}{48} = \frac{5}{6}$

Check your knowledge!

Question 1:

On any school day, the probability that John prepares a packed lunch for school is 0.6, and the probability that he eats from the school canteen is 0.4.

If John prepares a packed lunch, then the probability that he is late for school is 0.5.

If John eats from the school canteen, then the probability he is late for school is 0.3.

Given that John is late for school, what is the probability that he prepared his own lunch?

Question 2:

Dan is preparing a job application. He notes that:

- *48% of applicants receive an interview.*
- *10% of applicants receive a job offer, but 2% do so without requiring an interview.*
- *50% of applicants do not receive an interview or a job offer.*

What is the probability of an applicant receiving a job offer, given that they had an interview?

M7 - Probability

Question 3:

Susie has 2 spinners which can land on numbers 1-8. The first spinner does so fairly, but the second lands does not – it lands on numbers 2-8 with equal probability but lands on number 1 with a different probability.

When the 2 spinners are spun, the probability of that Susie gets a total of 2 is 1/24.

What is the probability of a total of 16 when the 2 spinners are spun?

Answers:

1. = 5/7 – Best to draw a tree diagram:
Total probability that Jon is late = 0.3 + 0.12 = 0.42, probability of preparing lunch and being late = 0.3, given Jon is late, probability he prepared own lunch is 0.3/0.42 = 30/42 = 5/7

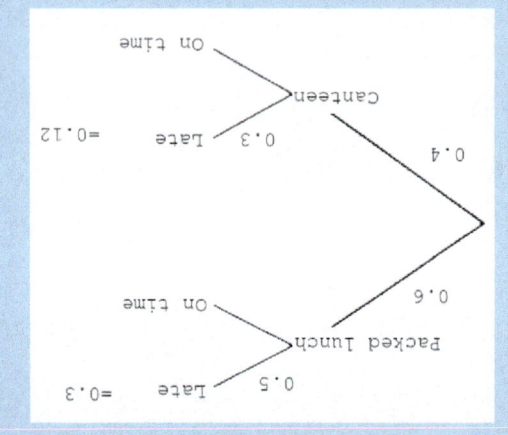

(tree diagram: Packed lunch 0.5 → On time 0.6 / Late 0.5 =0.3; Canteen 0.4 → On time / Late 0.3 =0.12)

2. = 1/6 – Best to draw a Venn diagram, 8% of applicants receive job offer and interview, 8/48 = 1/6

3. =1/84 – probability of total of 2: 1/8 × n = 1/24, n = 1/3 where n is the probability of a 1 on unfair spinner. Remaining numbers on unfair spinner have equal probability: 1 – 1/3 = 2/3, probability of each other number = 2/3 × 1/7 = 2/21. Probability of total 16 is probability of 2 8s: 1/8 × 2/21 = 1/84

The Complete BMAT Specification – Writing Task

Section 3 – The Writing Task

Well done for getting through the hard parts of the BMAT! Now onto section 3... The Essay. You'll have 30 minutes to write one side of A4 (around 550 words). This may seem scary for those who haven't written an essay since your English GCSEs, but this really is a piece of cake. Promise. Just follow the guide set out below 😊.

Basics

What does this section test?

1. The ability to communicate effectively in writing
2. The ability to organise your ideas, and present them clearly and concisely
3. The ability to support your ideas with evidence

Let's break that down.

- **The ability to communicate effectively in writing**
    - Here, examiners are looking for an essay that answers the question posed to you in full. They are expecting candidates (i.e., you) to provide them with an essay that addresses all aspects of the question. This includes providing a compelling counter argument and that leads onto a well-rounded conclusion to finish off the essay.
- **The ability to organise your ideas, and present them clearly and concisely**
    - This is where your plan comes in handy. Spending a few minutes at the start of the essay section to plan your thoughts will lend to a logical essay that flows through the arguments well. It's important that your essay makes sense – the examiner needs to understand how you arrive at your final conclusion and planning your points is a crucial first step to an excellent essay.
- **The ability to support your ideas with evidence**
    - Finally, you want to support your essay with evidence. Remember PEE on your paper? **Point, Evidence and Explain.** That's exactly what you need to do here. A well evidenced essay demonstrates good knowledge around the subject you have chosen and only makes your arguments stronger. This can be anything from your extra reading, as long as it is relevant to the subject of the essay.

> **6Med Tip:** read some example essays that have received both lower and higher marks to understand what makes a good essay. Annotate them according to the mark scheme to see if you can put yourself in the examiner's shoes.

Choosing questions

When you open this section of the BMAT, you'll find, on the page, three questions to choose from. The BMAT requires you to answer one of these questions in essay format.

The three question formats are as follows:

1. General
2. Medical
3. Scientific

All of the questions follow the same format – a statement or quote with instructions on how to respond. For example, in the 2018 past paper, the scientific question was:

> *"Rosalind Franklin said that science gives only a partial explanation of life.* Explain what you understand is meant by her statement. Argue to the contrary that science can give a complete explanation of life. To what extent do you agree with Franklin's statement?"

In this example you can see that there are 3 parts to the question: the statement in your own words, providing a counter argument and a conclusion. It is imperative that you answer all three parts in your essay as without one, you will lose marks. The essay is not negatively marked, but marks will not be awarded unless the examiner can clearly see that all facets of the question have been examined and communicated by the candidate.

So how do you choose the right question? First, you **must** read all of the questions in full before determining which one to answer. You must be comfortable with answering the question and with your knowledge base around the topic, in order to provide strong, evidence-based arguments.

> **6Med Tip:** In your preparation, try and plan for some essays even if you don't write them. This will encourage you to read up around the different topics and may be useful in the exam!

Many candidates applying for medical school will choose the medical question as it is the easiest one to provide arguments for – many of you will have done some extra reading already and can incorporate what you've learnt into your essay. Don't, however, hesitate to choose the general or scientific one if you think you'll produce a better essay.

In the event that you can't choose, or you don't feel confident with any of the essay topics in the exam, don't panic. Try and write out a point or two for each question and you might find that one of them naturally makes sense to you!

Planning

Use the **first five minutes** to plan your essay. This can be done in whatever way you're comfortable with. Planning is a crucial step to laying down your initial points and structuring you essay. You'll come up with more points than you need, particularly if you have some knowledge around the subject so this will help you choose the best points to include. If we were to plan for the 2018 question above, it might look something like this:

Rosalind Franklin said that science gives only a partial explanation of life.

Explain what you understand is meant by her statement.

- Science can't give us all the answers
- Hypotheses – cannot be proven? No real answers?
- What is life? Meaning of life, origins of life, etc

Argue to the contrary that science can give a complete explanation of life.

- For – lots of diseases we still can't cure
- Example – COVID-19, SARS and MERS
- For – confounding factors, we can't account for them, and they affect the results, bias, reliable, valid
- For – bad science? Andrew Wakefield – we can't answer questions if science isn't conducted properly?
- Against – science evolving
- Against – we know some of the mechanisms of life
- Example – plant reproduction systems
- Against – can't answer the abstract theories
- Against – we don't yet have the technology
- Example – RF used x-ray, we can now use CT or MRI or PET scans, etc

To what extent do you agree with Franklin's statement?
- I agree
- Science doesn't have to give all the answers
- Curiosity is necessary for building knowledge

Writing the essay

Writing should take about **20 minutes** if you want time at the end to check your essay. Remember that you only get one side of A4 to write your essay so don't leave too many spaces in between and if you have big handwriting, practice making it smaller so you can fit more in. Let's take our 2018 example and break that down.

> *Rosalind Franklin said that science gives only a partial explanation of life.*
>
> *Explain what you understand is meant by her statement. Argue to the contrary that science can give a complete explanation of life. To what extent do you agree with Franklin's statement?*

Explain proposition

Explain what you understand is meant by her statement.

This part of the essay should only be 2-4 lines long and should be the introduction part of the essay. The question is essentially asking you to put the statement into your own words. For example:

Here the statement implies that the questions we ask as researchers cannot be completely answered by the experiments we carry out.

The candidate puts the statement into their own words.

This is evidenced by the fact that we can never conclusively prove a hypothesis, we can only disprove it.

This is followed by a short explanation to introduce the essay.

The Complete BMAT Specification Explained
Section 3 – Writing Task

Formulate the counter argument

Argue to the contrary that science can give a complete explanation of life

A counter argument is expected to be slightly longer with both for and against arguments. We suggest two paragraphs for this part of the essay to make your essay more structured and make it flow better. It doesn't matter what order you put the points in, but make sure they are grouped together so it's easy to read and understand.

The most crucial part of this part is the evidence you provide. You must include some wider knowledge here to really strengthen your points. We suggest two examples, one that covers the for points and one that covers the against points. For example,

In the medical sciences researchers often look for answers to the mechanics of certain diseases. There is much we still don't know about serious conditions and this impacts of the level of care we are able to provide to patients.

> The candidate provides a point.

A pertinent example is the current COVID-19 pandemic.
> They then provide evidence to support the point.

Despite the virus being similar to the SARS Cov-1 and MERS, both of which have a plethora of research around them, healthcare systems worldwide were still severely under-resourced due to a lack of understanding about the biological mechanics of the virus.

> This is followed by the explanation.

See if you can highlight the points, evidence, and explanations in the following paragraphs.

Furthermore, it is impossible to test for all of the combinations of factors that would enable a researcher to prove a hypothesis. Confounding factors are factors that cannot be measured and controlled for, which means they will affect the results of the experiment and introduce errors and bias. This decreases the validity and reliability of an experiment. Thus, no experiment is ever 100% reliable or valid.

On the other hand, it can be argued that due to the ever-evolving nature of science, we may reach a point where we do know all the answers to life. As our knowledge grows and technology improves, we may be able to prove hypotheses and come to complete conclusions. For example, Franklin herself, used X-Ray crystallography to capture one of the first pictures of the helical structure of DNA – this would not have been possible 50 years prior to her time. In the same vein, we now have far more advanced imaging techniques that can capture the same pictures in greater detail.

It is also worth noting that, there is already a lot that we do know about the world around us. Science can provide us with details about the mechanics of life. For example, we understand how a plant reproduces through sexual and asexual reproduction and how it encourages that through the use of various physical characteristics i.e., bright petals. This demonstrates that although we may not be able to quantify the more abstract theories, we can still provide answers to many other questions.

In the paragraphs above, the candidate provides a point (highlighted in orange). They then provide evidence to support the point (highlighted in green) and then go onto explain (highlighted in yellow). This provides comprehensive, well supported points. There are two points each for the for and against arguments with a total of three examples used throughout the essay. Finally, we round off with our conclusion.

> **6Med Tip:** try and come up with at least two for and two against points to use in your essay

Conclusion

To what extent do you agree with Franklin's statement?

In the conclusion, you need to provide your opinion on the statement. Note that the question says, "to what extent". This gives you the option of agreeing, disagreeing or neither. It is acceptable to neither agree nor disagree with the statement, provided you can give a reason as to why. In your conclusion, you need to summarise your points listed above (but don't repeat them!) and end with a final sentence that rounds the essay off well. Remember to leave enough and space to add this part in – if you don't you'll lose marks.

I believe that the statement is true.

> The candidate provides their opinion on the statement – in this case, they agree

It must be said that perhaps the purpose of science is not to come to a complete answer at all. The fluid nature of science allows for curiosity and further questions on what has already been discovered. Without this, we would not already know so much about the world around us.

> They then give a short explanation that summarises the points above to support their opinion

Although Franklin may not have been able to answer all of the questions she may have had about the structure of DNA, she certainly paved the way for future work on the topic and other topics surrounding it.

> The essay finishes off with a sentence that completes the essay and brings it to a close

Quality of English

Another important aspect of the essay section is the Quality of English. This is part of the mark and is given a letter grade, with A being the highest mark received. In this, examiners look for fluency, good sentence structure, good grammar, varied vocabulary, and good spelling. Try and practise as many essays as you can and have different people look at them to give you feedback on the structure, content and grammar in the essay.

General Knowledge

Much of what you'll learn for section 3 will be from your own learning. It is important to stay up to date with current and past news topics. Some examples include:

> **6Med Tip:** read up on current healthcare news topics (BBC, SKY News, etc). You may be able to use some of these examples in your essay.

- Medical ethics
- Consent and confidentiality
- Informed decision making
- The biopsychosocial model
- Holistic vs paternalistic healthcare
- The slippery slope of medical ethics
- Postcode lotteries in healthcare
- Junior doctor strikes
- Brexit and the NHS
- The Bawa-Garba case
- COVID-19 and it's impact on the NHS
- Differences in healthcare systems around the world
- Private vs Public healthcare
- Medical technologies
- Common healthcare topics – obesity, diabetes, heart disease

We'll take a look at the first topic here, just to get you started.

Medical ethics

The basic principles of medical ethics are formed from the four pillars:

- Autonomy
  - The patient's right to make decisions about the treatment they receive. Thus, healthcare professionals need to have good communication skills in order to provide the patient with all the information they need to make an informed decision. This allows for more holistic healthcare in which the patient is empowered to take charge of their own health journey and advocate for their own needs.

- Beneficence
    - Do good. A healthcare professional must ensure that the care they provide is patient-centred and acts in the patient's best interests. A treatment must be evaluated on whether the outcome will truly be beneficial to the patient, and this must be communicated to the patient.
- Non-Maleficence
    - Do no harm. This means the patient must not come to any harm whilst under the care of a healthcare professional. This heavily ties in with beneficence as often, you may need to do harm in order to do good. For example, surgery is technically harming the patient, however, it is for the greater good. This is also true of the converse, you may withhold treatment if that would be harmful to the patient, for example, not performing CPR on a frail patient.
- Justice
    - This includes equitable resource and healthcare distribution.

If you use medical ethics in your essay, try and tie in at least two of the pillars. This will provide you with an essay that approaches the question in multiple ways and will look impressive to the examiner.

Checking your essay

This should be 2-5 minutes depending on how much time you've used already. Since you planned your points, you should only really be checking for any spelling or grammar errors. If you have made some mistakes, don't worry! Cross it out neatly (anything crossed out won't be marked) and rewrite it above the original sentence.

6Med Tip: anything in the margins will **not** be marked so don't write there!

Summary

In summary, you'll have **30 minutes** to write an essay on **one A4 piece of paper**. Use the **first 2-5 minutes to plan** your essay, the next **20-25 to write** the essay and the last **2-5 minutes to check** for any glaring spelling or grammar mistakes.

When writing your essay, ensure you **answer all parts of the question** and provide **at least two for and two against arguments**. Use **at least two examples** to illustrate your points and PEE on your paper!

In the conclusion, provide **your own opinion** and **summarise the points** stated above. Finish off with a **compelling statement** to top it off.

Bonus practice questions

"Our bodies are our gardens to the which our wills are gardeners."

~ Shakespeare

Explain what you understand is meant by this statement. Argue to the contrary that it is not only our will that is needed to keep our bodies healthy. To what extent do you agree with Shakespeare's statement?

Human knowledge is never contained in one person. It grows from the relationships we create between each other and the world, and still, it is never complete.

~ Paul Kalanithi

Explain what you understand is meant by this statement. Argue to the contrary that it human knowledge is contained in one person. To what extent do you agree with Kalanithi's statement?

In examining disease, we gain wisdom about anatomy and physiology and biology. In examining the person with disease, we gain wisdom about life.

~ Oliver Sacks

Explain what you understand is meant by this statement. Argue to the contrary that examining a person only gives you knowledge about anatomy, physiology, and biology. To what extent do you agree with Sacks' statement?

Laughter is the best medicine.

Explain what you understand is meant by this statement. Argue to the contrary that laughter is not a sufficient way of treating disease. To what extent do you agree with this statement?

As to diseases, make a habit of two things — to help, or at least, to do no harm.

~ Hippocrates

Explain what you understand is meant by this statement. Argue to the contrary that medicine requires more than just these principles. To what extent do you agree with this statement?

Master The BMAT Mark Scheme

Well done for making it to the end! We hope it was useful and that you feel more confident with the BMAT. The best way to utilise this book is to go back in and re-do the questions, then revise any knowledge you be may not yet be confident with. Doing the same questions over and over may seem boring, but repetition will drill those concepts into your head.

How does the mark scheme work?

The BMAT is scored in the same way for sections 1 and 2 and slightly differently for section 3. We briefly covered it earlier on in the book, but we'll go into more detail here. Put yourself in the examiner's shoes, especially for the essay section, and think about what they might want to see in your work.

Section 1 and 2 are positively marked (they won't deduct marks for wrong answers) and each question gets one mark, which means they all have the same weighting. Therefore, to maximise your marks, try and answer as many easy questions correctly as you can, rather than spending too much time on the difficult questions. The marks are then standardised to give marks ranging from 1.0 to 9.0. A score of >6.0 is considered to be above average and >7.0 is considered to be excellent. Generally, the average ranges around 4.0-5.0.

As a guide, in 2020, to score a standardised mark of 7.0, you had to get 29/32 questions right and to score a 5.0 you had to get 21/32 questions right. As you can see there isn't a large margin between the two, so it's usually a difference of 2-3 questions that will pull your mark up.

Section 3 is scored with a number and letter system. The number corresponds to the quality of the content of the essay and the letter corresponds to the quality of the English in the essay.

Numbers wise, 1 is the lowest and 5 is the highest. The average is usually around 3. We've explained this in a bit more detail using simple terms below.

1 – though there may be some relevant points, the answer doesn't really address the question and the essay does not flow well.

2 – the essay somewhat answers the question, but still does not address all aspects.

3 – this is the most common mark and addresses all aspects of the question, with a logical conclusion. There are flaws in the argument, but it is acceptable.

4 – this addresses all aspects of the question, flows well and there is a logical conclusion. There are minor flaws in the argument.

5 – this addresses all parts of the question, with strong arguments for and against the point. The conclusion is impactful and flows naturally. Very minor flaws that do not detract from the essay.

In terms of the letter system, you will be scored from A to E. A is the highest, E is the lowest.

A – Good use of English with fluent sentences and little to no spelling mistakes.

B – Good use of English with minor spelling mistakes.

C – reasonable use of English with spelling mistakes and some grammatical errors

D – reasonable use of English with spelling mistakes and grammatical errors

E – weak use of English with lack of fluency and flawed grammar

Knowledge Check

One last thing, before we go.

We know you've been working really hard with this book. Learning, revising, and testing yourself as you go.

However, just to be sure – we thought that we'd give you one more test.

Below, you will find practice questions, in the style of the BMAT for *every single part of the BMAT Specification.*

You can do them all at once, if you want – or, while you're revising, you can go to the specific section you're working on and test yourself using the practice questions for that particular section of the spec. Either way, these should give you the last boost you need for your exams.

So, if you want some extra practice, we're going to start on the next page with Biology, oh, and the answers are after those, as well (no peeking!)

Well, some peeking is okay, if you're really stuck.

Good luck!

6med

B1- Cells

Question 1

Which of the following statement(s) regarding cell structure is/are true?

1. All types of cell contain a nucleus.
2. Plant cells contain a cell wall made from cellulose.
3. Mitochondria are found in every cell type, providing energy for cellular processes

A- 1 only
B- 2 only
C- 3 only
D- 1 and 2 only
E- 2 and 3 only

Question 2

Which of the following definitions is incorrect?

A- Ribosome: the cell organelle responsible for protein synthesis.
B- Plasmid: rings of genetic material, found in the cytoplasm of prokaryotic cells.
C- Prokaryotic Cell: a cell that contains a nucleus, for example, animal and plant cells.
D- Chloroplast: an organelle containing both the green pigment chlorophyll and enzymes needed for photosynthesis.

Question 3

Which of the following comparison(s) between eukaryotic and prokaryotic cells is/are correct?

	Eukaryotic	Prokaryotic
1	Contain mitochondria.	Do not contain mitochondria.
2	DNA is contained in a nucleus.	DNA is found free in the cytoplasm.
3	Have a cell membrane, but no cell wall.	Have a cell membrane and cell wall.

A- 1 only
B- 2 only
C- 3 only
D- 1 and 2 only
E- 1 and 3 only
F- 2 and 3 only

B2- Movement Across Membranes

Question 1

Which of the following statements regarding diffusion is correct?

- A- Diffusion is the net movement of a substance from an area of low concentration to an area of high concentration.
- B- Diffusion occurs in solids, liquids and gases.
- C- In the lungs, oxygen diffuses from a high concentration in the blood to a low concentration in the alveoli.
- D- In the liver, urea diffuses from a high concentration in blood vessels to a low concentration in liver cells.
- E- When diffusion occurs, there is movement of particles in both directions (from both high to low, and low to high concentrations).

Question 2

Which of the following statement(s) regarding osmosis is/are incorrect?

1. As animal cells do not have a cell wall, the movement of water by osmosis can change their shape, potentially causing damage.
2. Osmosis is the movement of water molecules from a region of a high concentration of water molecules to a region with a lower concentration of water molecules, through a partially permeable membrane.
3. Water will move by osmosis from a dilute to a concentrated solution.

- A- 1 only
- B- 2 only
- C- 3 only
- D- 1 and 2 only
- E- 2 and 3 only
- F- All of the above
- G- None of the above

Question 3

Which of the following statements regarding active transport is incorrect?

- A- The movement of urea from liver cells into liver blood vessels occurs by active transport.
- B- Active transport, unlike osmosis and diffusion, requires energy to occur.
- C- The absorption of glucose from the intestinal lumen sometimes requires active transport.
- D- Active transport involves the movement of substances from an area of low concentration to an area of high concentration.

B3- Cell Division and Sex Determination

Question 1

Which of the following statement(s) regarding chromosomes is/are correct?

1. In mammals, including humans, females possess two copies of the X chromosome.
2. At all points of the cell cycle of a eukaryotic cell, the DNA in the nucleus exists as chromosomes.
3. Each chromosome in a pair contains the same types of genes.

A- 1 only
B- 2 only
C- 3 only
D- 1 and 2 only
E- 2 and 3 only
F- 1 and 3 only

Question 2

Which of the following definitions regarding the cell cycle is incorrect?

A- Haploid: used to describe cells that have a single set of chromosomes.
B- Gametes: the reproductive cells of an organism- in females these are called ova, and in males are called sperm.
C- Mitosis: a type of cell division producing daughter cells known as gametes.
D- Interphase: the period of the cell cycle occurring between each mitotic division, during which the cell grows and DNA is copied.

Question 3

Which of the following is not an advantage of sexual reproduction?

A- It results in variation, allowing a species to better adapt to a novel environment.
B- Only one parent is needed.
C- A disease is less likely to affect all the individuals in a population.
D- Sexual reproduction can be controlled by humans to suit various needs, such as the use of selective breeding to increase food production.

B4- Inheritance

Question 1

Which of the following definitions regarding genetic inheritance is incorrect?

- A- Allele: a different form of the same gene.
- B- Phenotype: the alleles an organism possesses for a particular gene.
- C- Heterozygous: when the two alleles of a particular gene in an individual are different.
- D- Haploid: used to describe cells that have a single set of chromosomes.
- E- Dominant: a type of allele that is always expressed in an organism's phenotype.

Question 2

The eye colour of a particular population is controlled by a single gene. The B allele is dominant and confers brown eyes. The b allele is recessive and confers blue eyes. If a brown-eyed individual with a heterozygous genotype breeds with a blue-eyed individual, what is the probability that they have a brown-eyed female offspring?

- A- 100%
- B- 75%
- C- 50%
- D- 25%
- E- 12.5%

Question 3

Which of the following statement(s) regarding genetic inheritance is/are correct?

1. Each characteristic of an individual is controlled by a single gene.
2. Some conditions, for example cystic fibrosis, arise from the inheritance of faulty alleles.
3. A recessive allele is only expressed in an organism's phenotype if there are two copies of it.

- A- 1 only
- B- 2 only
- C- 3 only
- D- 1 and 2 only
- E- 2 and 3 only

B5- DNA

Question 1

Which of the following statements about the structure of DNA is incorrect?

    A- DNA is a polymer made up from monomers called nucleotides.
    B- A nucleotide consists of a base, a common sugar and a phosphate group.
    C- Mutations to DNA bases will always result in the formation of a faulty protein.
    D- The bases in DNA nucleotides can be of 4 different types: thymine, adenine, guanine and cytosine.
    E- DNA consists of two separate strands, arranged as a double helix.

Question 2

Which of the following options would be the sequence of bases on the complementary strand to a section of DNA with the sequence: CGAACTCGAGGT

    A- GCTTATCGAGGT
    B- CGTTCTCGACCT
    C- GCTTGTCGTCCA
    D- GCTTGAGCTCCA
    E- CGAACTCGAGGT
    F- GCTTGAGCTCCA

Question 3

Which of the following statement(s) about DNA is/are correct?

1. A sequence of 3 bases in DNA codes for 1 amino acid when the DNA is translated into a protein.
2. Complementary base pairing means that thymine bases always pair with adenine bases.
3. All parts of DNA code for proteins.

    A- 1 only
    B- 2 only
    C- 3 only
    D- 1 and 2 only
    E- 2 and 3 only
    F- All of the above

B6- Gene Technologies

Question 1

Which of the following is not a difficulty associated with the use of stem cell therapies?

- A- If stem cells are grown in culture, they may become contaminated with viruses that may transfer to a patient.
- B- It is still unknown how successful stem cell therapies will be clinically.
- C- There are many suitable stem cell donors both available and consenting.
- D- It is difficult to both obtain and store embryonic stem cells.

Question 2

Which of the following is/are example(s) of genetic engineering in current use?

1. Engineering crops to become herbicide resistant.
2. Engineering bacteria to produce large amounts of insulin for the treatment of diabetes.
3. Engineering wild rice to produce beta carotene, becoming so-called 'golden rice'.

- A- 1 only
- B- 2 only
- C- 3 only
- D- 1 and 2 only
- E- 2 and 3 only
- F- All of the above

Question 3

Which of the following definitions regarding gene technologies is incorrect?

- A- Cloning: a method of producing genetically identical copies of a cell, tissue or organism.
- B- Stem Cell: a type of cell found in embryos, foetuses and a few types of adult tissue that can differentiate into many other cell types.
- C- Vector: the vehicle used to transfer genetic material from a donor cell or organism to a recipient cell or organism, for example, plasmids.
- D- Genetic Engineering: a method involving the transfer of genetic information from a donor cell or organism to a recipient cell or organism.
- E- In Vivo: a type of experiment done in glassware, for example, a petri dish or test tube.

B7- Variation

Question 1

Which of the following is not a stage in the process of natural selection?

- A- Some individuals become better suited to the environment in which they are, other individuals are less well suited so are less likely to survive.
- B- The environment in which the population exists has unlimited resources, so can support an unlimited population.
- C- Genetic variation between individuals of the same species occurs, for example, due to random mutations.
- D- The population becomes better suited to survive in its environment.
- E- Organisms reproduce and pass on their alleles to the subsequent generation.

Question 2

Which of the following is/are example(s) of natural selection?

1. Due to the overuse and inappropriate use of antibiotics, some bacteria have developed resistance to commonly used antibiotics.
2. The increased development of a dark sub-population of moths following increased pollution levels in the 19th century.
3. The prey species in a predator-prey relationship is likely to evolve to develop features that make it more prone to being hunted by the predator.

- A- 1 only
- B- 2 only
- C- 3 only
- D- 1 and 2 only
- E- 2 and 3 only
- F- All of the above
- G- None of the above

Question 3

Which of the following is not a source of variation in a population?

- A- Mutations spontaneously occurring during gamete production.
- B- Environmental factors such as diet and climate.
- C- The random fertilisation of gametes during sexual reproduction.
- D- The process of mitosis producing genetically identical daughter cells.

B8- Enzymes

Question 1

Which of the following statements regarding enzyme structure is incorrect?

- A- The substrate is the specific substance upon which an enzyme acts.
- B- Denaturation is when the molecular structure of an enzyme is altered, such as by extremes of pH or temperature, so that it can no longer catalyse.
- C- The active site of an enzyme is the part to which its specific substrate attaches in order for its reaction to be catalysed.
- D- The structure of an enzyme is unchanged at the end of a chemical reaction, allowing the enzyme to be reused in further reactions.
- E- Enzymes only catalyse reactions that involve the breaking down of substrates into smaller pieces.

Question 2

Various factors can affect the rate of an enzyme-catalysed reaction. Which of the following statement(s) regarding these factors is/are true?

1. The rate of an enzyme-catalysed reaction is directly proportional to the temperature at which it occurs.
2. Each enzyme has optimum activity at a specific pH value.
3. The rate of an enzyme-catalysed reaction is directly proportional to the concentration of a substrate.

- A- 1 only
- B- 2 only
- C- 3 only
- D- 1 and 2 only
- E- 2 and 3 only
- F- 1 and 3 only
- G- None of the above

Question 3

Which of the following statement(s) regarding digestion enzymes is/are correct?

1. Protease enzymes break down polypeptides into amino acids.
2. Carbohydrase enzymes are produced in saliva and the pancreas only.
3. Lipase enzymes break down lipids into fatty acids and glycogen.

- A- 1 only
- B- 2 only
- C- 3 only
- D- 1 and 2 only
- E- 2 and 3 only
- F- 1 and 3 only
- G- None of the above

B9- Animal Physiology

Question 1

Which of the following statements does not describe a way in which the efficiency of exchange systems is increased?

- A- The villi and microvilli in the digestive system provide a large surface area for nutrient absorption.
- B- Ventilation of the lungs allows the oxygen to be removed from the exchange surface area, and the carbon dioxide to enter the exchange surface area, maintaining a concentration gradient.
- C- The epithelium of the alveoli is only one cell thick, providing a short distance for the diffusion of gases.
- D- The network of capillaries in each villus of the small intestine allows the transport of substances to and from the site of nutrient exchange.

Question 2

Which of the following definitions is incorrect?

- A- Coronary Arteries: small arteries that supply the heart muscle with blood, allowing it to contract.
- B- Valve: a structure found in veins that prevents the backflow of blood.
- C- Ventricles: the two upper chambers of the heart receiving venous blood.
- D- Haemoglobin: the protein packed into red blood cells that binds to oxygen, allowing oxygen to be transported around the body.
- E- Pulmonary Vein: a blood vessel carrying oxygenated blood from the lungs to the left atrium of the heart.

Question 3

Which statement(s) regarding communicable diseases is/are correct?

1. Communicable diseases can be passed down through generations by inheritance of a faulty allele.
2. HIV is a virus which results in the development of AIDS.
3. Antibiotics are used to treat bacterial infections only.

- A- 1 only
- B- 2 only
- C- 3 only
- D- 1 and 2 only
- E- 2 and 3 only
- F- All of the above
- G- None of the above

B10- Ecosystems

Question 1

Which of the following definitions is incorrect?

- A- Species: all of the members of a specific type of organism that live in a certain geographical area.
- B- Primary Consumer: an organism that eats the producer in a food chain.
- C- Ecosystem: all of the organisms living in a certain area and the non-living parts of this environment.
- D- Abiotic Factors: the non-living factors of an ecosystem that affect its functioning, such as temperature and water availability.

Question 2

Which of the following statements regarding interaction between organisms in an ecosystem is incorrect?

- A- Producers are found at the bottom of most food chains and are consumed by the primary consumer.
- B- In a predator-prey cycle, the number of prey increases when there are more predators.
- C- There is almost always more prey than predators in a predator-prey cycle.
- D- Dead organisms are broken down by decomposers such as bacteria.

Question 3

Which of the following statement(s) regarding the carbon cycle is/are correct?

1. The decomposition of dead organisms by microorganisms removes carbon dioxide from the atmosphere.
2. The combustion of fossil fuels releases carbon dioxide into the atmosphere.
3. Carbon dioxide is removed from the atmosphere by plants photosynthesising.

A- 1 only
B- 2 only
C- 3 only
D- 1 and 2 only
E- 2 and 3 only
F- 1 and 3 only

C1 - Atomic Structure

Question 1

Which of the following statement (s) regarding atomic structure are correct?
1. A magnesium ion contains the same number of protons as a sodium ion
2. A copper ion in a blue copper sulphate solution contains three more protons than electrons
3. A fluoride ion contains the same number of electrons than an oxygen ion in magnesium oxide.

A) 1 only
B) 2 only
C) 3 only
D) 1 and 3
E) 2 and 3

Question 2

The following electronic configuration may apply to which elements and/or ions?
2, 8, 8, 18

    A) A potassium atom only.
    B) A Sodium ion only.
    C) A strontium ion or a rubidium atom.
    D) A strontium ion, a rubidium ion or a single krypton atom.
    E) A strontium ion, a rubidium ion or a single xenon atom.

Question 3

A student is assigned three different atoms and is told that they all belong to the same element. The atoms have different relative atomic masses. Why may this be?

1. The atoms are isotopes of one another.
2. The atoms are different ions of the same element.
3. The atoms have protons added or removed.

A) 1 only
B) 2 only
C) 3 only
D) 1 and 2
E) None

C2 - The Periodic Table

Question 1

Which of the following statement (s) regarding the transition metals are correct?

1. The transition metals belong to the same Period.
2. The transition metal ions all contain the same charge as they belong to the same group.
3. Each element belonging to the transition metals may donate electrons to form one ion with a specific charge.

A) 1 only
B) 1 and 2
C) 2 and 3
D) 3 only
E) None

Question 2

Which of the following statement (s) regarding Groups in the Periodic table is correct?

1. Transition metals belong to the same group.
2. A compound formed between a Group 2 ion and a Group 6 ion is ionic.
3. Atoms within the same group do not share electrons with each other.

A) 1 only
B) 1 and 2
C) 2 and 3
D) 2 only
E) 3 only

Question 3

Which of the following statement (s) regarding the halogens are correct?
1. Iodine is more reactive than bromine
2. A reaction between chlorine and MgF_2 would form magnesium chloride.
3. Bromine has a higher boiling point than chlorine.

A) 1 only
B) 1 and 2
C) 2 and 3
D) 2 only
E) 3 only

C3 - Chemical Reactions, Formulae and Equations

Question 1

Two aqueous solutions, namely sodium chloride and silver nitrate, are mixed together. Which of the following equation (s) correctly describes the reaction?

1. Ag^+ (aq) + Cl^- (aq) → AgCl (aq)
2. $AgNO_3$ (aq) + NaCl (aq) → AgCl (aq) + $NaNO_3$ (aq)
3. Ag^+ (aq) + Cl^- (aq) → AgCl (s)

A) 1 only
B) 1 and 2
C) 2 and 3
D) 2 only
E) 3 only

Question 2

A solution of barium nitrate is combined with aqueous sodium carbonate. Which of the following is the correct net ionic equation for the reaction?

1. CO_3^{2-} + Ba^{2+} → $BaCO_3$ (s)
2. NO_3^- + Na^+ → $NaNO_3$ (aq)
3. $2NO_3^{3-}$ + Ba^{2+} → $Ba(NO_3)_2$ (aq)

A) 1 only
B) 1 and 2
C) 2 and 3
D) 2 only
E) 3 only

Question 3

The reaction between carbon monoxide and hydrogen produces methanol. What effect would increasing the pressure have on the reaction?

1. The equilibrium will shift to the right.
2. The rate of reaction will increase.
3. More reactants will be produced.

A) 1 only
B) 1 and 2
C) 2 and 3
D) 2 only
E) 3 only

C4 - Quantitative Chemistry

Question 1

A student reacts 1.3 moles of magnesium metal with oxygen. 20.5g of solid powder is produced. Calculate the percentage yield of the reaction, to the nearest whole number.

A) 15%   B) 21%   C) 59%   D) 66%   E) 73%

Question 2

Lead (II) nitrate is combined with potassium iodide solution. What is the ratio of moles of lead (II) nitrate to the solid formed from the reaction?

A) 1:2   B) 1:3   C) 1:1   D) 3:2   E) 2:1

Question 3

Propane reacts with oxygen. What is the ratio of propane molecules to water molecules produced during the reaction?

A) 1:5   B) 1:3   C) 1:4   D) 3:8   E) 2:5

C5 – Oxidation, Reduction and Redox

Question 1

Aluminium metal is burnt under excess oxygen. Which of the following is the correct half equation for the reduction reaction?

A) $3O_2 (g) + 12e^- \rightarrow 6O^{2-} (s)$
B) $4Al (s) \rightarrow 4Al^{3+} (s) + 12e^-$
C) $4Al (s) + 3O_2 (g) \rightarrow 2Al_2O_3 (s)$
D) $O_2 (g) + 2e^- \rightarrow O2^- (s)$
E) $2Al (s) \rightarrow 2Al^{3+} (s) + 3e^-$

Question 2

Which of the following reactions is an example of a disproportionation reaction, and which species has been simultaneously oxidised and reduced?

1. $3Cl_2 + 6NaOH \rightarrow 5NaCl + NaClO_3 + 3H_2O$
2. $4HCl + O_2 \rightarrow 2Cl_2 + 2H_2O$
3. $Fe_2O_3 + 3CO \rightarrow 2Fe + 3CO_2$

A) Reaction 1; Na
B) Reaction 1; Cl
C) Reaction 2; O
D) Reaction 3; O
E) Reaction 3; Fe

Question 3

Which species act as the oxidising agent and the reducing agent in the following reaction, respectively?

$2NH_3 (g) + 3Br_2 (g) \rightarrow N_2 (g) + 6HBr (g)$

A) Br^-, H^+
B) Br_2, NH_3
C) NH_3, Br^-
D) N^{3-}, H^+
E) H^+, Br^-

C6 – Chemical Bonding, Structure and Properties

Question 1

Which statement (s) are correct regarding the properties of magnesium chloride?

1. This compound is held together by strong bonds formed by the sharing of electrons.
2. The forces that keep the compound together act in all directions.
3. Every positive magnesium ion has one constituent negative chloride ion.

A) 1 only
B) 1 and 2
C) 2 and 3
D) 2 only
E) 3 only

Question 2

A student is given an unidentified compound. She is told a limited amount of information regarding the compound. She knows it can conduct electricity, and has a melting point over 800 degrees Celsius. She is also told that the compound is held together by ions.
Which of the following statement (s) is true for the compound?

1. It is comprised of metallic bonding.
2. It may dissolve in water to form a solution.
3. It only conducts electricity in a solution.

A) 1 only
B) 1 and 2
C) 2 and 3
D) 2 only
E) 3 only

Question 3

Which of the following statement (s) is true for covalent bonding?

1. The carbon atom in methane donates all of its outer shell electrons.
2. Covalently bonded species have low melting and boiling points
3. The intermolecular forces involved in covalently bonded species are very strong.

A) 1 only
B) 1 and 2
C) 2 and 3
D) 2 only
E) 3 only

C7 – Group Chemistry

Question 1

The boiling point of radon is -67.5 degrees Celsius. Which of the following statement (s) is likely true for xenon?

1. It has a boiling point higher than -62 degrees Celsius.
2. It is often contained within fireworks due to its flammable properties.
3. The mass of a 150 cm^3 balloon filled with oxygen will be heavier than an 150 cm^3 balloon of xenon.

A) 1 only
B) 1 and 2
C) 2 and 3
D) 2 only
E) 3 only

The Complete BMAT Specification Explained

Knowledge Check - Chemistry

Question 2

A student is conducting an experiment. She adds an unknown gas to a solution of sodium bromide, and observes that the solution turns brown. Which of the following statement (s) are correct regarding this reaction?

1. Br becomes oxidised.
2. The unknown gas could be fluorine or chlorine.
3. The unknown gas must be more reactive than bromine.

- A) 1 only
- B) 1 and 2
- C) 1 and 3
- D) 2 only
- E) 1, 2 and 3

Question 3

A student is given an unknown element. He observes that the structure of the element is not brittle. The student adds the element to water, and observes effervescence, but no flame. Which statement (s) are correct regarding this element?

1. The element may be identified using a flame test.
2. The element could be any of the alkali metals.
3. The resulting solution will be a metal hydroxide.

- A) 1 only
- B) 1 and 2
- C) 1 and 3
- D) 2 only
- E) 3 only

C8 – Separation Techniques

Question 1

A student is looking to separate copper (II) sulphate crystals from solution. He decides that he will use the crystallisation separation technique. Which of the following statement (s) apply to this technique?

1. Continuing to heat the crystals after all the solvent has evaporated will likely produce larger crystals.
2. The resulting crystals should be blue in colour.
3. Removing all the water from the resulting crystals produces a blue powder.

- A) 1 only
- B) 1 and 2
- C) 1 and 3
- D) 2 only
- E) 3 only

The Complete BMAT Specification Explained

Knowledge Check - Chemistry

Question 2

A student is investigating the different types of separation techniques. They are looking to use fractional distillation to separate a solution containing two different species. Which of the following statement (s) are correct for this technique?

1. It may be used to separate a solution containing water and ethanol.
2. The species that remains in the flask containing the original solution will have a lower boiling point.
3. The fractionating column is hotter at the top than the bottom.

    A) 1 only   B) 1 and 2   C) 1 and 3   D) 2 only   E) 3 only

Question 3

Which of the following statement (s) applies to paper chromatography?

1. The mobile phase may be a coloured plant pigment, such as chlorophyll.
2. Paper chromatography only works when separating soluble substances.
3. Two substances that travel the same distance up the paper must be the same.

    A) 1 only   B) 1 and 2   C) 1 and 3   D) 2 only   E) 3 only

C9 – Acids, Bases, and Salts

Question 1

Consider the following reaction:
$2HNO_3 + MgO \rightarrow Mg(NO_3)_2 + H_2O$
Which of the following statement (s) apply to this reaction?

1. This is an example of a neutralisation reaction involving an acid and alkali.
2. This is an example of an exothermic reaction.
3. Mg is reduced.

    A) 1 only   C) 1 and 3   E) 3 only
    B) 1 and 2   D) 2 only

Question 2

A student finds some old chalk used for writing on the classroom blackboard. She adds this chalk to a beaker of dilute sulphuric acid. Which of the following statement (s) are correct concerning this reaction?

1. She should observe effervescence.
2. Inserting a thermometer into the acid should see a temperature rise following the addition of the chalk.
3. This reaction can test whether the chalk contains carbonate ions.

A) 1 only   B) 1 and 2   C) 1 and 3   D) 2 only   E) 1, 2 and 3

Question 3

Which of the following statement (s) is true for nitric acid?

1. It is a triprotic acid.
2. It reacts with $CuCO_3$ to form copper (I) nitrate.
3. To make a salt from sodium carbonate, you add excess nitric acid to sodium carbonate to form sodium nitrate.

A) 1 only   B) 1 and 2   C) 1 and 3   D) 3 only   E) None

C10 – Rates of Reaction

Question 1

Which one (or more) of the following changes will increase the frequency of collisions between reacting particles?

(a) increasing pressure
(b) adding a catalyst
(c) increases concentration of the product
(d) increasing temperature

A) a and b and d only
B) a and d and c only
C) a and d only
D) All the statements

Question 2

Calcium carbonate and HCl react to produce calcium chloride and hydrogen gas which is measured with a gas syringe. A graph of volume of hydrogen gas formed against time is plotted for the following two experiments.

-Experiment 1: Carried out at 35°C- 100cm^3 of 2mol dm^{-3} HCl and an excess of calcium carbonate.
-Experiment 2: Carried out at 20°C- 50cm^3 of 4mol dm^{-3} HCl and an excess of calcium carbonate.

Which of the following is true regarding the two reactions and their graphs?

A) Experiment 1 has a faster initial rate of reaction and it's line ultimately reaches a height that is double experiment 2.
B) Experiment 1 has the same initial rate of reaction as experiment 2 and its line ultimately reaches a height that is the same height as experiment 2's line.
C) Experiment 1 has a faster initial rate of reaction, and its line ultimately reaches a height that is the same height as experiment 2's line.
D) Experiment 1 has the same initial rate of reaction as experiment 2 and its line ultimately reaches a height that is the double the height of experiment 2's line.

Question 3

Which of the following describes the effect of a catalyst on the rate of a reaction?

	Effect on activation energy of reaction	Effect on collision frequency between particles	Effect on proportion of collisions which are successful
A	Decreases	No effect	No effect
B	Increases	Increases	No effect
C	Decreases	Increases	Increases
D	Increases	No effect	Increases
E	Decreases	No effect	increases
F	No effect	Increases	No effect
G	Decreases	No effect	Increases

C11 - Energetics

Question 1

Which one or more of the following are sources of error when measuring enthalpy change using temperature change?

(a) Incomplete combustion
(b) Calorimeter absorbing heat
(c) Heat lost to surroundings
(d) Heat gained by water

A) a and c and d
B) all of the above
C) a and b and c
D) a and c

Question 2

250g of water increases in heat by 12°C during a reaction. 5 moles of fuel were used so how much energy is transferred per mole of fuel burned? Specific Heat capacity of Water is 4.2J/g/°C

A) 12600J
B) 2520J
C) 3000J
D) 6000J

Question 3

Which one the following lines accurately portrays the activation energy of the reaction which has a catalyst added to it?

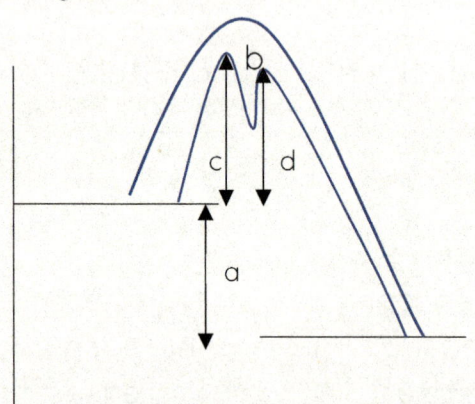

C12 - Electrolysis

Question 1

Which one of the rows below correctly identifies what is produced at the cathode and anode for different aqueous solutions?

	Electrolyte being electrolysed	Product at positive inert electrode (anode)	Product at negative inert electrode (cathode)
A	Sodium chloride	Hydrogen gas	Chlorine gas
B	Copper sulphate	Oxygen	Copper
C	Copper chloride	Oxygen	copper
D	Sodium chloride	Oxygen	Hydrogen gas

Question 2

Which of the following statements is correct regarding electroplating?

A) the cathode should be the plating metal
B) the electrolyte doesn't need to contain ions of the plating metal
C) the cathode should be the original metal
D) the anode should be the original metal?

Question 3

Which of the following statements is correct regarding electrolysis?

A) The electrode can be a molten electrical conductor which is in contact with the electrolyte solution
B) the potential difference in a circuit causes the cathode to become positively charged and the anode to become negatively charged.
C) Anions lose electrons at the anode to become atoms or molecules and the cations gain electrons at the cathode to become atoms or molecules.
D) there is no requirement for an electrolyte solution with free ions in electrolysis

C13 – Carbon/Organic Chemistry

Question 1

What is the percentage by mass of C in the tetrahydrofuran?

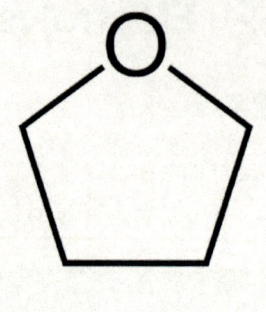

Molecular weights: C = 12, O = 16, H = 1

A) 60% B) 70% C) 82% D) 67%

Question 2

Which one of the following reactions of ethene is correct?

A) $C_2H_4 + H_2 = CH + CH_3$
B) $C_2H_4 + HCl = CH_3Cl + CH_4$
C) $C_2H_4 + HCl = CH_2ClCH_3$
D) $C_2H_4 + H_2O$ (steam) $= CO_2 + CH_4 + H_2$

Question 3

What is the name of the carboxylic acid with a total of 10 Hydrogen atoms?

A) Ethanoic acid
B) Pentanoic acid
C) Butanoic acid
D) Heptanoic acid

C14 - Metals

Question 1

Which of the following statement (s) regarding Group 2 metals is correct?

1. Be has the lowest boiling point of all metals in this group.
2. Mg may form an ionic compound with a chloride ion, with each Mg ion in a 1:1 ratio with each Cl ion.
3. A Ca^{2+} ion has the same number of electrons in its outer shell as a K^+ ion.

A) 1 only
B) 2 only
C) 3 only
D) 1 and 3
E) 2 and 3

Question 2

Which of the following statement (s) regarding Group 1 metals is correct?

1. Group 1 metals form alkaline solutions when reacted with a weak acid.
2. Sodium metal will react with water to form an aqueous salt and hydrogen gas.
3. Adding universal indicator to the solution formed after a reaction between potassium and water should turn it blue or purple.

A. 1 and 2   B. 1 and 3   C. 2 and 3   D. 3 only   E. 1, 2 and 3

Question 3

Consider the following reaction:
$Mg (s) + 2HCl (aq) \rightarrow MgCl_2 (aq) + H_2 (g)$
Which statement is incorrect regarding this reaction?

A) If potassium was used instead of magnesium, a more violent reaction could be expected.
B) If zinc was used instead of magnesium, a slower reaction could be expected.
C) The solution produced after this reaction is colourless.
D) The gas produced from this reaction could relight a glowing splint.
E) The solution formed could produce crystals.

C15 – Kinetic / Particle Theory

Question 1

Which of the following describes best what is occurring between A-B?

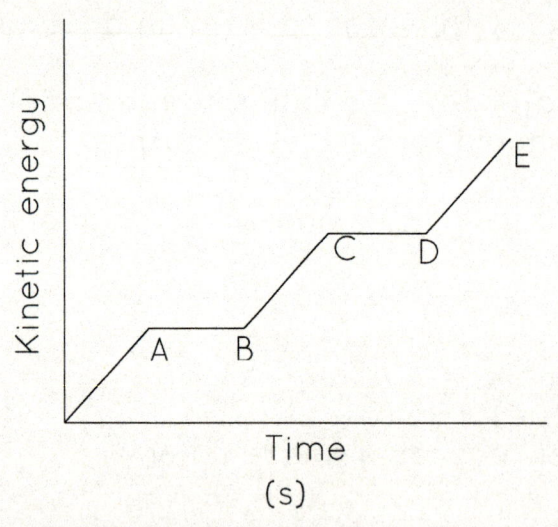

A) Liquid is evaporating into gas
B) Heat energy is being released as the temperature changes
C) Heat energy is being absorbed as the temperature changes
D) Heat energy is being absorbed but temperature doesn't change

Question 2

The melting point of platinum is 1,769 °C. The boiling point of platinum is 3,827 °C. The melting point of boron is 2, 453 °C. The boiling point of iodine is 3, 923 °C.

Which of the following is true at 2, 452 °C?

A) Platinum is a solid and Boron is a solid
B) Platinum is a liquid and Boron is a liquid
C) Platinum is solid and Boron is a liquid
D) Platinum is a liquid and Boron is a solid

Question 3

Which of the following characteristics is true for the states of matter?

	Characteristic	Solid	Liquid	Gas
A	Compressibility	Can't be compressed	Compresses easily	Compresses easily
B	Rate of diffusion	Does not diffuse	Diffuses slowly	Diffuses very quickly
C	Density	Low density	High density	Low density
D	Shape	Fixed shape	Fills container	Fills container

C16 – Chemical Tests

Question 1

A student heats copper metal with a Bunsen burner until a black solid powder is produced. They then add this powder to weak sulphuric acid and stir. What observations could be expected?

1. The sulphuric acid solution turns from colourless to blue after the powder is added.
2. Effervescence should occur when the powder is added to the acid.
3. Collecting any gas produced by adding the powder to the acid would produce a squeaky pop with a lighted splint.

A) 1 only
B) 2 only
C) 1 and 3 only
D) 2 and 3 only
E) None

Question 2

Which of the following statement (s) regarding metal cations is correct?

1. Magnesium reacts with NaOH (aq) to form a white precipitate.
2. Magnesium reacts with copper sulphate, turning the solution from blue to colourless.
3. Magnesium reacts with iron sulphate, producing solid iron.

A) 1 only
B) 1 and 2
C) 2 and 3
D) 1 and 3
E) 1, 2 and 3

Question 3

Two unknown metals are given to a student. She labels them Metal 1 and Metal 2 respectively.

Metal 1 is burnt with a blue Bunsen flame, turning the flame lilac.
Metal 2 is reacted with sulphuric acid, forming a blue solution.

Identify the metals.

A) 1: lithium, 2: potassium
B) 1: lithium, 2: copper (II)
C) 1: Potassium, 2: calcium
D) 1: potassium, 2: copper (II)
E) 1: Potassium, 2: lithium

C17 – Air and Water

Question 1

Which of the following statement (s) is true for the atmospheric gas methane?

1. It can be produced through landfill waste, farming or nuclear plants
2. It has created a hole in the earth's ozone layer
3. Reducing the amount of coal, oil and gas used as fossil fuels should help to reduce levels of methane released into the atmosphere

A) 1 only
B) 3 only
C) 1 and 3
D) 2 and 3
E) None

Question 2

Which of the following statement (s) regarding polluting gases is correct?

1. Sulphur dioxide is not directly harmful to human health but may cause acid rain
2. Nitrous oxides can be released from vehicle exhaust.
3. Sulphur dioxide is not released from naturally occurring phenomena. It is a product only of human activity.

A) 1 only
B) 2 only
C) 3 only
D) 1 and 2
E) 2 and 3

Question 3

Which of the following statement (s) are true for drinking water?

1. It contains chlorine gas.
2. Chlorination of water produces hydrogen gas.
3. Chlorine gas forms chloride ions when added to water.

A) 1 only   B) 2 only   C) 3 only   D) 1 and 2   E) 2 and 3

P1 - Electricity

Question 1

Concerning the properties of ammeters and voltmeters, which one of the following is true?

	Voltmeter	Ammeter
A	Connected in parallel Very high resistance	Connected in parallel Very high resistance
B	Connected in parallel Very low resistance	Connected in series Very high resistance
C	Connected in series Very high resistance	Connected in parallel Very low resistance
D	Connected in parallel Very high resistance	Connected in series Very low resistance
E	Connected in series Very low resistance	Connected in series Very low resistance

Question 2

If this battery supplies 6V and each lamp has a resistance of 1Ω, what will ammeter 1 and ammeter 2 read before and after Lamp A is removed and replaced with wire?

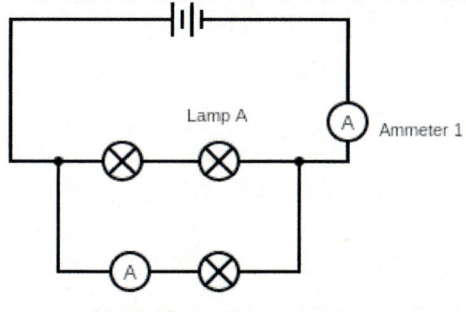

	Before	After
A	Ammeter 1: 6 A Ammeter 2: 3 A	Ammeter 1: 8 A Ammeter 2: 4 A
B	Ammeter 1: 9 A Ammeter 2: 6 A	Ammeter 1: 12 A Ammeter 2: 6 A
C	Ammeter 1: 9 A Ammeter 2: 4.5 A	Ammeter 1: 12 A Ammeter 2: 6 A
D	Ammeter 1: 4 A Ammeter 2: 2.666 A	Ammeter 1: 3 A Ammeter 2: 1.5 A
E	Ammeter 1: 2 A Ammeter 2: 2 A	Ammeter 1: 3 A Ammeter 2: 3 A

Question 3

Which electrical components are represented on the plots below?

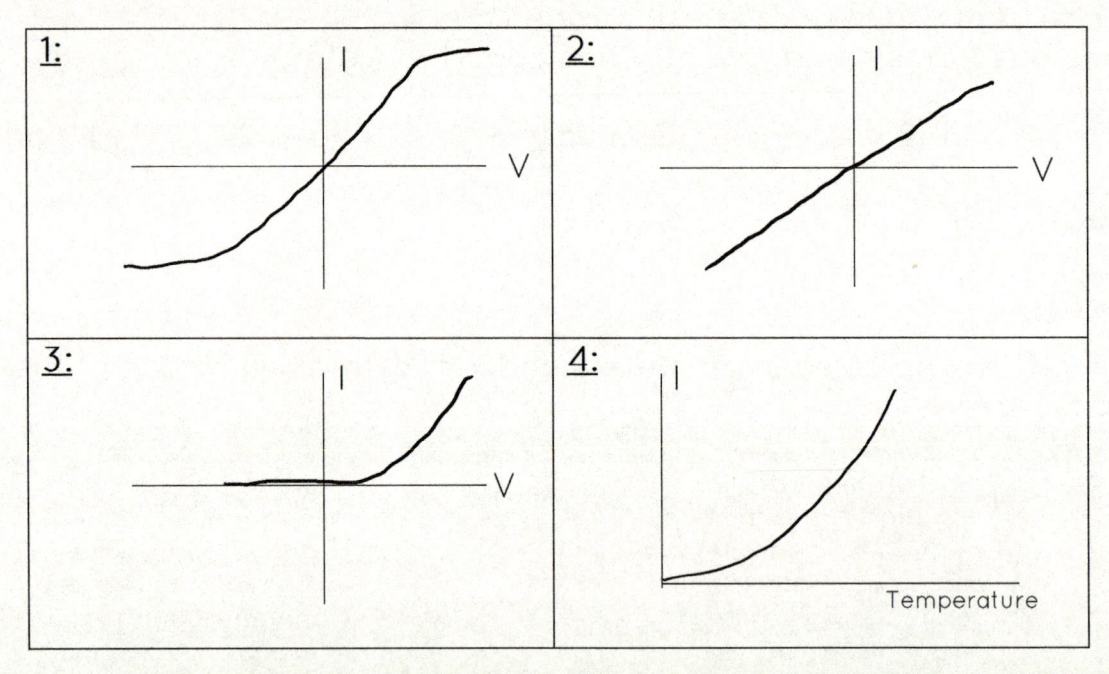

	1	2	3	4
A	Filament lamp	Ohmic resistor	Diode	Positive-temperature coefficient thermistor
B	Ohmic resistor	Non-ohmic resistor	Diode	Negative-temperature coefficient thermistor
C	Diode	Ohmic resistor	Filament lamp	Negative-temperature coefficient thermistor
D	Ohmic resistor	Diode	Filament lamp	Positive-temperature coefficient thermistor
E	Filament lamp	Ohmic resistor	Diode	Negative-temperature coefficient thermistor

P2 - Magnetism

Question 1

An alternating current is induced in a coil of wire when it is rotated in a magnetic field. What is the net effect on the frequency of voltage oscillation and amplitude of the induced electromotive force (emf) when the coil is rotated at twice the rate, the magnetic field strength is doubled and the number of coils is halved?

	Frequency of current reversal	Amplitude of induced emf
A	Doubled	Same
B	Doubled	Doubled
C	Doubled	Quadrupled
D	Halved	Doubled
E	Halved	Quadrupled

Question 2

When a current-carrying wire is placed in a magnetic field it experiences a force. Which of the following statements is true?

A) A force will only be generated when the magnetic field direction and current are parallel to one another
B) If the current is 10 A, the length of wire 2 metres and magnetic flux density 2 T the magnitude of the induced force is 14 N
C) Fleming's right-hand rule can be used to determine the relationship between force, magnetic field and current direction.
D) If the current is 10 A, the length of wire 2 metres and magnetic flux density 2 T the magnitude of the induced force is 40 N
E) Only direct current can be used to generate motion in an electrical motor

Question 3

Which of the following statement(s) on transformers is (/are) true?

1. For a step-up transformer, the primary coil has more turns than the secondary coil.
2. A direct current is induced in the secondary coil by electromagnetic induction
3. High voltages are used to minimise energy losses during long-distance transmission

F) 1 only
G) 2 only
H) 3 only
I) 1 and 2
J) 1 and 3
K) 2 and 3
L) 1, 2 and 3

P3 - Mechanics

Question 1

A 50kg woman is cycling along a road. She is generating 200 N of forward-acting force and is accelerating at 2 ms^{-2}. Assuming the friction between her tyre and road is the only other force present, what is the magnitude of this force? Acceleration due to gravity = 10 ms^{-2}

    A) 0 N
    B) 25 N
    C) 50 N
    D) 75 N
    E) 100 N

Question 2

Rinda is playing with her new remote controlled toy car which can travel forwards and backwards at variable speed. The velocity-time graph shows tracks the car's movement. At 5 seconds, what is the distance travelled by the toy from its start point and what is the total distance covered?

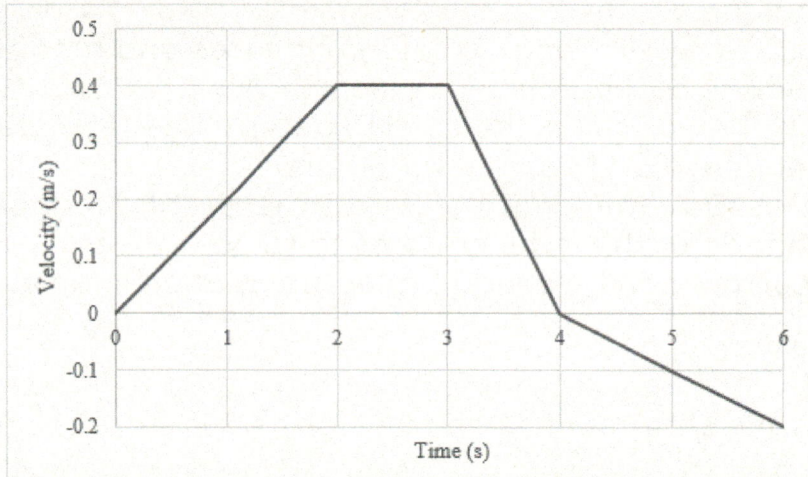

	Distance	Displacement
A	0.8 m	0.4 m
B	0.4 m	-0.2 m
C	1.2 m	0.8 m
D	0.8 m	-0.2 m
E	1.2 m	-0.4 m

Question 3

Two objects collide as shown in the image below, the green object is stationary after the collision. What is the velocity of the blue object after the impact? What is the magnitude of the force exerted by one object on the other?

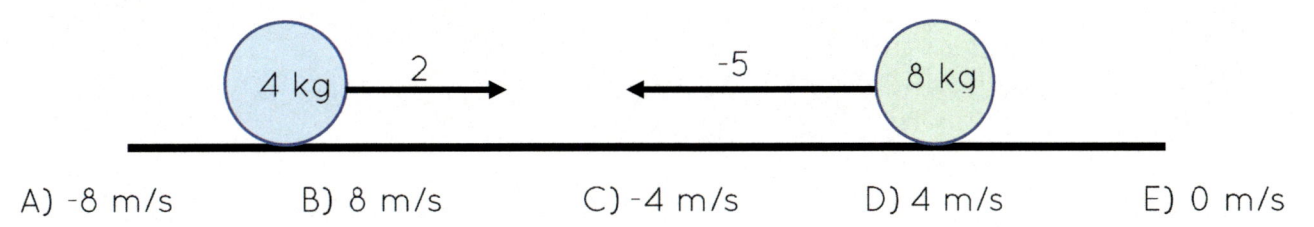

[Diagram: 4 kg object moving right at 2 m/s; 8 kg object moving left at -5 m/s]

A) -8 m/s   B) 8 m/s   C) -4 m/s   D) 4 m/s   E) 0 m/s

P4 - Thermal Physics

Question 1

An unknown substance is heated. 4800 J of energy raise the temperature of the 0.25 kg of the substance by 2°C. What is the specific heat capacity of this substance?

A) 2400 J kg^{-1} °C^{-1}
B) 4800 J °C^{-1}
C) 9600 J kg^{-1}
D) 9600 J kg^{-1} °C^{-1}
E) 19200 J kg^{-1} °C^{-1}

Question 2

Read the following statements about thermal energy transfers.

1. Metal is a good conductor of thermal energy
2. Convection is a process of heat transfer exclusively in gases
3. Thermal radiation is transferred by ultraviolet wave emission

Which are true?

A) 1 only   B) 1 and 2   C) 1 and 3   D) 2 and 3   E) 1, 2 and 3

Question 3

Which of the following would emit thermal radiation at the greatest rate?
F) A dark, hot, metal object in a cold room
G) A light, hot, metal object in a hot room
H) A dark, hot, metal object in a hot room
I) A light, cold, metal object in a cold room
J) A light, hot, metal object in a cold room

P5 - Matter

Question 1

The volume that an ideal gas occupies depends on:

    A) Its pressure, temperature, molecular weight
    B) Its pressure and temperature
    C) Its temperature and molecular weight
    D) Its temperature alone

Question 2

Which of the following is **not** true? When a gas is heated (in a fixed container)

    A) its particles gain more kinetic energy
    B) the pressure in the container is increased
    C) its particles collide more frequently with each other and the container wall
    D) particles move more slowly

Question 3

A balloon contains 1.2 L of air at $1*10^5$ Pa. The balloon is squeezed to reduce its volume until the volume of the balloon (still intact) is 0.8 L. If there is no change in temperature, what is the new pressure of the gas in the balloon?

A) 1.2×10^5 Pa   B) 1.5×10^5 Pa   C) 1.3×10^5 Pa   D) $2/3 \times 10^5$ Pa   E) 2×10^5 Pa

P6 - Waves

Question 1

A wave travels through air at a frequency of 100 kHz and wavelength of 3 km. Upon entering a new material, its new velocity is 2×10^8 m/s. What is its new wavelength?

A) 3000 m   B) 2 km   C) 2000 km   D) 0.0005 m   E) 20 km

Knowledge Check - Physics

Question 2

Which of the following is true of sound waves?

A) Sound waves can travel in a vacuum
B) A sound wave with a velocity of 330 m/s and frequency of 2 Hz has a wavelength of 660 m/s
C) Humans typically hear sounds between 20 Hz and 200 kHz
D) Increasing the amplitude of a sound wave will make it sound more high-pitched
E) Sound waves can be generated by a vibrating source

Question 3

Concerning the electromagnetic spectrum, which row in the table best describes the applications and relative frequency of the following waves?

	Infrared	Ultraviolet	Gamma rays
A	Use: medical tracer Frequency: middle	Use: TV remotes Frequency: lowest	Use: vitamin D production Frequency: highest
B	Use: TV remotes Frequency: lowest	Use: medical tracer Frequency: middle	Use: vitamin D production Frequency: highest
C	Use: TV remotes Frequency: highest	Use: vitamin D production Frequency: middle	Use: medical tracer Frequency: lowest
D	Use: vitamin D production Frequency: middle	Use: medical tracer Frequency: lowest	Use: TV remotes Frequency: highest
E	Use: TV remotes Frequency: lowest	Use: vitamin D production Frequency: middle	Use: medical tracer Frequency: highest

P7 - Radioactivity

Question 1

The following equations represent different types of radioactive decay.

i. $^a_b X \rightarrow {}^4_2 He + {}^{a-4}_{b-2} X$

ii. $^a_b X \rightarrow {}^a_{b+1} X + {}^{\ 0}_{-1} e$

Which of the following is correct regarding the nature of the decay and the minimum structures required to block the movement of the radioactive product?

	Process i	Process ii
A	Is α decay, and its radiation is blocked by a sheet of paper	Is β decay, and its radiation is blocked by aluminium
B	Is β decay, and its radiation is blocked by aluminium	Is α decay, and its radiation is blocked by a sheet of paper
C	Is α decay, and its radiation is blocked by a sheet of paper	Is γ decay, and its radiation is blocked by aluminium
D	Is γ decay, and its radiation is blocked by a sheet of paper	Is β decay, and its radiation is blocked by aluminium
E	Is β decay, and its radiation is blocked by a sheet of paper	Is α decay, and its radiation is blocked by aluminium

Question 2

Which of the following is **true**?

A) Distance travelled through air: γ radiation > α radiation > β radiation
B) Ionising power: γ radiation > β radiation > α radiation
C) Penetrating power: α radiation > β radiation > γ radiation
D) Mass and absolute charge: α radiation > β radiation > γ radiation

Question 3

Uranium-238 ($^{238}_{92} U$) undergoes a radioactive decay series of 14 steps before producing stable lead-206. After 6 alpha decays and 2 beta decays, an unstable, intermediate Pb species is produced. What is the symbol for this nuclide?

A) $^{214}_{84} Pb$ B) $^{210}_{82} Pb$ C) $^{226}_{86} Pb$ D) $^{214}_{82} Pb$ E) $^{210}_{92} Pb$

M1 - Units

Question 1

Evaluate
  0.08cm − 4.4μm
    Give your answer in standard form and in mm

A) 0.7956   B) 7.956 x 10⁻²   C) 0.756   D) 0.0756   E) 7.56 x 10⁻³

Question 2

Jonathan mixes 800g of sugar with 2.8kg of flour
Express the ratio of sugar to flour in its simplest form

A) 8:28   B) 28:8   C) 2:7   D) 1:2:7   E) 7:2

Question 3

Gina lives in Bristol and is driving to London. The distance from Bristol to London is 120 miles and Gina's car can travel 60 miles per gallon of petrol.

Petrol cost= £1.80 per litre
4.5 litres= 1 gallon

How much will it cost Gina to make a round trip to London?

A) £30.20   C) £31.40   E) £40.00
B) £16.20   D) £32.40   F) £33.70

M2 - Number

Question 1

Toffee sweets are sold in packets of 20. Fudge sweets are sold in packets of 28. Raed wants to buy the same number of toffee sweets as fudge sweets.

What is the smallest number of packets of each of the sweets he could buy?

A) 14 toffee and 10 fudge   D) 6 toffee and 4 fudge
B) 7 fudge and 5 toffee   E) 10 fudge and 14 toffee
C) 7 toffee and 5 fudge

The Complete BMAT Specification Explained
Knowledge Check - Maths

Question 2

Solve the following simultaneous equations
$$2Y = X + 10$$
$$Y = 2X - 7$$

Question 3

Find the smallest positive integer, k, such that 180k is a perfect square

A) 20   B) 5   C) 10   D) 9   E) 4

M3 - Ratio and Proportion

Question 1

Tom buys some football boots for £40. He sells them to his friend a year later for £28
What's his percentage loss?

A) 31   B) 32   C) 30   D) 29   E) 28

Question 2

A bank increased the rate of simple interest from 3.5% to 4% per annum. Alix deposited £5200 in the bank for 6 months at the new interest rate.
Find out how much more interest Alix would receive than if she has deposited the money before the interest rate changed.

A) £104   B) £91   C) £208   D) £26   E) £13

Question 3

Amy bought a bicycle for £1200. Each year it depreciates in value by 15%. How much is it worth in 3 years?

A) £700.28   B) £736.95   C) £867.23   D) £737.59   E) £373.95

M4 - Algebra

Question 1

If $x > 10000$ what is the closest value to $\frac{x}{3x+1}$

A) $\frac{1}{3}$ B) $\frac{1}{2}$ C) $\frac{1}{4}$ D) 0.66   E) $\frac{2500}{7501}$

Question 2

The curve $6y - 12 = 6x^2 - 18x$ is intersected at two points, A and B, by the straight line
$$y + x = 5.$$

Find the coordinates of points A and B

- A) (2,3) and (-1,8)
- B) (-4,5) and (-5,4)
- C) (2,8) and (-1,3)
- D) (-1,6) and (3,2)
- E) (4,5) and (-4,-5)

Question 3

Solve $-3 < \frac{x+3}{2} < 6$

- A) $-8 < x < 8$
- B) $-4 < x < 9$
- C) $-9 < x < 9$
- D) $-9 < x < 4$
- E) $-9 < x < 3$

M5 - Geometry

Question 1

Given that cos(60)= 0.5 find the length of AB

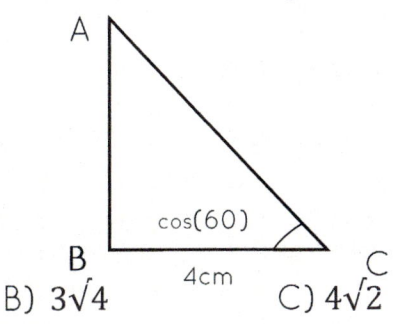

- A) $4\sqrt{3}$
- B) $3\sqrt{4}$
- C) $4\sqrt{2}$
- D) $\sqrt{16}$
- E) 48

Question 2

One side of a rectangle is 3π cm. The area is 22 cm^2
What is the perimeter of the rectangle to 3 significant figures?

- A) 22cm
- B) 22.5cm
- C) 23cm
- D) 23.5cm
- E) 24cm

The Complete BMAT Specification Explained

Knowledge Check - Maths

Question 3

A sector of a circle with centre O has a radius of 5.
The arc length of the sector is 10.
What is the area of the sector?

A) 23　　　　B) 25　　　　C) 26　　　　D) 30　　　　E) 25π

M6 - Statistics

Question 1

When designing a questionnaire it must be:

　　　　a. Easy to analyse
　　　　b. Easy to understand
　　　　c. Unfair (lead to bias)
　　　　d. Quick to answer

A) a,b,d　　　　B) a,b　　　　C) a,c　　　　D) b,c,d　　　　E) all

Question 2

What is the mean, median and mode of the following list of numbers (to 3.s.f):

$$1,1,2,3,4,5,5,5,6$$

A) 3.56, 4, 5　　B) 3.56, 4, 1　　C) 4.56, 3, 5　　D) 4.56, 4, 2　　E) 3.45, 5, 4

Question 3

Which statements are true:

　　　　a. Discrete data can only take certain values
　　　　b. Continuous data can only be between 0 and 100
　　　　c. Height is an example of continuous data
　　　　d. Shoe size is an example of continuous data

A) a,c　　　　B) a,b,c　　　　C) b,d　　　　D) c,d　　　　E) none

M7 - Probability

Question 1

Brandon has a bag containing 15 different sweets. She has 9 reds, 4 yellow sweets and 2 green.
Calculate the probability that she picks out 2 red and 1 yellow sweet in any order when she removes 3 sweets from the bag

A) $\frac{21}{5}$ B) $\frac{864}{2730}$ C) $\frac{673}{455}$ D) $\frac{2019}{455}$ E) $\frac{3}{15}$

Question 2

There are 9 boys and 11 girls in a class. All the students take a geography test. The mean mark for the boys is 44. The mean mark for the girls is 52. Susan was ill on the day of the test. She takes the test a day later and scores 45.

What is the overall mean mark for the whole class?

A) $\frac{242}{5}$ B) $\frac{1013}{20}$ C) $\frac{1013}{21}$ D) $\frac{242}{20}$ E) $\frac{96}{5}$

Question 3

Last year, a third of the population of Bristol admitted to having more than 5 bottles of beer a week. What is the probability that out of a random group of three people who live in Bristol, exactly one of them will have admitted to drinking more than 5 bottles of beer a week?

A) $\frac{4}{9}$ B) $\frac{1}{9}$ C) $\frac{1}{3}$ D) $\frac{4}{27}$ E) $\frac{2}{9}$

Knowledge Check Answers
B1 Cells

Question 1

B

1. Incorrect. Only animal and plant cells contain nuclei.
2. Correct.
3. Incorrect. Although mitochondria do provide energy for cell processes, bacteria do not contain mitochondria.

Question 2

C

A eukaryotic cell is the type of cell that contains a nucleus, prokaryotic cells such as bacteria have their genetic material free in the cytoplasm.

Question 3

D

1. Correct.
2. Correct.
3. Incorrect, some eukaryotic cells (plant cells) have cell walls.

B2- Movement Across Membranes

Question 1

E

- A- Incorrect, diffusion is the net movement from high to low concentration.
- B- Incorrect, diffusion can only happen in liquids and gases, as the particles in these are free to continuously move around.
- C- Incorrect, this described the movement of carbon dioxide. Oxygen diffuses in the opposite direction.
- D- Incorrect, urea in the liver diffuses from a high concentration in liver cells to a low concentration in the blood.
- E- Correct.

Question 2

G

None of the statements are incorrect - they are all true!

Question 3

A

- A- Incorrect, urea moves down a concentration gradient (by diffusion) from liver cells into the blood.
- B- Correct.
- C- Correct.
- D- Correct.

B3- Cell Division and Sex Determination

Question 1

F

1. Correct.
2. Incorrect, the chromosomes are only formed when DNA coils and condenses when a cell is about to divide.
3. Correct.

Question 2

C

- A- Correct.
- B- Correct.
- C- Incorrect, meiosis is the type of cell division producing gametes, which contain a single set of chromosomes and are all genetically different. Mitosis produces daughter cells that are genetically identical to each other and the parent cell.
- D- Correct.
- E- Correct.

Question 3

B

- A- Correct.
- B- Incorrect, two parents are needed for sexual reproduction. The need for only one parent is an advantage of asexual reproduction.
- C- Correct.
- D- Correct.

B4- Inheritance

Question 1

B

- A- Correct.
- B- Incorrect, this is the definition for genotype. Phenotype is the expression of the genetic makeup of an organism (the visible characteristics).
- C- Correct.
- D- Correct.
- E- Correct.

Question 2

D

Individual 1 genotype: Bb

Individual 2 genotype: bb

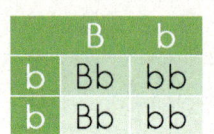

	B	b
b	Bb	bb
b	Bb	bb

There is a 50% chance of producing brown-eyed offspring (Bb). As there is always a 50% chance of offspring being male or female, this means there is a 25% chance of the offspring having both brown eyes and being female.

Question 3

E

1. Incorrect. Although some characteristics can be controlled by a single gene, it is more common that a characteristic is controlled by multiple genes.
2. Correct.
3. Correct.

B5- DNA

Question 1

C

A- Correct.
B- Correct.
C- Incorrect. Although some mutations have dramatic effects on the functioning of a protein, most do not. This can be because the mutation could be in a non-coding section of the DNA, for example.
D- Correct.
E- Correct.

Question 2

F

The complementary base to any C is G, and any A is T and vice versa. Therefore the complementary base sequence to CGAACTCGAGGT is GCTTGAGCTCCA.

Question 3

D

1. Correct.
2. Correct, and cytosine bases always pair with guanine bases.
3. Incorrect, there are coding sections of DNA that do code for proteins, and non-coding sections of DNA that can be used to switch genes on and off.

B6- Gene Technologies

Question 1

C

Options A, B and D all are difficulties associated with the use of stem cell therapies. Option C is not true. Even if this was true, this would be beneficial, not a difficulty.

Question 2

F

All 3 statements describe applications of genetic engineering in current use.

Question 3

E

Options A-D are all the correct definitions. Option E describes the term 'in vitro'. In vivo is when an experiment is done in a living organism.

B7- Variation

Question 1

B

Option B is incorrect. If the environment could support an unlimited population, there would be no 'selection pressure' allowing survival of the fittest organisms.

Question 2

D

1. Correct.
2. Correct.
3. Incorrect. Natural selection involves the evolution of a species so that it develops features that are more advantageous for its survival. In this case, prey species often evolve to develop features that make it less likely to be hunted and killed by its predator.

Question 3

D

- A- Correct.
- B- Correct.
- C- Correct.
- D- Incorrect. Although mitosis does produce genetically identical daughter cells, this does not result in any variation

B8- Enzymes

Question 1

E

Options A-D are all correct statements. Option E is incorrect at some enzymes can catalyse reactions that involve the joining together of multiple small substrates into a larger molecule.

Question 2

B

1. Incorrect. Although the rate of an enzyme-catalysed reaction increases with increased temperature, this is not a directly proportional relationship. As well as this, this increase in activity only occurs until a specific point at which the enzyme becomes denatured and its activity rapidly ceases.
2. Correct.
3. Incorrect. Although the rate of an enzyme-catalysed reaction increases with increased substrate concentration, this is not always a directly proportional relationship. As well as this, this increase in activity only occurs until a specific point at which the concentration of enzyme becomes a limiting factor.

Question 3

A

1. Correct.
2. Incorrect. Carbohydrase enzymes are produced in the saliva, pancreas and small intestine.
3. Incorrect. Lipase enzymes break down lipids into fatty acids and glycerol. Glycogen is a polymer of glucose molecules used for storage purposes

B9- Animal Physiology

Question 1

B

- A- Correct.
- B- Incorrect. Although ventilation contributes to the maintenance of a concentration gradient, it brings oxygen to the alveoli, and removes the carbon dioxide.
- C- Correct.
- D- Correct.

Question 2

C

- A- Correct.
- B- Correct.
- C- Incorrect. This describes the atria. The ventricles are the two chambers at the bottom of the heart that receive blood from the atria, pumping this blood into the arteries.
- D- Correct.
- E- Correct.

Question 3

E

1. Incorrect. Communicable disease are those that can be passed on between individuals by pathogens. This does not include inherited genetic disorders.
2. Correct.
3. Correct.

B10- Ecosystems

Question 1

A

- A- Incorrect. This describes a population. A species is the name given to a type of organism that is a basic unit of organism classification.
- B- Correct.
- C- Correct.
- D- Correct.

Question 2

B

- A- Correct.
- B- Incorrect. When there are more predators, the number of prey decreases as there are more predators to kill the prey,
- C- Correct.
- D- Correct.

Question 3

E

1. Incorrect. Decomposition releases carbon dioxide into the atmosphere.
2. Correct.
3. Correct.

C1 – Atomic Structure

Question 1

C

Statement 1 is incorrect. A magnesium ion contains the same number of electrons, not protons, as a sodium ion.

Statement 2 is incorrect. The copper ion in a blue copper salt solution is Cu^{2+}. It therefore contains two more protons than electrons

Statement 3 is correct. A fluoride ion (F^-) contains 10 electrons. An oxygen ion (O^{2-}) in MgO contains 10 electrons.

Answers - Chemistry

Question 2

D

A potassium ion has the configuration 2, 8, 8. A sodium ion has the configuration 2, 8. A rubidium atom has the configuration 2, 8, 8, 18, 1. A xenon atom has the configuration 2, 8, 8, 18, 18. Out of the options listed, only Sr^{2+} and Rb^+ ions, as well as Kr atoms have the configuration 2, 8, 8, 18.

Question 3

A

Statement 1 is correct. Atoms of the same element with different atomic masses have different numbers of neutrons to one another. This means that they are isotopes of one another

Statement 2 is incorrect. The charge of ions concern numbers of electrons, not neutrons.

Statement 3 is incorrect. Protons are not added or removed from atoms. Only electrons are added or removed from outermost electron shells.

C2 – The Periodic Table

Question 1

E

Statement 1 is incorrect. All transition metals belong neither to the same group or period.
Statement 2 is incorrect. Transition metal ions do not all contain the same charge.
Statement 3 is incorrect. Some metals can form multiple ions: Fe^{2+}, Fe^{3+} etc.

Question 2

D

Statement 1 is incorrect. Transition metals belong to many groups, specifically groups 3-12.
Statement 2 is correct. Group 2 elements are metals. Group 6 elements are non-metals. Metals donate electrons to non-metals, forming an ionic lattice.
Statement 3 is incorrect. Group 17 atoms commonly share electrons with each other to form a covalent compound.

Question 3

E

Statement 1 is incorrect. Reactivity decreases down the group.
Statement 2 is incorrect. Reactivity decreases down the group, so chlorine would not displace fluorine from the compound.
Statement 3 is correct. Boiling points increase down the group.

C3- Chemical Reactions, Formulae and Equations

Question 1

E

Equation 1 is incorrect. AgCl doesn't dissolve in solution to form an aqueous compound. It is a solid.
Equation 2 is incorrect, for the same reason.
Equation 3 is correct. This is an example of a net ionic equation.

Question 2

A

Equation 1 is correct.
Equation 2 is incorrect. Sodium and nitrate ions cancel out in the total ionic equation.
Equation 3 is incorrect. Nitrate ions cancel out in the total ionic equation.

Question 3

B

Statement 1 is correct. Composing an equation shows that 3 moles of reactants form one mole of product i.e. methanol. Increasing pressure favours the side with fewer moles.
Statement 2 is correct. Increasing pressure increases the number of collisions per second, increasing rate of reaction.
Statement 3 is incorrect. Less reactants will be produces as there are more mole of reactants than products.

C4 – Quantitative Chemistry

Question 1

D

$2Mg\ (s) + O_2\ (g) \rightarrow 2MgO\ (s)$
The ratio of moles of magnesium to magnesium oxide is 1:1. To work out the predicted mass of MgO produced, we do 1.3 x 24 = 31.2g.
(20.5/31.2) x 100 = 66.

Question 2

C

We must first construct a balanced equation:
$Pb(NO_3)_2\ (aq) + 2KI\ (aq) \rightarrow PbI_2\ (s) + 2KNO_3\ (aq)$
We can see that one mole of lead (II) nitrate reacts with one mole of solid product (1:1).

Question 3

C

We must first construct a balanced equation:
$C_3H_8 + 5O_2 \rightarrow 3CO_2 + 4H_2O$
We can therefore see that one mole of propane reacts to form four moles of water.

C5 – Oxidation, Reduction and Redox

Question 1

A

When electrons are added to an atom, this reaction is a reduction reaction. The answer is not D as writing out a full balanced chemical equation means that we must include 6 atoms of oxygen.

Question 2

B

Reaction 1 is a disproportionation reaction; Cl has been reduced in NaCl and oxidised in NaClO3. Reactions 2 and 3 are oxidation reactions; not disproportionation.

Question 3

B

Br_2 acts as the oxidising agent as the species is reduced from 0 to -1 in HBr. NH_3 acts as the reducing agent, as N is oxidised from -3 to 0 in N_2.

C6 – Chemical Bonding, Structure and Properties

Question 1

D

1. Statement 1 is incorrect. The compound is held together by electrostatic forces shared between oppositely charged ions. These ions do not share electrons with one another.
2. Statement 2 is correct. Electrostatic forces act in all directions in an ionic lattice.
3. Statement 3 is incorrect. For every one magnesium ion, there exists two chloride ions.

Question 2

D

1. Statement 1 is incorrect. It could have metallic bonding, but it also may have ionic bonding instead.
2. Statement 2 is correct. If ionic, it is soluble in water.
3. Statement 3 is incorrect. The compound could be metallic, in which case it will not dissolve in water and will conduct electricity as a solid.

The Complete BMAT Specification Explained

Answers - Chemistry

Question 3

A

1. Statement 1 is correct. The molecular formular of methane is CH_4. Carbon has four electrons in its outer shell, and shares each constituent electron equally with each of the four hydrogen atoms.
2. Statement 2 is incorrect. Although simple covalent substances have low melting and boiling points, giant covalent substances have very high melting and boiling points.
3. Statement 3 is incorrect. The covalent bonds within molecules are strong, but between molecules, the intermolecular forces are weak. This explains why many simple covalent substances are gaseous at room temperature.

C7 – Group Chemistry

Question 1

E

1. Statement 1 is incorrect. Boiling points for the noble gases increase down the group.
2. Statement 2 is incorrect. Noble gases are inert so are not flammable.
3. Statement 3 is correct. The density of noble gases compared to Group 16 gases is considerably less.

Question 2

E

1. Statement 1 is correct. Bromine loses an electron, changing from an oxidation state of -1 to 0.
2. Statement 2 is incorrect. Both chlorine and fluorine are more reactive than bromine.
3. Statement 3 is correct, as the brown gas is bromine. Bromine must have therefore been displaced by a more reactive element.

Question 3

C

1. Statement 1 is correct. The element could be a Group 1 or Group 2 metal, which will produce a specific colour when burnt under a blue Bunsen flame.
2. Statement 2 is incorrect. Potassium will produce a lilac flame with water.
3. Statement 3 is correct. This metal will react with water to produce a metal hydroxide and hydrogen gas.

C8 – Separation Techniques

Question 1

D

1. Statement 1 is incorrect. To produce large crystals, you should stop heating the solution before all the solvent has evaporated.
2. Statement 2 is correct. Hydrated copper (II) sulphate crystals are characteristically blue.
3. Statement 3 is incorrect. Anhydrous copper (II) sulphate is a white powder.

Question 2

A

1. Statement 1 is correct. Fractional distillation is used to separate miscible liquids that have different boiling points. This applies to water and ethanol.
2. Statement 2 is incorrect. The species that escapes the solution first and travels out of the separation apparatus has a lower boiling point.
3. Statement 3 is incorrect. The fractionating column is hotter at the bottom.

Question 3

D

1. Statement 1 is incorrect. The mobile phase is the solvent, not the substance which is being separated.
2. Statement 2 is correct. Insoluble substances will not form a solution so cannot travel in a solvent.
3. Statement 3 is incorrect. Two substances with the same Rf value are not necessarily the same.

C9 – Acids, Bases and Salts

Question 1

D

1. Statement 1 is incorrect. Although a neutralisation reaction, magnesium oxide is insoluble so is a base, not an alkali.
2. Statement 2 is correct. The reaction of acids with metal oxides is exothermic.
3. Statement 3 is incorrect. Magnesium does not change oxidation states.

Question 2

E

1. Statement 1 is correct. Effervescence should be observed as carbon dioxide gas is produced.
2. Statement 2 is correct. The reaction of acid and metal carbonate, such as calcium carbonate in chalk, is exothermic.
3. Statement 3 is correct. If effervescence is observed when chalk is added to acid, it is a sign that the compound contains carbonate ions, causing CO_2 gas production.

Question 3

E

1. Statement 1 is incorrect. The ratio of H^+ ions to NO_3^- ions in nitric acid is 1:1. It is therefore a monoprotic acid.
2. Statement 2 is incorrect. The copper in $CuCO_3$ has an oxidation state of two. Therefore, it would form copper (II) nitrate.
3. Statement 3 is incorrect. You add sodium carbonate in excess, not nitric acid.

C10 – Rates of Reaction

Question 1

C

1. Adding a catalyst doesn't increase the frequency (number) of collisions. It increases the frequency of <u>successful</u> collisions due to reducing activation energy. The overall number of collisions remain the same.
2. Increasing the concentration of the product decreases the frequency of collisions between reacting particles as they act as a <u>barrier</u> and reduce the frequency of the reacting particles coming in contact with each other.
3. Increasing pressure and temperature increases the frequency of collisions as they increase kinetic energy of reacting particles in a reaction, so C is the correct answer.

Question 2

C

1. Experiment 1 is carried out at a higher temperature so has a faster initial rate of reaction.
2. Both experiments have an excess of calcium carbonate so that does not affect the ultimate volume formed.
3. Experiment 1 has double the volume but half the concentration of HCl compared to experiment 2 so overall there are the same number of moles.
4. Therefore, the total volume of hydrogen gas produced is the same and both experiments lines will reach the same height.

Question 3

G.

Adding a catalyst reduces the activation energy of a reaction. Therefore, it increases the proportion of collisions which are successful but doesn't increase the collision frequency <u>overall</u>.

C11 - Energetics

Question 1

C.
 (a) is correct – especially for larger molecules being used as fuels, they may not burn completely.
 (b) Is correct as the calorimeter can absorb heat due to it acting as a conductor
 (c) Is correct as the material of the cup used e.g. polystyrene isn't a complete insulator so some heat can be lost
 (d) Is incorrect as heat is gained by water but this is not an error – it is used to measure enthalpy change!

Question 2

B

$Q = m c t$. $Q = 4.2 * 250 * 12 = 12600 J$. This is how much energy is transferred in total. To find out how much energy is transferred per mole of fuel, divide 12600 by 5 = 2520 J.

Question 3

C

A is the overall enthalpy change
B is the activation energy of the uncatalyzed reaction
C is the activation energy of the catalysed reaction as it is the highest point reached on the catalysed reactions line
D is not the activation energy as it is not the highest energy point reached on the catalysed reaction's line.

C12 - Electrolysis

Question 1

B

A is incorrect as hydrogen gas is produced at the cathode as sodium is more reactive than hydrogen.
B is correct as copper is less reactive than hydrogen, so the metal is produced at the cathode and at the anode, oxygen is formed unless halide ions are present
C is incorrect as the halide (chloride) at the anode loses elections to form the halogen chlorine
D is incorrect as at the anode, the halide (chloride) loses elections to form the halogen chlorine

Question 2

C.

The metal ions of the plating metal should be present in the electrolyte solution, so B is incorrect.

Metal ions are positively charged so will be attracted to the cathode meaning the cathode should be the original metal (that you wish to be coated) and the anode should be the plating metal. Therefore, the metal ions from the anode and electrolyte will be attracted to the cathode and cover it in the plating metal.

Question 3

C

A is incorrect as the electrode must be solid.
B is incorrect as the cathode is negatively charged and anode is positively charged.
C is correct. Anions lose elections and cations gain electrons.
D is incorrect as free ions are required in the electrolyte solution to complete the circuit.

C13 – Carbon / Organic Chemistry

Question 1

B

The relative atomic mass of tetrahydrofuran is 72 as it is 16 + 4*12 + 8. It has 4 carbon atoms, so the calculation is: (4* 12) / (16+ 4*12 + 8) = 48 / 72* 100 = 66.7%

Question 2

C

A is incorrect as when ethene reacts with hydrogen gas it forms ethane (C_2H_6)
B is incorrect as when ethene reacts with HCl it forms chloroethane (CH_2ClCH_3). Which is shown by C.
D is incorrect as when ethene reacts with steam it forms ethanol.

Question 3

B

If it has 10 Hydrogen atoms, 1 H is for the COOH group and 3 are for the first carbon which forms a methyl group (CH_3). This leaves 6 H's left meaning there are 3 CH_2 groups present. Therefore, the formula is C_4H_9COOH and it is pentanoic acid due to having 5 Carbons.

C14 - Metals

Question 1

C

1. Statement 1 is incorrect. The boiling point of Group 2 metals decreases as you go down the group. This means that Be has the highest boiling point of the Group 2 metals.
2. Statement 2 is incorrect. An Mg ion has a 2+ charge, and a Cl ion has a 1- charge. Therefore, there must be 2 Cl- ions for every one Mg2+ ion, making the ratio of Mg: Cl ions 1:2.
3. Statement 3 is correct. Both a Ca2+ ion and a K+ ion lose 2 and 1 electrons respectively to form a full outer shell. This means both ions have 8 electrons in their outer shell.

Question 2

C

1. Statement 1 is incorrect. Group 1 metals form alkaline solutions when reacted with water, not acid.
2. Statement 2 is correct. Sodium + water → sodium hydroxide and hydrogen.
3. Statement 3 is correct. This reaction will form an alkaline solution. An alkaline solution turns universal indicator either blue or purple.

Question 3

D

1. A is correct. Potassium is more reactive than magnesium, producing a faster rate of reaction.
2. B is correct. Zinc is less reactive than magnesium, producing a slower rate of reaction.
3. C is correct. Magnesium chloride is a colourless solution in its aqueous state.
4. D is incorrect. Oxygen relights a glowing splint, not hydrogen.

C15 – Kinetic / Particle Theory

Question 1

D

Before A, the substance is a solid. Between A-B the solid is melting into liquid. As it melts, heat energy is being absorbed from the environment to facilitate the particles moving further away from each other. There is no temperature change as there is no change in kinetic energy.

Question 2

D

Platinum - 2,452°C is between the melting and boiling point so platinum will be a liquid.
Boron - 2,452°C is below the melting point of boron so it will be a solid.

Question 3

B

A: liquids cannot be compressed so A is incorrect
B: is correct as solids cannot diffuse, liquids can diffuse slowly and gases diffuse very easily.
C: solids have high density, so C is incorrect
D: liquids don't fill containers; they take the shape of containers, so D is incorrect.

C16 – Chemical Tests

Question 1

A

1. Statement 1 is correct. The black solid is CuO (s). reacting CuO with sulphuric acid (colourless) should form copper (II) sulphate which is a clear blue solution.
2. Statement 2 is incorrect. Only aqueous copper sulphate and water (l) should be produced from the second reaction. No gas should be produced.
3. Statement 3 is incorrect, as no gas should be produced from this reaction.

Question 2

E

1. Statement 1 is correct. Mg (s) + NaOH (aq) → MgO(s) + Na (s) + H_2 (g). MgO is a white solid.
2. Statement 2 is correct. Copper (II) sulphate is a blue solution. Mg is more reactive than Cu so displaces Cu to form colourless magnesium sulphate (aq).
3. Statement 3 is correct. Magnesium is more reactive than iron, displacing the iron in the solution.

Question 3

D

Potassium metal burns with a lilac flame. Lithium burns with a crimson red flame. Copper (II) reacts with sulphuric acid to form a blue solution (copper sulphate).

C17 – Air and Water

Question 1

B

1. Statement 1 is incorrect. Although farming and landfill sites release methane, nuclear power plants produce no greenhouse gases.
2. Statement 2 is incorrect. Methane acts as a greenhouse gas but has not destroyed the ozone layer of the earth. This is due to artificial chemicals, such as CFCs, instead.
3. Statement 3 is correct. Fossil fuel extraction released methane into the atmosphere, so reducing their use should reduce methane emissions.

Question 2

B

1. Statement 1 is incorrect. Sulphur dioxide can be harmful to the human respiratory system
2. Statement 2 is correct. Incomplete combustion of atmospheric nitrogen in vehicle engines can emit harmful nitrous oxides
3. Statement 3 is incorrect. Sulphur dioxide can be released naturally, e.g. through volcanic activity.

Question 3

C

1. Statement 1 is incorrect. Chlorine gas dissolves in water, forming an aqueous solution containing HCl (aq) and HClO (aq)
2. Statement 2 is incorrect. Hydrogen gas is not produced when a halogen reacts with water.
3. Statement 3 is correct. Chlorine (Cl_2) dissociates in water to form Cl^- ions.

P1 - Electricity

Question 1

Voltmeter: instrument to record the potential difference (voltage) drop across a component. They are connected in parallel. Ideally, they have infinite resistance so as to prevent current flowing through them – any current that passes through the voltmeter (and not the component being recorded from) will lower the potential difference across the component that is being measured from.

Ammeter: measuring instrument to record the current in a circuit. They are connected in series so they measure the same current as the components from which they're connected with. They must have negligible resistance (ideally 0) so that they do not become part of the circuit and impact the flowing through that region of the circuit.

Question 2

B

Remember! When calculating resistance, the resistance of components in series is simply summed whereas for component in parallel the total resistance (R_T) = $\frac{1}{R_1} + \frac{1}{R_2} + \frac{1}{R_3}$ ....

   Where R_1, R_2, R_3 are the total resistance for each 'arm' of the parallel configuration.

   Therefore, the total resistance of any parallel combination will ALWAYS be less than that of any individual source of resistance

Before:
- Total circuit resistance = $(\frac{1}{1+1} + \frac{1}{1})^{-1} = \frac{2}{3}$
- Total current (reading at ammeter 1):
  - $V = IR \Rightarrow I = V/R \Rightarrow I = \frac{6}{\frac{2}{3}} = \frac{6*3}{2} = 9\,A$
- Ammeter 2: current will 'split' proportional to the resistance in each parallel arm such that the overall potential difference drop across each arm is the same.
  - As bottom arm has half the resistance as the top arm then the bottom must receive 2/3rd of the current (to ensure the total PD drop across each parallel line is 6 V)
  -
  - Ammeter 2 = $9 * \frac{2}{3} = 6\,A$

After:
- Total circuit resistance: $(\frac{1}{1} + \frac{1}{1})^{-1} = \frac{1}{2}$
- Total current (ammeter 1): $I = \frac{V}{R} = \frac{6}{\frac{1}{2}} = 12\,A$
- As both arms are now identical so share the 12 A equally, so ammeter 2 reads **6 A**

Question 3

E

On I-V plots, the reciprocal of the gradient represents the resistance. NTC thermistors have lower resistance at lower temperatures whereas filament lamps have lower resistance at high current (due to heating of the element).

P2 - Magnetism

Question 1

B

When a current-carrying conductor moves relative to a magnetic field, an EMF (ε, voltage) is induced. The magnitude of induced EMF is directly proportional to the rate of change of magnetic flux linkage.

$$\varepsilon = N\left(\frac{\Delta\phi}{\Delta t}\right)$$

Φ = magnetic flux = magnetic field strength * area swept through

Doubling the rotation rate doubles the rate of change of flux linkage, doubling the field strength (B) also doubles the magnetic flux whereas halving the number of coils (N) halves the EMF – thus the net effect of the 3 changes is to double (2*2*0.5) EMF. Doubling rotation rate doubles the frequency of reversal.

Question 2

D

Magnitude of induced force of an electric motor, F = BIL where field and current are perpendicular to each other. F = 2*10*2 = 40 N

Question 3

C

For each statement:

1. Step-up transformers always have more turns on the secondary coil. The ratio of the voltage of primary and secondary coils = the ratio of the coil number:

$$\frac{V_P}{V_S} = \frac{n_P}{n_S}$$

2. Transformers induce alternating currents in the secondary coil (it is the alternating current that causes the change in magnetic flux necessary for electromagnetic induction)
3. Energy loss is greater at higher currents so stepping up the voltage increases efficiency of transfer.

P3 - Mechanics

Question 1

E

This question is assessing your ability to understand the concept of resultant force and the relationship between weight and mass.

The cyclist's mass = weight/g = 50 kg

The relevant equation is F = ma

Enter the appropriate numbers and rearrange to solve for the force due to friction (which opposes the acceleration):

200 - x = 50 * 2
x = 100 N

The Complete BMAT Specification Explained
Answers - Physics

Question 2
C

Distance is the length of the total route travelled by an object during motion. It is a scalar quantity. Displacement is a vector quantity quantifying how far from the start point an object is; it can be positive or negative.

Distance: 2*0.4/2 + 1*0.4 + 1*0.4/2 + 2*0.2/2 = 0.4 + 0.4 + 0.2 + 0.2 = **1.2**

Displacement: (0.4 + 0.4 + 0.2) − 0.2 = **0.8**

Question 3
A

Remember: momentum (and velocity) are vector quantities so considering the direction is important. In this example, velocity from right to left is denoted as being negative. Assuming conservation of momentum:

$$(m_1 * u_1) + (m_2 * u_2) = (m_1 * v_1) * (m_2 * v_2)$$

Substitute the numbers in (stationary = 0 m/s):

$$(4 * 2) + (8 * -5) = (4 * x) + (8 * 0)$$

$$-32 = 4x \implies x = \text{-8 m/s}$$

P4 - Thermal Physics

Question 1
D

Specific heat capacity is a property of an object and is defined as the energy required to raise the temperature of 1 kg of a substance by 1°C and thus has the units J kg^{-1} °C^{-1}. E = mcΔt

For this substance, c = $\frac{E}{m\Delta t}$ = $\frac{4800}{0.25*2}$ = 9600 J kg^{-1} °C^{-1}

Question 2
A

Metal is a good conductor of heat. Convection can occur in all fluids (liquids and gases) so 2 is false. Thermal radiation is transmitted by infrared radiation (not UV) making statement 3 also false.

Question 3

A

Dark objects emit and absorb thermal radiation more readily than lighter objects. Energy transfer is also proportional to the temperature gradient and surface are (hence a hot object in a cold room would lose heat fastest).

P5 - Matter

Question 1

B

1 mole of any ideal gas occupies the same volume regardless of its molecular weight. The pressure of the gas will be influenced by both the volume of its container, its temperature and the number of moles. At standard temperature/pressure, 1 mole of an ideal gas occupies 22.4 L. This is formalised in the ideal gas equation:

$$PV = nRT$$

Question 2

D

As a gas is heated, its particles gain kinetic energy and thus move more rapidly. As they do so, they collide more frequently and with greater velocity with the container wall. This greater change of momentum, by definition, exerts a greater force on a given area of container wall which increases the pressure of the gas.

Question 3

B

The product of a gas' pressure and volume is a constant (Boyle's Law). Therefore,

$$1.2 * (1 * 10^5) = 0.8 * x$$

$$x = 1.5 * 10^5$$

P6 - Waves

Question 1

B

When waves pass between mediums of different optical density, both their wavelength and velocity change proportionally (decreasing when moving into optically denser materials) but the frequency remains the same. Therefore, upon entering the new material, one may rearrange v = fλ for:

$$\lambda = \frac{v}{f} = \frac{2 * 10^8}{100,000} = 2000\ m = 2\ km$$

Question 2

E

Sounds are generated by sources that cause vibrations of particles in a medium (usually, but not exclusively, air) and are transmitted from particle to particle and can thus not travel in a vacuum. A sound wave with velocity 330 m/s and f = 2Hz has a wavelength of 165 m (λ = v/f). Young humans are able to hear sounds between 20-20,000 Hz. Amplitude relates to volume, whereas pitch is determined by wave frequency.

Question 3

E

EM spectrum waves all travel at the speed of light (in a vacuum). Components of the EM spectrum include (from lowest to highest frequency or wavelength):

- Radio waves (uses: communications, radio, TV)
- Microwaves (uses: heating water/food, satellites)
- Infrared (uses: TV remotes, heating lamps)
- Visible light (uses: vision, photography)
- Ultraviolet (uses: tanning lamps, endogenous vitamin D production by skin)
- X-rays (uses: medical imaging)
- Gamma rays (uses: radiotracers in medical imaging, killing cancer cells and instrument sterilisation)

P7 - Radioactivity

Question 1

A

There are 3 main types of radioactive decay of unstable atomic nuclei:

Particle	Equation	What blocks it?
α (^4_2He)	$^{219}_{86}Rn = ^{215}_{84}Po + ^4_2\alpha$	Paper
β ($^0_{-1}\beta$)	$^{14}_6C = ^{14}_7N + ^0_{-1}e$	3mm aluminium
γ	Nuclear structure unchanged	Several metres of concrete/lead

Question 2

D

- α: most ionising but does not travel far in air. Greatest mass (4) and charge (+2)
- β: middle ionising and travels further than α but less than γ in air. Negligible mass (1 electron) and charge (-1)
- γ: least ionising but travels very far (as not a physical particle) in air. These waves have no mass nor charge.

Question 3

iv

Each α decay reduces mass number by 4 and atomic number by 2, each β decay increases atomic number by 1 (without changing mass number).
Therefore,
- New mass number = 238 - (4*6) = 214
- Atomic number = 92 - (6*2) + 2 = 82

M1 - Units

Question 1

A

0.08cm = 0.8mm
4.4 μm = 0.0044mm
0.8-0.0044= 0.7956

Question 2

C

800g:2.8kg
800:2800
8:28
2:7

Question 3

D

120 x 2= 240
240÷60= 4
4 x 4.5= 18
18 x £1.80= £32.40

M2 - Number

Question 1

C

Find common multiples of 20 and 28

20 x 1= 20
20 x 2= 40
20 x 3 = 60
20 x 4= 80
20 x 5= 100
20 x 6= 120

20 x 7= 140
28 x 1=28
28 x 2= 56
28 x 3=84
28 x 4=112
28 x 5= 140

Question 2

B

2(2X-7)=X + 10
4X - 14= X + 10
3X= 24
X= 8
Y= 2(8) -7
Y= 9

Question 3

B

Divide 180 by its smallest prime
180÷2= 90
Repeat the process till the answer = 1
90÷2=45
45÷3= 15
15÷3= 5
5÷5 =1
2 and 3 appear as primes twice therefore 180= $2^2 \times 3^2 \times 5$
Therefore as 5 is not squared to make 180 a perfect square k=5

M3 - Ratio and proportion

Question 1

C

(12÷40) x 100 = 30

Question 2

E

5200 x 1.04= 5408
5408-5200= 208
208÷2= 104
5200 x 1.035= 5382
5382-5200= 182
182÷2 = 91
104-91= 13

Question 3

B

1200 x 0.85³ = 736.95

M4 - Algebra

Question 1

A

Divide both the numerator and denominator by x

$$\frac{1}{3+\frac{1}{x}}$$

As x>10000, $\frac{1}{x}$ is going to be very small and as x gets bigger it will get closer and closer to 0 so is effectively negligible

Question 2

D

$6y-12=6x^2-18x$
$y-2=x^2-3x$
$y=x^2-3x+2$
$y=5-x$
solve simultaneous equations

Question 3

C

-6< x+3< 12
-9< x< 9

M5 - Geometry

Question 1

A

$\cos(60) = \frac{4}{AC}$
$0.5 = \frac{4}{AC}$
$0.5 AC = 4$
$AC = 8$
$8^2 - 4^4 = AB^2$
$AB^2 = 48$
$AB = \sqrt{48} = \sqrt{16 \times 3} = 4\sqrt{3}$

Question 2

E

$\frac{22}{3\pi} = 2.334$
$2(2.334) + 6\pi = 23.518$ cm $= 23.5$ cm

Question 3

B

Circumference of full circle $= 2\pi r = 10\pi$
Arc length $= \frac{x}{360} \times 10\pi$ $\quad\quad x° = \frac{360}{x}$
Area of circle $= 25\pi$
Area of sector $= \frac{360}{\pi} \times \frac{1}{360} \times 25\pi$
$= 25$

M6 - Statistics

Question 1

A

Question 2

A

Question 3: A

A

Discrete data has set values whereas continuous data can be any value not just been 0 and 100. Shoe size is discrete but height is continuous

M7 - Probability

Question 1

B
R= red Y= yellow
Y+ R+R
R+Y+R
R+R+Y
$P = 3 \times (\frac{4}{15} \times \frac{9}{14} \times \frac{8}{13})$
$= \frac{864}{2730}$

Question 2

C
Total score of the boys= 9x 44=396
Girls excluding Susan= 52x11=572
Total score with Susan's= 572+45=617
New mean= (396+617)/(9+12)=1013/21

Question 3

A

People drinking 5 bottles of beer a week= 1/3
People not drinking 5 bottles= 2/3
All the combinations of the 1 of the 3 people admitting to drinking 5 or more bottles=
Yes no no= 4/27
No yes no= 4/27
No no yes = 4/27
Probability that exactly one person out of three admits to drinking 5 or more bottles of beer = 4/27+ 4/27+ 4/27= 4/9

Final Words

Well done for making it to the end of this guide to the complete BMAT specification! We hope it was useful and that you feel more confident with the BMAT. The best way to utilise this book is to go back in and re-do the questions, then revise any knowledge you be may not yet be confident with. Doing the same questions over and over may seem boring, but repetition will drill those concepts into your head.

Now that you are fully up to speed with every part of the BMAT, you can work your way through practice materials and make sure you are completely comfortable with the exam. 6med runs BMAT courses every year which can help you evolve your understanding even further – you can find more information at 6med.co.uk

Here are some tips for test day:

1. **Be well rested**
   - Getting a good night's sleep before the exam is key. Cramming the night before won't help (we know because we've done it), so rest up and sit the exam with a well-rested brain.
2. **Have a good breakfast**
   - A substantive breakfast will fuel you through the exam. You don't want your mind to be distracted by your rumbling stomach! Eat something that will fill you up for longer and make sure to hydrate as well.
3. **Stay hydrated**
   - Take some water with you into the exam as you may need it and won't be able to get up from your seat to go and get some.
4. **Go to the toilet beforehand!**
   - You won't be able to go during the exam so make sure you go beforehand.
5. **If you're unsure about the exam conditions, call the exam centre**
   - If you have any questions about the exam conditions, call your test centre to confirm. It's better to be prepared. Different centres will have different ways of conducting the test, so make sure you check specifically with the one you're taking the BMAT in.

What happens next?

After you sit the BMAT (whichever sitting you choose), you'll get your results a couple of weeks after. Your scores will have been sent to the universities you've applied to first and you'll then get calls for interview based on how they use the scores. Remember that the BMAT is a single component of the entire application process so even if you didn't do as well as you hoped, you still have a good chance with your grades and your interview.

Ideally in the time between doing your test and getting your results, you should be thinking about starting interview preparation (take a break first though!). You'll need a lot of time to do plenty of interview practice so that your interview skills are top notch. We have plenty of resources to help you with that too, so check our website out if you're interested. We're sure you'll all do well and will come out of the exam with the best marks possible.

Thank you for choosing 6Med and we wish you all the best for your BMAT and your future in medicine!

Printed in Great Britain
by Amazon